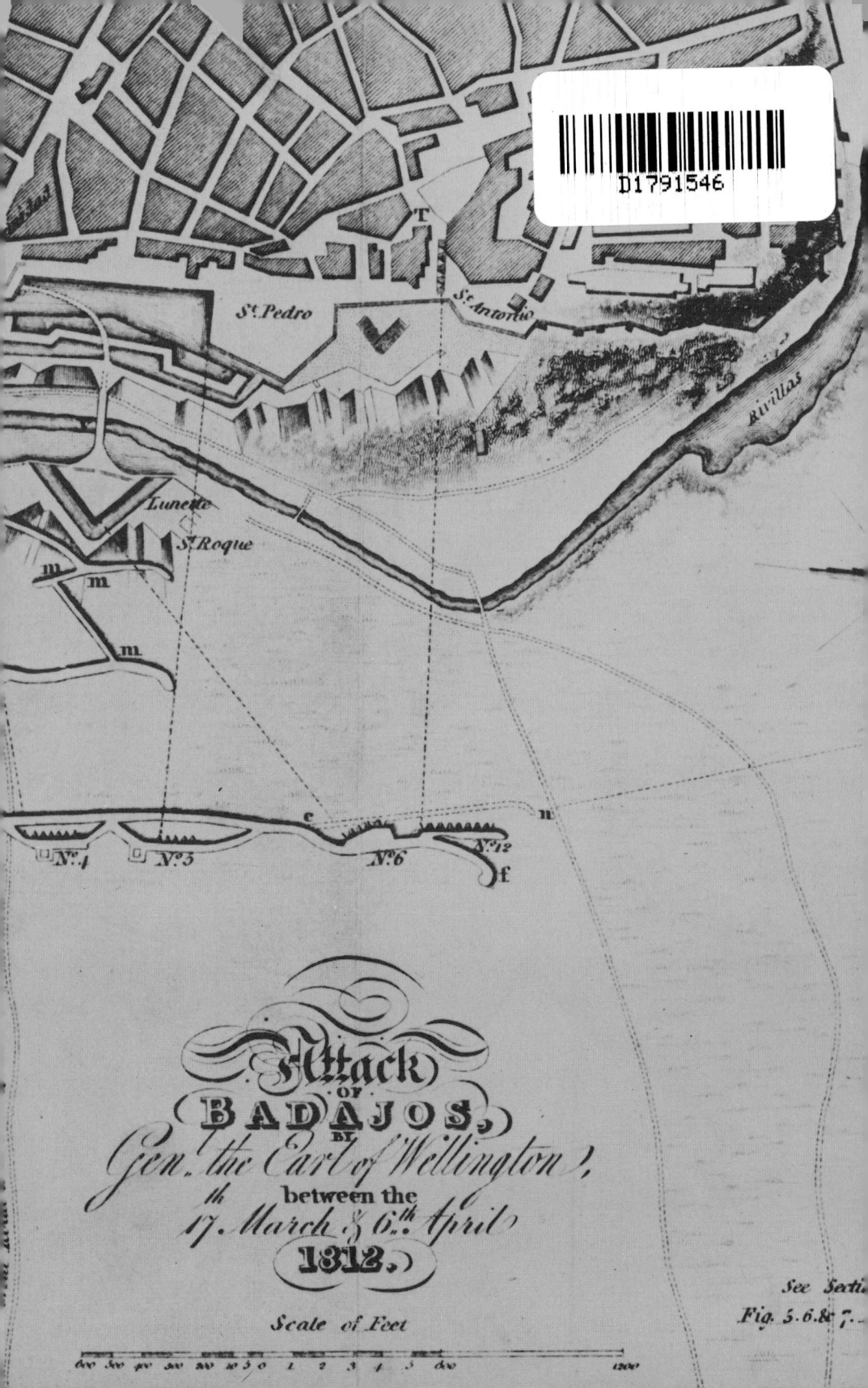

INTELLIGENCE OFFICER
IN THE PENINSULA

INTELLIGENCE OFFICER IN THE PENINSULA

Letters and Diaries of
Major the Hon Edward Charles Cocks
1786–1812

JULIA V. PAGE

Foreword by David Chandler

HIPPOCRENE BOOKS INC
New York

SPELLMOUNT LTD
Tunbridge Wells

*Dedicated to the memory of Charles Cocks
and his staunch friends William Tomkinson and Hugh Owen*

In the Spellmount Military list:

The Uniforms of the British Yeomanry Forces 1794-1914 Series:
The Sussex Yeomanry
The North Somerset Yeomanry
The Yorkshire Hussars
Westmorland and Cumberland Yeomanry
3rd County of London (Sharpshooters)
Duke of Lancaster's Own Yeomanry
Yorkshire Dragoons
Lovat Scouts

Riflemen Form
History of the Cambridge University OTC
The Yeomanry Regiments – A Pictorial History
Over the Rhine – The Last Days of War in Europe
Yeoman Service
The Territorial Battalions

In the Nautical list:
Sea of Memories

© Julia V. Page 1986

First published in the UK in 1986 by
SPELLMOUNT LTD
12 Dene Way, Speldhurst
Tunbridge Wells, Kent TN3 0NX
ISBN 0-946771-71-5 (UK)

First published in USA 1986 by
Hippocrene Books Inc, 171 Madison Avenue,
New York, NY.10016
ISBN 0-87052-310-4 (USA)

British Library Cataloguing in Publication Data
Cocks, Edward Charles
Letters & diaries of Major the Hon. Edward Charles Cocks.
1. Peninsular War, 1807-1814 — Personal narratives
I. Title   II. Page, Julia
940.2'7   DC231

All rights reserved. No part of this publication may be reproduced, stored in a retrieval system or transmitted in any form or by any means, electronic, mechanical, photocopying, recording or otherwise, without prior permission in writing from Spellmount Ltd, Publishers.

Designed by Mike Wicks
Typeset by Picton Print, Bath Road, Chippenham, Wiltshire
Printed by Staples Printers Rochester Limited, Love Lane, Rochester, Kent.

Contents

	Page
Author's note	10
Introduction	12
1. Southern Spain 18 September 1808 – 6 May 1809	19
2. Oporto 9 May – 11 June 1809	27
3. Talavera 2 July – 18 October 1809	33
4. Andalusia 9 December 1809 – 27 January 1810	43
5. Cadiz 29 January – 24 February 1810	53
6. Between the Coa and the Agueda 22 March – 19 July 1810	59
7. Wellington's Eyes and Ears 20 July – 25 September 1810	67
8. The Fighting Squadron 27 September – 18 October 1810	82
9. The Lines of Torres Vedras 27 October – 25 December 1810	90
10. No Man's Land 5 January – 11 March 1811	97
11. Fuentes d'Onoro 30 April – 19 May 1811	101
12. Badajoz 1811 22 May – 10 June 1811	111
13. Reflections 16 June – 9 July 1811	120
14. More Reflections 1 July – 8 August 1811	127
15. Catching up on Correspondence 12 August – 31 August 1811	133
16. Heartache 1 September – 2 October 1811	139
17. Autumn Activities 11 October – 20 December 1811	147
18. Ciudad Rodrigo 27 December 1811 – 30 January 1812	158
19. Winter Letters 1 February – 15 March 1812	167
20. All Points of the Compass 4 April – 23 May 1812	173
21. Salamanca 10 June – 6 August 1812	182
22. Sweet Success 16 August – 26 September 1812	191
23. Siege of Burgos September – 6 October 1812	197
24. 8th October 1812 and its aftermath	204
Appendices	
Appendix A Gibraltar	207
Appendix B Cocks's library	211
Appendix C Observations on piquets; Of attacking small parties of the enemy; On chains of posts; Hints for a patrol	212
Appendix D List of guns at the 1812 siege of Badajoz	224
Appendix E The siege of Badajoz 1812	226
Appendix F Military Ideas, Sections 1, 2 & 3	235
Sources	242
References	246
Index	250

List of Plates

1. Edward Charles Cocks. From a miniature by J. C. D. Engleheart c1808 at Eastnor Castle, Herefordshire.
   (The Hon. Mrs B. A. F. Hervey-Bathurst)
2. Thomas Somers Cocks. From a miniature by W. J. Thomson.
   (J. V. Somers Cocks, Esq.)
3. The Duke of Wellington by Goya. Painted after the capture of Madrid, 1812. (Apsley House)
4. Reigate Priory today.
5. Oporto, looking up river from the Serra Convent. The old seminary where the troops landed is beyond the curve in the river.
6. The River Coa at Castel Mendo where Cocks and his party helped the peasants destroy the mills in August 1810.
7. Wellington's Headquarters at Pero Negro in the Lines of Torres Vedras.
8. View from Santarem towards Malhaquejo where Cocks harrassed Massena's forging parties in November 1810.
9. Obidos, from whence Cocks waged war on the enemy, January – February 1811.
10. Fuentes d'Onoro. The battle raged within its streets in May 1811. Camille Siego owned a house here.
11. Almeida. This fortress was abandoned by Brennier in May 1811, after the battle of Fuentes d'Onoro.
12. Frenada. A village between the Coa and the Agueda and Wellington's headquarters for a while.
13. Villa Velha. The crossing point over the Tagus used continually by the army.
14. Salamanca today.
15. Tordesillas today, showing the remains of the old bridge.
16. The Escurial Palace outside Madrid. Cocks and the 79th were billeted here.
17. Peninsular War c1812. Light Dragoons: *A Glimpse of the Army*. (National Army Museum)

List of Maps and Line Illustrations

The maps are merely sketches in order to give the reader an idea of Cocks's travels and the approximate positions of the army. The details are taken from a variety of sources, including his own maps; however, some places defied identification and cannot be shown. Distances are always difficult to calculate, but one of his leagues is possibly between $3\frac{1}{2}$ to 4 miles. Additionally, in Peninsular narratives, the problem of accurately spelling the names of the towns and villages always arises, but, in this case, they have been left as Cocks wrote them because, despite variations, the meaning is clear. Likewise, the spelling of Somers confusingly varies according to the individual. Before his elevation to the peerage Cocks's father always signed himself John Sommers Cocks, his sons and nephew invariably wrote Soḿers, while today the family has discarded the accent. At no time have the two names been hyphenated.

Page

1. The Cocks Family Tree ... 14
2. The Peninsula ... 22
3. Oporto Campaign ... 26
4. Cocks's March to, and from, Talavera ... 32
5. Battle of Talavera ... 35
6. Southern Spain, December 1809 – January 1810 ... 42
7. Cadiz, January 1810 ... 52
8. Spain and Portugal ... 58
9. Between the Coa and the Agueda Rivers, Northern Section, June – July 1810 ... 61
10. Between the Coa and the Agueda Rivers, Southern Section, June – July 1810 ... 66
11. Between the River Coa and Guarda, August – September 1810 ... 69
12. The Mondego Valley, September 1810 ... 75
13. Marshal André Massena, Duc de Rivoli, Prince d'Essling ... 81
14. Retreat to the Lines of Torres Vedras, Autumn 1810 ... 83
15. Skirmish on the road to Busaco ... 86
16. The second siege of Badajoz, June 1811 ... 113
17. Portalegre to Merida, June – July 1811 ... 119
18. Cocks's diagram, 29 June 1811 ... 124
19. Part of Cocks's letter to his brother John Somers, describing his first weeks in Spain, 29 April 1809 ... 138
20. Ciudad Rodrigo, January 1812 ... 157
21. Jacquier's Hotel matrimonial declaration, February 1808 ... 160
22. Storming of Ciudad Rodrigo, 19 January 1812 ... 164
23. Eastnor Castle in the 19th century ... 178
24. Salamanca campaign, June – July 1812 ... 181
25. Battle of Salamanca ... 189
26. St Michael Hornwork, Burgos, September 1812 ... 194
    Endpapers: The siege of Badajoz, April 1812.

Foreword

'SPAIN,' runs an ancient adage attributed to Henri IV of France, 'is a country where small armies are defeated and large armies starve.' The involvement of the Anglo-Portuguese Army under Wellington in the Peninsular War was of great significance on several counts, not least the support it was able to afford the truly critical partisan and guerrilla struggles of popular resistance to the French occupation. The waging of campaigns amidst a largely barren terrain against a foe that at one time numbered over 320,000 men posed immense problems – but one positive factor was the superb intelligence network that Wellington was able to establish. This was based upon 'correspondents' hidden in the cities and towns, and on news and captured despatches provided by the numerous guerrilla chieftains, together with direct observation by well-mounted British 'galloping officers' hanging hazardously on to the skirts of the French armies in the field and reporting back their findings, thus permitting their commander-in-chief to guess accurately what lay '. . . on the other side of the hill'.

One such officer, employed on mainly intelligence duties from 1809 to 1812, is the subject of this book, the Hon. Edward Charles Cocks. At different times and places he found himself on attachment to Spanish regular forces, operating with his 16th Light Dragoons (today the 16th/5th Queen's Royal Lancers) on the outpost line, and increasingly conducting special missions for Wellington, with whom the young officer established what can only be termed a special relationship.

Indeed, it is amazing that Cocks has not attracted a book to himself before this, as his letters and diaries contain a wealth of fascinating and valuable information that adds a considerable amount to our understanding of the Peninsular War in general and the crucial intelligence aspect in particular. Perhaps it is because he generally writes in a prosaic style rather than in the colourful narrative form (however exaggerated) of a Marbot or a Harry Smith whose writings and opinions have long been appreciated. Cocks was – as Julia Page makes abundantly clear – a highly 'educated officer' in the military sense of the term, in other words a dedicated professional soldier. It was probably this aspect of the man, together with his superb front-line courage and unusual intellectual attainments, that first attracted Wellington's attention, then his admiration and trust. And it is the evolution of Cocks into a fully professional officer that the author has rightly taken as her central theme. Not that the young officer was 'all work and no play'. We find him attending balls and entertainments, on one occasion travelling overnight over a mountain to attend one such event only to find an urgent order of recall awaiting him. In late 1811 he lived with Josepha, a young Spanish girl, and when, next year, the victorious army entered Madrid after the battle of

Salamanca, '... he had never been kissed by so many girls in one day'. But he was serious-minded about his profession, unlike so many of his younger officer-comrades. And this is a serious book about the emergence of a professional officer – a chrysalis process completed by late 1811 when he was aged 25 – and the author's many years as a British Army Officer's wife has enabled her to penetrate Cocks's evolution with a telling degree of understanding and appreciation. Her work with the letters and diaries has been exemplary, including the rediscovery of the 'lost' journal for 1812; and although she modestly describes herself as an 'amateur military historian', there are many 'professionals' who will admire her thoroughness and application. For, from the first time I met her on a Captain Gordon Battlefield Tour to the Peninsula that I was running in 1977, I have rarely encountered a more dedicated researcher into a military biographical subject. This book is a monument to her application and zeal.

Although the saying 'Only the good die young' is hardly applicable to participants in major wars, it remains a fact that many fighting soldiers are young men, whether good or bad, or – like most of us – the usual somewhat indeterminate mixture. It is also tragically true that many of the most talented seem to be struck down by some inelectuable Fate. In the First World War one thinks of 'Boy' Bradford, VC, and the poet Rupert Brooke. Nor is intelligence and undercover work by any means the safest employment for an officer. At Sandhurst an anteroom in Victory College is named after a graduate officer, Captain Robert Nairac, GC, captured and brutally killed after torture in Northern Ireland on 15 May 1977. Cocks avoided this fate, but it was his gallantry as a fighting soldier, which made him volunteer for hazardous services on many occasions, that led to the newly-appointed Brevet and Regimental Lieutenant-Colonel of the 79th (Cameron Highlanders), to which he had transferred from the cavalry in mid-1812, to be shot down repelling a French sortie on the fortress of Burgos on 8 October 1812 – ironically the very same day that his new promotion was published in *The London Gazette*.

Wellington's grief at this loss of a highly gifted subordinate officer is in no way to be discounted. At the graveside he turned to General d'Urban and remarked that: '... had Cocks outlived the campaigns, which from the way he exposed himself was morally impossible, he would have become one of the first Generals in England.' The future Great Duke was not a man who made such comments lightly. And from a close study of this fine book, the reader may well come to agree that Wellington was right.

DAVID G. CHANDLER
MA (Oxon), FRHistS, FRGS
Head, Department of
War Studies, RMA
Sandhurst, and
President of the
British Commission for
Military History.
April 1986

Author's Note

I WOULD LIKE to offer my warmest thanks to the Hon. Mrs B. A. F. Hervey-Bathurst for her generosity in allowing me unlimited access, not only to Charles Cocks's own documents, but all the eighteenth-century Eastnor archives. I shall not forget the day we read his teenage essays, gazed in some awe at the experiments in his science text book and chuckled over the sketches in his history rough note book. Nor the coming to light of the Burgos journal, absent-mindedly replaced by an ancestor on a library shelf instead of back in the muniment room, its red leather binding camouflaging its contents. But perhaps the greatest excitement of all was the recovery of some letters belonging to Charles's cousin. Known to have been sold by a kinsman in 1934, they suddenly turned up at an auction and are now safely in the Castle. Indeed, every year something new comes to light and this book may well produce more.

I am deeply grateful, too, to Mr John V. Somers Cocks, the great-great-grandson of Thomas, Charles's chief correspondent. He willingly opened his archives and gave me every support and his *History of the Cocks Family* became my bible. Both he and Mrs Hervey-Bathurst patiently answered dozens of questions and directed me to other possible sources of information besides giving me portraits of Charles and Thomas and several members of the family. Gratitude is also owing to Lord Somers whose kindness and encouragement was much appreciated. Without their co-operation and close interest the book could not have been written.

A particular word of thanks must go to the military historian, Mr David Chandler, whose wise counsel and infectious enthusiasm has proved so invaluable. The memories of the ten-day Peninsular battlefield tour will remain with me always, as will his kindness in explaining the intricacies of eighteenth-century warfare and bringing home to me the immense difficulties under which the armies fought.

Amateur historians have to feel their way and I am indebted to the Director and Staff of the National Army Museum, particularly Mr Peter Boyden of the Department of Records who directed me to the National Register of Archives wherein I discovered the diaries' existence; without his early advice the search would have been lengthy.

I would like to thank the staff of the several Record Offices up and down the country who eased my path: that of the House of Lords, Worcester and Hereford, Gloucester, Greater London, West Sussex; Mrs Doughty at the Surrey office; Mr Chesterman at Chester; and, last but by no means least, the Public Record Office.

Libraries, too, have played their part: the British Library, the British Newspaper Library, the Victoria Library at Westminster, the Old War Office Library and, my help in all times of trouble, the Librarian of the Royal United Services Institute for Defence Studies, Mr Richard Tubb, who bore nobly with my requests; I thank them all most heartily.

For details of Cocks's parliamentary career I am grateful to The History of Parliament Trust, and for information on the Cocks, Biddulph Bank to Barclays Bank Ltd, in particular Mr Handford.

Without Mr R. C. F. Catterall's professional diagnosis I would not have learned the nature of Charles's handicap and thus the key to his determination, and my special thanks go to him.

As I well know, schools are busy places, but the Headmaster and Staff of Reigate Priory School were kindness itself and I would like them to know how much I appreciated their hospitality and interest; their information was very useful.

There have also been many who, in one way or another, have helped me on my way: Lord Combermere who allowed me to see the Stanhope Papers; Mr Heald of Bevere House, Bevere, who took me over his flat, once part of Cocks's grandfather's home; Sir Robert Ricketts who told me about Gibraltar; Major General W. Cooper who painstakingly explained about fascines, gabions and flying bridges; Madame E. Grove who translated some of Cocks's childhood French; and Colonel George Gillberry who strove by every means at his disposal to decipher an important page in the diaries. I thank them all most sincerely for their interest and assistance.

Others without whom the research would have been the poorer are Mrs David Rasch, Miss Caroline Neale, the late Mr E. Holland-Martin, Major General R. Darkin, Major General N. Spellor, Brigadier M. B. Page, Mr R. B. Page, Major Digby Smith, Mr Chris Abrahams and Mr & Mrs G. J. Moore. I greatly appreciated their help.

There are also the friendly helpful people behind desks, and at the other end of telephones, or initials at the close of letters, without whose help I might have missed a trick or two. To these unnamed I am grateful.

Lastly, I doubt if I can thank my sister, Miss Angela Newman, and my friends, sufficiently. They have shown remarkable understanding and forbearance with my enthusiasm for Charles Cocks, and whilst I am sure there were times when they wished him at the other end of the world they never wavered in support. There are no words to express my gratitude to them, it goes too deep.

Maidstone   JULIA V. PAGE
April 1986

Introduction

ONE EVENING IN June 1855 two men sat reminiscing after dinner, Sir John Rennie was in Oporto and had become acquainted with Hugh Owen, a British officer who had served with the Portuguese during the Peninsular War and thereafter stayed on. Over their port that warm night Owen began to speak of Charles Cocks, a colleague of his who had fought a very unusual war, often working exclusively for Wellington behind enemy lines, and on one occasion with the very safety of the army dependent on his expertise, yet withal a man of vision who still found time to think up methods for improving army training and overall reform.

Aware that he was intriguing Rennie and guessing he would like to hear more, Owen continued the tale by letter the following morning, enlarging on Cocks's life in the period he had known him and concluding with the comment that he felt Napier's *History* had failed to do him justice despite the historian's tribute to 'this gallant and zealous officer ... of modest demeanour, brave, thoughtful and enterprising, [who] lived and died a good soldier,'[1] dismayed that he should have ignored 'his unequalled search after a scientific knowledge of his profession.'[2] 'I had hoped,' Hugh went on, 'to have seen it recorded that Major the Honourable Charles Somers Cocks was not only the never tiring, confidential outpost officer of Wellington but he was both, in cavalry and infantry, the pattern soldier of the British army,' adding: 'This is not the language of flattery to him for he is gone –nor to his family for I know them not.'[3]

Rennie returned to England unable to get the story out of his mind, disturbed that a distinguished career should have gone almost unnoticed. He found Cocks mentioned briefly two or three times in Wellington's Despatches, also in a History of the King's German Legion whose outpost officers were clearly never going to forget him, but that was all; Owen's letter seemed the only record of a gifted man and in an effort to redress the balance he had it published in pamphlet form, distributing copies among his friends as well as to the Cocks family, one of whom, a soldier too, read his copy amidst the ruins of Sevastopol.

In 1866 Field Marshal Viscount Combermere's widow published her late husband's memoirs. Combermere, then Stapleton Cotton, had been Wellington's Cavalry Commander in the Peninsula and, since he had known Charles Cocks from the day he joined his regiment, there were frequent references, tantalisingly short on detail yet hinting at ability.

And then came silence until 1894 when more emerged: William Tomkinson, his lieutenant and close friend, who held him in the greatest affection and probably understood him better than any, had kept a diary in which he not only described many of their shared experiences but also included a moving tribute when his comrade was killed. Too modest to publish in his lifetime, it was left for his son to do so† but by then Cocks had faded from living memory and only the *Saturday Review* picked up his qualities and gave belated honour where it was due. 'Cocks, one perceives,' wrote the critic, 'had by special dispensation of Providence, grasped the fact that there is such a thing as the "business of soldiering". The prevailing faith hitherto had been that an officer was a gentleman who condescended to do vulgar, mechanical things like a common, professional person.'[4] And apparently that was the last of the evidence. When early twentieth-century historians came to write his part in the war they believed they had only Owen and Tomkinson, Cotton and Wellington to go on and the essence of Charles Cocks eluded them; of his other activities and how he came by his qualities they did not know nor the nature of the improved training which Owen had mentioned.‡

But it so happened Cocks had written a diary as well, running to eleven volumes over three years, with whole sections devoted to his ideas, and along with 180 letters, 138 of them from the Peninsula – once scattered but now together – it has lain almost undisturbed in a muniment room except for a brief period when the family sent it to Napier in the hope that he might use it for his history. However, the family's hopes were dashed as that part of the book applicable to Cocks had been completed but, eventually, with the coming of a national policy of registering archives, both diary and letters were offered for inclusion in the index, thus, at last, becoming known to those who cared to look.

Running to thousand upon thousand words, when transcribed filling seventeen modern files, the journals are an extraordinary record of daily occurrences, observations, topographical detail and, even more importantly for Cocks himself, a continuous discussion on the war. In conjunction with his reading he came to use them as a way of teaching himself military science, endlessly debating tactics and often spending hours comparing previous campaigns, both ancient and modern, with the present, and questioning the decisions of the various commanders.

The events are generally written in the past tense from memoranda kept daily and sometimes hourly, but the delay proves a bonus because by then he had usually gathered additional information and could assess the situation more objectively.

During the early months of the war he taught himself Spanish and it played havoc with his English syntax but one grows accustomed to his style. The character and personality of the man shine through the eccentric phrasing and, taken as a whole, the journals testify to his perseverence, ambition and intellect.

Edward Charles Cocks was born on 27 July 1786 in Great Marlborough Street, London,[5] to John Sommers Cocks, heir to the Somers barony, and Margaret

---

†*The Diary of a Cavalry Officer, 1809–1815*, by William Tomkinson and edited by his son, James Tomkinson. 1894.

‡Few even got his name right and many still refer to him as Charles Somers Cocks. Owen began the mistake, possibly because in 1841 the Cocks family assumed the surname Somers Cocks by Royal Licence; before then, excluding Charles, it was customary to give the boys in the family Somers as a second Christian name.

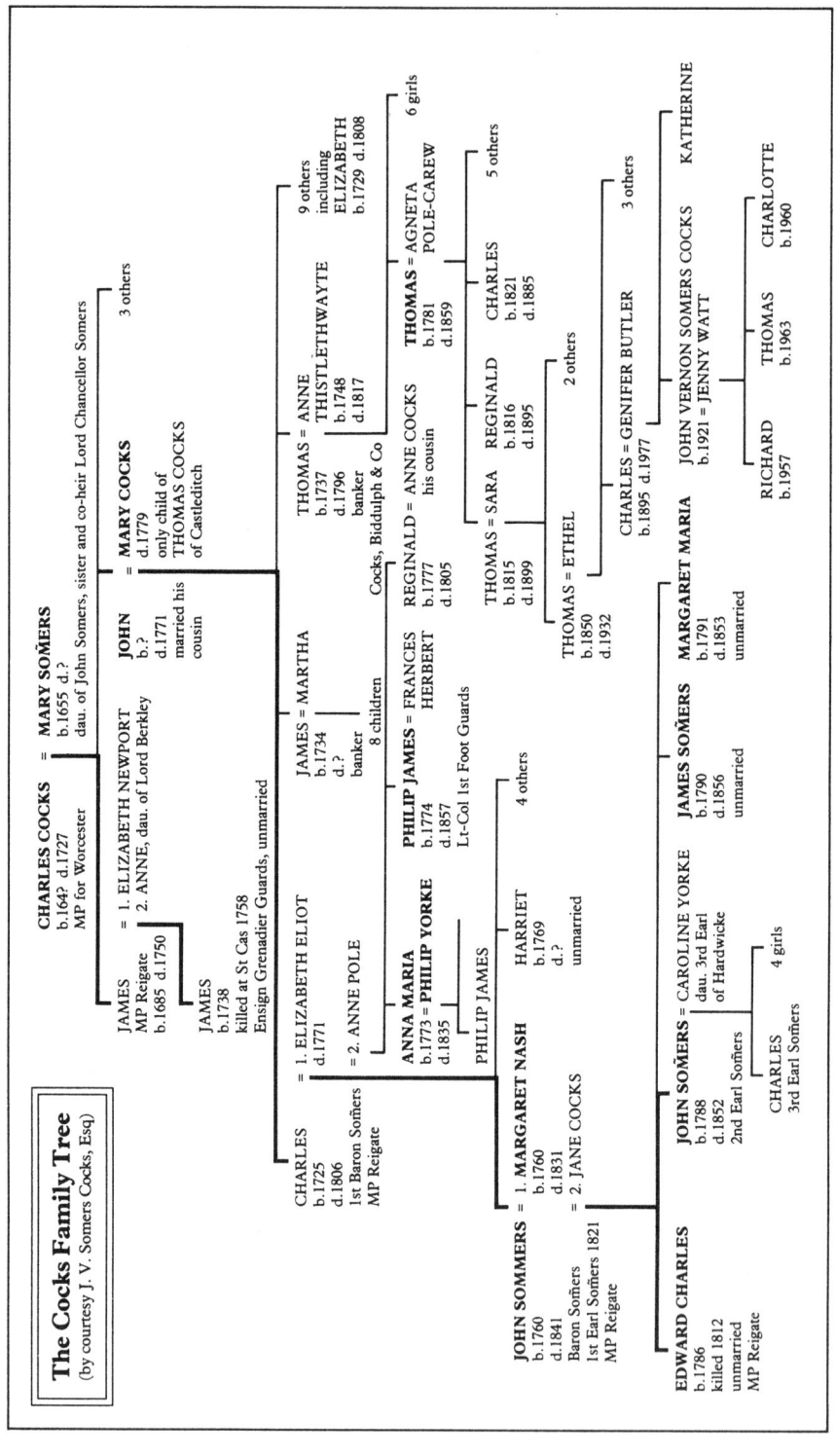

Nash, the daughter of Treadway Nash, of Bevere, Worcestershire, a scholar, pluralist and compiler of the county's first history, and a fortnight later he was baptised in St James's church, Piccadilly.[6]

The Cocks family may have originated in Kent but are only positively identified from Tudor times when they appear in villages the length of the Cotswolds escarpment.[7] In 1600 Richard Cocks, a successful merchant, purchased the manor of Castleditch, over at Eastnor, Ledbury, and from then on the family steadily moved from trade into the professions. The marriage of Worcester's Cocks MP to Mary Somers, a local attorney's daughter, towards the end of the century sealed their fortunes for all time because she was the sister and co-heir of John Somers, William III's trusted Lord Chancellor.[8] And along with the bulk of Somers' money came the constituency of Reigate which, together with their kinsmen, the Yorkes, the family was to represent for well over a hundred years.

The eighteenth century found them principally in law, politics, the church and the army but during the middle years, in partnership with their neighbours, they established the Cocks, Biddulph Bank in Whitehall (now incorporated in Barclays although the branch name remains the same) and by the time John Sommers Cocks succeeded his father as Member for Reigate in the 1780s the family was soundly based and universally respected, both in London and the provinces.

Unfortunately, such a promising ancestry could not prevent natural tragedy and Charles (the Edward was never used) came into the world burdened with clubfeet, thereby causing his early childhood to be entirely dominated by efforts to correct them.[9] Right from the start they were bound together with plaster in order that as he kicked with a baby's natural action, one might knock the other straight, a treatment so successful that at the end of nine months only one leg had to be fitted with a splint, made, incidentally, by a trussmaker who never saw him, constructing it solely from measurements and a drawing. Three years later this, too, had triumphed and by 1789 his feet were pronounced, 'well or, at least, pretty well,'[10] the residual deformity presumably being hidden by his boots.

But the experience may have left its mark. Early infancy is the peak learning period when the foundations of personality and character are laid. Against the background of pain it required enormous determination to learn to walk with the weighty appliance inhibiting movement, and the struggle to do so possibly gave birth to the iron resolution which marked his career, of seeking advancement through his own efforts rather than patronage as was the custom. By nature highly ambitious, the disability could have provided an additional spur. Subjected, inevitably, to the helping hand in infancy he sought the solo path in adulthood: 'I do not want an introduction to Lord Cathcart, *nor any introduction to anybody else*,'[11] he declared forcibly to his mother in 1804, a decision greatly at variance with his contemporaries.

He became the eldest of four: John Somers born in 1788,[12] James Somers in 1790[13] and Margaret Maria in 1791,[14] and at this period in their lives a happier or more lovingly united family it would be hard to find. They had him educated at home, 'Private but very good'[15] Tomkinson described it, but with no one around his own age he may have been lonely. His great friend and cousin, Thomas Somers

Cocks, lived in London and he could have done with the hurly-burly of school life. 'Without it,' he once told an uncle, 'one sets out in the world without any friends of one's own standing.'[16] John Sommers Cocks owned a town house in Hertford Street but rented a series of properties close to Eastnor (Bromesberrow Place, Bromesberrow; Down House, Redmarley; & Highnam Court, Gloucester) and Charles mostly spent his days in the country, visits to the Nash grandparents at Bevere playing an important part in his upbringing. Dr Nash enjoyed his eldest grandson's company and Charles probably owed his intellectual discipline as much to his grandfather's scholarly logic as to his tutor.

War against France broke out in 1793 when Charles was $6\frac{1}{2}$ and John Sommers Cocks, a moderate Whig, supported Pitt in Parliament, and at home became one of the leading lights in the Worcestershire Provisional Cavalry, rising speedily from captain to colonel. Suddenly all the talk round the dinner table was military; musters, uniforms, manoeuvres – heady stuff for a small boy. He was ten when the French landed in Fishguard, catching only the excitement as the Worcester garrison marched out to the sound of the guns but the Duke of York's Helder expedition three years later found him more mature, writing seriously to his mother in French about the campaign,[17] albeit culled from the newspapers, and from then on it was generally accepted he would join the army.

During his teenage years he seems to have divided his time between London and the country, beginning a hunting journal, regularly taking his gun after the rabbits, and breeding horses, yet he remained somewhat solitary. John Somers, his younger brother, had gone to school, to Westminster, and James and Margaret Maria were too young for anything but games. Thomas' seniority by five years was in a way another disadvantage because, having missed the companionship of a crowd of boys at school, with his cousin he skipped the teens as well, mixing principally with adults. In consequence he left home a somewhat shy boy when it came to making friends with his own age group.

The peace of Amiens may have delayed his joining the army but when war again appeared likely his father purchased a cornetcy for him in the 16th (Queen's) Light Dragoons;† Dr Nash put up some of the money and he was gazetted in April 1803.[18] The regiment was stationed in Ireland and after an overland journey to Holyhead and a, 'tedious passage of 25 hours', he landed in the capital at ten o'clock in the evening of 10 June 1803.[19]

The 16th Light Dragoons formed part of the Dublin garrison and were currently commanded by Lt-Col Sir Stapleton Cotton – shortly to become a brigadier. Cotton was devoted to his regiment and profession and possessed many virtues, but vanity and snobbery marred him and he positively fawned over Cocks, vacating his own office for him because of the scarcity of barrack accommodation,[20] thereby not only thoroughly embarrassing Charles but also placing him at a disadvantage when it came to making friends and it was not until after the furore of Emmet's rebellion a few weeks later that the boy finally settled and was accepted. 'I have liked my regiment and my brother officers infinitely better since the row,' he told them at home, 'it has brought us more together.'[21]

---

†Now the 16th/5th Queen's Royal Lancers.

In all, Cocks spent nineteen months in Ireland, in Dublin and then Gort, his own studies augmenting the regimental training, the private but very good education having laid down habits of concentration and discipline. The box of books, destined to accompany him to the Peninsula, included at this time de Saxe's 'Reveries' and histories of the eighteenth-century wars and he approached their contents methodically. Cotton soon discovered there was more to him than aristocratic connections and on one occasion, as part of his outpost training, sent him around Gort to sketch the countryside, with results good enough to show the District Commander.[22]

By mid-1804 admission to staff college and promotion were occupying Cocks's mind. The former eluded him because one had to be nineteen before application and by the time he was eligible his circumstances had changed, while the latter was not easily accomplished either. In January 1805 all the cornets, bar the most senior, were dispersed on a recruiting assignment across the kingdom, with the reward of instant promotion without purchase once a quota of ten had been realised. The race was on but he was given Birmingham, a notoriously difficult area, and was not gazetted before August, six weeks behind his brother John Somers, who had joined the regiment half a year after him.[23] The delay also meant he had to refuse the Lord Lieutenant's invitation to become one of his ADCs. The 3rd Earl of Hardwicke, as a Yorke, was a kinsman of the Cocks family and, failing Charles, he promptly turned to John Somers, whose lucky year it certainly was. But it may have been a happy escape, the pomp of Dublin Castle was not Cocks's idea of military service. Attending a levée the previous year he had remarked it was 'a shocking, stupid thing, nothing but bowing'[24].

The remainder of 1805 was spent recruiting and emerging from adolescence and when the 16th returned home in December the boy had gone forever.

At the start of the following year Lord Somers died and John Sommers Cocks entered the Lords. After some family persuasion Charles agreed to stand for Reigate in his place, with the proviso that if the 16th were posted overseas he would go too, and the successful election took place in November. He sat on the Commons benches from 1807-9 as a passionate, albeit silent, Whig, voting for the relief of the Irish Catholics from their disabilities and joining the Opposition condemnation of the Danish invasion,[25] he and his friend Frederick Ponsonby making an unlikely pair to be found voting against an expedition both would have given their eye teeth to join.[26]

Charles became a captain, by purchase, in the 48th Foot on 25 December 1806[27] but by 12 March 1807 had exchanged back into the 16th.[28] Towards the end of that year, too, his father bought Reigate Priory,[29] its proximity to London giving the family a country home close to the metropolis. It was also convenient for Charles as regards the regiment, although with Parliamentary duty taking precedence the 16th scarcely saw him.

And so his life might have continued, politics and the army competing for his time, but Napoleon's infiltration of Spain and Portugal and the subsequent outbreak of the Peninsular War in 1808 changed everything.

The 16th were encamped at Woodbridge, Suffolk, in September when news of their Portuguese posting arrived and it drove all thoughts of politics from his head. Overnight he resurrected the singlemindedness of his Irish years. He sent for his books from home, began teaching himself Spanish, summoned a serjeant for a daily bout with the swords, endlessly practised shooting, both on foot and from the saddle, and attended every parade to brush up on drill procedure, even those for the newly joined. Owen remembered that, 'When Sir Stapleton Cotton exercised the Regiment and the Horse Artillery in outpost duties, he always took the advanced guard; that as "Eclaireur", he might himself learn, and teach us, according to "the King of Prussia's instructions".'[30] Tomkinson, for his part, recalled the innumerable games of cards played in their spare time and Charles's reluctance to accept his winnings. He and Charles also played Piquet in the Peninsula, to the extent that the cards became so thumbed they each knew what the other held.[31]

In November the regiment, brigaded with the 14th Light Dragoons under Cotton, marched to the west for embarkation and the latter sailed immediately, leaving the 16th to await their turn. However, events were moving so fast in the Peninsula that the government delayed their departure. Wellesley's auspicious start to operations in July had ended in the controversial Convention of Cintra and now Sir John Moore, his successor, was at Salamanca facing difficulties which were to result in the retreat to Corunna. The idea of landing a force at Cadiz and co-operating with Spain in Andalusia was beginning to appear more sensible but the Spanish were proving exceedingly awkward allies.

With the monarchy in Napoleon's hands, the upper classes had formed a Supreme Junta at Seville but corruption and indolence negated their efforts and few battles were won although, given the patriotic fervour of the lower classes and better direction, they might have been more successful, and an inkling of this was appearing in Moore's despatches.[32] Suspicious of each other, the Junta also distrusted Britain and her intentions and the English diplomats were not always very wise either, thereby compounding the problem. Meanwhile, General Sir John Cradock was about to take over the command of the British troops remaining in Portugal.

Cocks's opening letter is self-explanatory and written the day the embarkation orders arrived, whilst the second, from Exeter three months later, is an angry outburst against the Tory government for its seeming incompetence and torpor over Spain, the root of his fury lying in frustration at still being in England and out of touch. By January, thoroughly put out by the continued delay, he went back to London and obtained permission to go on ahead of the 16th but the winter storms held him up and it was 1 March before he finally arrived in Lisbon. Sir Stapleton immediately offered him a place on his staff but, instead, Charles proposed a fact-finding tour of the Spanish southern armies, to which both Cotton and Cradock readily agreed.[33]

He went first to Seville and then Grenada, but two more Spanish defeats, at Ciudad Real and Medellin, upset his arrangements and he doubled back to reach General Cuesta at Monasterio. However, events overtook him him once again because news of Soult's capture of Oporto coincided with his arrival, and he left at once to re-join Cotton,[34] now at Leyria, pausing only for twenty-four hours to see the British Ambassador.

CHAPTER ONE
Southern Spain
18 September 1808 – 6 May 1809

18 September, Woodbridge. To his Mother:
Dearest Madam,
 The orders are at last arrived for our proceeding immediately on service. I have been disappointed so often on this subject that I can scarce bring myself to trust my good fortune. It has been almost the first wish of my heart, but one which I have lately despaired to see accomplished, to serve with my old regiment, with comrades whom I love and who are attached to me. Will you have the goodness to direct Nickolls† to join me immediately . . .

> By December the situation with Moore and his force at Salamanca had become critical and the Government hardly knew what to do for the best, but, in the end, events decided for them with the retreat to Corunna and they held their hand for a while. Cocks saw the hesitation as a possible withdrawal from Spain and thus operations against Buonaparte and feared his dream of active service was fast fading.

18 December, Exeter. To Thomas Somers Cocks, Esq:
My dear Thomas,
 . . . Our transports with those of the Heavy Brigade embarking at Portsmouth have been ordered to Vigo to receive the Hussars, the 14th go with them but are not to disembark but to proceed to the Tagus. It is said the vessels are then to come back for us but this hope can be only regarded as most precarious . . . If Government pretends to say that it is now waiting for fresh information before it takes further steps they cannot keep that ground a moment. Energy, despatch, almost rashness, is necessary to drive courage into a multitude, if the Spaniards have once reason to believe that we despair, even that we hesitate, they will rise no more . . . I have always flattered myself that, aware of the impossibility of openly opposing the progress of the French along the champagne country, Government had, nevertheless, resolved to fan the flame whilst one ember continued alight. Had British officers, soldiers and arms been distributed throughout all the provincial armies their example would have greatly assisted in keeping them together . . .‡ France might have poured her legions over the Pyrenees, they might have marched round and round Spain but enemies would have sprung up in their rear faster than they could have reduced them in front and their atrocities would have heightened the national resentment. Some of the wilder parts of Spain would have maintained their independence, the existence of the nation

---
†His servant.
‡In fact the Spanish refused all offers of troops in 1808.

would have been ascertained and some favourable opportunity would have arisen when a fatal blow might be struck. As it is, however, they seem to have no intention of this sort. If Sir John Moore with his 40 or 50,000 cannot keep the field against Buonaparte with 150,000 – a thing impossible – they appear to intend giving the matter up and quietly walking up to the Treasury Bench; they will say they have done all they can for Spain and Europe. As for the defence of Portugal, it is said to be out of the question.

For myself, let the Regiment go or not, the end of January shall not see me in England . . . All my mornings I learn Spanish, hunting I have given up and I have been little out shooting. Adieu . . .

6 February 1809, Falmouth. To Thomas Soṁers Cocks, Esq:
My dear Thomas,
You may conceive how much against my inclination I am still detained in this place by a cursed SW. What have I done to offend Appolus I know not, nor am I aware that Juno has conceived any secret spite against me which might induce her to play off her old tricks by bribing the huffing God. Yesterday and the day before I was tantalised by the wind's veering to the W and once to the N of the W, but today it has settled in its old point and is blowing a severe gale.

In one respect I have been fortunate, for the weather since my arrival here has been tremendous. A West Indian packet was obliged to put back today after being at sea a fortnight. Several vessels have drifted and gone ashore in the harbour itself. The *Primrose* sloop of war and a transport with part of the 7th were lost a few days before I came here. Meantime I fear that the port of Lisbon should be shut against me. As in this case I shall probably proceed to Cadiz, I have obtained letters of credit on that port to the amount of £150 from Messrs Fox, Merchants in this town and have given them a draft to that amount on you.† I was obliged to take this precaution lest I should sail before I could hear from you.

Last Tuesday I boarded the *Ferdinand 7* off Falmouth and brought a Mr Tyrrel on shore who came on board her. He had been from Cadiz to Sevilla and through the Sierra Morena to Lisbon. He was with General Cuesta about the 16 January; Cuesta had about 23,000 men with him and was fortifying the passes. The hatred of the French is strong and universal among all ranks of Spaniards. But their armies are in a state of disorganisation and very deficient in officers, particularly Engineers, arms and accoutrements. When he left Lisbon, January 24, the 14th were on board Transports waiting for orders. Since that period the winds have been constantly adverse and it has been impracticable to convey intelligence from hence to the southwards so that unless the Commander-in-Chief in Portugal has discretionary orders, or that the arrival of the French hinted the necessity of the immediate departure of the British, it is probable Cotton and the 14th are still waiting in the Tagus.

If I could have read a leaf or two in the book of fate I could have spent this fortnight more pleasantly than I have. À solo in an Inn at Falmouth does not offer

---

†Thomas Soṁers Cocks was a banker with the family bank of Cocks, Biddulph & Co, and he transacted all Cocks's financial business.

many amusements . . . Remember me to all present and acquaintances. Adieu, you may depend on hearing when I reach the other side of the water. Do not mention my Cadiz scheme ! . . .

14 February 1809, Falmouth. To Thomas Somers Cocks, Esq:
My dear Thomas,
This is indeed a horrid place ! Would you believe it, the girls are contemptible. If you address them in a morning they are shocked at the idea of walking at night and if you speak to them in the dark, Good Lord, they set up their backs like a cat worried by a terrier. What can be the cause of this astonishing degeneracy I am unable to ascertain, and I know not whether any cold-blooded Sea Monster formerly haunted these shores, daily demanding the sacrifice of a virgin . . . ? I believe Andromache's Sea Monster was a native of Britain, I know Tassio places one in Ireland, perhaps he meant Falmouth, various have been my conjectures. This fact, only, have I been able to ascertain for sure, that I have lived in celibacy since my arrival. Dreadful sclrospection . . . †

Tonight, tonight is to be the crisis of my fate. At one o'clock the moon changes and with it I am assured, the wind will probably alter; it is now within three or four points of fair. And when once it shifts it has been so long fresh that I am told there is every chance of its remaining fair . . .

21 February, Falmouth. To his mother:
Dearest Madam,
The wind has, at last, shifted to a fine breeze from the north and we shall be underway in a few hours. A packet arrived here last night six days from Lisbon where everything was quiet and the French not expected . . . you may conceive I have no time to turn . . .

Unfortunately, it was yet another false hope and in fact he did not leave until 24 February.

2 March, Lisbon. To his mother:
Dearest Madam,
We reached this place last night after a delightful passage of ten days and I have met with a very hearty welcome from all friends . . . The French are to the north of Portugal and have passed the river Minho in small numbers . . . The hatred of the French throughout Portugal appears from everything I have *heard* for, of course, I have not yet had time to judge for myself, to be very universal. The levée en masse comprises of considerable numbers but wretchedly armed and wretchedly officered. Buonaparte has returned to Paris and his brother is firmly seated on the throne of Spain. The French have advanced twelve or fourteen thousand men to the Tagus and are endeavouring to pass at the Ponte del Obispo. Cuesta had a superior Spanish force to oppose them . . . This is all *hearsay* but is generally believed here. I shall probably set off for Spain in a few days to obtain intelligence of the state of organisation in Andalusia. My destination will,

---

†Throughout his Letters and Diaries Cocks frequently made up words or adapted ones to his use.

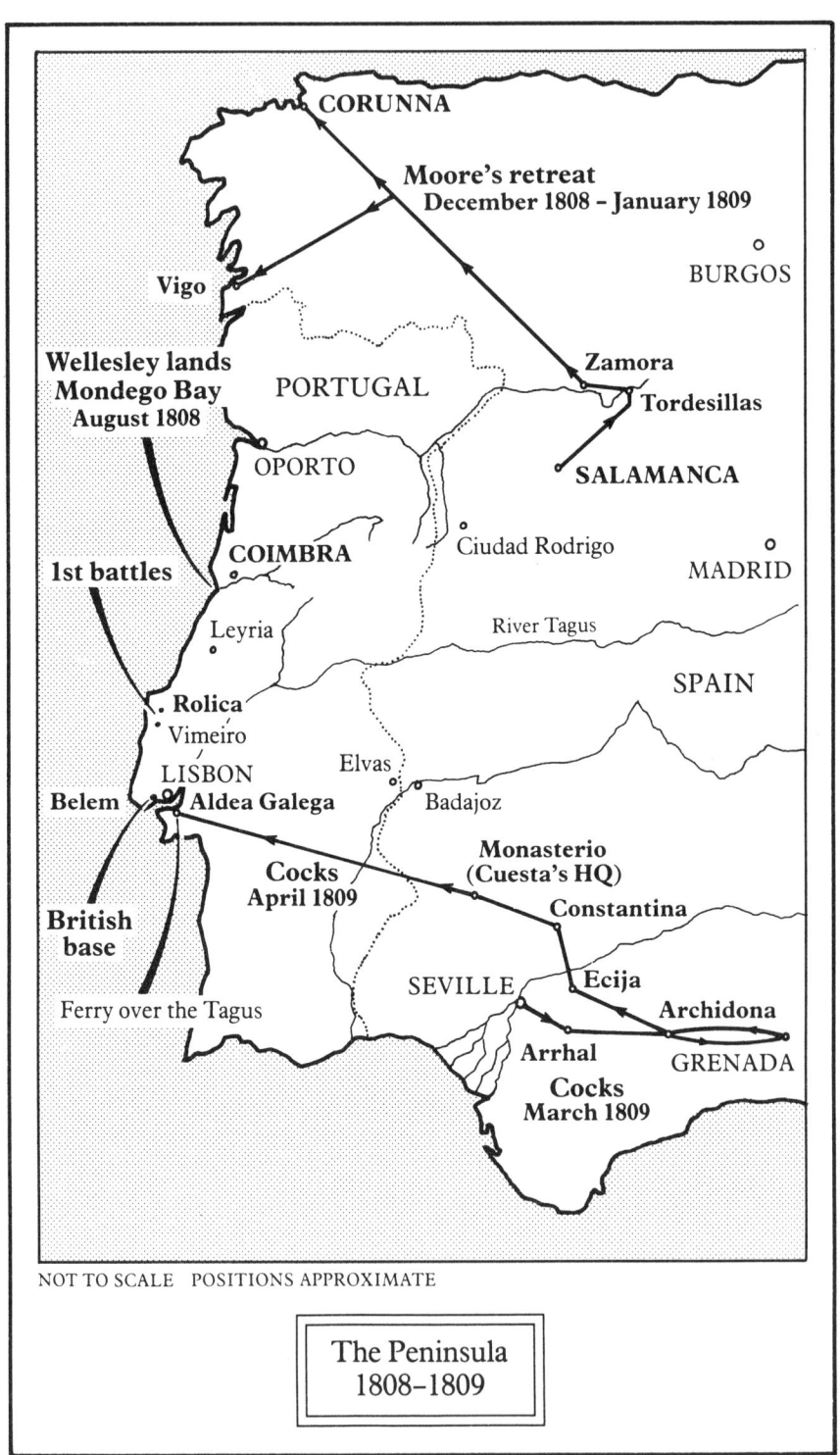

however, in some manner depend on Sir John Cradock whom I see tomorrow. As I think this likely to be an employment of activity and amusement I have preferred it to being on Cotton's staff, which he very handsomely offered me the instant of my arrival. As I am, *at present*, here *unofficially* I will thank you to mention it as little as possible and on no account to *quote* any political reports I may detail . . .

22 March, Sevilla. To his mother:
Dearest Madam,
    I had intended to have despatched another tremendous letter of four pages but I am so much hurried today that I find it impossible. As I keep memorandums, my next will contain all I meant to have said.
    Now! I set off tomorrow early for Grenada in company with a very gentlemanly Englishman, Mr Bailey, either his father or brother is in Parliament. I shall take the first opportunity of writing from that place but as there is no British minister there, the communication will become much more uncertain and it will probably be some time before my next letter may reach you. I am improved in my Spanish but there is an English regiment here, the 40th, and I hear too much of my own language; in Grenada I hope I shall neither hear or see anything but what is Spanish. I have been much pleased with this city where there are some good pictures. Remember me to everybody, I am called here Senhor Capitano Don Eduarte Carlos Cockings! . . .

1 April, Grenada. To Thomas Somers Cocks, Esq:
My dear Thomas,
    I have no doubt you are already informed of my perambulations from Lisbon to Sevilla . . . as time is rather precious I shall continue with my March from Sevilla . . .
    We slept the first night at Arrahal . . . the second at Assuna, an handsome town, and the next day reached Alamenda where a regular deputation waited on us to compliment us as Englishmen. The same spirit is observable everywhere as far as I have travelled. The rising generation are brought up amid excretions of the French and blessings on the English. Spain is deficient not in zeal, not in the determination to undergo all extremities rather than submit to a foreign yoke. She fails in the organisations of the energies she possesses; her officers, composed of gentry, brought up in indolence and inactivity, have too often set an ill example in the moment of action. Her government too, as an executive body, has been collected without order and without regularity and acts without resolution, dispatch or unanimity . . . I propose remaining here some days longer, when I shall go up to Urbino's army in La Mancha . . .

21 April, Lisbon. To his mother:
Dearest Madam,
    Excuse the hurry with which I write. From Grenada I joined General Cuesta's army in Estramadura but hearing that the enemy had entered Portugal conceived it my duty to return here. I made a most fatiguing march, having been

fifty three hours on horseback almost without intermission. I am perfectly well and not the least the worse for it. I am now on the point of starting for Leyria, where the army is ...

29 April, Coimbra. To his younger brother, Captain The Hon. John Somers Cocks:
My dear Somers,

For the last fortnight or three weeks I have been so hurried that I have scarce had time to write to anyone. You probably heard of my being in Grenada. I there bought two horses and proceeded to join Cuesta's army where I intended serving as a volunteer. My route was by Archidona, Ecija and Constantina; the country was most romantically beautiful, being the wildest part of the Sierra Morena. I met with no other adventure than being detained at Irreza† as a French spy. I was the second stranger that had ever appeared there since the revolution, the first had correct passports but afterwards turned out a spy. The Magistrate of the place was a most sagacious blockhead and had inferred from this circumstance that correct passports wore a suspicious appearance, on this ground he detained me. Unfortunately, on examining my portmanteau he found some receipts of my groom for hay and corn at Falmouth, which being written very ill he, with great gravity, pronounced to be *Memorandum Cyphers*. The business began to be serious as the mob in their zeal for England seemed inclined to insult me. At Constantina I met with a different reception. Being the first Englishman who had ever appeared there the town seemed actually mad with joy. I was stuffed with eatables and overwhelmed with civilities of every kind. On my arrival at Cuesta's army I was received by the old boy very kindly. Headquarters were at Monasterio, our advanced posts at Medina, Fuente di Carlos, etc. Our numbers did not exceed 14,000 men but strong reinforcements were daily expected and the Infantry were tried men who could fight.

I was disappointed on being obliged to leave this corps but hearing that Soult had entered Portugal in force, taken Oporto and was marching on Lisbon I conceived it my duty to join Cotton. We are at present in a state of inaction as Sir A. Wellesley has superseded Sir John Cradock but has not yet joined us. You may conceive our anxiety to know [his] schemes. I am at present returning with Cotton from Trant's corps at Agueda on the Vouga. Yesterday morning he went out to make a reconnaissance. We pushed considerably within the French patrols but they had withdrawn their videttes in the night and we could see nothing of them ...

2 May, Coimbra. To his uncle, The Rev Philip Yorke:
My dear Uncle,

... We are now at Coimbra, 17,000 strong, and expecting reinforcements, eight leagues from the Vouga. Operations have been for some days at a standstill, in consequence of our change of general. Thank God, Sir Arthur Wellesley arrived this morning and Soult must make haste to pack up his plunder in Oporto. With regard to our future operations little is known. Sir Arthur has discretionary orders to enter Spain but at present he cannot leave Victor on his right ...

---

†Unidentified.

6 May, Coimbra. To his father:

My dearest Lord,

... The 16th Light Dragoons† came up with the army yesterday but as the general‡ wishes to keep me on his staff I shall not join them for the present except occasionally. Sir Arthur Wellesley has taken the command of the army and inspired fresh spirit into every breast. I believe there are upwards of 20,000 British troops in Portugal. A corps is detached under General Mackenzie to Abrantes to keep in check Victor and some floating columns of the enemy which are between the Tagus and the Guadiana.

The Portuguese keep possession of the bridge of Amarante, Soult is at Oporto, his advanced corps extend to the Vouga. We march tomorrow and have reason to think we are on the eve of a movement of some importance. Sir Robert Wilson is at Pedro de Sal, General Beresford with a brigade of British infantry, a squadron of the 14th Light Dragoons, a troop of Germans, 20,000 Portuguese infantry and 2,000 cavalry is marching on Viseu.

The bridge over the Vouga in our front is occupied by the Portuguese. Their troops are superior to what I expected, at least in appearance, but I fear their officers are bad. A regiment has been attached to each British brigade ... Your lordship will excuse the haste in which this letter is written. I have just got an order to march and have, at this moment, not even a table to write on but, hearing that a packet goes tonight, am unwilling to lose the opportunity.

I remain your lordship's most dutiful and affectionate son,
    E. Charles Cocks

---

†The regiment arrived in Lisbon on 16 April.
‡Sir Stapleton Cotton.

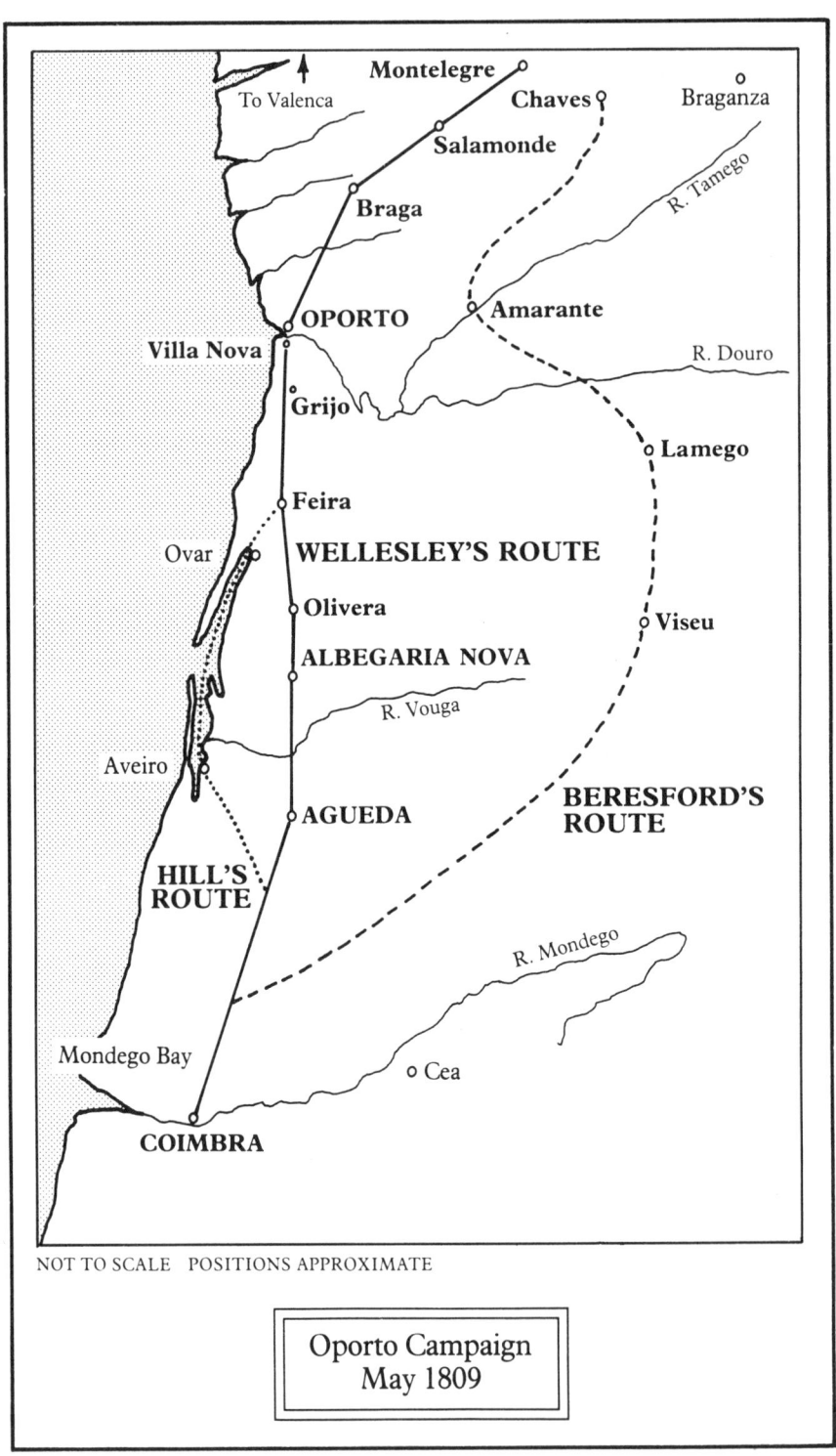

Oporto Campaign
May 1809

CHAPTER TWO

Oporto

9 May – 11 June 1809

WITH THE AIM OF attacking Soult in Oporto before turning his attention to Marshal Victor on the Tagus, Wellesley marched his army of 18,000 out of Coimbra on 7/8 May. He divided his force into three, taking the main body on the direct route himself and sending Major-General Hill's brigade off to the left through the lagoons to Ovar before linking up with him again near Oporto, while, at the same time, despatching Marshal Beresford's Portuguese regiments – he had been appointed by the Portuguese government to command and train them – away to the right to seal off the escape routes east. The 16th Light Dragoons were with Wellesley.

Despite eventual success, the next fortnight saw inexperience causing many mistakes, and not the least when Sir Stapleton found himself ordered to begin the advance at night on the 9th rather than by day as he had been led to believe, and several units lost their way.† Cocks was also concerned to see the troopers miss opportunities during skirmishes and downright dismayed when muddled orders produced a dangerous confusion at Grijo on the 11th and William Tomkinson was severely wounded.‡ Between the 9th and 20th Cocks remained with Cotton and the brigade as they pursued the French from the Vouga to the Douro, and beyond, and he watched the capture of Oporto from the grandstand position with the staff by the Serra Convent.

It is doubtful if Wellesley and Cocks had ever spoken whilst in England, the difference in age and political persuasion giving them no reason to do so, but now Sir Arthur was anxious to learn all he could of the situation in Spain and Charles's recent visit to the south, together with Cotton's obvious confidence in him, soon bridged the gap.

★ ★ ★

12 May Villa Nova: . . . the column marched off at five and reached Villa Nova about six. This is the suburbs of Oporto, situated on a hill immediately opposite the town and separated only by the Douro. It had been said that the French had an advantageous position in Villa Nova which they had intended to defend, but no traces of it appeared and it would only have been madness to oppose the British with the Douro directly in their rear, over which, in case of a retreat, they must have crossed by a narrow bridge.

Half a mile to the right was a large convent and beyond this an open

---

† Cocks's notes, written later, describe this in detail and great indignation.
‡ He had to be evacuated to England and did not return until 1810.

space of ground all commanding the other bank of the Douro that was likewise very high and could only be ascended by a long flight of steps. Immediately opposite, on the summit of the bank, was an old convent and some houses from whence a road led to the back of Oporto. Each side of this road, which was confined by hedges, there were some large enclosures. Between the convent and the town there was an extent of 4 or 500 yards.

On the head of the column arriving at Villa Nova, Sir Arthur established a battery on the open space of ground and sent the advance, under General Paget, over the river at the point opposite the second convent. They were conveyed in boats which some Portuguese boatmen brought from the Oporto side. It was never publicly known how they escaped the vigilance of the French or how far the business had been preconcerted with Sir Arthur.†

The Buffs passed over first, huzzaing as the boats shoved off, and reached the top of the steps without opposition, but were soon after attacked. They threw themselves into a house and maintained their ground. However, it was a critical moment. Sir Arthur appeared very anxious, but fortunately reinforcements arrived and the enemy retreated a little way up the road where they again made a stand. We could see the rising smoke, which pointed out when the heads of the columns were engaged, alternatively advancing and retrograding, while, beyond, large columns of cavalry were seen in action. From their direction it could not be ascertained whether they were commencing a retreat or coming down on our infantry. Our battery did little execution and occasionally injured our own men, while one gun, which the enemy had brought into action upon a height, appeared to annoy the British column.

Meantime, General Hill and General Murray had passed the river higher up, at separate fords, and the Guards, with two squadrons of the 14th, had crossed opposite Oporto. General Hill had with him the cavalry piquet of the preceding night, commanded by Major Hervey‡ of the 14th Dragoons; his arrival decided the affair, the enemy evacuated Oporto. Major Hervey followed them and charged by order of General Stewart§ under great disadvantage. He lost several men and horses and was himself so severely wounded in the arm as to render amputation necessary.

13 May Villa Nova: . . . this morning was occupied in repairing the bridge and provisioning a brigade of infantry which, with two squadrons of cavalry, was destined to accompany General Murray in the pursuit. Intelligence had been received from General Beresford that General Loisson had abandoned Amarante after having burned the whole of it and that he was in possession of the ruins together with the bridge. Sir Arthur was likewise informed that the Duc d'Dalmatia,†† on ascertaining this and being joined by Loisson, had destroyed all his

---

† In fact it was fortuitous. The French overlooked 3 wine barges, concealed by a bend in the river, and a barber alerted the British and helped float them across.

‡ Felton Hervey was a friend of Cocks. The owner of the Cocks diaries was born a Somers Cocks and is married to Hervey's descendant.

§ General the Hon. Charles Stewart, Lord Castlereagh's half brother.

††Marshal Soult.

artillery and whatever baggage he could not convey on mules and taking the mountain road had made for Guimares, intending from thence to cross into the road leading from Braga to Chaves and Monte Allegre. In fact this was his only resource for there are but three roads from Oporto towards the north and towards Spain, namely by Amarante by Chaves, or Monte Allegre and by Valenca.

14 May Sir Arthur resolved to march by the Braga road, with the Brigade of Guards, with that of General Cameron and the cavalry, and endeavour to meet the enemy. The troops were successively supplied with three days' rations and marched off as supplied. The infantry were in front, then the 16th and 20th Light Dragoons and last of all the 14 Dragoons, followed by the squadrons of the Portuguese.

15 May the column reached Braga, distance eight leagues, early on the following day.† It rained the whole of this afternoon and from this time continued to do so daily.

16 May the troops left Braga soon after daybreak... the cavalry were in front and then the Guards, their route lay through Carvalho and Igreja Nova towards Monte Allegre. The day was very rainy and the road narrow and bad. The rearguard of the French had passed the night a little more than two leagues from Braga, from this point the pursuit became more animated, smoking villages attested the recent passage of the enemy...

The province of Tras os Montes through which the column was penetrating is composed wholly of mountains, the foot of one of these is washed by an impetuous stream, rushing along a deep ravine. This stream winds round the projections of the mountain and two of the principal of these are in a direct line, about a mile distant from each other, but the road, which has to pass round intermediate projections or tongues of land, doubles the distance. As you turn the point of either you see the other, with the intermediate ground; the road was nearer the river than the summit. It was very narrow but not otherwise bad.

On the farthest point of these projections is situated the village of Salamonde. In front of it, on each side [of] the road, was the rear guard of the French, 1,500 strong. Observing that the British dragoons were in no force, they took no other precautions than sending out a piquet of cavalry rather more than half the distance towards them, and proceeded in lighting their fires and cooking their dinners.

In rather more than an hour Sir Arthur arrived and spent some time in making his arrangements. He thought it necessary to treat the enemy with great respect. The light companies of the Guards with some of the 60th were sent by the back of the mountain to occupy the summit, and the remainder of the Guards advanced by the road. All these preparations took a great deal of time; when the Guards commenced their attacks scarce half an hour of daylight was left. The enemy precipitately retreated, indeed, it is more than probable they never thought of serious opposition and only assumed a show of resistance to cover the retreat of their main body.

---

†Apart from the 14th Light Dragoons who had lost their way and arrived later, exhausted after a dreadful night.

To the rear of Salamonde the road crossed the river, there are two bridges, one immediately below the village, the other farther on by two miles. The enemy crossed by the first of these but the light companies, in eagerness of pursuit and in the dark, missed the road leading to it and vainly pushed on to the second.

The enemy did not, however, wholly escape, the parapet of the bridge had been destroyed and the bridge itself otherwise injured by the Portuguese peasantry. In their hurry, many of their men and horses fell over the sides and perished and the greater part of their baggage was left as plunder to the British.

General Beresford was perfectly aware of these bridges. He had sent his aide de camp word to destroy them but the Portuguese peasantry refused to assist him, effectually alleging that it was their only road to market. He then attempted to defend them, but with such men that was equally impracticable.

This was a curious circumstance, for why was Colonel Murray as QMG so ignorant of the road beyond Salamonde that he could give no directions to the Guards when General Beresford was so well acquainted with the country, and when a few questions directed at any Portuguese peasant would probably have given sufficient explanation? There was no want of men to ask, for there were many round the column. Again, why did General Beresford run wild upon Chaves, where the French never thought of going, and not send a sufficient force to destroy or defend these passes, the only danger the enemy had to apprehend? I am almost certain he had sufficient time, particularly had he not halted two days at Amarante.

Note 10 March 1810 General Beresford was three days without intelligence of the passage of the Douro through the negligence or stupidity of the dragoon who conveyed the despatch.

17 May ... the cavalry and a part of the infantry reached Monte Allegre. The latter had been so fatigued in their exertions on the 16th that, on the first of these days (17th and 18th) they did not advance little more than a league. (The enemy) entered Spain, his route was marked by men and horses, dead and dying. A few prisoners were picked up by the army and some were massacred by the Portuguese. At Monte Allegre the French had the cruelty to murder their Portuguese guides lest they should be of any use to their pursuers ...

18 May ... At Monte Allegre the pursuit was given up ...

11 June, Coimbra. To Thomas Somers Cocks, Esq:

My dear Thomas,

Long before you receive this letter you will have talked over the capture of Oporto till you have tired yourself of the subject... The passing of the Douro was wonderfully fine, we marched on quietly to the river as if no enemy had been near. How it was contrived I know not, but some Portuguese instantly managed to bring boats off, General Paget's brigade passed over and ascended with three cheers by a winding path up the hill on the other side ...

Hervey of the 14th is recovering slowly, his right arm is gone, he behaved very gallantly. Stewart had endeavoured to monopolise his part as well as that of a charge of the 16 Lt.Dns the day before but depend on it from me, whatever Sir A. Wellesley may choose to say, his only merit on either day was being Lord

Castlereagh's brother. On both occasions when he came within sight of the enemy he said, 'There's your enemy, charge them,' and *went* back.† I need not caution you on no account to quote any opinions I may give on speculative points. I am too young a soldier to venture my ideas except to a particular friend, as to facts, I do not care.

   Your affectionate cousin,
      E. Charles Cocks

---

†To be fair to Stewart this appears the only reference to this behaviour.

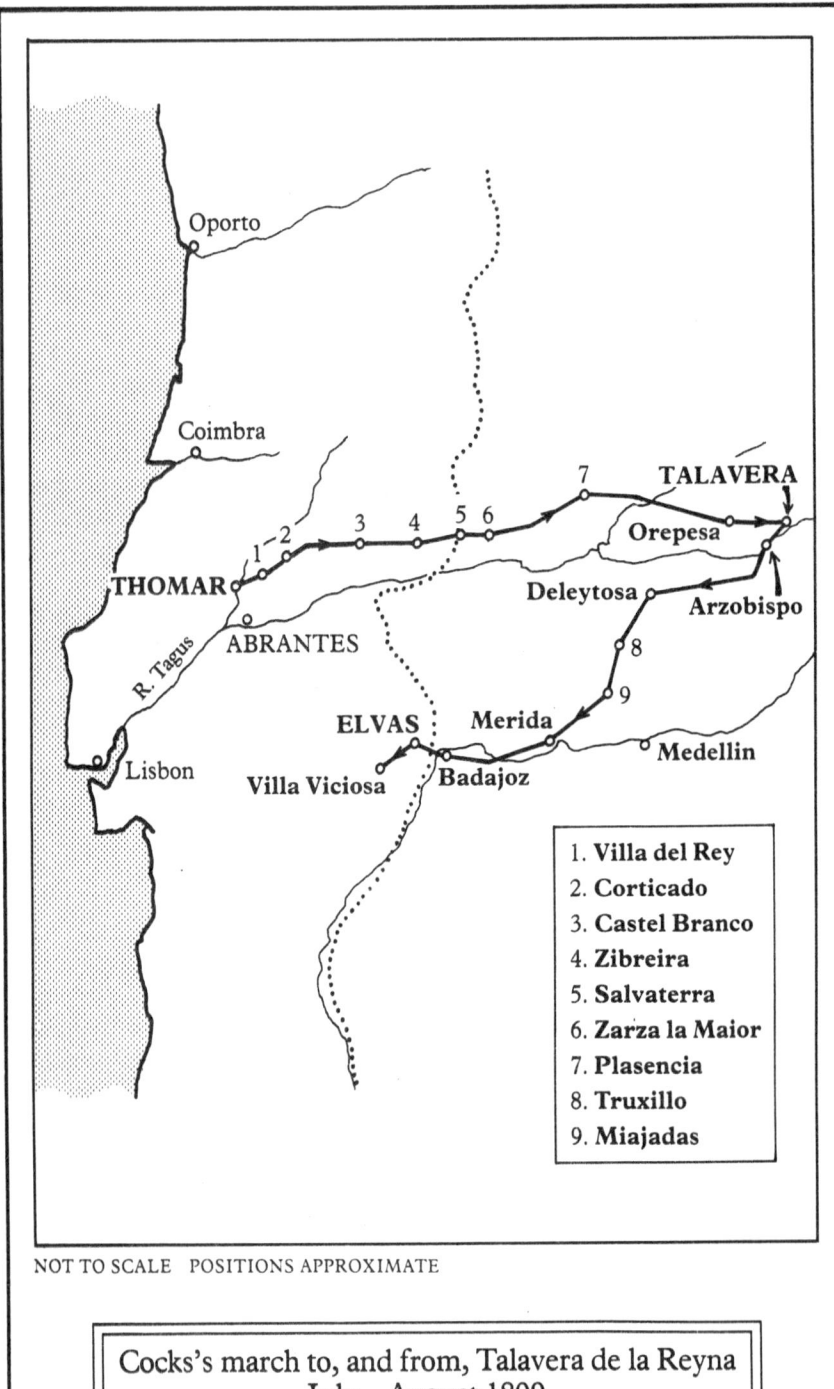

Cocks's march to, and from, Talavera de la Reyna
July – August 1809

CHAPTER THREE
Talavera

2 July – 18 October 1809

AT THE END of the Oporto campaign the army returned to central Portugal to recuperate, the 16th finding themselves at Thomar, while Wellesley at nearby Abrantes began preparations for an Anglo-Spanish operation along the Tagus valley towards Talavera de la Reyna, at the same time commencing the lengthy but imperative task of reorganising and training his army. The shortcomings noticed by Cocks were equally obvious to him, multiplied many times over.

Charles used the breathing space to jot down his own account of recent events on some odd bits of paper but, when the march for Spain began, abandoned them and started a proper diary, heading it 'Journal from leaving Thomar, July 2nd 1809', and henceforth maintaining it became a feature of his life. At first he tended to enter information only likely to be of use in operations, for example: descriptions of roads, towns, villages, attitude of the peasants, availability of food, forage and water, the nature of crops, geographical features such as fords and defiles and whether tracks were practical for artillery, etc; but after Talavera he began to discuss the campaigns and their possible outcome.

Wellesley, meanwhile, planned the July operation on the understanding that he and General Cuesta – Cocks's late acquaintance from Andalusia – would unite at Orepesa for a combined attack on Victor's position at Talavera and that the British would be victualled once they crossed into Spain. Had Cuesta possessed his ally's ability all might have been well, but he was old, obstinate and given to jealousy besides commanding an ill-officered, undertrained army. The Supreme Junta, too, was faltering, split by dissention, and its promises of food and carts were inadequately kept, in consequence of which the British were nearly annihilated by starvation, let alone enemy action. Additionally, a plan to attack Victor on 23 July, which could have been decisive, failed to materialise because Cuesta changed his mind at the eleventh hour and when he did come round to it the moment was lost. But the enemy had gained precious time and brought up formidable reinforcements so, when the battle finally took place, 20,000 British faced 46,000 French, and the 34,000 Spanish had to be given a safe position where their unsteadiness could do least harm.

Following the hard-won victory, the situation took an even unhappier turn because Wellesley learnt that Soult was advancing through the passes in his rear to cut his communications, and both he and Cuesta were forced to retreat across the Tagus at Arzobispo and seek haven in the mountains lest they become caught between the re-forming remnants of the defeated enemy and Soult's fresh troops. In the confusion, feelings ran high against Cuesta whom it was felt could have made a stand.

Adding to the toll of battle by now the British were starving and stricken with disease and among the most seriously afflicted was Cocks. He was placed in a cart alongside others and when it reached the makeshift hospital at Deleytosa five days later, he alone had survived. The conditions there were so appalling that, 'only the worst of our sick and wounded were left'[1], but fortunately someone, possibly Cotton, relayed his plight to Wellesley who gave permission for both he and Belli, also of the 16th, to go on ahead to a permanent hospital being set up at Elvas, on the Portuguese border, and when Lord Somers heard later of this kindness he resolved never again to support Whig criticisms of the Commander in Parliament.[2]

Cocks spent a fortnight at Elvas and, once his strength returned, minutely inspected its fortifications† before joining the 16th at Villa Viciosa where the regiment was recuperating, encamped in the Royal Deer Park. 'I regret my gun dreadfully,' he told James, 'I brought one out with me but it was stolen in the north of Portugal. There is plenty of game here, partridge, hares and red and fallow deer, wolves, etc.'

The following selection starts in July at Orepesa where, after the long march from Portugal, the army met up with its Spanish Allies.

★ ★ ★

21 July ... A Spanish officer, to whom I have just spoken, assures me that the day before yesterday the numbers were 45,000, including 10,000 cavalry in his army; I believe he exaggerates... Various reports prevail respecting the number, position and intentions of the enemy... In the evening we were out for the inspection of General Cuesta, the infantry formed one beautiful line on the Talavera side of Orepesa, near the Madrid road. The cavalry were on the right and the whole force was upwards of 20,000 and moved on afterwards about two miles...

25 July, Camp near Talavera. To his father:
My dearest Lord,
We have just missed a most favourable opportunity of striking a decisive blow in favour of the independence of Spain. Victor's corps, amounting to 20,000 men, after retreating before Cuesta from the south, took up a position near Talavera, behind the river Alberchi... On the 22nd Sir Arthur wished to attack the enemy the next day but Spanish delay prevailed over British promptitude and the engagement was deferred a day. On the 24th we advanced at daybreak but the prey had escaped, in the night the whole French army had made their retreat.

As circumstances have turned out it is most unfortunate that Sir Arthur did not attack the enemy with the British troops only on the 23rd, we should have had every advantage and consequently the most reasonable hopes of victory... Two circumstances, however, excuse Sir Arthur. He had been all along deceived in the number of the enemy. Sebastiani's corps was supposed to have joined, which

---

†His account in the journal runs to 1,324 words and includes the system of water supply, the type of soil, 'relative to mines', and the length of the defensive walls.

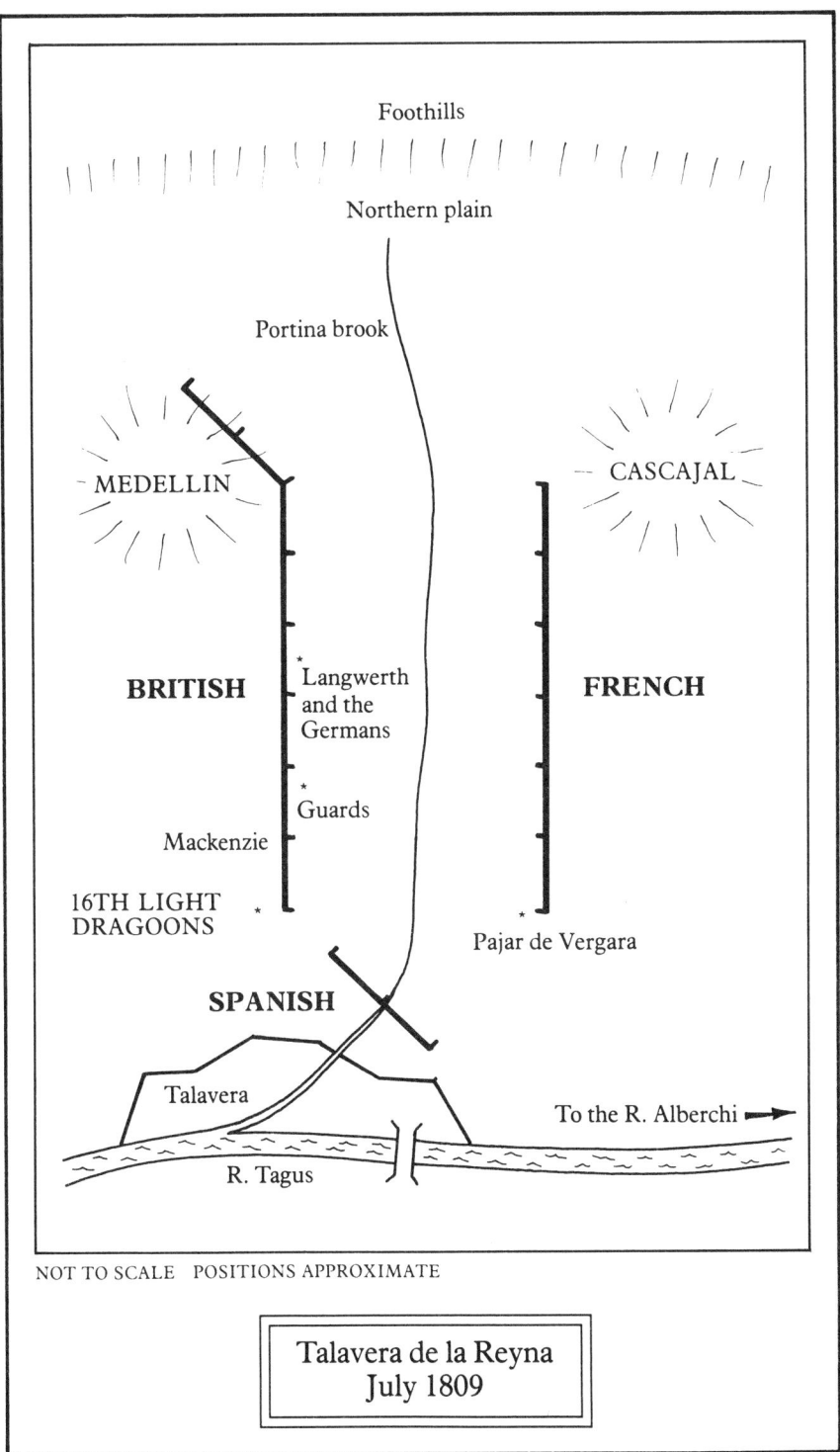

would have made them 35,000 and secondly, it seemed inexplicable why the enemy should choose to wait one day within a league of us if they had not made up their mind of fighting us in their present position . . .

30 July, Encampment near Talavera de la Reyna. To his father:
  My dearest Lord,
    On the 27th and 28th of this month I had an opportunity of witnessing a general engagement, obstinately and bravely contested, and which perhaps reflects as much honour on the British arms as any which have taken place for some years . . .

On the 25th the enemy occupied a position about six leagues beyond the Alberchi, here they were joined by Joseph Buonaparte and every French soldier in this part of Spain. Their number was doubled. This day the Spaniards advanced, the British were detained for want of provisions.

The 26th the French attacked the Spaniards, who lost a few hundred men and fell back in some confusion. The enemy were now so infinitely superior to the British and so little reliance could be *comparatively* placed in our allies that Sir Arthur was compelled to adopt for the moment a defensive conduct. This object was to draw the enemy on to attack him where the ground would be in his favour and this he effected in a masterly manner.

On the 27th our advanced posts beyond the Alberchi were attacked, the whole of our cavalry were out and covered their retreat. We were so closely followed by the enemy, indeed so briskly that had it not been for General Mackenzie's gallant conduct our baggage would have been lost and the army attacked before Sir Arthur had finished his arrangements.

By night the army was formed in the position Sir Arthur had chosen and the enemy coaxed on so far that they had only the option of attacking us or retreating disgracefully and under every disadvantage. Our left flank occupied a steep hill, General Mackenzie's brigade was thrown back at right angles to our line to receive their [?], the most important of the whole, below this, was a plain, where part of the cavalry was posted. This plain was crossed by ditches which made it difficult to charge. From the plain to the river Tagus was a chain of olive groves and vineyards. These were occupied in part by the Guards and the remainder by the Spanish army.

The town of Talavera and the Tagus was on our right. The enemy made three desperate efforts during the night to get possession of the hill on our left but failed. A little before daybreak a most tremendous cannonade began on that point; the enemy were infinitely superior in artillery. The firing continued till nine or ten when it slackened for an hour or two and then recommenced about two.

The French made a famous effort against the centre of the line where the Guards were. They covered themselves with glory but numbers at one time made them fall back, when the Spanish infantry covered their retreat very handsomely. Their cavalry, too, charged and took two pieces of cannon, two generals and many prisoners.

The enemy now gave up the centre and strained every nerve against the left. At one moment they had nearly carried their point, General Anson's brigade of cavalry were ordered to charge. A ditch broke them as they advanced and in consequence they failed in breaking the [front?] the enemy offered to them, yet they terrified them so effectually they dared not advance. I regret to add in this charge the 23rd Light Dragoons were nearly cut to pieces, of 450 men not 120 were left fit for duty. Of 8 captains, 6 are killed, wounded or prisoners.

The action was doubtful till near five; at this moment you may conceive our joy to perceive all parts of the enemy's line beginning to retreat. The firing continued till dusk when the whole of the enemy made off. We knew not, however, that night the extent of our victory, we did not think it improbable we might have been attacked the following day and we were ill-prepared for this. We had lost some capital officers, the men were in high spirits but some of the regiments were faint from fatigue and want of food. But the enemy had been thoroughly discomfited, they fell back at once 4 leagues and are now retreating, I believe, on Toledo. 25,000 Spaniards are ready to stop them there.

Our loss is said to be about 3,000 and that of the enemy 8,000 but I do not speak with any certainty. The enemy had mustered every man they could collect, I believe even the corps from Galicia and Asturias was present. My own regiment had not an opportunity of charging and did not lose above 10 or 11 men and a good many horses. My favourite horse was wounded under me but is likely to do well. The gallant General Mackenzie, the man who did more than anyone towards our victory, is killed, Colonel Gordon is likewise dead. Everybody deeply regrets Mackenzie. Sir Arthur's staff suffered, he was the whole time in the most critical part of the action.

The consequences of this victory cannot be calculated, the French will probably retreat towards the Ebro or perhaps not make a stand till they get there. They have sent back all our wounded prisoners . . .

30 July A mere trifling disorder which brought on a violent fever and which attacked me from this day prevented me from reviewing the field of battle and ascertaining many interesting facts.

17 August, Badajoz. To his father:
My dearest Lord,
    No man could ever be more deceived or disappointed than I believe nearly the whole British army have been in the consequences of the battle of Talavera. The fact is everyone to the Commander-in-Chief was ignorant of the immense force still retained by the French in Spain.

We remained five days quietly in camp at Talavera. Our loss was much more considerable than at first believed† . . . so bloody an action has seldom been fought.

On the 5th day information arrived that Soult had marched from the north and occupied Plasencia, a town directly in our line of communication with Portugal. Sir Arthur instantly determined to march against him, leaving Cuesta to maintain the position of Talavera. Victor's beaten army had retired to considerable

---

†Modern figures give the British casualties as 5,365 and the French 7,268.³

distance. When Sir Arthur had advanced two days he received at once two species of intelligence, that Soult had been joined by the divisions of Ney, Kellermann and Mortier, making his force upwards of 40,000 men – a number infinitely too great for the British to cope with – and also that Cuesta had abandoned shamefully, without the appearance of an enemy, the position of Talavera. He [Wellesley] had now but one course to pursue, instantly retire a day's march, collect his sick and wounded, cross the Tagus and destroy the bridges. This was effected with the bridge of Almarez. The Spaniards were left in charge of the bridge of Arzobispo. Sir Arthur retreated by forced marches for four days to Deleytosa, across the mountains, destroying part either of his stores or his artillery.

At Deleytosa he halted. We had always believed that the whole disposable force of the French in this part of Spain was contained in Victor's army, which we beat; we even thought Soult was there.

For my part, I was attacked by a fever a day or two after the battle; the fatigues and severe privations I was forced to undergo during our rapid retreat, of course, made me worse. But since, by the kindness of the Commander-in-Chief, I have enjoyed considerable indulgences in my mode of travelling and got leave to go before the body of the sick, a great convenience. I have all my servants with me and am recovering in strength. My fever has nearly left me and my appetite is daily growing better ...

5 September, Villa Viciosa. To Thomas Somers Cocks, Esq:

My dear Thomas,

... I meant to have written you an account of our fine fight at Talavera but between my illness and being heartily tired of writing the same description over and over, I never made up my mind to it. Nothing was ever more fortunate, as it afterwards appeared, than a circumstance the whole army regretted at the time, the retreat of the French on the night of the 23rd and our inability to follow them for want of supplies. Had we advanced, Victor would have fallen back on Sebastiani and occupied a position with 42,000 men in our front, covering the bridge of Toledo. Soult would have occupied Talavera – and the fine position in which we eventually fought – in our rear with 35,000 men and the Tagus would have been on our right without either bridge or ford. Our only resource would have been the sabre and the bayonet, the Dons would not have relished this work and 19,000 half-starved English would have had to make their way through one of those armies, probably that of Soult.

Nothing can account for the infatuation our generals displayed respecting Soult. His approach was known at Plasencia, six days before he entered it and advice was sent off to Sir Arthur. This was repeatedly confirmed. On the 5th their advanced guard made some prisoners in Naval Moral, five leagues from Orepesa where our Headquarters were, yet at six in the evening their numbers were grossly miscalculated and their approach not known.

Cuesta misled Sir Arthur by false intelligence, it is said he was at one time doubtful whether he should retreat by the Puente de Arzobispo; the French have behaved nobly to our prisoners ... I regret poor Ross of the Guards, I spoke to him just before he was wounded, the shot came from his own men who did not see him in their front. Gordon, who was with Lord Hardwick in Ireland, was knocked off his horse by a shot through the neck and, as they were conveying him off, a shell fell on him and instantly burst; it carried off his thigh and killed the four men who were carrying him. He lived an hour. Hawker of the 14th is wounded. Water was dreadfully scarce. We could procure none except what was foul. I believe this was one cause of the number of sick. Poor Neville of the 14th Dragoons, a son of Lord Braybrooke, sunk under the fatigue and privation and died about 10 days afterwards. Had the French pressed us in our retreat we must have lost a dreadful number, as it is our army is nearly annhilated for a time ... our men could not bear the forced marches, excessive heat and scarcity of provisions combined ...

Headquarters are at Badajoz and our army is cantoned on the frontier of Spain. I hear Sir Arthur says if the French mean to have Spain to themselves they must *drive* us out ...

Will you have the goodness to procure for me the following articles ... a writing case of Russia leather, strong with a good lock and stored with paper, six black lead pencils, a piece of Indian ink and some camel hair brushes, a piece of india rubber and six memoranda books with *metallic* pencils. Two: A two-foot portable military telescope by Dolland. Three: A pocket compass by ditto. Four: Stockdale's largest map of Spain and Portugal done on canvas and folding in a case ... Would you also order Cobbett to be regularly sent in future and all his papers from the 20 January last, bound in a book ... with any pamphlets you may think worth the carriage and any good accounts of Moore's Spanish expedition. Adieu, excuse all the trouble I give you ...

11 September, Villa Viciosa. To The Hon. James Someŕs Cocks:
My dear James,
In the last budget of English papers, which we received a few days ago, is the gazette account of the battle of Talavera. Sir Arthur Wellesley's account is more remarkable for length than clearness, or even precision. I know not what other papers have done but *The Times* have added comments calculated only to favour errors. I shall notice two. *The Times* calls upon us to admire the conduct of the Spaniards and the Germans. The former are represented as having repulsed the French cavalry on the evening of the 27th and having materially contributed to the safety of the left on the 28th.

In the first instance they were not seriously attacked but, nevertheless, a fair proportion ran away – the officer leading – the instant the firing commenced. In the second they were used only for show. A line of Spanish cavalry was formed in the rear of the British lines and since the enemy could not tell to what nation they belonged they served to add to our apparent force.

For the Germans, they behaved in several instances extremely ill. At one period of the 28th the whole of their infantry ran fairly away. Poor Langwerth seized the colours and, planting them, called to the men to form. He was killed in attempting to rally them. Colonel Dereham was equally unsuccessful. He got 40 or 50 round the colours but the instant he went to collect others these set up. Had not the 16th been moved up opportunely there would have been a gap left in the line. The Germans formed in our rear . . .

> That autumn Cocks joined Cotton's staff at cavalry headquarters in Merida and immediately made friends with three or four Spanish families, visiting them regularly – something he was to do everywhere he stayed. He found their social life very different from home, 'Spanish women are tender, but rather from constitution than sentiment,' he noted, 'lounging rather than living away their time . . . Taking chocolate in bed, getting up and dressing, sitting in a graceful attitude in the Salla, gobbling down dinner, sleeping, talking, going to Mass; such are the chief occupations of the Spanish fair. Generally uneducated, they are destitute of settled principles and information and though their constitutional vivacity . . . often renders their conversation brilliant, yet it is only the conversation of the passing hour . . .' But it passed the time agreeably and he was a great believer in social intercourse. Conducting an affaire too, was part of the scene, but it proved more difficult than he had imagined. Courtesans apart, most of the married women already had a 'cortejo' and supplanting one of them took all his powers of address.

18 October, Merida. To The Hon. James Somers Cocks:
My dear James,
   . . . Since my health has been perfectly re-established I have begun to long again for operations rather more active than those we are at present engaged in. But after all, there is nothing like the life of a soldier in the field. Privations are scarcely felt when experienced in common with so many others; your little comforts, and even absolute necessities, acquire a double relish from the consciousness that next day you may want them and perhaps a reflection that the day before you were without them. Luxuries – when they do come your way – are enjoyed without fear of satiety; or dread of enervation. Ennui, that great foe to human happiness, is set at defiance, your mind is constantly animated, your body continually in proper exercise and, except a confounded fever lays hold of you, you enjoy a flow of spirits which is perhaps partly caused by the idea that you are more usefully and mainly employed than idly lounging at home.

   Yet, how few are there, particularly in dragoon regiments, who will thus fairly consider their situation. English officers come out eager to fight, are disappointed if an action does not immediately take place and anxious to get home after it is over. They forget that the objects of the campaign are oftener accomplished by patience and perseverance than by the most brilliant success. They seem not to consider that they have voluntarily entered the service and are receiving the pay of their country and that unless they perform what is required of them cheerfully, and to the best of their ability, they are not doing their duty. Throughout the generality of my regiment I am happy to observe that a proper spirit reigns, but I have been often mortified by hearing officers of other regiments, particularly of cavalry, expressing in the most undisguised terms, their disgust at this country and their indifference as to the event of the war here, and only hoping a speedy return for themselves. It must, indeed, be allowed that we have not met with much cordiality among our allies. The Junta are weak, the military heads are ignorant or treacherous, the executive agents of government are often avaricious and corrupt and the Spaniards have also failed both in their promise of supplies and effective military co-operation. But are we here for motives purely disinterested or because the interests of Spain and England tend towards the same centre? Certainly from the latter cause. Therefore, however untoward and irritating these circumstances may be, we should not be lukewarm in fighting and exerting ourselves for England merely to show a spiteful revenge towards the Spaniards. For my part, they have done so much; I see so many remains of a great and noble people and I have received so many personal kindnesses that I feel heartily interested in their fate. Nor do I despond. If Buonaparte is released from his war in Germany he may pour his Myrmidons over the Pyrenees; he may, perhaps, march to Sevilla and he may overturn the present miserable government, but he cannot root out the spirit of independence which pervades the population. It is true the Spaniards, at present, cannot beat the French, for a mob cannot beat an army, particularly if that mob be led by a fool or a traitor, but it is equally true that the French cannot conquer the Spaniards.

I trust my letters have been received from Villa Viciosa begging that Boverick may be sent out to me . . .†

Believe me, your truly affectionate brother,
 E. Charles Cocks

---

†His servant.

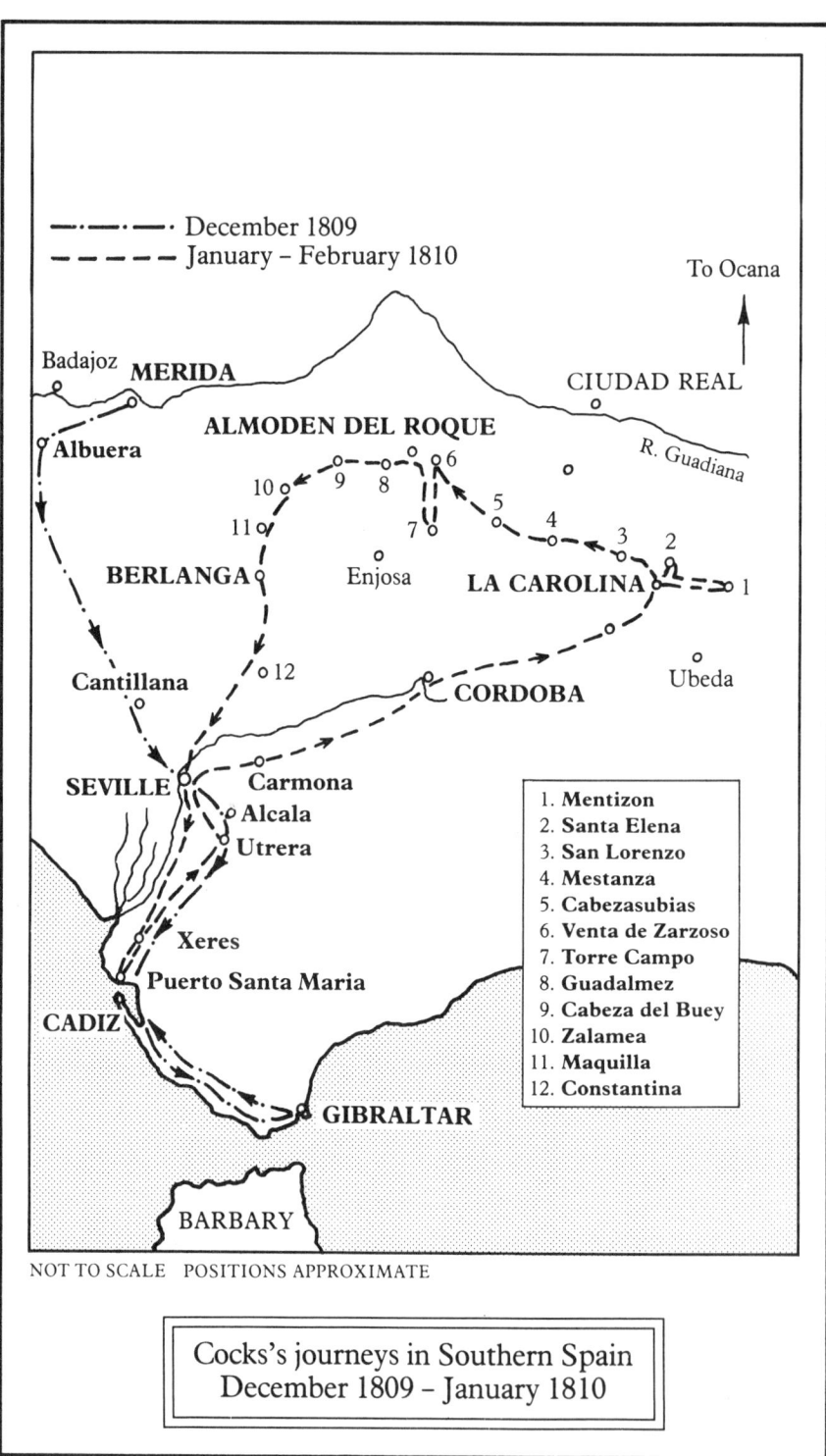

CHAPTER FOUR
Andalusia

9 December 1809 – 27 January 1810

AT THE BEGINNING of December Cotton had to return home for a few weeks to settle some legal affairs and invited Cocks's company as far as Cadiz, extending it into permission for a resumption of his tour of southern Spain. It still appeared likely that operations would shift to Andalusia and La Mancha and, with a dearth of good maps, a detailed reconnaissance of the Sierra Morena and its defensive positions could prove vital.

They left during Advent, stopping off in Seville for a lightning trip round the city and a memorable, candlelit concert in the cathedral: 'The music, vocal and instrumental was exquisite,'[1] Charles noted. At Xeres the next day a Mr Gordon, renowned for his hospitality to travellers, took them over his farm and into his wine vaults to sample some sherry, before directing them to a nearby Carthusian convent to view its collection of Murillos.

★ ★ ★

9 December . . . We embarked at Puerto Santa Maria for Cadiz, crossing the bay which is about two leagues over . . .

Cadiz is situated on a peninsula connected with the continent by an isthmus of more than 3 miles in length and from only 3 to 500 yards in width. The country beyond the isthmus as far as Chiclana is salinas or salt marshes. It appears not unlike the bogs of Ireland, and the isthmus, with a part of this bog, is separated from the main by a deep cut, over which the road is carried by the Puente de Zuarzo. During the war with Spain the gunboats used sometimes to slip out from this cut on our vessels and it also served as a retreat for Spanish merchantmen which, when light, might be floated through it . . . Cadiz ought never to be taken as long as herself or her allies are in possession of the sea . . . The Isla de Leon affords the finest position for an entrenched camp . . .

> Cotton sailed almost immediately leaving Cocks to continue to Gibraltar and spend a few days examining its fortifications, his resulting account running to several thousand words.†

20 December, Three Anchors, Gibraltar. To The Hon. Miss Margaret Maria Cocks:
My dear Sister,
    If all the devils in pandemonium had regaled themselves in this house last night it would probably have been quieter than it actually was. I arrived here very much tired late yesterday evening and after dinner went early to bed. A few hours

---
†See Appendix A.

after I was awoken by a din, something resembling what I have pictured to myself of an earthquake, in fact it resembled an incessant rain of chairs and other heavy materials upon a wooden floor, mixed with the crash of various glasses and voices the most discordant and inhuman.

The scene at the inn in Don Quixote must have been peace and quiet to it. I jumped up in my bed and looked for my pistols but in listening more attentively discovered that some Irish ship owners and masters were regaling themselves in the next room. As far as I could discover by their conversation the bone of contention was an unfortunate expression of the company. Someone had slipped his chair from under him, upon which the *slippée* remarked to the *slipper* that he was a 'rascally blackguard'. The president declared this out of order, on which the slippée again rejoined, complementing the chair with the epithet of a liar. Pistols were talked of across the table, nothing separated me from them but a temporary partition and I momentarily expected the appearance of a ball through the thin, deal boards. However, whether it was wine, brandy or gin, I know not, but at length their senses seemed lulled into forgetfulness, their discord into peace and their howls into unbroken silence, while I, relieved from my perturbation, turned in my bed and snored at my leisure.

I left Cadiz the 18th, perhaps there are no people in the world prouder of their native city than the inhabitants of Cadiz. Situated on a peninsula, the whole of which is occupied by the buildings, and connected only with the main by an isthmus 3 miles in length and only 2 or 300 yards in breadth, they feel a sort of proud independence which teaches them to look only to themselves for defence. There is a gaiety and neatness in the houses which is very different from anything I have seen in other parts of the Peninsula. The streets are scrupulously clean, I know no city in England which equals it in this respect. The walk round the ramparts, which are washed by the sea, is delightful. Perhaps the view of the bay could be improved if there was more relief on the opposite side but unfortunately the shore in the further part is very flat.

The public buildings of Cadiz are handsome, they are building a new church which is too splendid amidst its crowded and studied ornaments, it loses that solemn magnificence which should always characterise sacred edifices, the gothic architecture is more suited to a church than the Grecian.

There is a very good theatre at Cadiz. In our old theatres the massive appearance of the front of the boxes has always struck me as a great fault. I believe the proprietors were aware of the cumbersome heavy air this gives though they mistook the cause. They endeavoured to remedy the fault by lightening the supporting pillars; this produced a contrary effect, the theatre looked the more heavy when the want of proportion was contrasted between the supports and what was supported. In Cadiz the front of the boxes is formed by balustrades and the improvement is undoubtedly great. There is no part of Spain where the British interest is more fairly established. Nothing goes down but what is English. It was not the fault of the inhabitants that General Sherbrooke was not admitted last year; in fact it was as much as the government could do to keep the populace in order and the Governor lost his life in the attempt. Many of their favourite plays are translations from our stage, the other night we had *The School for Scandal* but

I did not know it in the playbills as they have changed the name, and unfortunately I came into the house just as it was over.

Adieu, my dear sister, do not forget your brother Charles.

Cocks spent Christmas in Cadiz, thoroughly enjoying himself in more ways than one: 'I have lived a most Cyprian life,' he told Thomas gaily, but on 31 December set out for the Headquarters of the Spanish Army of the Centre, situated at La Carolina, astride the great road for Seville which ran from the northeast.

Events were coming to a head in Andalusia. The previous autumn the Supreme Junta had appointed a General Areizaga to command this particular army, but once again its choice was unfortunate. 'As irresolute in danger as presuming out of it,' according to Cocks, at the battle of Ocana, 'he lost all presence of mind,' suffering a resounding defeat[2]. And as Charles left Cadiz the French were already concentrating for a two-pronged attack through the passes of the Sierra Morena – their destination Seville. Naturally unaware of the approaching crisis, he made a leisurely journey across Andalusia, exploring every town, noting each one's history and talking to every person he could. The morning of 11 January he examined Bailen, the scene of one of the few Spanish victories in 1809, and that afternoon reached La Carolina.

11 January 1810 Bailen: 2½ leagues. Half a league short of the town you pass the spot where Dupont surrendered, it lies to the left of the road among some olives. It is not easy to account satisfactorily for the little resistance made by the French ... there is nothing remarkable in the ground that could occasion their embarrassment... La Carolina: The approach to the town is particularly good, it lies through a double row of elms and is flanked by groves of mulberry trees. The road we had marched had been constantly superb all the way from Cadiz. La Carolina is the point through which the great road passes from Madrid to Sevilla. Something above 20,000 men are collected here. They have, besides, an army under the Ducque de Parque in Castille and a corps of 12,000 under the Duc d'Albuquerque in Estramadura, but to the main army is entrusted the defence of the Sierra. It is commanded by Don Carlos de Areizaga, a man as presumptuous in safety as timid and irresolute in danger. He has thirty leagues – or upwards of one hundred miles of mountain to guard, crossed by four roads practicable for artillery and by innumerable paths practicable for cavalry and infantry, and turned by a road which goes round the end of the Sierra on the right. I have dined with Areizaga and conversed with him and, under these circumstances, he expressed himself perfectly confident that he should be able to defend his position ...

12 January Went to reconnoitre Despana Perros.

This was the vulnerable pass through which the great road ran to Seville.

14 January Left Carolina to reconnoitre Mendizon ... At Venta Nueva I was told this was the venta where Cervantes has supposed Don Quixote to meet with the adventure of the enchanted Moor, but this story does not agree with the map published in one edition ...

In the venta I found the Headquarters of Brig-Gen D. Caspar de Vigodet. I liked this man's manners, he appeared collected without arrogance and conscious of his exposed situation without fear ... The troops were much superior to the half-starved, unhealthy wretches I saw at Despena Perros. He had 900 cavalry, which were in good condition, but most of them in want of carbines... they had, in general, received their rations, bread, bacon and aquadente up to the current day.

> The following day the French began their advance. Victor and 20,000 men were to move on Almoden del Roque and cross the Sierra Morena to Cordova while, a day or so later, Joseph Buonaparte, nominal 'King' of Spain was to attack Areizaga, drive him from Despena Perros, and go on to form a junction with Victor for the march on Seville.

16 January The enemy are on the alert, for 2 or 3 days they have made great demonstrations on the left and parties have been heard of in the direction of Lunca. Today's accounts state Victor, with upwards of 20,000 men as being in full march for Almoden del Roque. This is far from improbable and will place them in the rear of the Spaniards, who will be cut off from Sevilla. If they also push a corps by Segura on Baeza and Ubeda the Spaniards will likewise be cut off from Grenada and completely trapped. These manoeuvres will certainly be very daring unless they have something in Castile to keep the English in check, but probably their reinforcements have already arrived. The only measure the Spaniards can adopt is an immediate retreat on Grenada; they will secure themselves in strong and unexplored mountains and, if the French advance on Sevilla, will be ready to act on the left of their line of operation.

This measure, however, a blind confidence will probably prevent their adopting. Two months will probably see their army dispersed, the miserable Junta overturned and Andalusia invaded. This will be a trial of Spanish patriotism. I have seen and dined with Areizaga. His arrogance is disgusting in the man who lost the battle of Oçana. His conversation is composed of wild assertions unsupported by arguments or facts. He cleans his teeth, shaves well, talks fast et voila tout.

> Clearly it was time to be off and where better than towards the enemy. Cocks decided to try to cross the line of advance and gain as much information as he could to send to Wellington.

17 January Having bought a horse of Roche† I set out, accompanied by two dragoons of Fernando 7‡, in order to reconnoitre the movements of the French on the left.

San Lorenzo: 5 leagues, 3 hours. On this march you pass three brooks, two of which in rainy season might probably be dangerous. The road is with difficulty passable to a horse, though I had been told in Carolina a regiment of cavalry had marched by it. It rained the whole day ... Nothing can be more impracticable than this part of the Sierra.

18 January Majenza: 4 leagues, $4\frac{1}{2}$ hours. Brig-Gen D. Francisco Capons commanded here. He had about 2,000 infantry. He was a gentlemanly, intelligent man.

Cabezasubias: 2 leagues, 3 hours. A small but comfortable village. I procured

---

†Colonel Roche, one of the British liaison officers with the Spanish.
‡A Spanish regiment.

only wheat here for my horses, but having a day's barley gave them half and half.
19 January Abrazatortas: 2 leagues, 3 hours. Venta de Sarzozo: 4 leagues, 4 hours. The Venta lies a little to the left, I shall not easily forget the Venteso's features, Zabarter would have chosen his countenance as an example of cunning, shrewdness and desperate villainry.
20 January As I had by this time acquired as much information as I could hope for in this direction, I was anxious to cross the route of the enemy and forward my intelligence to Lord Wellington.† I had at one time intended to cross between Abenojaer and Zazauela but had been recommended at Abrazatortas to pass near Enjosa as this gave me a better opportunity of learning something more of the enemy, and I readily acceded to it. It lay by Torrecampo: 3 leagues; Torre Mulano: 2 leagues; Enjosa de Cordoba: 5.

As I understood the enemy occupied Torre Campo, I left the Venta at midnight in company of some smugglers who were pursuing the same route. It froze very hard and was dreadfully cold. After proceeding a league, on arriving at the summit of a hill I saw the fires of the French encampment at Torre Campo. I still hoped to be able to pass round them but, continuing my route by a stony, bad road, I learnt at a mile that 2,000 cavalry were at Torre Campo and that the rest of the Cita Villas‡ were full of French detachments and it became necessary to give up this route. The smugglers concealed themselves in the mountains and I returned to the Venta, which I reached by daybreak.

I found the Venteso in better humour. As he thought it likely the French would be in his house that day and drink his wine without paying for it, he determined to prevent them by drinking it himself. The wine had softened his rugged disposition and he told me he knew a peasant perfectly acquainted with the country, and he sent for him. A robust young man appeared, with a countenance pleasing and lively, nor did it belie him for he proved most active and intelligent. We determined to push on by Alosmillis, a village on the Cordoba road, three leagues from Almoden.

We again left the Venta about an hour after daybreak, I had procured two days' barley for my horses. We had three leagues to the road by which the French were marching; our guide led us by an unfrequented path through a wood. Half a league short of the road we met some peasants who informed us some of the enemy were actually marching along the road. We concealed ourselves in the wood and sent the guide forward to reconnoitre. We waited upwards of an hour and at length our guide returned, he had explored the road and even the village of Alamillos. All was now clear of the enemy, those we had heard of were a few, straggling dragoons. We passed the two roads by which the French had marched and, an hour after dark, we reached a small village called Guadalmez to the left of the road from Almoden to Cabeza del Buey and 3 leagues from each place. We were thoroughly fatigued, our horses and ourselves had been 19 or 20 hours in action, almost without interruption.

The enemy had been in Gualmez two or three days before and I had an

---

†After Talavera Wellesley had been made a Viscount.
‡The collective name for the towns in the valley.

opportunity of ascertaining the parties sent out to impose requisitions; they consisted of 40 dragoons or hussars and upwards, according to the size of the village. They generally appeared about 9 or 10 o'clock in the morning, never at night, and having formed before the town and fired a shot or two to terrify the inhabitants, they sent in an officer and three or four men to transact the business with the magistrates.

21 January Cabeza del Buey: 3 leagues, 4 hours. This is a considerable town of 2,000 families, the road we pursued was nearly a bridle path. For the first 2 leagues our road had run by the side of a small river and through a valley, about half a mile broad; during the last league it crossed a mountain. The day was dreadful, the snow fell the whole march and when we arrived was some inches deep.

When the French first arrive in a province they put the whole under requisition, a measure which they repeat till it produces no effect. Their commissaries then come forward, who always pay in ready money and never break their word. The inhabitants eagerly seize this opportunity of getting money for their concealed grain and thus the country is completely drained. They sometimes conclude with a requisition for money, which brings the great part of their coin back to their own pockets.

21 January, From Cabeza del Buey. To Lord Wellington:
My Lord,
    In compliance with the wishes of Colonel Roche, in a letter from whom I have the honour to enclose, and my own earnest desire to render myself of any use to the service that lay in my power, I left Carolina the 16th ult, and passing the Spanish cordon, crossed the route pursued by the French corps which has entered Andalusia.

The Sierra Morena to the west of Almoden branches off into various ramifications, diverging from each other. The most northern passes in nearly a direct line to Santa Marta, on the road between Badajoz and Sevilla, the most southern inclines to the Guadaquivir and follows the course of that river. Between these and the intermediate ranges of mountains are plains, some leagues in width and producing considerable supplies.

In the northern branch of the mountain is situated Almoden del Roque, a point of union to most of the communication between Estramadura and La Mancha on the one hand and Andalusia on the other. This was the extreme of the Spanish line and occupied by General Serain. His division consisted nominally of 4 or 5,000 men but, in reality, was composed of only a few hundred, ill-armed and worse clothed.

From Almoden proceed two carriage roads to the south, one by Cordoba, the other by Llerena and Monasterio to Sevilla. From Cordoba to Almoden is 22 leagues and from Sevilla 39. Both these roads are bad, particularly that to Cordoba, but both practicable for artillery. The road to Sevilla is called the Camino de los Plate and is the route by which the quicksilver is transported from the mines of Almoden. Besides these, there are other routes practicable to cavalry both to Cordoba and Sevilla.

The advanced guard of the enemy entered Almoden on the 16th ult having marched by Abenojar and Zazuela. General Serain fell back without resistance to Campo Alto, a pass 4 leagues to the north of Cordoba, and where he has been reinforced by troops from that and the adjacent cities.

On the 17th the 1st division of French infantry occupied Almoden, the cavalry were pushed forward to Alamillo and Santa Euphemia, it was, in fact, dispersed in every direction. I believe it may be estimated at 4,000 and the infantry at 5,000, with 30 pieces of artillery. Passports opened from Almoden were signed by Pilgash, Chef de l'Etat, Major du Premier Corps d'Armee.

The 2nd division, said to be commanded by Soult, marched the same day from Abenojar. On the 19th, after a day's halt, the advanced cavalry, crossing the second range of mountains, entered the plains where Los Suit Villas or Los Pedroches de Cordoba are situated; these are seven towns each distant a league from the other. Puerto Blano, which is the principal, contains near 2,000 inhabitants; 2,000 cavalry were encamped at Torre Campo, about 8 leagues from Almoden and the remainder were cantoned in the other towns. One division of infantry followed the cavalry, the remainder with the artillery pursued the carriage road by Santa Euphemia and Puerto Blano.

During the 16, 17, 18, 19th, they put almost every town in requisition within the distance of 5 or 6 leagues; on the 20th the cavalry were again en route.

I feel mortified that I cannot give your Lordship more certain accounts of the number of enemy, but no dependence can be placed on the flying rumours in circulation and the Spanish officers whom I have seen, although pushed forward for the express purpose of reconnoitring, are too torpid or too cautious to gain information.

Comparing, however, the various accounts I have received in the different towns where the enemy has passed, I do not think his force on the 20th, south of Almoden, exceeded 20,000 and on that day he had no troops either in Almoden or Alamillo. Had I fortunately left Carolina two days sooner I might have concealed myself 3 leagues from Almoden in a point which commands the road and seen the whole of his left column defile at the distance of 400 yards.

It will scarcely seem probable to your Lordship that, with this movement only, the enemy thinks of penetrating to Sevilla but perhaps he expects that this movement on the left of the Spaniards will compel the latter to abandon their present position and, in that case, another column will pour down through Despena Perros along the great road by Bailen and Andujar. Cordoba is nearly equidistant from Despena Perros and Almoden del Roque and will then be the point of reunion.

As was happening, even as he wrote.

This project will answer the double purpose of facilitating his subsistence and of rendering every position between Carolina and Cordoba untenable. In the event, too, of a sudden and hurried retreat from Carolina it will be impossible to collect the Army of the Centre. 6,000 of their best troops are at Montezon, 11 leagues east of Carolina and 2 leagues from Villa Manriques; the remainder is dispersed in corps of one, two and three thousand men between Montezon, and Mestanza, a distance of 28 mountain leagues and without any facilities of communication.

The Duc of Albuquerque is marching by Maquilla and Guadacanal towards Cordoba. I understand he has 10,000 infantry and 12,000 cavalry. He has sent his guns, etc to Llerena. There is a road practicable for infantry and cavalry by Guadacanal to Cordoba, which is distant 15 leagues and in Cordoba he will find a sufficiency of artillery.

As your Lordship may possibly wish to receive further information of the enemy's movements in this interesting moment, I shall overtake the Duke of Albuquerque's army and, in case I meet no other British officer, remain with it until I receive your Lordship's orders. As the British army is now in cantonments and as I speak and write Spanish, I should be most happy should your Lordship think to continue me upon this service.

The peasantry of the Sierra Morena are bold, active and intelligent and there are among them men who might be made extremely useful in gaining accurate information.

I fear some time will elapse before your Lordship will receive this letter, there being no regular post from hence . . .

22 January Zalamea: 5 very long leagues. The carriage road comes in here from Merida, by which Cuesta's artillery retreated when he occupied the position of Monasterio in the spring of 1809. The weather continued extremely severe, the snow remained very deep, a circumstance which had not been known in this part of Spain for many years . . .

23 January Maguilla: 6 leagues . . .

24 January Cazala: 7 leagues, by Berlanga & Guadacanal . . .

25 January Cantillana: 7 leagues, by Pedroso . . .

26 January Sevilla: 4 leagues. After crossing the Guadaquivir by a ferry the road is good but through a deep country. The Duc d'Albuquerque had established his Headquarters at Brenes, one league from Cantillana. He never entertained a hope of reaching Cordoba before the enemy, his only aim was to cover Sevilla. In this he has succeeded. His march, in which he has traversed Estramadura and the Sierra Morena, has done him and his army the greatest credit. Though I have been following him for several days I have not seen twenty stragglers . . .

27 January, Sevilla. To Lord Wellington:

My Lord,

I had the honour to address your Lordship from La Cabeza del Buey, enclosing a letter from Colonel Roche and reporting to you that by his design I had followed the enemy to Almoden. I likewise informed your Lordship that from thence I should proceed to the army of the Duc d'Albuquerque, there to await your Lordship's orders.

Had I known the dates of the Duc's march I could never have flattered myself that he would have reached Cordoba before the enemy. Instead of attempting it he marched by Cazala and Pedroso, across the Guadaquivir at Cantillana and established his Headquarters at Alcala de la Guadaira, 2 leagues from Sevilla. It is, however, with regret that I inform your lordship that he has done this without the least hope of effectually defending or covering the city. He has only 8,500 men, including 1,200 cavalry, the junta of Badajoz having robbed him of his batteries to garrison that city. Perhaps the scattered troops, which have been collected from various points may be estimated at 4,000 more, but what are there to oppose the enemy whose advanced posts are in possession of Ecuija and have put Louisiana under requisition?

Your Lordship has, no doubt, been already informed that on the 24th ult a revolution took place in Sevilla. The greater part of the Central Junta are under arrest. The Conde de Montijo and Palafox have been liberated and, with the Marquis de Romana and Saavedra, compose the executive government which is normally entrusted to the Junta of Sevilla.

The Marquis de Romana has left Sevilla to assume the command of his army in the room of the Duc del Parque. This change, however, appears to have produced no effect in the Sevillians; all who were able have left the city and there does not appear to be the least intention of determined opposition. Mr Frere has gone to Cadiz. All communication is so completely cut off with the Army of the Centre that nothing certain is here known respecting it. It is reported that it has fallen back on Jaen but it is also reported that it has dispersed.

Tomorrow I shall be able to give your Lordship more certain intelligence† but I did not like to omit this opportunity of writing as I am certain of your Lordship's receiving this letter.

I remain, my Lord, with respect,
  Your Lordship's humble servant,
    E. Charles Cocks, 16th Queen's Light Dragoons.

---

†Unfortunately Cocks lost the copy of this third letter.

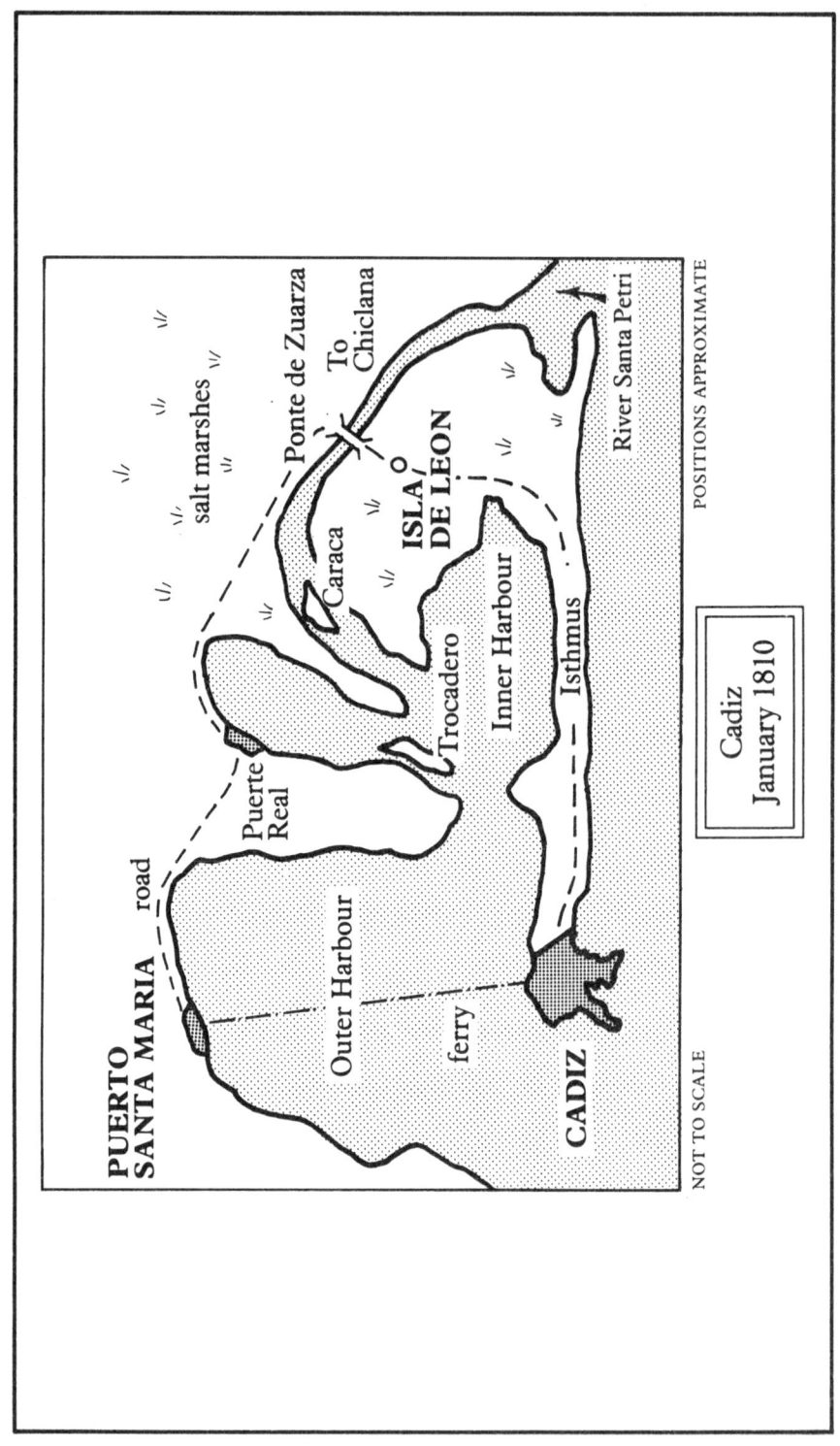

CHAPTER FIVE
Cadiz

29 January – 24 February 1810

29 January Left Sevilla and went to Alcala. The French had pushed forward their advanced posts to Carmona, which was evacuated about 11 o'clock. They also advanced a column towards Utrera as far as Marchena. It was absolutely necessary to retreat ... The greater part of the Spanish muskets were unserviceable and the English ones with which some of the regiments were provided have touch holes too small for Spanish powder ...
30 January At midnight the army was again in motion, falling back on Las Cabezaz and Lebrija. Coming out of Utrera in the dark I missed the route of the army and pursued the only road I knew towards Xeres ...
31 January Left Xeres and went to Puerto Santa Maria. The alarm had now become general and men, women and children were flying in all directions. At first they tried to cross the water to Cadiz but, it becoming impracticable to obtain boats and some having even sunk from being overloaded, the fugitives pushed on towards the Isla by land. The gates of Cadiz presented an affecting spectacle, so many people wished to seek refuge in the city that a contagious fever must have been the certain consequence of a siege. It became necessary to shut them and crowds were in vain entreating to be admitted ... Fort Catharina and the Fort at Matagorda, the two principal batteries on the north side of the Bay of Cadiz, were given up to our navy to be destroyed. This duty was entrusted to Captain Lindsay of the *Triumph* but it was performed very imperfectly, particularly at Fort Catharina where only the embrasures in front were thrown open. The Spanish ships and hulks with French prisoners were moved out into the outer harbour among the British Squadron.
1 February Went back to Puerto Santa Maria for my horses and was unable to repass the bar.
2 February Went to the Isla de Leon. Castanos had established himself here. Albuquerque, who arrived the day before, had brought about 11,000 men. I went on to Cadiz ... 1,000 are expected from Gibraltar.
3 February Went to Headquarters and took possession of my billet. Headquarters were established in the town of Isla. It is considered that the French can only attempt the passage of the river Santi Petri in three points, namely by the Puenta Zuarza, by the Point of Santi Petri, and the right of the Carraca and to the left. Between these points the banks of the river are so boggy that it is inaccessible on each side ...
5 February The French entered Sevilla the 1st and had about 24,000 in the neighbourhood. The servant of O'Farrell, who deserted to Carmona, left his master at Cordoba. He was a spy employed by the Spaniards and only entered

O'Farrell's service that he might learn all he could. Among the papers he brought away was a plan of [Marta's] to disembark on the Isla near Santi Petri and between that point and Torregorda the strand there is perfectly good. The man says the French have now received 10,000 reinforcements, a number not sufficient to compensate for the loss in the various actions since Talavera. All other accounts agree with this, yet I cannot believe, under such circumstances, they would venture to invade Andalusia although I am aware they had, at this moment, a great inducement, namely to prevent the meeting of the Cortes and the forming of a more regular effective government. If this has been their inducement their plan has failed for unless they take Cadiz their very invasion has caused the erection of a military government, a form of all others most to be dreaded by them.

6 February Visited Santi Petri. Placing your back to Cadiz, the beach to the right of the road forms a triangle with the road of which Torregorda is the vortex, and part of the beach out to the right of Puente de Zuarza the base. Immediately to the right of the town of Isla is a hill called the Sesso de Martyrs, partitioned into fields, but except this hill the whole of the above triangle is impracticable marsh except the beach itself. It consequently falls that the cut can be passed nowhere except opposite the end of the beach at Santi Petri. A new battery has been erected there of 12 guns, I believe 24-pounders, which will be finished in a day or two and is ready to fire tonight. It is composed of sandbags and faced with straw.

The old battery which defended the mouth of the cut against an attack from the sea side will be repaired. The island opposite the mouth is already provided with 10 pieces of artillery, 2 mortars and 2 howitzers, the cut is 15 yards deep here at low water. 3,000 men are stationed at Santi Petri and 14 gun boats have been brought down to assist in the defence. It is impossible to pass here except in boats but how are these boats to be built? The opposite beach is under the fire of the battery and even if boats can be procured the batteries must be silenced before a plan of this sort can be effected. There is a third battery of six guns immediately in front of the Sesso de Martyrs called the Galinera.

7 February About 10 o'clock the Generale was beat. I went with Campbell to the Puente de Zuarza, the fire proceeded from the Carraca. We went there. The artillery officer had been only firing to ascertain the range of his guns and this he had done without even reporting his intention! The Spaniards will do nothing while such unmilitary practices are tolerated.

The Carraca lie out of the Isla, beyond the cut, but they are covered by another cut, the whole of the ground in front is salinas or salt pans, impracticable even to men on foot. Their only communication on the land side is with the Isla de Leon, crossing the cut by a ferry. Three or four paths which formerly led to the front as far as La Reservi - or road from Puerto Real to the Isla - have been cut through to the breadth of 6 or 8 feet. In the Carraca are several pontoons and plenty of timber. If the enemy could ever arrive here they might easily cross to the Isla for there are no batteries covering the ferry. The Carraca are defended by two batteries, one of eight 18-pounders, the other fourteen 24-pounders. The first was provided with 300 cartridges for the battery and 50 rounds of round and 30 of case shot, per piece. It was composed of dry fascines and turf, faced with wood and consequently perfectly inflammable.

On our return we learnt that 1,000 cavalry with some artillery had gone round by the mountains and taken possession of Chiclana. They had pushed a piquet towards here and used the pontoon there, which had been carelessly left on their side. The Duc sent to order that they should be dislodged and the bank destroyed. Never were 30 dragoons treated with more ceremony. After three quarters of an hour's consultation, 200 infantry, 50 dragoons and 3 pieces of artillery were marched to the river side. A little desultory firing dislodged them and the pontoon, after a vain attempt to burn it, was carried off in triumph. The enemy have their most advanced post in Venta de Afuesa, about a league off towards Puerto Real.

8 February Visited Torregorda. This is a point of some importance, the roads to the Isla and Santi Petri unite here and the whole of the beach towards the latter point is open to the fire of the fort. It is a small round tower situated in the middle of a small brick redoubt. Towards the town side the sand has been built up so high that it is almost liable to insult. There are some embrasures on this side which can be of no use as the fort must not be expected to hold out anytime after it is turned.

In a memoire given in today by Campbell and a Spanish engineer of the name of O'Loughlin, it is proposed to provide the fort with 3 guns for the 3 embrasures, pointing towards Santi Petri, to place one howitzer in the redoubt and 2 on the top of the tower to stop up the embrasures looking towards Cadiz, and to surround the whole with a strong [barricade]. In the event of a retreat towards the Contedura this tower may be very useful.

The enemy have been endeavouring to erect a battery at Matagorda, near where Fort Louis formerly stood, but he has been hitherto prevented by the fire of the shipping.

9 February The bridges beyond the Puente de Zuarza have been broken down and two advanced batteries erected. Our advance posts are just in front of the bridge.

10 February The Spaniards endeavoured this morning to destroy the two ferry houses towards Chiclana but, the enemy firing two cannon shot, they desisted. An English boat disembarked last night and attacked a party of 40 Frenchmen. They killed one and took ten, the prisoners say the French are preparing boats near Puerto Real and Sebastiani commands on the left . . .

11 February The batteries of the Puente de Zuarza amused themselves this morning by endeavouring to break down the ferry houses and by firing at some straggling parties of French cavalry. This was a shameful waste of ammunition, particularly when the Junta of Sevilla prevailed on Mr Frere to apply yesterday to Gibraltar for 500 quintels of powder.

12 February General Stuart's brigade arrived this day from Lisbon, composed of the 79th, 87th and 94th regiments, with two companies of artillery.

13 February The 79th disembarked this morning as did our company of artillery which was marched to the Isla. The barracks on each side the land post are destined for those of the British who remain in Cadiz. Some firing took place all day at the bridge; the Spaniards were employed in pulling down the houses which might cover the enemy; a few were killed on each side.

14 February The Spaniards had erected a sixth battery on the causeway, beyond the bridge, of two 24-pounders. This will keep the enemy a little further off and check their throwing shells into the town. The 79th marched in here this morning and are quartered in the Conventuo del Carmen.

15 February Visited the Galinera. It is a wooden battery; with 7 iron 18-pounders and behind it the Spaniards are erecting another small battery. It is of no great use except to cover the navigation of the Rio de Santi Petri and keep up the communication between Santi Petri and the Isla. The enemy appear erecting batteries on the road towards Chiclana. Ten gunboats have been put under the command of British Lieutenants and each received 10 English seamen, besides their Spanish crew. Six of them were very active this morning towards the Chiclana road.

16 February In consequence of information from Whittingham† that the enemy were on the borders of Portugal and that the British army were in motion I resolved to leave Cadiz and take the opportunity of the *Myrtle* sailing, to go to Lisbon and from there join my regiment.

17 February Captain Landemann of the Engineers, who was employed last year to take a plan of Cadiz, showed me a scheme of his to form an artificial harbour with jetties near the signal house and making store houses in the rocks. Such a harbour might be secure from shot but I doubt if it could be made sufficiently capacious.

18 February Went on board HMS Sloop of War the *Myrtle*, Captain Innes, of 18 guns.

19 February The enemy has been for some days endeavouring to repair the batteries at Fort St Catharina and Matagorda, the remains of the fort seemed to mask their work. At Matagorda a Spanish hulk was moved opposite the fort, it was left under the command of her captain but manned with 150 British seamen. The Spanish captain, however, quickly resigned his command declaring, according to the sailors' story, that it was impossible to serve with men who knew so little of their duty as to run a ship alongside a battery at the distance of 4 or 500 yards.

A vain attempt was made to check the progess of the work at Santa Catharina by sending the ship launches, with each a gun on board, to fire at the troops there. Guns in such a situation can produce no effect and only subjected the boats to the mortification of being obliged to run whenever the enemy brought a gun against them. Weighed anchor at 4pm.

24 February, Lisbon. From Boverick, his servant, to Mrs Gardener:‡
Madam,
Yesterday I had the pleasure to see the Captain arrive safe and well in Lisbon, in fact I never saw him look so well, it was an agreeable surprise to me and

---

†Colonel Samford Whittingham, later Lt.-Gen. He was English but commanding the Spanish cavalry at Cadiz. He and Cocks had met the previous year in Seville and he accompanied Charles from Talavera to Arzobispo.

‡Unidentified, but certainly from Castleditch; Cocks once asked 'particularly to be remembered to Mr Gardener'; so they may have been employed by the Cocks family.

everyone for Capt Swetenham had told me about three hours before that there was not one in the regiment knew where he was and he thought I should not see him for a month, indeed, I find he has had many narrow escapes.

He came from Cadiz to Lisbon in the *Myrtle* Sloop of War in six days. The French are close to Cadiz with 45,000 men and the English have taken possession of the place so that there is no fear for Cadiz whatever. We go up to the army tomorrow morning. It is the opinion of most people that we shall not be able to stay long in this country. I have been up so far as Abrantes sometime since, in the hope to see the Captain, but while we was [sic] on the journey the regiment got the route and was marched for Coimbra and I was obliged to return with all my luggage to Lisbon, and since that, all the baggage for the use of the British army that was in stores in Lisbon is put on board the ships in the river incase of a start.

The dragoon that was with the Captain tells me that when the Captain was ill of a fever after the battle of Talavera he was so weak for sometime that the man was obliged to carry him about on his back, but he has the character of having done more for the service in the time than any officer in the army. He has been more than once selling gin, etc amongst the French lines, but I have not had time to get any particulars as we are so busy preparing for our departure. I will write again when anything particular occurs.

I remain, with best wishes for you all,

   Yours, etc, F. Boverick

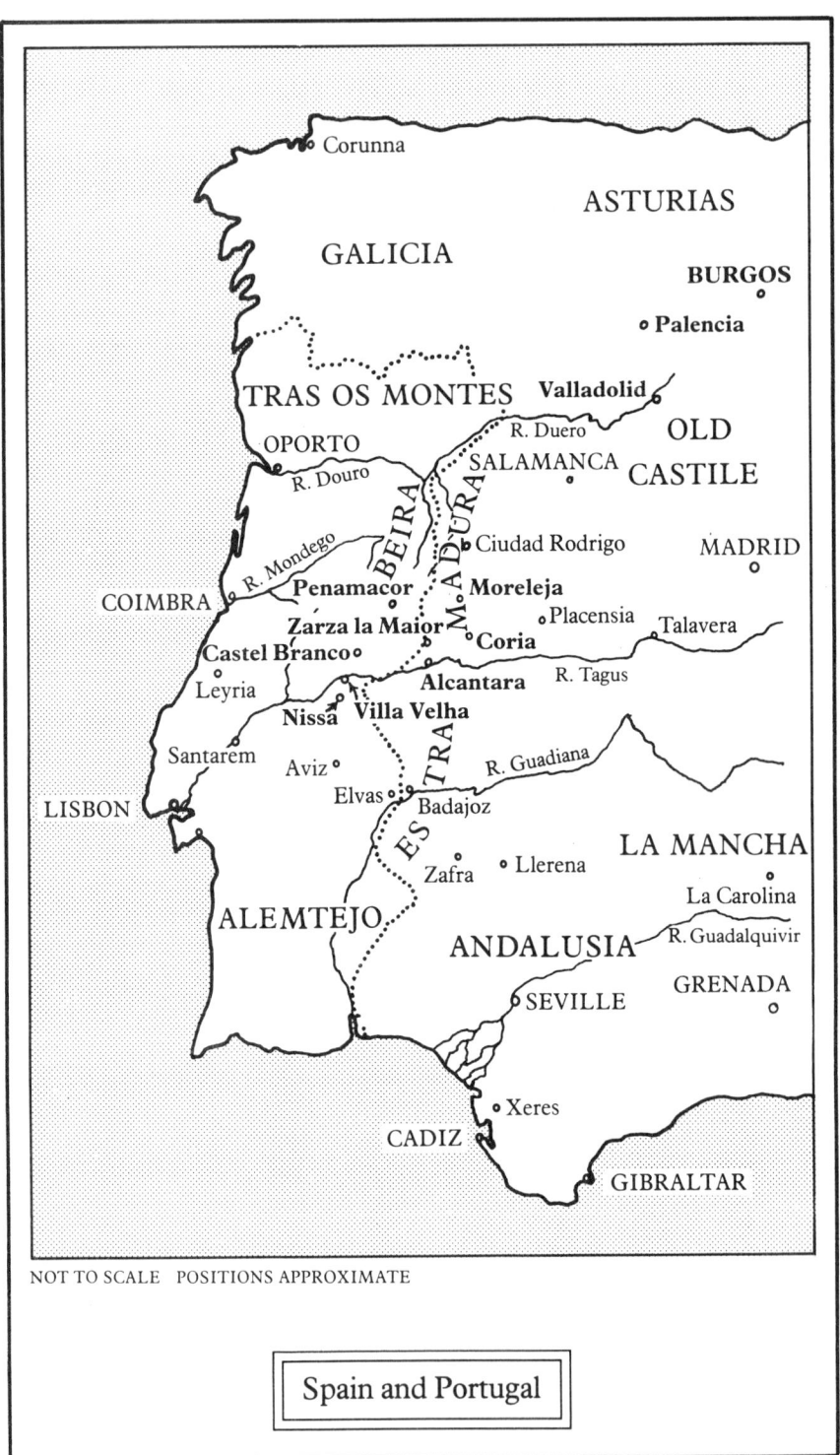

Spain and Portugal

CHAPTER SIX
Between the Coa and the Agueda

22 March – 19 July 1810

IT WAS OBVIOUS that 1810 would see another invasion of Portugal and with the Spanish so unreliable Wellington temporarily abandoned joint operations and moved back to defend the long frontier between the two countries, at the same time making secret preparations for a shorter defensive position close to Lisbon should he have to retreat.

Three practical roads led to the capital, from Ciudad Rodrigo, Zarza la Maior and Badjoz; he himself had the first under surveillance while General Hill, with Marshal Beresford and his Portuguese as a back-up†, was guarding the other two, but none of them alone could hope to withstand a concerted attack and his plan hinged on early intelligence of the route and the speed with which he could concentrate to block it. Charles thought it a 'desperate game' but since Frederick the Great had once made a similiar, successful defence in Germany he hoped it was not impossible, prophetically believing that if all else failed they might hold the line between Santarem and Leyria. No more than Wellington did he accept evacuation from Portugal as necessary: 'It will not be a competent excuse for retreat to say we are outpowered by numbers or attacked in too many parts at once, for it has long been evident whenever we were attacked it would be by very superior numbers advancing on different points yet, in spite of this, we have engaged the Portuguese in determined measures of resistance, entailing upon them expense and hatred of the enemy, we are bound to abide the trial with them and not pusillanimously desert them because the moment of danger has arrived.'[1]

Cocks found the 16th in cantonments at Santa Combadao, outside Viseu, he himself going to Ovão close by, and in the light of his recent experiences spent the spring retraining his troop. Cotton arrived back in April, accompanied by a now fit Tomkinson, but with heavy rain halting all operations it was June before the brigade moved up to take over the outpost duties and support General Craufurd's Light Division between the Agueda and Coa rivers, opposite Ciudad Rodrigo. The area they guarded was a wide, undulating plain, covered with cornfields, pasture and woods, dotted with farms and villages which, after some miles, gave way to a barren, rocky, moorland plateau cut by the fast flowing Coa, deep in its gorge and difficult of access. Few bridges spanned the streams and rivers but fords abounded, dependent on the water level, rains affecting them all very quickly.

Craufurd's headquarters were at Gallegos and he defended the line from Barba del Puerto to Campillo, thereafter the Spanish taking up the chain with their guerillas. By June the French had already gained a foothold over the Agueda and

---

†Among them Hugh Owen, who had transferred from the 16th.

were encamped on the slopes by Carpio and Marialva on the Azava tributary and all the activity in that month and early July centred round these villages and their adjacents. With Cotton having been appointed Wellington's Commander of Cavalry, Cocks accompanied him to Craufurd's introductory briefing.

From the advanced vedettes it was possible to make out Ciudad Rodrigo, now under siege, and hear the dull crump and thud of 15 to 25 balls an hour reverberating across the river. 'It is a bitter pill to us to sit with crossed arms and view this rich prey fall into the hands of the enemy,' Cocks wrote, 'but our corps is much too small to attempt anything of itself and though the army is within two days' march Lord Wellington does not seem inclined to attempt anything and I believe circumstances justify him in this cruel inaction.'[2]

Wellington was possibly expecting a quick, determined attack on his position but the French decided otherwise. This was their third assault on Portugal and, brooking no further failures, Napoleon appointed Marshal André Massena to command. 'He is a general of reputation and not likely to be sent on a thriftless errand,' Cocks commented.[3] Massena chose the Ciudad Rodrigo route but elected to take his time and capture the town and its Portuguese counterpart, Almeida, before tackling the road to Lisbon, in the meanwhile keeping his hand hidden by sending General Reynier to threaten the other two routes.

At the end of June the 16th, who shared the duty with the 1st Hussars, the King's German Legion, were principally finding the piquets for the highly sensitive fords and bridges over the Agueda and Azava. Massena, anxious to take advantage of the rich forage and also discover whether Wellington intended giving battle for Ciudad, was regularly probing the line. 'About seven o'clock,' Cocks recorded for 30 June, 'the enemy's cavalry advanced in considerable force and their attention appeared to be of attacking us, they soon dispersed, however, and began to forage; about twelve they retired. A heavy column of infantry occupied the hill above Marialva all day, they retired at dusk; at ten they sent forward two regiments of Chasseurs who encamped halfway down the hill and threw out their piquets and sentries. The latter came at dark down to the river bank.'[4]

He was duty officer that night and Lt Alexander, on piquet at Mollino de Flores – the ford over the Agueda – mounting three double vedettes with a serjeant and twelve, unwisely sent all six of his relief out at the same time leaving only himself and the serjeant to guard the ford and when, after an hour, none had returned he fled to Cocks's post with the tale that the enemy had passed the river.[5] Cocks had no choice but to give the alarm before investigating. Luckily the men were only lost, but no one was amused and Craufurd put Alexander under arrest.†

★ ★ ★

1 July This morning no cavalry were in sight except a regiment or two foraging. Three guns and a howitzer were to the right of Carpio and the Chasseurs in the same position as yesterday. They continued quiet all day except for some occasional firing from the advanced vedettes; we were very jealous whenever the

---

†This unfortunate young man made another mistake later in the war.

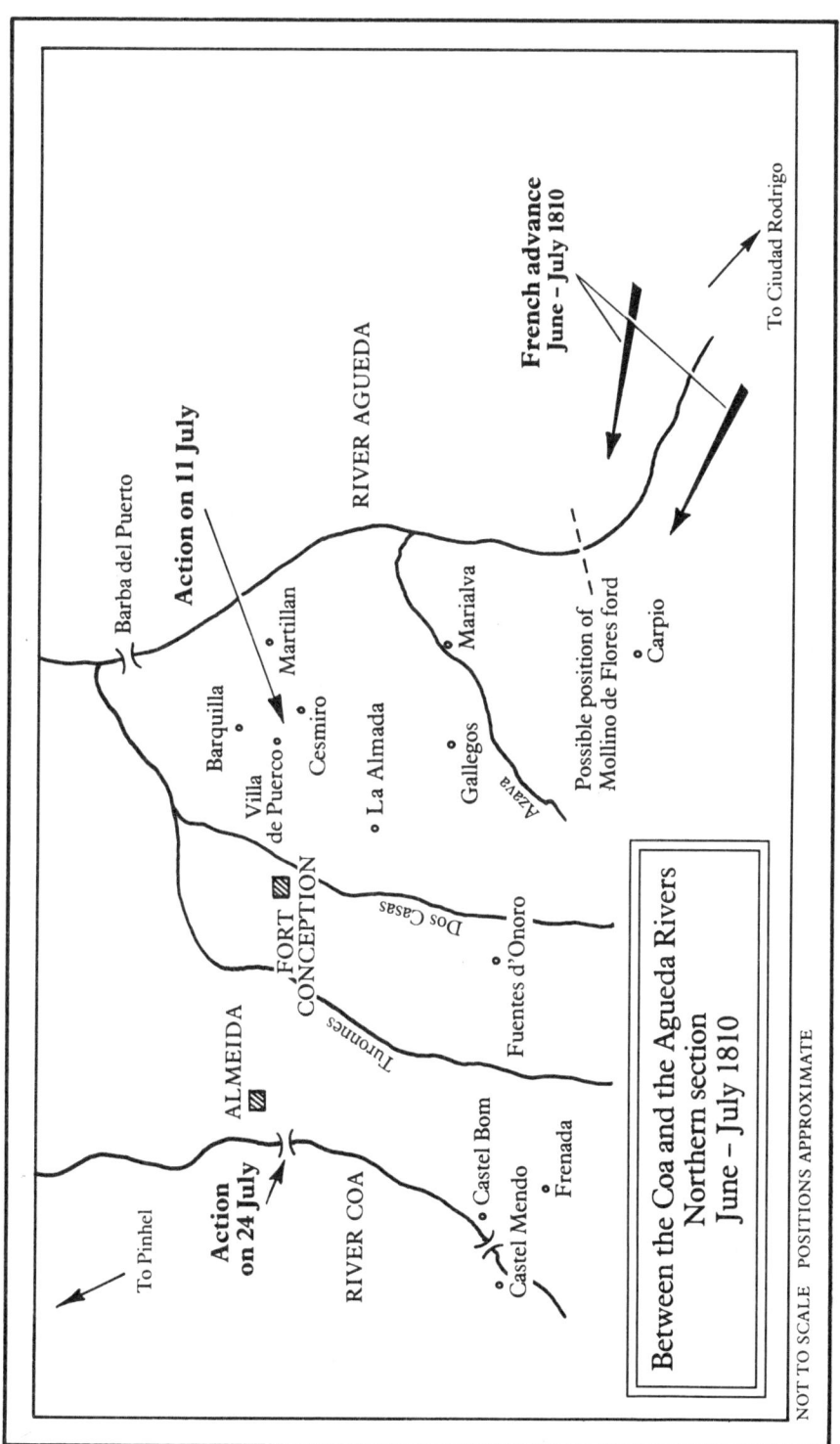

occasional firing from the advanced vedettes; we were very jealous whenever the enemy appeared to be trying the ford . . .

2 July The enemy brought down a regiment of cavalry this morning and encamped them with their right on Marialva, this makes our situation very ticklish, it appears superior to our 3 squadrons and is not 400 yards from our vedettes.

3 July Four squadrons of the enemy came down this day; and reconnoitred Carpio ford. At sunset they made an attempt to carry off some cars we had thrown across the Marialva bridge.

4 July At daybreak this morning, just as we had turned out and taken up our usual ground, the enemy attacked the piquets at Marialva bridge, Carpio and Mollino de Flores. He had 2,000 cavalry supported by infantry and artillery. We were ready for them with Krokenburgh's† squadron of Hussars and two Squadrons of the 16th. The infantry and Spaniards were at Alamada. Of course we retreated as the enemy appeared and fortunately not a man of the piquets was cut off . . . About $\frac{1}{2}$ a mile in rear of Gallegos is a marshy brook, crossed by a manor bridge and behind this Krokenburgh made a rally with the skirmishers and dashed several times very gallantly at the advance of the enemy as they attempted to cross. Three French officers, a serjeant and some men were sabred and one dragoon taken with his horse. The enemy might have been stopped here longer had he not turned our right. Our artillery served with considerable effect and did execution in their crowded columns. We had two 6-pounders under Lt Macdonald of Capt Ross's troop of Horse Artillery.

Almost a mile further to the rear, as the enemy began to press us very hard again, we met the infantry and Elder's Caçadores pouring a running fire into him; this completely checked him. The enemy's artillery hardly ever got into action . . . The Hussars behaved particularly well. It would be unfair not to bear unqualified testimony to their courage, zeal and knowledge of their duty. They have not such good seats as English dragoons but their horses are under better command and, I think, better taken care of . . . Our advanced posts now occupy the line of the little river Dos Casas, from Fuentès to Castilegos . . .

5 July We moved this evening a mile to our rear and occupied a wood. Ciudad Rodrigo still holds out. The enemy's object in attacking us yesterday was probably the forage near Gallegos. He will not have the same temptation here but should he advance upon us suddenly, in force, our retreat will be more critical. We cannot make a stand either at Fort Conception or Alamada and we must retire to the Coa across 2 leagues of open country where, unlike yesterday, there will be no woods to shelter our infantry. There are, it is true, 3 bridges to our rear, at Castel Bom, Almeida and on the road to Pinhel, but we must keep a good look out to our flanks or the enemy will be in our rear.

8 July Ciudad Rodrigo appeared on fire at midnight and from one till nine or ten there was heavy firing at intervals. Some French cavalry occupied Cesmiro and Villa de Puerco this morning, plundering everything. We turned out to cut them off but the birds were flown.

---

†Captain Krokenburgh of 1st Hussars, KGL.

9 July, Encampment near Fuente de la Conception. To Thomas Someers Cocks, Esq:

My dear Thomas,

With a beard of four days' growth and a shirt resembling Queen Isabella's shift, I mean to fill up the time till it grows hot enough to bath in writing letters. The quiet of our situation is particularly calculated for any sedate operation of this nature, for except the eternal squealing and fighting of mules and the thundering of the batteries, pro and con, at Ciudad Rodrigo there is scarce any noise to interrupt me, unless indeed anything else like a horse should break loose and run over my hut or the enemy should make a movement in which case our cat-like General Craufurd is sure to turn us out.

You see by my mention of the batteries at Ciudad Rodrigo that that resolute town still holds out. For sixteen days has it been bombarded yet, as far as we can observe, its fire is still kept up with the same alacrity, yet it is very ill-provided with artillerymen or with officers of any description.

Two circumstances only were in its favour. The first is that the enemy, aware of its weakness and ignorant of the disposition of its intrepid governor, held it in too great contempt and only brought down against it 18 or 20-pounders and 9 mortars, with a scanty supply of ammunition. The other circumstance is common to all Spanish towns. From their construction it is scarcely possible to set them on fire. It is a heartbreaking thing to us to remain inactive spectators of this gallant defence, especially as some of the prettiest girls in Spain are in the town. What care would we take of them if we had them here. We would build them such nice huts! And keep them so warm at night! And now these French foutres will have them all. I am very glad I never was in Ciudad Rodrigo or I should feel ten times more.

We are on very good terms with the French. The night before they attacked us at Gallegos I had a long conversation with a French officer, a little brook only divided us. Both parties made a point of never firing on single officers in this way without calling to them first. The French are very badly off for rations, a mess of four men only receive one lb of bread and $\frac{1}{2}$lb of flesh per day; we are capitally off. The French desert by every opportunity, even native Frenchmen. We are acting here with some of the German Hussars. Though I have not a very high opinion of the infantry belonging to the German Legion, yet I must bear the most unqualified testimony to the courage, skill, zeal and marked good conduct of the cavalry – the fact is, the first are foreigners of all descriptions and exactly the same species of troops except being finer men, as the French armies – the cavalry are old Hussars, almost all Hannoverians, and many of them men of great respectability. These men are perfectly to be depended on and understand outpost duty better, and take more care of their horses, than British dragoons.

We are living here almost at free quarters for as we know the enemy will be here before long we make a point of conscience to leave him as little as possible. Since we were driven in on the 4th ultimo, from Gallegos, we have been much quieter and been allowed to have our baggage with us and we get hot breakfasts. But our clothes are never off our backs or our saddles off our horses. I must confess I enjoy this sort of life, there is a wildness and continual occupation of mind and body which delights me . . .

10 July The enemy had a party of cavalry and infantry in Villa de Puerco again this morning. Later a reconnoitring party examined our front.

11 July Having conceived the idea of cutting off any party of the enemy General Craufurd assembled six squadrons in our camp, the evening, the 10th.† We moved off soon after 11pm and, crossing the ford, circled round by Alamada in order to get beyond Villa de Puerco. Ciudad Rodrigo preserved a dead silence and it became more and more apparent it had surrendered. Had this been foreseen it is probable we would never have attempted what we we were about, but as it was we were far too engaged to give it up.

We reached Villa de Puerco and formed in close column of squadrons beyond it a little before daybreak and well concealed in a hollow. As the sun rose some infantry and a troop of dragoons were discovered in a large plain, covered with corn, beyond the village. We advanced in column of division, right in front, but as we had a defile to pass it tailed a good deal; the Hussars were first under Krokenburgh, then the 16th, then the 14th. The French infantry were just opposite the defile behind the brow of a hill, and nearly concealed in the corn ... The Hussars and Ashworth's, of the 16th, charged, but they got a heavy volley which knocked down 13 or 14 men and nearly as many horses, and they then wheeled to the left and made at the distant enemy cavalry. The third squadron emerging – Belli's – followed their example, the sun was directly in our eyes and from the circumstance, and the dust, we could see nothing, and indeed, except the first two squadrons who had charged, no one knew whence the enemy volley had proceeded.‡ These three squadrons rode at the cavalry and took nearly 40 with their horses; very few got away. The fourth squadron, the 14th, was stopped by General Craufurd and ordered to charge the enemy infantry and it is impossible to do justice to the intrepidity of this enemy body. They stood this second charge as well as the first, knocked down some by running fire and bayoneted others. Col Talbot led the squadron. When he saw the enemy had formed an oblong he endeavoured to bring his right flank forward and charge the upper face of the square. He moved on like a lion, had his horse killed close to the enemy, and fell himself, fighting sabre in hand in the middle of the square; this was not broken and the 14th was repulsed. In the dust and confusion the enemy got off through the corn into the woods.

It is probable that General Craufurd was hurried by the idea of Ciudad Rodrigo having surrendered, those officers to whom he spoke say his manner was that of a man who had lost his presence of mind. It is certain that had we only surrounded and watched the infantry and sent for the guns – which were in the neighbourhood and could have come up in twenty minutes – we should have annihilated them had they not first surrendered. But this I feel convinced they would have done but they had no opportunity, they were charged the instant our cavalry appeared and had not time to throw down their arms. Other things were

---

†One Squadron, Hussars; 3 of the 14th; 2 of the 16th, and another sent round by Barquilla, which Craufurd forgot, and later thought they must be the enemy.

‡Gossip declared that the 16th had 'avoided action on purpose', and Cotton, Cocks and Wellington united to put a stop to it. See Combermere Vol. 1.

ill-managed. General Craufurd appeared to have forgot his own arrangements and our own squadrons were repeatedly pointed out to us as enemies.

On the whole it was very mortifying that an affair, ably planned and favourably carried on to the moment of action should, in the end, turn out so ill through a too great precipitancy in the execution. We returned to camp at about 8 am and learnt that Ciudad Rodrigo surrendered at six yesterday evening.

17 July It is strongly reported that the greater part of the French army in our front is moving to the south. Capt Grueben and Cornet Wisch have been detached some days to penetrate towards the Agueda and ascertain the truth.

19 July I was detached with 30 men of my troop to the right and, taking Cornet Wisch under my command, was directed to watch the motions of the enemy on that flank.† The point of most consequence was Fuente Guinaldo, where the roads branch off to the south and south-west.

---

†By Wellington's own order.

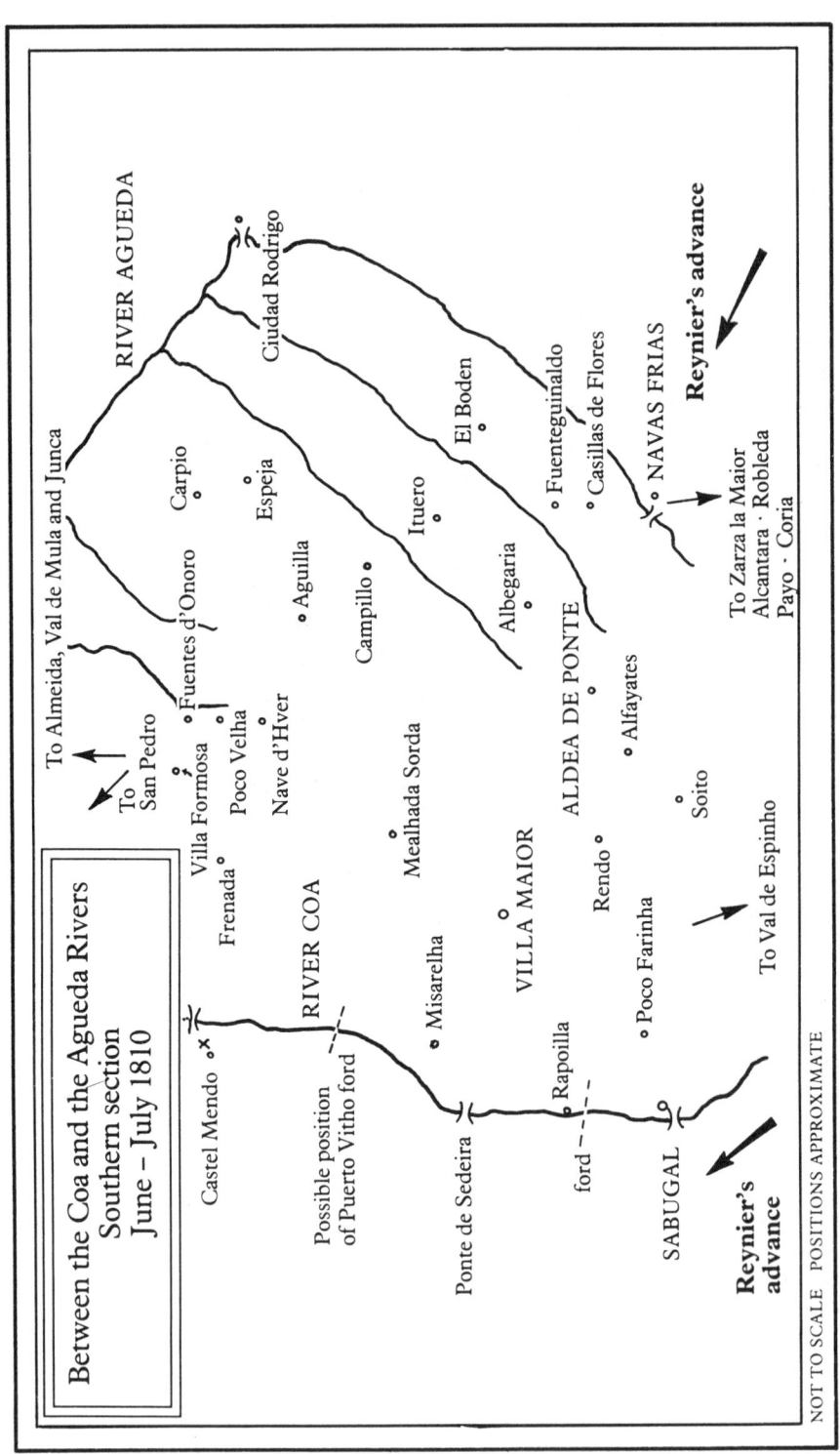

CHAPTER SEVEN
Wellington's Eyes and Ears

20 July – 25 September 1810

WITH ALMEIDA now under threat it became imperative for Wellington to know by which route, or routes, the French would advance, and whether Massena and Reynier would be operating in unison or no. Should the thrust be down the Mondego valley, there was a choice of only two roads, one either side the river, the northern atrocious and the southern practical for all arms. No one could conceive Massena would take the former but with Reynier the unknown factor the Commander could take no chances, the French could attempt both roads, and he depended wholly on Cocks's early information to give him time to concentrate appropriately.

* * *

20 July Villa Maior. Saw Cornet Wisch ... 11,000 men under Reynier are marching from Alcantara and reached Coria and Moreleja yesterday. Their advanced guard is at Payo and it is said they are to halt four days there. Coria is five leagues from Payo.

21 July Firing was heard to our left and an Hussar came in to report the enemy had driven in our cavalry and Fort Conception was blown up. General Slade, who is with the Royals behind the Coa, has promised to send an officers' party† to Soito, this will secure our right. General Craufurd is at Junca.

22 July Sent my party, consisting of one Subaltern, one serjeant and 16 dragoons to Mealhada Sorda while I went myself to Aldea de Ponte and almost to Navas Frias. Went to Don Julian Sanchez's‡ encampment and agreed with him mutually to communicate intelligence. Returned to Mealhada Sorda. General Craufurd's Headquarters are in Almeida and our cavalry is in the neighbourhood, the enemy has been in Val de Mula, San Pedro and Villa Formosa but does not occupy them at present. I am informed by the Town Major of Ciudad Rodrigo, who has escaped from the enemy, and from peculiar circumstances is likely to have accurate intelligence, that the enemy has formed the following plan of campaign.

His first object is Almeida, he then means to establish a line of posts from Astorga, through Zamora, Ciudad Rodrigo and the passes of the sierra to Zarza la Maior. When all this is organised, which it is supposed it will be by two months at farthest, their columns will advance from Galicia on Oporto, through Almeida, in the interior of Portugal, and through Castel Branco on Lisbon.

---

†The number varied from between 6 and 8 and 50 to 60.
‡The guerrilla leader who had escaped from Ciudad Rodrigo in June.

23 July Remained at Mealhada Sorda; the enemy is in force at Fuentes and beyond Nave de Hver, towards Aguila. Passed the night in an old convent near Mealhada Sorda whence there was a road to the ford at Puerto Vitho. I never remember such a night as this, the heaven was in a blaze with lightning and the rain fell in torrents. I got all my horses and men into a chapel.

24 July Came back to Villa Maior; four deserters from the 27th Regiment surrendered to us. They were well clothed but, like all the rest, complained bitterly of the want of provisions. A report came in from the left that the enemy had invested Almeida; that place was firing this morning and I should not be surprised if the news were true as the enemy has pushed our troops from Gallegos and Carpio.

25 July The Royals and the Fusiliers who were on the bank of the Coa have fallen back. Capt la Motte of the former writes me word that General Craufurd has passed that river. The enemy does not occupy Pueblo, Campillo, Albegaria or Casillas de Flores, but a considerable number of troops passed through Espeja yesterday on their way to Almeida; some guns have been heard in that direction.

26 July During the night I received two despatches from Cornet Wisch on the right, stating that Reynier had advanced in the evening of the 25th and occupied Navas Frias, pushing on his advanced posts in the direction of Sabugal to Valverde and almost to Val de Espinho . . .

> His report of this reached Wellington the same day. At 7.20 that evening Wellington wrote to General Craufurd concerning its importance, but at the same time commenting, 'the fact is not sufficiently ascertained to enable me to move General Hill.'[1]

. . . My situation now became uncomfortable, the enemy was certainly beyond my left and probably beyond my right and, although he could not cut me off from the river Coa, he might easily catch me on the other side. I determined to fall back. I ordered Cornet Wisch to Poco Farinha to look after Reynier, and myself went to Sedeira Nova. None of the orderlies I had sent off for the last two days had returned, nine men were absent and it only left me one serjeant and nine more. Soon after my arrival in Sedeira a patrol I sent to my left fell in with some French infantry and killed one. I moved to a hill behind Sedeira and occupied a ruined convent called O Convento de Nosses Senhora de Monte. In the evening I got orders from General Cole, who commanded in Guarda, to attach myself to his division reporting to General Slade.

I now heard that our infantry had been engaged on the 24th; General Craufurd had remained until the last moment beyond the Coa and been forced over with some loss . . .

> Despite a warning from Wellington to retire earlier behind the Coa, Craufurd hung on and paid for it. This was the action at Almeida bridge over the Coa on the 24th when the Light Division fought so magnificently.

. . . At night I fell back to Richioso, receiving orders to take post at Marmeliero. *27 July* (His 24th birthday) Occupied Marmeleiro. There are four points in front of me where the enemy can cross the Coa: Sabugal, Roquemadou, Rapoilla de Coa, and Seixo de Coa. Vendes, the Ponte de Sedeira where I crossed yesterday. The enemy has not yet appeared near the river in this direction, his line extends from Navas Frias, where Reynier is, by Frenada and Castel Mendo to Pinhel. Our

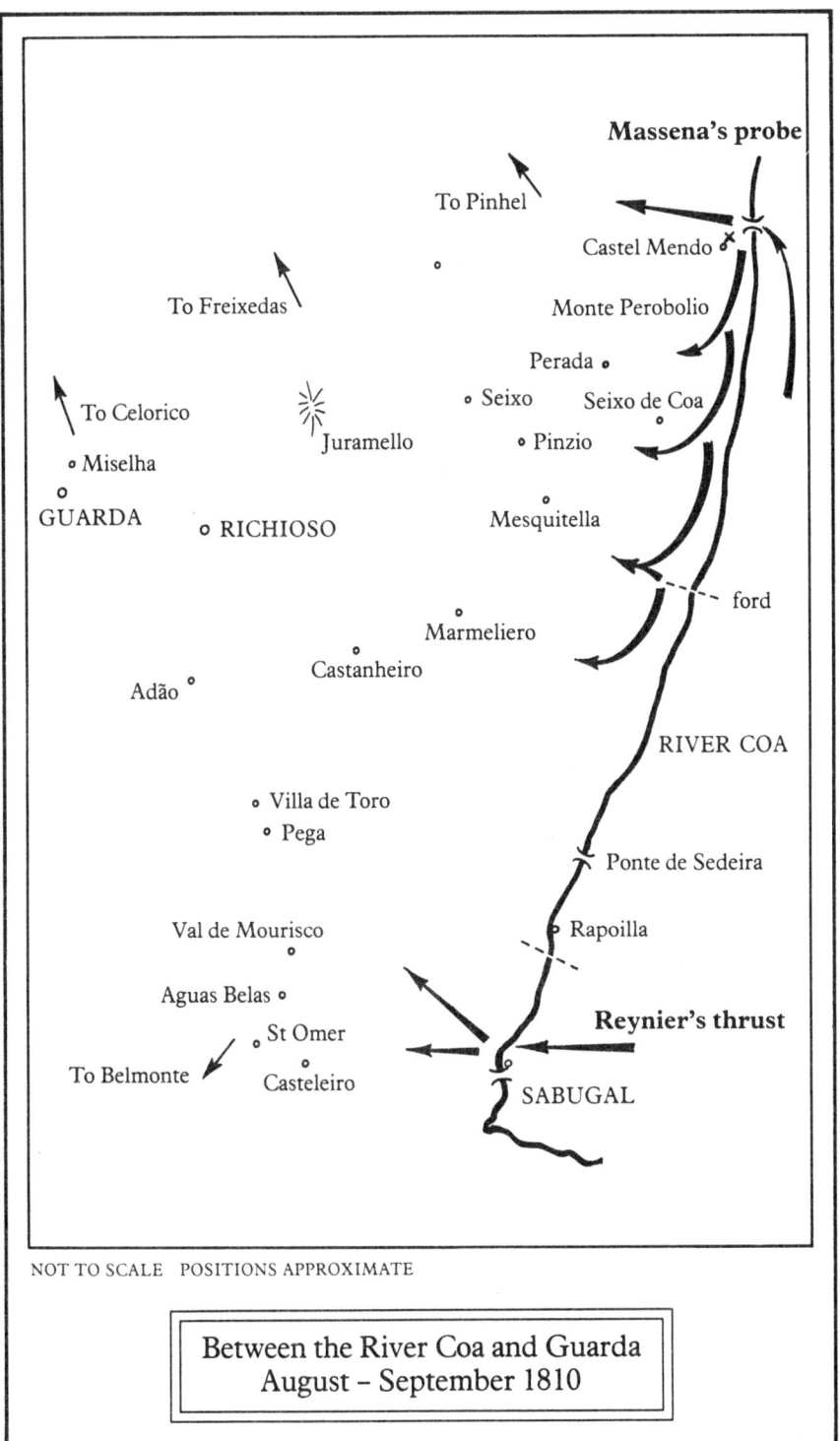

Between the River Coa and Guarda
August – September 1810

Headquarters remain in Alverca, with our advanced post in Freixedas.

Cornet Wisch has fallen back to Sabugal, fearing to be cut off by Valverde; I sent him to Villa de Pega, looking out for the roads from Sabugal and Rapoilla to Guarda. I shall remain, myself, in the neigbourhood of Richioso and Marmeliero, looking out to Castel Mendo, Ponte de Sedeira and Seixo de Coa and communicating with a post we have at Juremello† on the left. Cornet Wisch will retire on Guarda. I shall fall back on that place and Freixedas when driven in or ordered.

28 July Everything was perfectly quiet, pressed 16 skins of wine.

29 July Moved at daybreak to Richioso.

> He remained in this new camp for a month. Tomkinson, in his diary written later, reminisced that 'It was a most excellent camp, the trees affording capital shade; and from the length of time we had been there each man had a good hut and the encampment wore the appearance of a small village. We were much safer from any sudden attack; the men and horses both continued healthy from having plenty to eat and something to employ themselves with. The men got as much rye bread, mutton, potatoes, and wheat flour from the adjacent mills as they wanted, and the horses as much rye in the ear and thrashed as they could eat, and now and then some wheat, nearly ripe. Cocks and myself had nothing with us but a change of linen, a pot to boil potatoes, and the same to make coffee in, with a frying pan, which were carried on his led horse. We never wanted for a single article excepting wheat bread, which failed us occasionally and with a person not accustomed to rye, it does not agree. We could always march in five minutes, never slept out of our clothes and never enjoyed better health; half past two in the morning was the hour we got up.'[2]

... The enemy patrols every day to Perada, he is extremely cautious, he never ventures to stir without infantry and all his outpost duty is performed by parties composed of the two arms. About 1pm thirty or forty French dragoons and a company of infantry entered Castanheiro, about three miles from me. The peasants of Richioso were very anxious to get rid of me as I annoyed them by taking rations. They took advantage of the neighbourhood of the enemy and came running in from all quarters crying out the town was surrounded by the infantry and cavalry. I got my people together as quick as possible but a party of Royals, who had been put under my orders and who had seen no service, were so long in turning out that had the report been correct I should have been awkwardly situated. It fortunately proved false. I secured some of the alarmants and had them well flogged.

In the evening I moved about two miles to the point where the roads join from Castel Mendo and the Ponte de Sedeira to Guarda and bivouacked under some chestnut trees. Don Julian is at Alfayates. A few Spaniards from his party have attached themselves to me under a Bohemian officer of the name of Strenuwitz.

30 July A patrol which I sent out yesterday, one serjeant and three men, has not returned and is I fear taken by the enemy. I patrolled this morning to Castenheiro where I could hear nothing of the enemy. Two deserters came in who said the 6th and 8th corps d'armée were at Almeida. The 6th was reviewed yesterday which is generally a signal for advancing. The 8th is destined either to besiege or watch

---

†Juramello is now tree covered and lies to the right of the Guarda/Frenada road.

Almeida. Reynier with the 2nd has moved towards Zarza la Maior. Occasional firing at Almeida.

31 July The enemy has evacuated all the villages between this and Castel Mendo and the peasants even say he has left that place ... General Hill, who had moved up to Belmonte, has fallen back in order to keep opposite Reynier ... I do not think he will now advance on us but that other corps are forming in the north or on the Tagus to turn our flanks ... I believe there is occasion to expect he intends advancing by the line of the Tagus through Zarza la Maior. It will be necessary to keep a look out at Penamacor.

1 August For some time I have observed increasing symptoms of neglect and dislike in the Portuguese peasantry towards us; they think we are retreating and deserting them and conceive this a proper moment to show all the rancour which has long been brooding in their breasts. I do not blame them for disliking us, the contempt with which Englishmen treat them is a sufficient excuse for it, but I despise them for the manner with which they have hitherto fawned on us and not dared to show their dislike till they think they are getting rid of us. Today, two of my patrols were attacked in two separate villages, a man of each is badly wounded. I immediately visited each village with a party, seized some of the inhabitants whom I considered as culprits and have sent them on to General Cole at Guarda.

> Tomkinson related: 'They shot Thompson through the body and kept the dragoon of the Royals with them, tied the whole day to a tree, releasing him in the evening, when he returned to us, reporting what had happened. Capt Cocks, with the party, went out, found Thompson lying amongst the rocks dreadfully bruised with stones and shot through the lungs. He was brought home and will never again be fit for service.'³

2 August ... The enemy occupied Penamacor this morning with 2,000 men. This is a demonstration to harrass us, Penamacor is not a likely point for invasion. I hear the Portuguese Caçadores behaved extremely well with Craufurd at Almeida bridge. Cox, too,† had made some sallies from the town with success. This is well, if the Portuguese fight, the French have a troublesome lot before them.

3 August The enemy pushed forward parties from Penamacor as far as Aguas Belas. From some prisoners and deserters I find that the 6th Corps, covered by the 8th and commanded by Marshal Ney, is destined for the siege of Almeida...

> On this day Wellington requested Cotton to 'relieve the horses of Cocks's party and give him Light Dragoons or Hussars instead of the Royals. He might possibly experience some inconvenience if all his men were relieved and still greater inconvenience if his detachment were much diminished; and he in a most important situation in front of the right of the position of the area, and on the communication between the enemy's corps.'⁴

4 August A Spaniard from Salamanca says some hundred men marched in on the 30th and 31st from Puerto de Banos. Don Julian says the enemy's troops in their direction received orders yesterday to release a deserter from the 3rd Hussars confined there. The enemy has left the neighbourhood of Aguas Belas.

5 August By two peasants from Castel Mendo I learn the enemy has not above 100

---

†The governor of Almeida and about to come under siege.

or 150 infantry in that town, with nothing in front. The peasants annoy them considerably. They are the more enraged as there are many Spaniards in the French army.

7 August, Encampment near Richioso. To his father:
My dearest Lord,
I trust this letter will find you perfectly recovered from your indisposition and that the keen air and wild beauties of the Highlands will have had their full effect. For my part I am leading a life still wilder, being detached from the army with sixty or seventy men composed of all regiments to watch the enemy on our right. I have 16th and 14th Dragoons, Royals, Hussars and Spaniards under my command. At present, as the enemy is quiet, I am also. This is an interesting service, being very independent and giving me the means of knowing all that is going on. I surprised a company of sixty French yesterday, with twenty dragoons, had the ground been at all in my favour I should have taken a good many of them. But there were so many stone wall enclosures and rocks close to the village where they were that most of them got off and I could only secure a serjeant and three men and a horse, although a good many shot were fired. As this was the first time I had been engaged in an enterprise of my own planning and conducting I felt well satisfied with even this very moderate success. It seems the decided intention of the enemy to besiege Almeida; I believe the trenches will be open tonight . . .

Reynier's corps, which had marched up from Estramadura as if it meant to join the troops in the front, has moved to the south and is threatening the passes of Castel Branco. General Hill is watching him with a superior force. The French are not fond of working during the great heats, they cannot stand them, they are miserably off for provisions. From two or three pounds of bread is all they allow eight men. Meat they are obliged to plunder as they can, they are hourly employed in collecting all the grain they can, grinding and baking it. They wish to avoid the August suns, the necessity of establishing magazines and collecting greater numbers will, I feel convinced, delay their great attack on Portugal till the middle of September. They will then move in a variety of points, meanwhile they will reduce Almeida and very probably Badajoz and Elvas. Some of the Portuguese regiments which have been raised and disciplined by British officers have been engaged in different affairs and have in every instance conducted themselves perfectly well . . . Our army in general is very healthy and the weather is not hotter for the time of the year than in England. Last year at this period we were low and the great mountains lay to the north of us; now, on the contrary, we are in a high country, open to the north and sheltered from the sultry gales to the south . . .

11 August . . . it is reported the enemy has occupied Soito and Alfayates, I know not what this means.

12 August The enemy does not occupy Soito, he came to Alfayates fair, which took place a day or two ago and, surrounding the town, carried off everything of value. Don Julian is put on British pay, he has about 240 horsemen with him of whom nearly half have lances. He will be stationed on my right to form the chain in that direction.

13 August Don Julian is encamped near Adao, he means to occupy Sabugal, Villa de Toro and Marmeliero. The enemy came to Seixo this morning.

14 August A deserter came in in the evening, he says the batteries at Almeida are expected to open tomorrow, being the Emperor's birthday ...

16 August I had concerted with the peasants at Misurelha and Seixo de Coa to make an attack on the mills of Castel Mendo this morning. I marched at 2 am and was joined at Monte Pereobolio by 80 or 100 peasants. I halted immediately opposite Castel Mendo, having first ascertained that the enemy did not occupy Freixel or Mesquitella. The peasants went down to the mills and about 25 Frenchmen turned out from Castel Mendo and a few from the mills. The peasants succeeded in destroying five mills.[5]

> At 6.30 that evening Wellington in Celorico wrote to Cotton, 'I find by the telegraph from Guarda that Cocks and his detachment, and the ordenanza, have destroyed the mills near Castello Mendo.'[5]

21 August I patrolled this morning with twelve men through Perada in the direction of Suli to discover how far the enemy's posts extended that way. Just as I got to Leomil I saw two or three scattered dragoons retiring whom I took for vedettes falling back. I halted the patrol and galloped in with one hussar to reconnoitre; however, they were not vedettes but dragoons returning from foraging. I fell in with an officer and seven men and had I four or five dragoons I could have taken them all they were so encumbered with trusses; as it was, I could only ride up and fire at the officer and, I believe, wound his horse.

The vedettes, with a piquet of twenty, were a little further back.

21 August 1810, Encampment near Richioso. To Thomas Somers Cocks, Esq:
My dear Thomas,

I hope you received safe, a letter I wrote up to about a fortnight ago, The enemy has opened the trenches before Almeida but his batteries are not yet ready. Since the 15th, when the trenches opened, the deserters say he has lost a hundred men nightly by the fire of the town. All is quiet this morning and I suspect he is summoning the place previous to opening his fire tomorrow. His ignorance and want of information is astonishing; in his first summons he addressed Governor Cox as a Portuguese. Deserters come in by handfuls, between 40 and 50 have passed through my post in the last month. I have had one or two little skirmishes and yesterday was very near taking an officer of the 15th Chasseurs ...

22 August This night Almeida threw a good many light balls.

23 August Towards evening the cannonade recommenced at Almeida. I moved off at dark with the intention of trying to cut off the enemy's piquet near Suli but when I arrived he had changed his position and I marched all night for nothing.

24 August The enemy was foraging in Amoriero.

25 August A piquet of the Royals is stationed during the day at Castenheiro falling back at night to Iona[?], I shall change my encampment as this piquet is partly in front.

26 August I marched this morning with 45 men to attempt to surprise the enemy's foragers in Amoriero or Freixo and I very nearly cut off 15 Chasseurs à

Cheval in the latter place, but they escaped me by an accident. They made off to an encampment on a hill above Leomil where they were joined by 40 or 50 men. I drove the whole party about two miles hoping to make the enemy show his face but I only saw one squadron turning out. I carried off everything worth the trouble from the encampment, among other things 4 sacks of bread and biscuit and some barley.

27 August I moved my encampment to Nossa Senhora de Monte; a patrol of the enemy's came and drove in my vedettes.

28 August It is reported that Almeida has surrendered. I was ordered to my old encampment but such a hurricane of rain with thunder and lightning came on that I put the party up in Albardo[?].

29 August A deserter came in this morning and I have likewise seen a Portuguese soldier who was taken by the enemy in Almeida and afterwards escaped. They both give nearly the same account. On the 26th the batteries opened. The place, which is particularly exposed to bombardment, suffered dreadfully. At night a skit entered the magazine in the bastion, which blew up. The place ceased firing. The French would grant nothing to the garrison but their lives and the honours of war, which was accepted on the 28th.

Reynier has moved to Sabugal but cavalry outposts are called in nearer Guarda.

30 August There has been some skirmishing near Freixedas and the enemy has destroyed the telegraph there; a squadron of the Royals charged with success.

31 August The enemy has been to Villa de Pega and near Villa de Toro but today's reports speak of him retiring. I think this is only a demonstration.

> The same day Wellington, in Celorico, wrote to the British Ambassador in Lisbon: 'The enemy talked of attacking Guarda this day but it is now half past ten and I have just received a telegraph message from thence stating that a patrole had come in and there was nothing new.'[6]

2 September The enemy is encamped near Sabugal, Nave and Alfayates. A considerable quantity of artillery has passed down to the south, this must mean something. If light it must be intended for Reynier, he has artillery at Plasencia already; therefore, if he wants more he must have something in hand. I should not be surprised if, while he is occupying Sabugal, troops are marching down behind him through Penamacor. Reynier's corps, thus reinforced, will be ready for an advance by Castel Branco or the siege of Badajoz. This evening the enemy made a reconnaissance forcé on the side of Alverca and a general attack was expected; our army moved to the rear. All the cavalry near Guarda was called in and the infantry evacuated that place. The heavy cavalry, 2 squadrons of the Royals, marched with them. My party only occupied the town.

> The warning beacons were lit along the range of hills and Tomkinson wrote: 'We slept in the street, not thinking it safe to put under cover. From lighting the beacon, several houses had taken fire; and there not being an inhabitant in the town two or three were burnt down. I was too tired to get up and see the fire.'[7]

3 September I received orders to retire on Prados, leaving a small party in Guarda.

> Wellington wrote to Cotton from Celorico at 8am that day: 'Capt Cocks is upon Prados with a piquet of observation upon Guarda ... He will retire upon Linhares ... It might

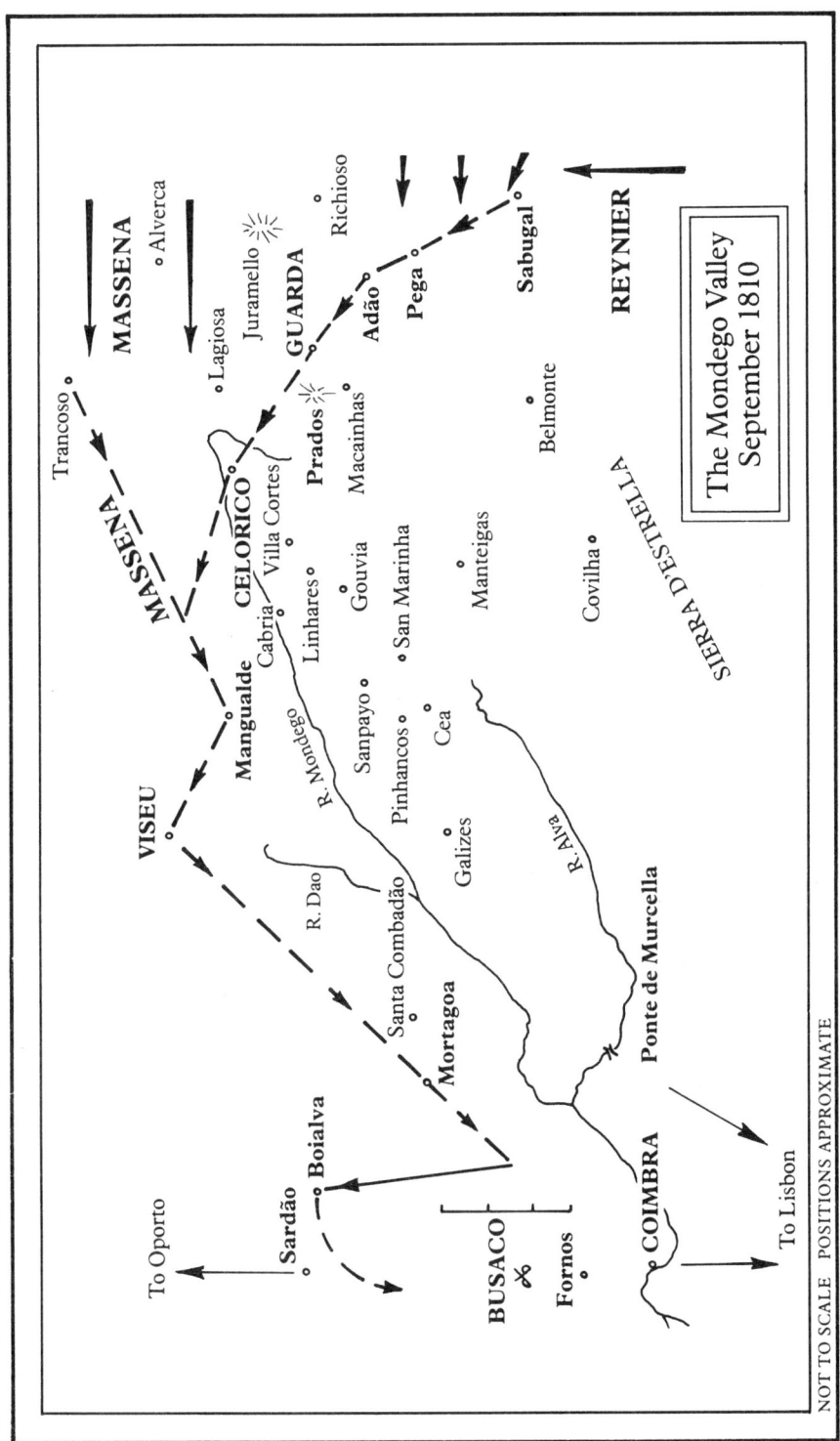

be advisable to strengthen him a little so as to enable him to strengthen his post at, and to patrole from, Guarda, to obtain better intelligence of the enemy's movements ... I believe [General] Cole has left the English key of the telegraph at Guarda with Cocks; if he has not I shall desire him to send it to him.'[8]

4 September ... all is quiet at Guarda, the enemy has not advanced in that direction.

5 September Received orders from Lt-Gen Cotton to re-occupy Guarda, increasing the party there to 25. The remainder of my party continued at Prados under Lt Tomkinson. I put all my people and horses in a house and yard out of the town on the Prados road. Don Julian is between Guarda and Belmonte, occupying that place. He patrolled yesterday to Sabugal, the enemy's nearest post is the large convent beyond Alfayates.

6 September No fires could be seen last night from the hill of Juramello; the peasants report that the enemy is advancing from Pinhel on our left.

> The same day Wellington wrote to Cotton from Gouvia: 'I wish you would strengthen the party upon Guarda and get Cocks to go out to the front towards Sabugal and discover what they are about; whether they have really moved cannon from Almeida by Sabugal; whether it is cannon of a heavy calibre; whether the troops of Ney's corps have moved that way; and let me know the number of any regiment that has marched and I shall know to what corps it belongs.'[9]

8 September The enemy came today with a patrol of 30 cavalry and some infantry and plundered Richioso and Perada ... They enquired repeatedly what troops were in Guarda. My party was increased to 48 and Lt Badcock, 14th Light Dragoons joined me.† Lt Tomkinson joined his regiment.

9 September I patrolled by Villa Mendo, Marmeliero to Villa de Toro. My intention was to go on, either in the direction of Alfayates or Sabugal ... but at Villa de Toro I saw about 300 infantry and some dragoons entering Pega, about half a mile from me. This was at 1pm. I learnt from the peasants that the enemy entered Alfayates in force yesterday and marched from thence this morning. As it is three leagues from Alfayates to Sabugal and four from thence to Guarda, I had no idea the enemy would advance beyond Pega today and had some idea of waiting at Villa de Toro to see if more came. Thinking it, however, of consequence to give immediate information to Lord Wellington, I returned to Guarda at the trot. As I passed the woods near Adao I heard a drum, I had not been in Guarda above an hour when, at half past four, the head of the enemy's column appeared in sight, they had marched seven leagues without halting. There were 800 infantry and 50 cavalry ... but when my piquet began to skirmish they fell back and the infantry pushed forward.

10 September At daybreak some of the enemy's vedettes were in sight. I got a Portuguese to go into the town and from him learned that the enemy had evacuated it. I got in about 11 and found some of the Heavys there, who had got earlier information of the enemy's departure; in this there was some want of alertness on my part ... It was probably a reconnaissance to ascertain whether it

---

†Lovell Badcock became a major general in middle life, and for family reasons assumed the surname of Lovell.

was true that we had abandoned Guarda. This was a point of great importance since without the place we could not seriously maintain ourselves in advance of Celorico.

10 September. To Lord Wellington (Daybreak):
  My Lord,
    I had the honour to report yesterday at 4 pm that the enemy was advancing by Alfayates and Sabugal on Guarda and had reached Pega at 1 pm. I afterwards sent off an orderley at half past five to report that the enemy was obliged to leave Guarda. I think altogether I saw about 50 or 60 dragoons. The infantry came out of the woods from two points, marching in files and straggling a good deal; the cavalry preceded them. When my piquet began to skirmish they fell back and the infantry advanced. I observed two mounted men about three miles from Guarda, upon the Pena Maior road. I cannot tell whether they were flankers or the advance of another column, nor am I quite sure they were not peasants. I am about a league from Guarda towards Mantugua†. The peasants say the enemy talk of marching on to Celorico. I hope to find some point whence I can command that road perfectly.
    I apprised Sir S. Cotton of the movements of the enemy. I brought with me every one of my party.
    I have the honour to be, etc.
      E. Charles Cocks
My party fell in with a patrol of the enemy just before daybreak, between this and Guarda.

> Lovell Badcock wrote to his father: 'I was three times nearly taken, once with four men cut off from the rest of the Party but succeeded in joining them again by leaping some fences ... I had the misfortune to lose a stirrup which broke from the tree of the saddle whilst I was galloping with some French Chasseurs so close at my heels that one of them cut the Croup of the Man's horse next to mine.'[10]
>
> Wellington spent the whole day writing to his commanders about these moves. At 2 pm he sent to Cotton: 'I have just received your letter of 10 am. I enclose one which I have received from Cocks. Both accounts appear to agree pretty well. If the enemy advance in concert I think they will take possession of Guarda with a stronger force. I conclude that Cocks will have returned to Guarda. You will observe that he retired by the road to Manteigas, to which I see no objection when he shall retire again. But if he does so, there should be likewise a post on Prados to observe the enemy and also one at Linhares, otherwise they would be on the great road before you would know it ... Desire Cocks to have the road from Guarda to Manteigas examined and let me know what kind of one it is ...'[11]

11 September I patrolled to the front to Villa de Toro and Pega; near the latter I saw a considerable body of French cavalry and a party pursued me, nearly cutting me off at Adao ... I do not think I can be quiet long in Guarda though it is very probable the enemy has no serious intention of advancing and only means to drain the rich plain in my front.

---

†Possibly Manteigas.

12 September About eight I heard two shots in the plain and saw Lt Badcock returning and a column of the enemy following him ... We had some sharp skirmishing in Guarda and I retreated; a squadron followed me as far as Macainhas. This was the best French cavalry I have seen, the men were Bavarians, well mounted and rather dashing fellows ... They only remained a few hours in Guarda and then returned to the plain and I re-occupied the town.

Significantly, General Reynier arrived in Alfayates this day.[12]

13 September The enemy is plundering all the villages in the plain; I believe this was his principal object and that his advance yesterday was only intended to ascertain there was nothing dangerous for his dispersion.

15 September About 9am I discovered about half a mile from the foot of Guarda hill a few French dragoons dismounted, and on looking accurately with my glass I perceived a dismounted squadron half a mile beyond them, near the woods. Within the woods I saw a large force of French cavalry also dismounted, and still further a column of infantry, marching in file about two miles long. I soon after received advice that a detachment was moving on Pacos to my right. Fearing I might be cut off I determined to retreat on Prados. It was clear the enemy was now advancing seriously and I did not think it worth while to wait for him especially as by his two visits to Guarda he had acquired sufficient knowledge of the locality to know how to intercept me. I fell back to Miselha, from hence I had an excellent view of the Celorico side of Guarda hill and soon discovered that the enemy's column did not halt in Guarda. I fell back to Prados ... I found the enemy had sent a squadron to Macainhas to prevent my patrolling up to Guarda but had marched no column in the direction of Manteigas.† I heard that our outposts had been driven in to Celorico and Lagiosa, another column of the enemy having moved by Alverca.

> Wellington wrote to Cotton at 'twenty minutes before 5pm, I have heard from Captain Cocks ... that the enemy were pushing down Guarda hill,'[13] and later that evening the enemy's route for the main advance into Portugal became clear. Writing to Beresford, he said: '... the enemy moved upon Guarda this day in strength and apparently in earnest, as they have crossed the hill and are on this side as far as Lagiosa ... The lady sent to your headquarters says that Massena was to be this day at Pinhel, tomorrow at Trancoso. I enclose a note which she brought from Alorna‡ to his wife, which rather shows that the route of the main body is by Viseu.'[14] Or, as all the British were aware, by the northern and most atrocious road.

17 September Last night our cavalry fell back to Pinhancos and the army is in full retreat to occupy the position of the Ponte de Murcella. I went at daybreak to the Carvalhos Quinta, some singular looking trees on top of the mountain of Linhares. My orders were to remain in this neighbourhood and watch the motions of the enemy on the plain. I received information that a party of the enemy's cavalry had moved yesterday on Fornos. The column in advance is said

---

†The significance of this was that Manteigas lay on the good, southern route to Lisbon and apparently the French were ignoring the road.

‡The Marquis of Alorna was a Portuguese Quisling.

to be commanded by Soult, nephew of the marshal. A piquet of the enemy occupied Linhares; his fires were very numerous last night at Celorico, the plain between that place and Guarda and about Guarda itself.

18 September Last night there were no fires at Guarda, the rear of the enemy has passed that place and he appears to be concentrated around Celorico. About 9am I could distinguish two columns in motion, 1,000 infantry with five squadrons encamped round Villa Cortes and a large column with a quantity of ammunition and wagons moved on the Fornos road. It is evident that the principal part of the army is marching on Viseu.

19 September Last night we counted 270 fires, principally towards Fornos. I could discover nothing of the enemy today from the hill, except a few cavalry near Fornos. The detachment at Villa Cortes had moved off towards the Mondego soon after daybreak. I descended into the plain and found that the whole of the enemy was off. The small column at Villa Cortes crossed the Mondego at Cabria and thence joined their army. They have committed considerable excesses and killed several peasants.

20 September ... by all I can learn the enemy has marched in three columns, by Guarda, by Alverca and by Trancoso ... The greatest part of the cavalry horses are said to be in bad condition and the artillery horses worse. They could scarcely get some of the pieces up Celorico hill.

> Cocks's orders were possibly delayed as to his future movements but Wellington had written to Cotton this day: '... You see that the enemy have all crossed the Mondego and I propose that you should cross tomorrow ... Be so kind as to leave on this side of the Mondego an intelligent officer, either Krauchenberg or Cordemann or Cocks, with about a squadron to observe the enemy's movements between the [river] Dao and the Mondego and do you take care to keep up a communication with him.' This same day he mentioned Cocks in his despatches home: '... it is but justice to mention the zeal and intelligence with which the duty of the outposts has been performed by Capt Krauchenberg and Cornet Cordemann of the 1st Hussars and by Capt the Hon. C. Cocks of the 16th Light Dragoons.' Both these letters were dated 20 September 1810, the second addressed to the Earl of Liverpool, Secretary of State.[16]

21 September Received orders to march to Galizes, eight leagues off in the direction of the Ponte de Murcella. Arrived there in eleven hours, this road has been made excellent†. I hear the enemy entered Viseu the 19th and his advanced guard is near Santa Combadao. Oporto is certainly open to him and there is a bad road open to Coimbra, but he has thrown the Mondego between him and Lisbon, he has not advanced much in the final reduction of Portugal, and he must keep open communications with Spain.

22 September I expected to meet with orders, but none have arrived ... I cannot conceive why I am left except to watch that the enemy, after demonstrations on the right bank, does not suddenly advance by the left, but I am too far from the army to communicate any intelligence and he would cross the river between me and the Ponte de Murcella.

23 September My patrol did not return and I began to suspect the enemy

---

†This was the southern route the French had rejected.

occupied some point on the road to Ponte de Murcella. I decided to try and get there but thought it safer to move at night. I set off at sunset with a guide but as he was slow and the road easy I dismissed him. This was a great error and I think it may be laid down as a military maxim never to do that by night which may be done by day and never to march in country you do not perfectly know without a guide. Neglecting these precautions I lost my way and determined to return.
Note I might have proceeded with safety and the fires I saw were some of General Hill's Portuguese cavalry.

25 September, Ponte de Murcella. To The Hon. Miss Margaret Maria Cocks:
My dear Sister,

Since I wrote last we have had some interesting scenes in this quarter and by what I can observe the next fortnight will help to afford a little matter for the historian. My last letter was dated Guarda, it is reckoned the highest city in Europe and is situated on a point of the chain of mountains where all the roads meet from one side of the country and then branch off again for the other. The French turned me out twice before they really moved upon the place and each time I re-entered it. At length, on the 15 September, I observed after breakfast five French dragoons dismount at the foot of the hill holding their horses. This seemed very odd. I got my glass out and a little further, near a wood, I saw a squadron dismounted and, in the wood, two or three regiments, also dismounted, and again behind them a column of infantry in motion. From the point where their head was to the point of the hill to which they reached was two miles. I now began to think the thing serious. The French moved also on other parts of our line and our whole army fell back. I had a most interesting duty. The road of the enemy lay through a large plain, on one side of which is an immense mountain. On this mountain lay I, and very much at my ease counted the divisions which marched at the foot. Unfortunately their principal force did not take this route but I, one day, saw 5,000 infantry and 2,000 cavalry perfectly, with all their baggage and etcs.

This advance has caused most horrible confusion. The Portuguese have such a dread of the French, they desert the villages for leagues on each side of their route. Though one must feel for these unfortunate people, driven from their homes and their habits of indolence, into mountains and activity, yet sometimes in these gangs of fugitives one meets with such curious combinations and such extraordinary demonstrations of dread that it is impossible to help laughing. Fancy to yourself, but first recollect that the scene lies in a grove of pine trees, with firs and brambles about knee high. Fancy to yourself an elderly, fat woman in a flowered satin petticoat trudging away, in one hand a parasol, in the other a lapdog. Then two boys, knock-kneed and trembling, with countenances devoid of every colour but a pasty yellow; a footman, like an old English serving man, with his shoes in his hand, then two misses with fans, crying 'Jesu Maria'; three serving maids, with bundles, howling; two bullocks lowing; a car with the wheels squeaking and a peasant in a cocked hat and a long gun, more frightened than the whole party. Fancy all this trudging through the firs taking *me* for a Frenchman and setting off in every direction.

I believe Marshal Massena, Prince d'Essling, is in a scrape and I flatter myself we are likely soon to give him, with all his titles, a sound drubbing. He has tried to outmanoeuvre our gallant Wellington, and he has hitherto completely taken in the Frenchman ... Adieu, my dear Sister wish us good luck and plenty of plunder, and believe me,
   Your ever affectionate brother,
      E. Charles Cocks

Marshal André Massena, Duc de Rivoli, Prince d'Essling.

CHAPTER EIGHT
The Fighting Squadron†

27 September – 18 October 1810

Cocks met up with General Hill at the Ponte de Murcella and was ordered to rejoin the army on the long, broad summit of Busaco, to the north-east of Coimbra, where Wellington was concentrating. And with such a magnificent defensive position the ensuing battle was almost a foregone conclusion. The terrain being unsuitable for cavalry, only the infantry were locked in combat, the French struggling uphill and the Allies firing down. 'At daybreak,' Charles wrote, 'the enemy advanced in two columns to attack the hill. The 2nd corps d'armée, Reynier, was principally engaged, General Simon led the column which advanced by the Mortagoa road on General Craufurd, the other column attacked General Picton, who was supported by General Hill. After two hours' sharp firing, during which the 52nd and the 95th and a Portuguese regiment made a very brilliant charge, the enemy was completely repulsed.'[1] But not defeated. Learning of roads around Busaco, to the north, by which he could reach the main Oporto/Lisbon highway and outflank Wellington, Massena set out in drenching rain to march through the night of the 28th, while Cocks, similarly, a few leagues to the west, was ordered by Wellington to reconnoitre Massena's movements.

★ ★ ★

28 September Intelligence was received that the 6th and 8th Corps were marching to gain the Oporto road by Boialva and Avelans de Camino. I was sent to ascertain the fact but lost my road in the dark and did not reach Boialva in time.

29 September Soon after daybreak I had discovered the head of the enemy's column marching by Boialva. Our cavalry had moved the preceding night to the plain near Avelans de Camino and it was now all sent back to Mealhada except for two squadrons of the 3rd Dragoon Guards who were left at Avelans de Camino. The enemy continued to advance, and about twelve or thirteen squadrons and 14,000 infantry had descended the mountain when the approach of the head of the enemy's column obliged me to quit the spot where I was reconnoitring. The greater part halted near Boialva while six or eight squadrons, with some infantry, advanced to Avelans de Camino. I obliged the two squadrons there to fall back on the rest of the cavalry. I saw no artillery descend the mountain and therefore conclude that has gone the road by Sardao. The road was so bad that the whole of the French cavalry led their horses down the hill.

30 September We retreated near two leagues to Fornos. Our infantry have crossed the Mondego and it is understood to be Lord Wellington's intention not to defend

---

†Tomkinson relates how the men 'called Cocks's squadron The Fighting Squadron'.

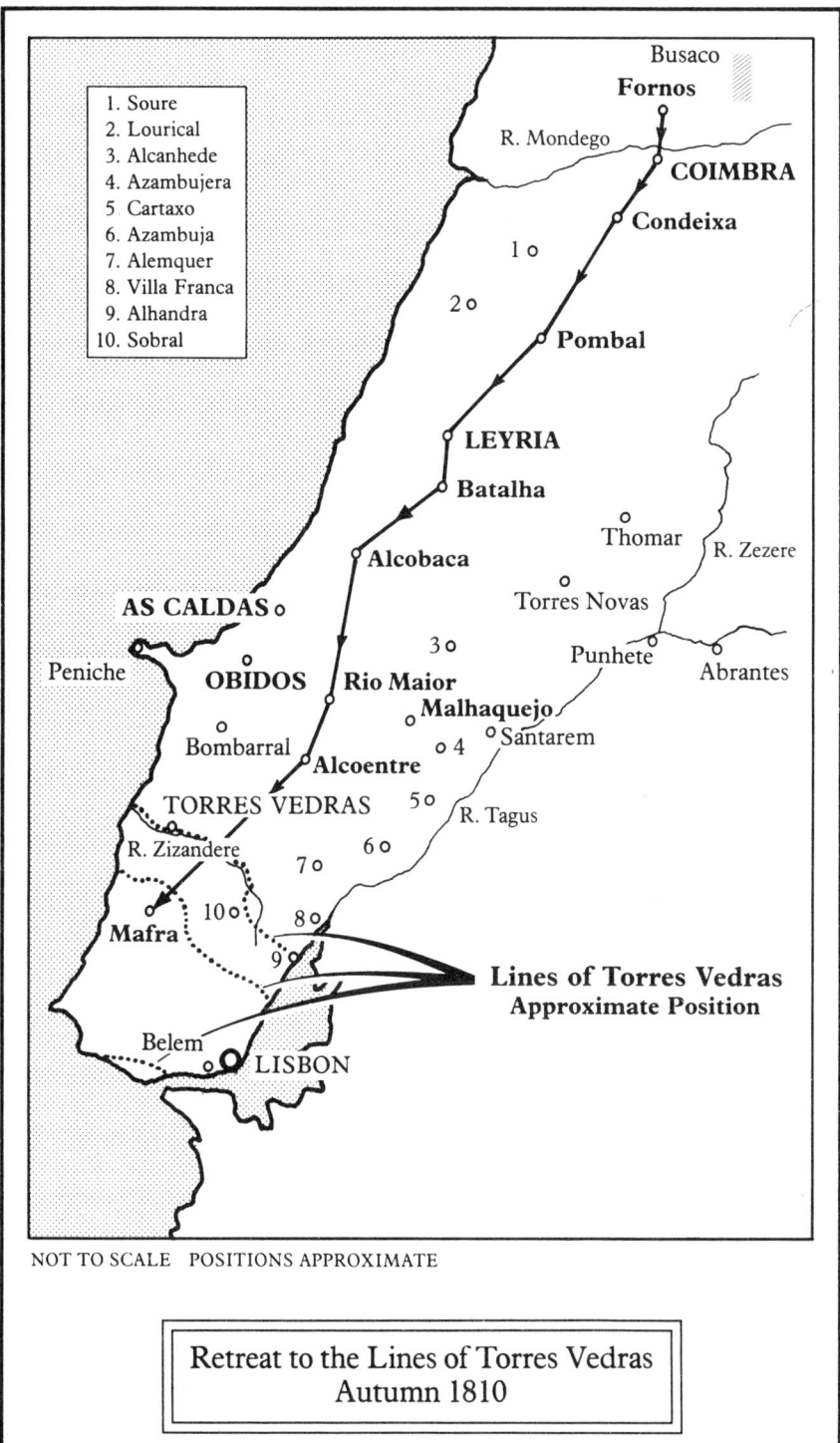

Retreat to the Lines of Torres Vedras
Autumn 1810

that river, which can be forded in a variety of places. It is said he means to fall back on the ultimate position near Villa Franca.

In the evening I was sent with a patrol to gain intelligence on our left. I found a number of fires at a distance of two leagues but, hearing a drum in a wood close to me, did not think it prudent to advance; it was clear the enemy had brought infantry to his outposts, which indicates his intention to advance. I rejoined the cavalry at midnight.

1 October Half an hour after daybreak the enemy attacked our piquets. General Anson's brigade had been imprudently left in a wood from whence the only road by which we could retreat was narrow and bad and the enemy came on in force and rather pressed us. Captain Krokenburgh of the Hussars, who was on duty, was wounded so I took command of the rearguard. Eight hussars were nearly cut off but we charged and saved them and although three or four of the enemy were sabred we were ultimately driven back and lost a hussar, besides several being wounded.

Our cavalry formed in the large plain by Coimbra. The enemy's cavalry was checked by our guns but after an interval his infantry advanced on our right, by the high road to Coimbra. It became necessary to retreat by the ford in our rear and we experienced the mortification of showing the enemy our line of cavalry without awaiting his attack. Perhaps this would have been imprudent from the beginning because the ground was not very favourable . . . but then we should not have formed line; we should not have shown our teeth unless we meant to bite . . .

5 October Camp of Leyria. To Captain The Hon. John Someers Cocks:
My dear Someers,

You have, of course, already seen in the papers the affair of Busaco, as honourable to the troops immediately engaged as favourable to the cause and its results, and this is not merely because we repulsed the enemy with considerable loss – at least 5,000† – but because it has afforded a proof that Portuguese infantry are to be depended on . . .

The way in which Lord Wellington took up that position was acknowledged by everyone to be most masterly, it completely frustrated the first plans of the enemy and obliged them to make a circuitous route in order to reach Coimbra. As there was no position on this route, and as it is in our interests to draw the enemy as far as possible into Portugal – unless any imprudence on his part offers a favourable opportunity by fighting – we have retired to Leyria but not without a very sharp skirmish near Coimbra, at the passage of the Mondego . . . I was more sharply engaged than I have been any time this year, a ball struck my mare but the blanket saved her. We charged the enemy with a few of our rearguard, in the river, and nearly took the colonel of the French dragoons. I hope we shall come across that regiment again; they refused quarter to one of our hussars and we mean to pay them.

The enemy is now in the vicinity of Coimbra and I think it doubtful whether he does not consider himself as having done enough for this campaign. Perhaps, after

---

†In fact a couple of hundred or so less.

plundering the rich country of the Mondego, he will retire on Oporto and take up his winter quarters behind the Douro, where we can hardly disturb him this year. This would be the worst thing he could do for us but if, on the other hand, he advances, I think he will be obliged to fight us in a position of our choosing, and with a trifling disparity in numbers. I have no fear as to the issue and take my word for it, if we ever beat Massena high up in Portugal half his troops will not get back. Not a straggler will escape the peasantry and, acquainted as our light troops are with the country, his will be no enviable situation . . .

6 October Fell back on the high road to Lisbon to about two leagues short of Rio Maior. The enemy did not press us but in the evening he drove in our piquets and a few men were wounded . . .

7 October General Slade's brigade took the rearguard today and we fell back quietly to about a mile beyond Rio Maior; the enemy continued to follow us but at some distance.

8 October The rain set in this morning and lasted the whole day. The cavalry retired to Alcoentre and our piquets were left at Rio Maior.

About twelve the enemy attacked them but though our general was apprised of this he conceived they would halt short as they had done the two preceding days. Perhaps we forgot that we had been making short marches and that it was not certain the enemy would do likewise. Besides, the country after leaving Leyria had become so barren and so short of forage and water that it was almost necessary for them to push on.

By 4 o'clock repeated reports had arrived and there was firing close to the town. The baggage moved out in the greatest hurry and the 16th were ordered to turn out, with the Hussars and Royals in support. The guns had been imprudently put up in the town and were in danger as the enemy were advancing in force.

About forty of the 16th who were first mounted, galloped off to support Capt Bull's guns. However, a squadron of the Royals came up, contrary to orders, with the same intention and we were all mixed together. Captain Murray, who commanded the squadron on piquet which was driven in, finding himself supported, charged the enemy who had already entered the town and this completely checked them. A good many were sabred and twelve prisoners taken but we lost nothing, everything was got off safe. We skirmished with the enemy till dark and he dismounted 40 or 50 men and opened a sharp fire on us; we had a man and horse wounded. The cavalry fell back to Quinta de Torres while Captain Linsingen's squadron was left on piquet, supported by mine.

9 October At nearly 12 o'clock I received a report from Captain Linsengen that the enemy was driving him in and unfortunately, in endeavouring to bring off a man whose horse was killed, he allowed the enemy to press too close to him. 31 French Houssards were sabred but he lost 15 or 16 men and horses besides, some wounded, and was driven in on me in great confusion with the enemy close in his rear.

I formed my squadrons off the road, on the brow of a hill, and threw out some skirmishers. The enemy, however, came on so fast that I found it necessary to charge, and drove them back twice but the Hussars, whose horses were quite

Skirmish on the road to Busaco.

tired, were unable to support me and we were ultimately overpowered. Many of the enemy were cut down and two prisoners brought off and three or four horses, but we lost three men and six horses.

Note: When they have the worst of it the French cavalry have a way which must not be allowed. They cry for pardon but still keep galloping to the rear, or perhaps throw themselves on the ground, and it is impossible to get the prisoners off when you are certain of being attacked yourself by a superior force. We were obliged to cut down or shoot several who did this . . .

10 October Last night was dreadful, it poured all night and in the morning our cavalry were put under cover in Carrigada, falling back in the evening to Povo. The whole of our army is close to the lines and the infantry are to occupy them while the cavalry retires behind to shoe up and re-fit.

11 October The 16th and Hussars marched to Mafra. We had been almost constantly in the field without even tents, for near four months, and our late, long marches had completely worn out our shoes. Two or three days more such would have ruined us by laming every horse . . .

13 October, Mafra. From F. Boverick to Mrs Gardener:
Madam,

We arrived here two days ago and the fate of Portugal seems to be drawing to a crisis and the British army are in high spirits as to the result. We are enjoying a day or two in quiet here, behind our line of defences which are strong and numerous, which the cavalry very much needed as we have covered the retreat all the way. Neither the Captain or myself have had our clothes off now for more than four months and very seldom under any cover but the sky.

I mentioned in my two last letters several affairs wherein the Captain had a distinguished share, but what has occurred within these few days has been highly to the honour of the 16th but much more so to my master, who has charged the enemy repeatedly against five times his numbers and always drove them with great loss to them.

Many of these affairs I have been eye witness to as I always waited till I was driven out.

Five days ago the Captain led his own squadron with success and returned and took a fresh squadron and led on, with equal success, in the last charge, which was on a long bridge which I had not long crossed. He took nineteen prisoners besides a number of killed and wounded with very little loss to himself. And as to his own person, there is certainly a protecting genius attends him for he has never got the least scratch and, including himself, we have but three captains in the regiment fit for duty, but he continues in excellent health and spirits.

There is talk of our brigade being relieved by one that is coming out and our going to England. This is now the pheasant season at Castleditch and I hope you are very merry . . . This is the height of the shooting season here as well, though a different kind of game and what our men call 'fine sport' . . .

18 October Last June a variety of opinions prevailed in the army. Some thought we should not be attacked, others that we should be overrun in a moment; others again, that this campaign was only to open the frontiers and pave the way for a grand attack under the Emperor.

The most common opinion, however, and certainly my own, was that the enemy would advance with two columns when the harvest was got in, and, acting simultaneously on the Tagus and Mondego, would render any position on either of those rivers untenable unless connected with a corresponding one on the other.

These ideas were grounded on the erroneous opinion, universally entertained, of the great superiority of the French numbers. Most officers expected that they would bring into the field two for one and the preparation for embarkation at Lisbon gave credit to this sort of language. Lord Wellington did not discourage it and, I rather think, wished everything should wear the appearance of his having no intention of making serious resistance.

When the campaign opened no French force was heard of disposable for the operations in Portugal except the 2nd, 6th and 8th Corps d'Armée, commanded by Reynier, Ney, Junot and under the orders of Massena, Prince d'Essling. Their strength amounted nominally to 75,000 but could scarcely be really estimated at more than 60,000 and men became so unreasonable in their expectations of success as they had before been ceaseless in despondency. It was, nevertheless, very evident that Lord Wellington had no intention of maintaining himself on the frontiers. On the slightest indication of the enemy to advance, our infantry was removed considerably to the rear and our cavalry only left to maintain an apparent position close to the enemy.

Commonsense pointed out that it would be the height of imprudence to engage the enemy where his retreat would be assured and ours, in the event of disaster, was not. I believe the enemy was deceived by this system of manoeuvring. I have very little doubt that he believed our army and not our outposts only were close to him, both at Ciudad Rodrigo and Almeida. When, at length, all saw that whenever the enemy advanced we were to retreat, a variety of opinions prevailed as to the distance this retrograde movement intended to extend. The Ponte de Murcella was commonly talked of but then this position was completely turned by the Viseu road – but there can be no doubt that Lord Wellington looked forward to the enemy marching by this route. In the instructions I received at Guarda I am particularly directed to watch it. When it was ascertained that this was not their intention, Lord Wellington occupied Busaco.

This position is one of the most perfect for defence I have ever seen and crosses the regular road from Viseu to Coimbra by Mortagoa, but it is likewise turned by its left, by the roads of Boialva and Sardao. I do not think Lord Wellington at first expected Massena would be so imprudent as to advance by Mortagoa but when he found he was really marching by this route, that he had neglected those of Boialva and Sardao, and was actually attacking Busaco, I believe he flattered himself that he would not persevere. I am inclined to this opinion by his not giving the people of Coimbra more notice of the danger they were in, through which they lost the opportunity of removing a great part of their effects. This seems the only instance in which Lord Wellington does not appear to have exactly foreseen the movements of his opponent.

At length, the manoeuvres on Sardão and Avelans de Camino rendered it absolutely necessary to retreat behind the Mondego, an operation easily effected as the detour the enemy was obliged to make enabled us to gain a good day's march.

For a moment it was believed we should stop behind the Mondego but a little consideration showed that this was out of the question. Besides the bridge at Coimbra there are at least three fords over the Mondego lower down the river; one, a league from the town where our cavalry crossed, another at Montemor, and a third still lower, I believe, near Figuerra. If any of these fords had been forced, the troops defending the bridge and the two fords higher up the river would have run into considerable danger of being cut off. Besides, it was by no means desirable to give the enemy an opportunity of halting on the banks of the Mondego, the country between Coimbra and the sea being one of the most fruitful tracts in Portugal.

Lord Wellington's projects were now explained. Amid the variety of conjectures, no one had supposed he could reconcile it to the Portuguese to defend their country by only covering their capital, yet the instant it appeared he had so done everyone was struck with the advantages. When one army seriously undertakes to conquer a country and another, as seriously, resolves to defend it, it is evident that however they may for some time amaze each other by manoeuvring, it is only the event of a battle which can decide the contest, and that the manoeuvring can be no otherwise useful than it brings on the battle under circumstances favourable to the one or the other.

Now, where can we fight more to our advantage than near to Lisbon? We are supplied without difficulty, as to all essentials we instantly get rid of any sick or wounded and receive any reinforcements which arrive without fatiguing them by a march. If we are beat we are close to other positions which will cover our retreat. If we conquer, can the French army have to encounter a more desperate operation than a retreat through an exhausted country where every peasant is armed and thirsting after their blood, and when they will be followed by troops quite fresh, piqued at having retired so far before them and not a little delighted to turn the tables on their foe?

Went to Lisbon and visited the theatre of Rua des Condes. Lisbon looks thin, I cannot conceive where all the people are gone. From all parts of the country they have been crowding here and yet they are not to be found. I believe a great many have crossed the river. I understand the enemy has been feeling different parts of our position but our infantry is under canvas.

CHAPTER NINE

The Lines of Torres Vedras

27 October – 25 December 1810

SAFE BEHIND the Lines of Torres Vedras, that well kept secret, the British were triumphant. The long retreat was at an end and instead of ignominious evacuation, harried by the enemy, they were able to draw breath in comparative comfort. True, many officers expected the army to be withdrawn and several requested home leave, possibly doubting if their services would be required in an active capacity in the Peninsula again. But Cocks was not one of them. Throughout his time in Spain and Portugal he firmly believed that the French would be ultimately defeated, not even the darkest hour could induce pessimism. If one pursued a steady, logical course, alert to every possible situation and ready to meet it, then victory must follow.

So far as his own character and development were concerned, maturity had set in and he was older than his years, but the sheer physical effort of campaigning was taking its toll, even of him, and he was glad of the break.

* * *

27 October, Amiel. To The Hon. James Someṙs Cocks:
My dear James,
   After a very quiet ten days at Mafra, a town quite in the rear to which our brigade was sent to shoe up and refresh itself, we were ordered here. Amiel is a little village close to Ramahal and a league in front of Torres Vedras.

The ignorance of the French has been really wonderful, there is very little doubt that even Massena himself advanced into Portugal under the false persuasion that he should meet with no serious opposition from us. On every occasion there is reason to believe he has had miserable information as to our numbers and designs. The French army was so completely deceived that a French officer, whom we took one day and whom I met in the evening at dinner at Sir Stapleton Cotton's, asked the General's leave to go to England with his baggage, not having the least doubt that he would immediately be put on board.

From two or three circumstances I am inclined to suspect the enemy thinks of moving shortly to the rear, it remains to be seen whether he will try and attack before he retires. I am of the opinion he will do nothing more than possibly make demonstrations in order to conceal his moving off.

The 16th were engaged on several occasions during the retreat, on the 5th and the 9th we charged repeatedly. A French hussar, with whom I was engaged and whom I had wounded, struck me the deuce of a blow on my sabre wrist with his sword. Luckily, the flat only hit me and had no other effect than of deadening my hand, by which means he got off. I was lucky enough, with Capt Atty of the Germans, to lead the last charge; we took an officer, 21 men and 16 horses.

The Marquis of Romana's corps now forms part of our army and a regiment of Spaniards – infantry – is attached to our brigade – 212 strong. The men are very good, I saw part of them engaged the day before yesterday and they behaved most bravely but the greater part of their officers are a miserable set.

We are badly off for captains, having only three left out of eight, two wounded, two sick and one on the staff. Our duty, however, is not very severe now. Before we went to Mafra there were several days and nights dreadfully wet, for sixty hours I do not believe I was dry. The weather now is very fine though frosty and cold at night. In about three or four weeks the rainy season may be expected. Boverick is not very well and I have been obliged to send him to Lisbon . . .

3 November Amiel. To The Hon. Miss Margaret Maria Cocks:

I have been often accustomed to write to you, my dear Margaret, on those books I happen to have lately read. Books are, however, not very portable articles in a campaign and I believe my library is, at present, reduced to an odd volume of Vergil, Dulles' *Mathematics*, an odd volume of *The Spectator*, the *Spanish Duty* and *Robinson Crusoe*. This is the more unfortunate as we have plenty of leisure time upon our hands, the 130,000 men who are here assembled to fire and sabre at one another remaining all perfectly quiet and, except the generals, going on just as unconcerned as if the one party were in London and the other in Paris.

A poor man, however, sometimes raises in half an acre of poor land behind his cottage what a rich one can scarcely stuff into half a dozen of garden mould and, on this principle, I was resolved to try what I could make of *Robinson Crusoe*, and when I came to read it I was really astonished at the wonderful ingenuity and luxury of the author's fancy. The incidents, however extraordinary, grow out of one another in the most natural manner. The character of the hero is perfectly consistent and I am convinced, were we not in the habit of attaching childish ideas to it and were not above wanting that spice and relish to all works of fancy, that it would stand very high among British novels. Defoe had a great taste for this species of writing. He has written the *Memoirs of a Cavalier* in the same style and just as well as *Robinson Crusoe*; indeed, to a soldier they are more interesting.

I wonder how long we shall remain in our present situation? The weather is much like what we have at this season in England, cold and frosty mornings and nights with sunshiny days and now and then a day of rain. My quarter is rather cold, having neither window, nor door, nor fireplace. Pray thank my mother for a pound of excellent tobacco she sent me, which arrived in high order and of which I now feel the comfort. We live very well, having plenty of mutton, beef, fowls, turkey, coffee, butter, bread, potatoes and figs. My cellar – alias pigskins – is stocked with sherry, Collares, an excellent wine of this country like claret but not so strong, and some draught wine. Perhaps I never told you that wine in this country is carried in pigskins, dried and stripped of their hair but retaining their original strength. The mouth is sewed up and the liquor generally drawn by one of the ears or a foot. The prudence of not putting *new wine into old skins* is exemplified for new wine sometimes ferments and then the skins, unless they are very strong, burst. Old skins are the best as they never give the wine taste, which unseasoned ones always do . . .

PS: *The Lady of the Lake* has never arrived.†

4 November Amiel. To his father:

My dearest Lord,

I trust it will not be attributed to vanity if I ask your Lordship whether you have seen the approbation with which Lord Wellington has mentioned some part of my conduct.‡ The chief motive an honourable and modest man feels for deserving public praise is the pleasure he knows it will naturally give his friends; with his comrades it signifies little, they form their opinions of one another from their own knowledge, not the despatches of the Commander-in-Chief.

I am unable to give your Lordship any light on the probable result of operations here, that they will be eminently successful no one appears to doubt but to what degree or in exactly what way defies conjecture.

Massena, deceived by false information and the artful measure of his opponent, is undoubtedly in the greatest of military difficulties. How far his abilities will get him out is now the question. A French officer, a prisoner, with whom I was conversing, said of him that he *had been* a good general but was now in his dotage . . .

8 November My troop was ordered to Moita to relieve Linsingen's of Hussars. The other troop of my squadron was there and therefore completed by this change. I had discretionary power to remain at Moita or march to Obidos.

Moita is an open village particularly exposed to a night attack of infantry as there are a number of ravines and gullies leading to it. It is scarcely possible to secure it properly with cavalry and there was no infantry either to furnish night piquets or to co-operate with me in any attack on the enemy's foraging parties. Besides, every man on duty must have been exposed to the weather.

Obidos is a walled town and was garrisoned by 300 militia and recruits under Major Fenwick. It was furnished with seven pieces of artillery. A night attack was out of the question as the wall was too high for an escalade and it would have been necessary to breach it. It was admirably situated to keep the enemy's parties in check, being beyond his right and a little to his rear. I had no hesitation in preferring Obidos. It was safer, the men and horses were not harrassed and I considered myself to be more likely of use, the only risk was that the enemy might think it worth while to march two or three thousand men in the night and occupy all the roads. It is scarcely possible, however, that they should do this without our being apprised in time by the peasants. Let the worst come to the worst, I think I can break out with the cavalry and get round the Lake of Obidos to Peniche and from thence to Vimeiro to the Lines.

---

†Scott's recent work.
‡He had been mentioned in despatches.

12 November Obidos. To his mother:
Dearest Madam,
Since my last letter my squadron has been ordered to Moita and from thence to this place, Obidos. It is 4 leagues from Torres Vedras and 12 from Lisbon. We have most capital quarters and no duty but to scare away the straggling parties of the enemy who come after provisions to the different villages near us. We attacked a party yesterday and took 17 of them. We had only 12 dragoons and 8 or 9 armed peasants but they made no resistance and most of them declared they were delighted at being made prisoners. 'Toutes les choses s'en a présent très mal arrangée dans l'armée français,' was the observation of one . . .

13 November Our infantry have a report that an attack upon the Lines will take place but some of the French deserters say Massena has ordered the army to make itself comfortable for the winter. He has some troops near Rio Maior and the prisoners complain very much of want, yet still we hear of great quantities of eatables being brought in from the rear.

14 November The enemy would have suffered much more considerably from the want of supplies had our commissioners been enjoined to buy up everything for ten leagues in front the lines. General Blunt, the Governor of Peniche, asked the Capitao Mors some time ago what time would be necessary to remove all the grain between Leyria and the Lines. Their answer was six weeks but they had only a few days' notice when we fell back last month. It is clear vast quantities must have been left to the enemy.

This evening it was discovered the enemy was in motion.

> During the next few days Massena gradually shifted his position but everyone's hopes that he was retreating were finally dashed. Time revealed it was all merely a rearrangement.

23 November, Malhaquajo. To Thomas Somers Cocks, Esq:
My dear Thomas,
You have already learnt by the papers that the French moved off from their position in front of our Lines the night of the 13th. I do not think he, in general, suffered so much as has been represented. Individual instances of want extending perhaps sometimes to regiments or brigades I have certainly met with but, on the whole, since he has been lying opposite to us here he has had bread, he has had wine, he has had forage and only latterly was he deficient in meat. However, his means of supply were failing every day, he could do nothing but break his teeth against the Lines and altogether a retreat was unavoidable . . . For the last five days we have been stopped by the position of Santarem, the most perfect, perhaps, on a small scale that can be imagined and which has been occupied by the 2nd Corps.

During these five days he has made strong demonstrations on our right in the directions of Leyria and Rio Maior, so that it appeared by no means certain that his object was not to draw us from our Lines and then fight us under circumstances unfavourable to us.

This morning, I believe from several things, he has abandoned Santarem but it is not yet ascertained and, even if he has, these five days will have given him time to get off everything but the sick and perhaps some artillery behind the Zezere, where we shall again be checked. I believe Lord Wellington has never been deceived by the manoeuvring but still it was necessary to proceed cautiously when so much was at stake. A proof, however, that he has not been frightened is that he has ventured to send General Hill by the south of the Tagus to Abrantes, which I trust will prevent the enemy from remaining behind the Zezere... We have been rather on the starving order for the last two days, no bread, very little meat and rainy weather. I console myself with my pipe and a huge fire. Adieu. Tell everybody to remember me...

24 November Everything remains in status quo...

11 December It appears clear from our long inactivity that Lord Wellington has no intention of forcing Massena from his position. Barring the mortification naturally felt at lying so long before an enemy without doing anything, I am convinced that he is right. The general and main object of the French is the conquest of the Peninsula, and to resist and frustrate their efforts the more troops we draw from Spain into Portugal – providing we ultimately prevent their conquering the latter country – the more chance shall we give the Spaniards of reinstating their affairs and not the less shall we be ultimately successful in Portugal.

If we had driven Massena back into Spain Drouet's corps would not have been sent for and would be disposable for operations in any other part of Portugal. It is too late for us to follow Massena into Spain this campaign and we are, therefore, not losing any time, for our army is well put up and except a few light troops on the outposts as comfortable and as little harrassed as if Massena were a thousand miles off.

This is not the case with the enemy; his system is conquest and offensive war. When he is not going forward he is going backward. If he was in Spain, part of his force, the 8th Corps for example, might be employed against the guerillas. Even the mere circumstance of so considerable a force being in the country would keep a large tract in subjection, which is now aiding the cause of the allies. Where he is now, he does not prevent a single soldier joining our standard. In point of facility of subsistence we are much better off than we should be if we had driven the enemy any further and had to watch him nearer the frontier. Besides, the more the supplies of Portugal are drained this year the more difficult will her conquest be the next – if the enemy should receive sufficient reinforcements to make a second attempt.

When the value of the stake between the opposing generals is considered their mutual caution is not surprising. If a plan occurs to Lord Wellington by which he can obtain his object without any risk, he is certainly right to pursue it even though the risk might be but small pursuing a contrary system.

Massena, with the army he has, clearly regards an attack on our lines as hopeless. Lord Wellington will fight him nowhere else. He cannot subsist himself forever in Portugal though he may gain time. In this end, therefore, he must retreat and in the meantime his army is suffering privations which will probably render it very sickly and may eventually disorganise it.

But supposing Massena is anxious to retain his ground in the hope of receiving sufficient reinforcements to venture an attack on the Lines? Still is the defensive plan full of advantage for, when Massena again advanced we should fall back, but the less distance we sally from our Lines, the less distance we shall have to march to regain them. And, of course, the more numerous and effective will our army be when it occupies its position.

I know not what number of troops might be efficient to attack our Lines with a chance of success, or what chance the enemy has of procuring them, but of this I am assured, that while we can defend that position the longer we detain the French in Portugal, and thus the more we shall profit our cause and the more deeply we shall wound theirs...

22 December, Malhaquejo. To Thomas Somers Cocks, Esq:
My dear Thomas,

You will infer from the shape of this letter that paper is running short. I expect, however, some from Lisbon and my next epistle shall be more secundum artem... I am now going to trouble you with a few commissions, for the length of this campaign has made great havoc with my equippage.

First, Egerton, the bookseller; Gilbert, bootmaker, Old Bond Street; and Cunningham, hosier, corner of St James's Street, Piccadilly; I should be much obliged to you to settle with.

Second, would you order me a new hussar saddle with accoutrements complete, from Whippy. There is a new hussar saddle at my father's in Cavendish Square; I should ask this to be also fitted up and sent out at the same time. I wish the pads for the valises to be made very large and fixed to the saddle. The saddle to be strong, roomy and extremely high in the withers. Will you tell Whippy to remember that a saddle for service must not be made like one for a gingerbread field day but strong and calculated to save in every respect the horse's back and withers.

Third, would you order a new helmet from Hawkes. I wish it to be very light and very low. If he has forgot my measure then there is an old hat of mine at Cavendish Square.

Fourth, a new sabre and belt from Prosser. It should be roomy in the handle and not too heavy at the point. Will you be so good as to have it proved. My present sabre is a very bad one. It should not be *too broad* at the point. I have no particular liking to Prosser and if you know any cutler esteemed better it would perhaps be desirable to employ him. I do *not* like the handle roughed with fish skin.

Fifth, four pairs of new hussar boots, not open, from Gilbert, three pairs of laced half boots with spurs to them all.

All these things will make a pretty good package and had better be sent out together. I know I need not apologise to you for the trouble I am giving you.

The only thing I want more are a few books, would you send me these,

Spenser's *Faerie Queen*
Shakespeare
Pope's work
Warton's *History of English Poetry*
Percy's *Ancient Ballads*
Spectator
Blair's *Lectures*
Milford's *Grecian History*
Stewart's *Elements of Philosophy of Human Mind*

Of course, pocket editions where they can be procured and all bound as they take up less room.

There is a work published of which I forget the name, on the new system of tactique, Egerton has published a translation of it but I should prefer the original.† Any new military book that stands high I should be very glad of ...

24 December The last three weeks have been without interest, one day could only be distinguished from another by the rumour of the peasants or the arrival of a straggling prisoner or deserter.

25 December The more I think, the more I am convinced it is our policy to be quiet unless the enemy can starve us by the occupation of Aldea Gallega, which at present there is no ground to fear ... I have no doubt Lord Wellington might have driven Massena out of Portugal this year, but then next campaign the enemy would have advanced with the further advantage of knowing the country and our plans ... It is a proof of Lord Wellington's enlarged views that he dares for the present to disappoint the country at home and most of the army here, in the hope of distant but more important successes. He has often shown himself a brave and dashing officer, he now proves that he is more.

Poor Fenwick has died of his wounds.‡

---

†*Traite de la Grand Tactique* by A. de Jomini.
‡He had co-operated with Major Fenwick, an infantry officer, at Obidos and thought very highly of him.

CHAPTER TEN
No Man's Land

5 January - 11 March 1811

AT THE BEGINNING of 1811 Cocks was ordered again by Wellington to patrol the area around Leyria and As Caldas da Rainha and disperse or capture the foraging parties which were regularly combing the country for supplies. Together with two squadrons, one of the 16th and one 1st Hussars, upon occasion joined by an infantry back up, he spent January and February chasing these marauding bands.

* * *

5 January Marched from Rio Maior to As Caldas with my squadron and Dekin's squadron, Hussars. This town, formerly the spa of Portugal, is totally deserted by its own inhabitants but full of emigrants from other places, but the population, the excellence of the houses, and cleanliness of the streets made it infinitely preferable to the miserable villages I had lately seen. It is one short league in front of Obidos and four long leagues from Alcobaca ... General Blunt, with the greater part of the garrison of Peniche, is at Alferesao, driving the country between that place and the river of Alcobaca.†

6 January Went to Alferesao, this road is quite impracticable for artillery at this season of the year and cavalry could scarcely pass it in the night; it crosses two streams, one bridge has been carried away and the other is only passable with difficulty for men on foot; some of my patrol swam in crossing ...

8 pm: A report has reached me that the enemy has entered Alcobaca in force. I have sent a patrol of a serjeant and eight for information.

7 January Patrolled at daybreak on the upper Alcobaca road. I found it bad in particular places and it is here and there not practicable for artillery but it might easily be rendered so. In general it has no foundation either of stone or wood and as the soil is remarkably fine sand, after rain it becomes full of quicksands. The country is hilly with deep ravines, but open.

At Sella, one league from Alcobaca, I found my patrol ... There is a common in front and then enclosures and some French were plundering a small village on the edge of them. I had ten men with me and determined to attempt to capture them as a prisoner might give me valuable information, but they fled on my approach. The enclosures were so impracticable that I could only make two grenadiers prisoners. Having observed the next village, Visitaria,‡ from several different points and observing nothing about it, I conceived it was evacuated and entered with the intention of getting a view of Alcobaca. I must confess I was so persuaded

---

†Blunt commanded infantry and it was he who lent Cocks a back-up.
‡Unidentified.

there was nothing in there that I was careless. I was a few yards in front of my party and had gone nearly through when, turning a corner, I found myself close to two French dragoons. They both fired but missed me and, at the same instant, near thirty dragoons sallied from a hollow road and made at us. My party went about and I formed that once but the enemy was too strong to handle and off we went, ventre à terre, rather to our mortification. The enemy was afraid to venture further than the edge of the enclosures where he then formed forty dragoons and a strong company of infantry. I formed opposite. We looked at one another a short time while the officer of cavalry and I exchanged pistol shots at a very respectable distance, and then each went off.

26 January, As Caldas. To the Hon. James Somers Cocks:
My dear James,
... We have had some trifling skirmishes with the enemy in this neighbourhood; in the last two days the two squadrons I command here have killed one man and taken twenty-three, also seventeen horses, two mules and fifteen donkeys, the latter laden with corn. These Hannoverian Hussars are the best cavalry we have, especially against cavalry. The 16th is brigaded with them, they have been our masters. Perhaps our officers have surpassed theirs but our men are not equal to them.

The French had an old proverb, 'Tenez chauds les pieds et la tête et pour le reste, vivez en bête,' but I am in want of both books and boots, lining for the head and covering for the feet – badly off at the extremities while my centre is better provided. This is the best market of any town within the reach of the war, neither fish nor flesh are wanting, but the French army is certainly beginning to feel great want. They may, perhaps, have cattle in store but no more is to be found in the country, every vegetable is consumed within their reach and sickness thins their ranks ...

3 February I have received information from a variety of quarters that it is the common conversation in the French camp that the army is to cross the Tagus near Punhete very shortly. I hear there was a girl in Alcobaca yesterday who had been living with a French Artillery officer. She left him the day before yesterday in consequence of his telling her he was going with the whole army over to Alemtejo and she might either go with him or return home.

22 February, As Caldas. To The Hon. Miss Margaret Maria Cocks:
My dear Margaret,
Our time is now passing so quietly that it is scarce possible to find materials for a letter. For the last month I have scarcely seen a Frenchman or heard a shot fired and altogether I think it very likely we shall continue as quiet till the fine weather sets in, which we cannot expect before April or May. Meantime our horses are getting into capital condition.

My family party here consists of my friend Tomkinson, who has been with me all the campaign, and a little squinting fellow of five foot two inches but withal extremely diverting and a very good officer. I had a squadron of hussars but it has been ordered away and I have only my own squadron and a battalion of Portuguese infantry. The most disagreeable part of this quarter is the distress we are obliged to witness among the peasants. The real inhabitants of this town have mostly left and it is peopled by immigrants from other villages in the possession of the enemy. These immigrants subsist by bringing off grain in the night from stores they know of within the enemies' posts and where there are two or three stout young men in the family they do tolerably well, but where a family consists of very old or very young people and gets sickly they absolutely are in danger of starvation. There is so little arrangement in the Portuguese government that no assistance is given to these unfortunate wretches, dispirited, fatigued and starving; fevers are continually breaking out among them and unless some caution is adopted I really think there is danger in the summer of an epidemic disorder in this part of Portugal.†

I wish John Bull, when in a grumbling humour, could see a few of the scenes which daily occur here, and I believe he would be very well contented to pay his taxes and have his home to go to. I believe the distresses of the enemy are great

---

†He and Tomkinson organised a soup kitchen in As Caldas, with some success, and Wellington, writing to Beresford on 3 March, comments, 'It is almost useless to write to the [Portuguese] Government . . . they will not do what we desire them, indeed, I doubt if they can. Cocks has already informed me of this disorder at Caldas and I have removed the dragoons from there . . .' Likewise he wrote to the British Ambassador to see if he could help.¹

and increasing; I know of some instances, but probably they have been accidental ones, when French soldiers have eaten asses and cats. It is thought the south of the Tagus will be the seat of our next campaign.

Is Agneta† still with you? Do not forget my love to her and sprinkle it all round you like holy water ...

NB: Since writing the above, two hundred French cavalry have had the impudence to come this way foraging. They set off when they saw me but I got fourteen men, eleven horses, three mules and some donkeys and all their plunder. I lost one man and one horse ...

> And so the operations might have continued until Massena's eventual retreat but for the fact that, out of the blue, Wellington received a letter from Lord Somers requesting Charles's presence at home. The Rev Nash had died bequeathing him a sizeable estate and there were urgent legal matters requiring attention. That the Commander was dismayed is evident in the letter he sent Cocks:
>
> 'You must be as well aware as any expression of mine can make you, how severely we shall feel here the loss of your assistance and services; and I am convinced that you will not desire to go if the occasion for your going is not of that urgent nature which would render your remaining any longer with us an injury to your family and yourself. I therefore leave it to you to determine what you will do; and although I have lately referred all applications for leave of absence to the Commander-in-Chief, I will give you leave if you wish it. If you do go I only hope that you will return to us as soon as you can ... I have received the account of your last success, which is very satisfactory.'[2]
>
> Charles was equally aghast at the news but felt he had no option and Wellington avoided the thorny subject of leave by deputing him to carry the despatches.

3 March Embarked for England. I carried despatches for Marquis Wellesley and Lord Liverpool and had a passage on board the *Sea Flower*, a gun brig, Lt Stewart.

7 March Met with a severe gale of wind and threw some guns overboard.

Though the wind was fair Lt Stewart lay to, being afraid to make the shore in the night, and in the morning the wind veered to the north-east and we were driven off Guernsey.

10 March Landed at Plymouth and immediately set off for London.

11 March Reached London and delivered my despatches.

---

†Agneta Pole-Carew, whom Thomas was courting.

CHAPTER ELEVEN
Fuentes d'Onoro

30 April – 19 May 1811

IN ALL HE WAS AWAY six weeks and it is possible his father brought pressure to bear on him to resume a political career.† For over a century the Cocks's had produced more politicians than soldiers and Lord Somers was anxious for his heir to follow in his footsteps. But Charles had long ago decided otherwise; the old, childish ambition had hardened into adult determination. On the emotional side, he loved the army with its cameraderie and physical challenge, while the theoretical side offered the intellectual stimulus his active brain desperately needed, witness the astonishing volume of writing he achieved in 1811-12, often penned under difficult circumstances.

However, in May 1811 promotion above all things was uppermost in his mind. He searched the lists for vacancies. Thomas and his father – despite the latter's preference – contacted army agents, rumours of possible majorities were checked, and Wellington, only too aware of the injustice of his several outstanding young officers having to wait their turn whilst less deserving men in England gained the coveted rank, used his powers to bestow brevet rank,‡ which at least acknowledged worth. Charles, himself, seized every opportunity to gain experience and, since he mixed regularly with the most senior officers, he was able to listen to many arguments and debates as well as contribute to them. Thus, while his reputation grew in the ranks as a 'Come on' man, who would lead with resolution and – even better – success, he also stood out at staff level because he knew what he was talking about. Small wonder he appears to have been a frequent guest at Wellington's table. John Somers, now in the 2nd Dragoon Guards, accompanied him back, Cotton having offered a temporary position on his staff, and the pair of them examined the line of Massena's retreat. During his absence the French had given up the struggle to exist before the Lines and the two armies were now back in roughly the same position as the previous summer, opposite Ciudad Rodrigo, with the outposts along the Azava and Agueda, and it was certainly a fortuitous moment to arrive because the battle of Fuentes d'Onoro was about to begin.

★   ★   ★

30 April Our outposts are on the Agueda and part of our cavalry which had been sent to the rear has been hurried up. Almeida has been closely invested for some time. It is understood that it was not the intention of the enemy to have retained

---

†He may have feared history would repeat itself. The young Cocks heir in the 1750s had been allowed to join the army, only to be killed a few months later.
‡He could not really influence regimental promotion.

this place but their rearguard [in the retreat] was so closely pressed by our people that Brennier, with 1,500 men and the greater part of the field artillery, was unable to get away and therefore shut up in it. Massena's movements are probably with a view to relieving this officer. He has made several reconnaissances over the Agueda and there have been one or two sharp skirmishes at the Puente de Marialva.

1 May Gallegos: The enemy made a strong reconnaissance this morning and our cavalry was turned out, it occupies a chain of cantonments from Villa de Puerco to Fuenteguinaldo. I must confess I find myself very happy being once again with my regiment. If we fight soon I am confident we shall beat Massena; there is neither union, confidence nor good will in the French army and all these in ours, but in this open country our want of cavalry will cramp all our movements and prevent us from gaining any material advantage. The object of contest is, however, whether or not Massena will be able to relieve Almeida and if we prevent his doing this we ought to be very well satisfied.

2 May Soon after daybreak as near as I could judge, 8,000 infantry and 1,200 cavalry passed the bridge of Ciudad Rodrigo and compelled our outposts to fall back. It is confidently reported in our army that Massena has positive orders from the Emperor to fight and keep the position of the Coa . . . What Napoleon orders we cannot know but I think it is imprudent for Massena, with an army not very superior in numbers, inferior in artillery, of late often beat, discontented and out of heart, to attack our army in the spirits it now is, and this imprudence is increased by his having two rivers in his rear. If he had not so much cavalry it would be madness. I think, therefore, his object is only to create a diversion and relieve Almeida.

Note Our outposts were on the heights in front of Fuentes. Headquarters still continued at Villa Formosa.

3 May About eight o'clock the enemy was in motion and our army took up a position behind Fuentes. Our right was covered in front by that village, composed of the 1st Division while on the right of it were six squadrons of Slade's brigade and the whole of Anson's. Erskine's division, with two squadrons of Slade's brigade, were on the left towards Fuerte de la Concepcion covering the Almeida road.

At two o'clock the enemy's columns appeared and some skirmishing commenced near the village of Fuentes. At half past three one 9-pounder was brought into action. At half past six the enemy advanced in close column beautifully at a run, charged the village and succeeded in getting possession of it for a few minutes but he was driven out by the 79th and 71st. The firing ceased at dark.

Nave de Ver was occupied by Don Julian who had 500 cavalry and 1,000 Spanish infantry. The French cavalry, having demonstrated and patrolled that way, our brigade was ordered to support the Spaniards but they had already retired.

4 May The heights occupied by the two armies were separated by the river of Dos Casas which flowed through Fuentes d'Onoro. Higher up, that is to the south, this river was rather a morass and about four or five miles off in this direction was the village of Nave de Ver, on a very commanding ground and central to all the roads from our and the enemy's side of the country. The possession of the village was of consequence to both parties as without it neither could manoeuvre on the flank of the other; it was occupied this day by Don Julian.

This day was spent in trifling skirmishing between the cavalry, which wearied our horses and answered no other end than ascertaining the enemy's force, but I should have thought we had known this already. Massena reconnoitred our left. General Hay was too polite and he would not allow Bull to fire on him when within range of case shot.

5 May Early in the night the Light Division was moved to the left but Lord Wellington afterwards received information that the enemy was strengthening his left and he immediately made a corresponding movement. The Light Division was thrown into the woods extending from thence towards Poco Velha. A battalion of Caçadores under Colonel Dickson occupied that village.

On the extremity of the woods to Nave de Ver the country was open but crossed by the morass I have already mentioned. The rear of the ground we occupied was a valley full of enclosures and beyond that a range of high ground, on the crest of which was the Cassil road from Almeida towards Alamondillo. A little within this road, in rear of our right and beyond the valley, was a commanding height and on this it was intended to throw back our right in case it should be turned by the enemy's superiority in cavalry. On each side of the Cassil road the country was perfectly unembarrassed.

About half an hour after daybreak the enemy formed strong columns of cavalry opposite the open ground between Poco Velha and Nave de Ver. The heads of columns of infantry were likewise seen issuing from the road to support.

At six the enemy advanced with the cavalry strongly supported by infantry and guns towards the morass, and the columns of infantry on Poco Velha and the surrounding woods. Two squadrons of our brigade had been advanced to the morass under Major Meyer of the 1st Hussars to watch the enemy. Injudiciously and contrary to orders, they crossed the morass, charged the advance of the enemy and were overpowered by numbers. Capt Belli, 16th Dragoons, wounded and taken, Lt Blake killed with six men, Lt Weyland and Capt Krauchenberg [*sic*], 1st Hussars, with 30–40 men wounded.

The enemy's cavalry advanced and crossed the morass while his columns of infantry drove our troops from Poco Velha; a sharp skirmish ensued in the adjoining wood. The enemy showed about forty squadrons or near 4,000 cavalry; we had Anson's and Slade's brigades forming 1,010 men, serjeants included. Of these, two squadrons of Slade's had been detached to the left and two of Anson's had been nearly annihilated. On the right we had not above 800 cavalry, they were drawn up fronting outward to the right, echelon.

At half past seven the woods to the left, in rear of Poco Velha, were still maintained and the 7th and Light Division supported the right of the cavalry while Bull's guns played on the advancing columns of the enemy.

The object for which we were contending was the maintenance of the blockade at Almeida but in our position we had so few communications to the rear and beyond the Coa that Lord Wellington wished to maintain the line of Sabugal. To do this he weakened his position by extending it too much.

At eight, four squadrons under Colonel la Motte, the enemy's picked men, made a charge and drove in our guns; their left was gallantly broke by the Chasseurs Britanique. Two squadrons of Slade's were ordered to charge but some of Don Julian's people were galloping in front of the French and being driven in. By an unfortunate mistake, Slade's squadron, seeing these fugitives, took the whole body for Spaniards and halted. They were charged, a mêlée and much sabring took place, and I was concerned to observe the tide stretched back to our line. The French were said to be drunk but their officers led them bravely. They had never seen British cavalry and rode forward till they were cut down. Many individuals got up to the formed squadrons of our reserve and were there killed. At this moment we had not 550 cavalry formed and these were divided in the centre.

Note It is the opinion of some officers that no troops who behave well can be penetrated by the centre because the advancing enemy is necessarily turned by both flanks. It is possible the fear of such a manoeuvre might have checked the enemy. Had he followed the blow the moment would have been critical, but his support did not follow his advance. The remains of Meyer's squadron got round their flank, charged their rear, and the four squadrons were cut to pieces except for their commanding officer, Colonel la Motte and forty men, who were taken. The enemy showed no dash.

Massena probably thought he could not depend on his infantry and that if his cavalry were defeated he was lost. Perhaps, too, he did not expect this advantage and had merely advanced his cavalry to cover his infantry and artillery while passing the morass and woods. It is certain he did not follow up his blow and I think he might have done. This column was halted.

Note† I heard Lord Wellington say afterward at his table he thought he had never been in a worse scrape.

Lord Wellington, however, thought he had attempted too much, gave up the communication with Sabugal and contracted his line. We evacuated the woods, the cavalry were back behind the right of our infantry and the 7th Division occupied the heights on the Cassil road, forming an angle with the rest of our line and fronting outward.

The enemy occupied the woods opposite our right and their right was in front of Fuentes. Some severe skirmishing took place between the tirailleurs of the two armies and an attempt to seize some of the enemy's cannon by three squadrons of Slade's brigade failed. The French made some desperate attacks on the village of Fuentes and obtained a momentary possession, but we regained and kept it. The lines were not engaged ...

Note The enemy lost about 5,000 men, 2,904 wounded entered Ciudad Rodrigo the following day. Of these 154 had been amputated on the field. The French never amputate unless the limb has been already destroyed. Our loss was between 1,700 and 1,800, of whom 150 were cavalry including a great many officers. Poor Knipe was mortally wounded. The 79th took a good many prisoners, altogether the French took 200.‡

---

†It is never clear from the Letters and Diaries when Cocks came to the end of a *Note*.
‡Weller lists the loss as Allies: 1,545; and French: 2,192.

I think this day gave Lord Wellington a higher idea of the effect of cavalry as an arm in battle. Though in India he had done a great deal with cavalry, yet in his European battles the infantry had decided everything and perhaps this had contributed to overrate his confidence in them. It is certain that our cavalry had always been no more than was sufficient for outpost duty and even this body, harrassed as it must be under such circumstances, of late has been badly supplied. It is true the country behind the Coa is not fit for the operations of cavalry but Lord Wellington always expected to act again in front of it. To make cavalry of effect in battle it is always necessary to have some regiments in reserve. Could not a brigade have been kept in Oporto and Braga when we were in the Lines?

6 May The enemy did not move this morning and our position was something like a Z. Putting out of the question the division covering the Alamada road, our left may be said to be on Fuentes and from thence our line forms a re-entering angle towards the point of the hill where the 1st Division was supported by the Light Division. Hence our right was flung back across the valley to the height on which General Houston was posted on the 7th Division. I should conceive if the enemy attacks the Guards it is intended for General Houston to manoeuvre on his left flank. If he attacks General Houston he will expose himself to be cut off from his point of retreat.

The day was spent in covering the Guards from the enemy's cavalry by hors de coup. Some fleches were constructed to cover the artillery and the village of Fuentes was strengthened. General Craufurd's division, the Light, relieved General Picton there. The enemy made his reconnaissances towards our right and the Cassil road; I think he will attack us tomorrow.

7 May About midnight an officer of the cavalry on duty reported that the enemy was moving a column to their left and although Lord W said it could not be the case a patrol was sent off which ascertained it to be a mistake.

I had the command of this patrol and an accident occurred which shows how careful everyone should be in reports. I had a squadron with me, the greater part of which I left just in front of our outposts and pushed on myself, with a few men, along the Cassil road, leaving two or three men at every crossroad to prevent being cut off. Just between dark and light, skirmishing began in my rear and the intermediate men came galloping in, saying I must be quick or I should be taken, as a French column had come up to a crossroad in my rear, and one man said he had seen a squadron advancing at a gallop. Fortunately, he placed the squadron in a direction I knew was impossible it could be, and I was convinced the report was false. On riding back I found my reserve and some Spanish infantry, which had been thrown into Frenada, skirmishing with each other, each taking the other for French. I immediately sent off to prevent the alarm which the firing might have occasioned.

The enemy remained perfectly quiet this day and I do not think he will attack us, for every day he must be more distressed for provisions and he has now given us time to strengthen our position.

8 May When it was light the enemy was discovered to have evacuated the woods near Poco Velha and fallen back to the high ground beyond Fuentes. His cavalry was assembled near Nave de Ver, which they afterwards evacuated, and his piquets near Aguila. I was sent to Fuente Guinaldo to observe his future movements and bivouacked near the town.

9 May Patrolled towards Ciudad Rodrigo; the enemy did not appear in motion. Several convoys of wagons have gone backward and forward since the 5th.

10 May This morning I got intelligence that the enemy was retreating on Ciudad Rodrigo. I went to rising ground about two miles from that place and saw him moving in two columns by Carpio and Gallegos. By two o'clock the greater part of the army had crossed the bridge, leaving twelve squadrons encamped on the plain with a chain of vedettes in rear of Carpio and Marialva. These vedettes convinced me that the whole had passed. Most of the columns which crossed the bridge continued their route to Salamanca while the remainder encamped behind Ciudad Rodrigo. At night there was a great light behind the town.

11 May Two hours after daybreak all the French cavalry which had remained on the plain, except four squadrons, crossed the bridge. Their piquets and vedettes were called in close to the town. The lights about the place disappeared before daybreak and the troops moved off for Salamanca.

Don Julian passed the Agueda and followed in observation of them.

12 May By the information I received today I learnt that the whole of the French army has marched for Salamanca except for 3,000 infantry in Ciudad Rodrigo and 800 cavalry encamped under the walls.

It appears that on the 8th and 9th the great many stragglers who passed the town were officers and men with arms but apparently without orders. I am convinced there never were troops worse disposed to fight than French infantry.

On the 10th the army passed, the Imperial Guards arriving at about eight o'clock, followed by the whole force. A small column took the San Felices road. Their killed, wounded and prisoners in the affairs of the 3rd and 5th could not amount to less than 5,000. The 800 French cavalry made a reconnaissance towards Espeja, two squadrons in advance got roughly handled by Elder's Caçadores and left the dead on the spot.

Note This night, by some unfortunate mistake or neglect, the garrison of Almeida under Brennier made their escape, crossing the Agueda at Barba del Puerco. They lost about one third, or five hundred. Brennier commanded them. Previous to their departure they blew up some of the work but all the mines did not take effect; however, the fortifications are still materially injured. Had Lord Wellington's orders been executed not a man would have escaped. It is the more unfortunate as it will give Massena a pretext for saying that he succeeded in the object for which he advanced, but in point of fact, the escape of the garrison is an isolated piece of good arrangement, wholly unconnected with his movements. At the time they went off he had been completely foiled and the garrison was in our power.

13 May The French cavalry has moved from Ciudad Rodrigo with about 1,000 infantry, leaving 2,000† in garrison under Renant, mostly foreigners. Don Julian is halfway to Salamanca.

---

†These figures were amended a few days later.

15 May, Fuenteguinaldo. To Thomas Somers Cocks, Esq:†

My dear Thomas,

You have probably heard how fortunate I was in sailing the instant I arrived in Falmouth and, being only eight days in my passage to Lisbon, reached that place the 13th and left it the 15th. I expected to have found the army in perfect tranquillity but when I reached Celorico I heard that Massena had again advanced. I joined my regiment the first of May.

I can give you no account of Massena's retreat further than what you are already in possession of. It appears to have been well conducted and the country was much in favour. Lord Wellington's manoeuvres were masterly. The loss of the French in Portugal must have been enormous; with Bessiére's reinforcements Massena could not muster 40,000 effective men. The corps which composed this army probably brought 125,000 from France.

The French had not expected that we should cross the Coa and we advanced so suddenly that 1,500 men under Brennier, a detachment of artillery and staff corps and, I believe, most of the field artillery, were shut up in Almeida and cut off. Massena could not brook the loss of all this and determined to advance by positive order from the Emperor and maintain the position of the Coa.

On the 1st the enemy made some demonstrations in front of Ciudad Rodrigo and established himself in front of the Agueda. His army which, at first, had fallen back to Salamanca, was all brought forward and consisted of about 30,000 infantry and 1,000 or 1,500 cavalry of the old army and 2 or 3,000 infantry and 3,000 cavalry brought up by Bessières, Duc d'Istria. The latter were all fresh troops from France and brought for the purpose of beating the British cavalry, very well mounted on Spanish horses. They included several squadrons of the Imperial Guard; they had likewise forty pieces of artillery.

Our force was 32,000 infantry, 1,000 British cavalry, 150 Portuguese and 48 guns. The cavalry horses were very weak as it had been impossible to bring forward stores and they had lived chiefly on grass.

The greater part of one division was employed in a blockade of Almeida, further diminishing our force. In artillery, however, we outnumbered them in guns, having twelve 9-pounders medium and two troops of superb horse artillery, the artillery cattle being in excellent condition.

On the 2nd our outposts retired to Espeja and Alamada, with very trifling skirmishing. On the 3rd the army took up its position. A deep ravine, with a little river, Dos Casas, covered our front and in front of our right was the village of Fuentes d'Onoro, surrounded by stone wall enclosures.

The French formed on the opposite side about 2pm. We were separated by the ravine which only could be passed in front through the village. We expected to be attacked.

At half past three they attacked the village and it was defended by part of the 79th. Just before dark a strong French column charged and got possession of the village but were immediately recharged and driven out by the 79th and 71st.

To our right and the French left, the country was perfectly open and

---

†Although in some respects repetitive, this is another account of the battle.

unembarrassed except by a long morass. At the end of this morass, four miles to our right, was Nave de Ver, a village on a very commanding situation occupied by 500 Spanish cavalry and 1,000 of their infantry – By the by I did not include this force before – this infantry was of the line, the cavalry, irregulars. A little before dark a considerable body of French cavalry moved in this direction and Anson's brigade was sent to support the Spaniards, but they retired at night.

On the 4th the Spaniards again occupied Nave de Ver and the day was spent by the cavalry in manoeuvring and by the infantry in eating their dinners and sleeping. They had the best of it. Towards evening the enemy strengthened his left and at dark our 7th Division occupied a chain of woods near Poco Velha and Nave de Ver.

On the 5th, at daybreak, we observed the enemy advancing his cavalry between Poco Velha and Nave de Ver, supported by masses of infantry. The Spaniards abandoned Nave de Ver and the French cavalry advanced to the bog. Two squadrons of ours – one my old squadron but of which Belli had taken the command, the other Bergmann of the Hussars – both under the command of Major Meyer, Hussars, charged five French squadrons. I did not see this but suspect it was imprudent, the object was to cover the Spaniards' retreat but our squadrons were so weak – about 55 each – that the odds were too great, especially as the French advance was sure to be picked men and drunk.

Belli charged first. He was overpowered; a French officer cut him down and took him but was then killed himself. Lt Blake was killed, Weyland run through the body, Krauchenberg of the Hussars wounded, two serjeants and five or six men killed on the spot and about thirty badly wounded. About fifty French were cut down. Our people, however, did not come about till ordered and were then covered by the Spanish cavalry, but what with the wounded and those taking care of the wounded the squadrons were reduced to nothing.

The French cavalry were now on our right and advancing. They drove in the Spanish cavalry and charged after them. The Spaniards made for the 14th and Royals, with the French pell mell behind them. The Royals and the 14th, or rather part of them, saw only the Spaniards who were in front and almost suffered themselves to be charged by the French. The consequence was a complete confusion: Spaniards, French and British, all mixed, man to man hacking and sabring. At this moment the remains of the two squadrons under Meyer got in the rear of the French and charged them. The reserve of the French cavalry behaved in the most dastardly manner, had they come on with the same spirit as the advance the moment would have been critical, and even some of our guns were in danger, for I did not see any of our cavalry formed except three squadrons of the 16th and as many of the Hussars. Fortunately we kept our people quite steady and ready for whatever might happen. This was not easy as many of the French were in our rear and charging like drunken madmen through our intervals and our men wanted to cut them down, there being an order to give no quarter. The result of all this was that the advance of the French cavalry was annihilated.

General Stuart engaged a French officer in single combat and took him, and the colonel who commanded the brigade was taken. In the meantime, other French cavalry had been repulsed most gallantly by the Chasseurs Britanique; the

Brunswickers behaved particularly well too and the French were for a time checked.

Lord Wellington rather threw back his right and we momentarily expected the action would become general but the enemy contented himself with making some desperate attacks on Fuentes, constantly without success and skirmishing sharply till 4 pm when we remained quiet, the two armies about half a mile from each other, the vedettes about two hundred yards, and open plain betwixt us.

During the skirmishing, part of the 14th and the Royals made an attempt to take some guns but without success; Captains Knipe and Mills and other officers wounded.

The enemy had completely failed in his object, which was possession of the village, the key to the whole position. He probably thought that by turning it by the right he would compel us to evacuate it, but our communication with it was secure from the left of the line. He has lost about 1,000 killed and 3,000 wounded; 500 cavalry have been killed and wounded.

The 6th the enemy did not attack us, our infantry strengthened the position, fleches, etc. Trant arrived with 10,000 Portuguese Ordenanza and took up the blockade of Almeida while the troops employed on that duty joined us. The enemy made some reconnaissances on our right where the country was fit for his cavalry.

Everybody in the army fully expected an attack next morning, the 7th, but to our infinite surprise Massena remained perfectly idle and it became evident he did not mean to attack us. Every day we were getting stronger and he was uselessly losing time. From what has since come to my knowledge, I am convinced that his wish was to have fought us but his army would not fight, and he was controlled by Bessières and Marmont.

On the 8th the enemy fell back and this and the following day vast numbers of his infantry went off without leave or licence for Salamanca.

On the 10th the French army crossed the Agueda and on the 11th the whole was en route for Salamanca, leaving 3,000 men in Rodrigo with 800 cavalry in the suburbs. The 6th Corps covered the retreat.

Thus, for all was beautiful in the different affairs, the enemy had lost a good 5,000 men while our loss did not exceed 1,700, including 9 or 10 officers and 150 men of cavalry. They had failed in two objects, viz: occupying the line of the Coa and relieving Almeida, but now a most provoking incident occurred. An English general delayed executing the order he received to occupy the bridge of Barba del Puerco and the garrison of Almeida slipped out at the moment when reduced to extremity and got off with the loss of only 3 or 400 men. Do not show this letter . . .

15 May, Fuenteguinaldo. To The Hon. Miss Margaret Maria Cocks:
My dearest Sister,

It was useless to write on my march up from Lisbon and I must have carried the letter in my pocket as the first days after my arrival I was rather employed.

Considering how much I have missed, I was tolerably fortunate in the moment when I arrived as I witnessed all the movements and skirmishes belonging to the affair of Fuentes. I call it affair for I know not what you will think of it in England,

I scarcely think it deserves the name of a battle. I experienced mortification the day before, when Belli came up and took command of the squadron I had always had last year and I was removed to the command of another. This squadron under Belli's command was early and severely engaged while the one I commanded scarcely suffered at all and did not charge. Belli himself was cut down by a French officer and taken. The business was principally of cavalry and the French outnumbered us, three or four to one in that arm. In infantry they were nearly equal, and in artillery inferior. The only point where the infantry were seriously engaged was in the village of Fuentes: it was taken and retaken with the bayonet several times.

I am now detached but we are very quiet, the whole French army has retreated to Salamanca. I have received a letter from you dated April, we have balls here every night, there is no other English officer but there is a Spanish regiment here...

16 May Ordered to Gallegos where I joined my squadron. Two divisions and Lord Wellington himself have gone to reinforce the army of Alemtejo.†

19 May Went with a flag of truce to Ciudad Rodrigo. I was not allowed to pass the bridge but I saw Belli, who was not materially hurt. Eighteen battalions of the 9th Corps have moved off by the Escurial to join the Army of Estramadura.

---

†Badajoz had fallen to the French in March after the Spanish governor had basely surrendered to Soult.

CHAPTER TWELVE
Badajoz 1811

22 May – 10 June 1811

FUENTES D'ONORO had been a doubtful victory and Almeida's loss completed Wellington's discomfiture. But a sixth sense warned him worse was to come and, leaving a covering force to take care of the frontier in the north, he rode at a punishing speed to Badajoz where Marshal Beresford was laying siege, en route learning of the battle of Albuera with its frightful casualties and as questionable a success as Fuentes. The capture of Badajoz now loomed large. If he could secure the town before the enemy advanced to its relief he would not only forward his own plans but provide a positive victory for his critics at home to chew over.

Being part of a quiet covering force was never Charles's idea of soldiering and he accepted Cotton's offer of the temporary position of DAQMG† to the cavalry as an excuse to accompany him south, and, with Sir Stapleton's further approval, act as a volunteer officer with artillery in the trenches in order to find out how sieges were conducted. The following journal entries are his day-to-day account of the experience.

★ ★ ★

2 June ... the trenches were completed last night, the first parallel was likewise finished and the batteries. The parallel was completed on the north of the river.

3 June Last night the platforms of the batteries were laid. General Picton's attack is directed against a part of the town which is only covered by an old Roman wall and, like those of Merida, formed of tapis work, that is of composite stone 30–35 inches long and 15 square at the end, composed of a number of pebbles cemented together by mortar. From the length of time it has been erected it is probably strong. The wall appears 30 feet high and is situated on a steep height and strengthened by towers.

The point intended to be breached is a little to our right of the old castle. As there was no ditch, covered way or glacis on this side of the town a breaching battery was erected in front of the first parallel to hold fourteen 24-pounders, two 10-inch howitzers – dismounted and placed on mortar frames – and four 8-inch howitzers; the guns were all brass and brought from Elvas. Four guns were advanced in an old house in front of the centre of the battery.

On General Houston's side were four batteries connected by a parallel in front and opposite to Fuerste San Cristobel. They were numbered from left to right:– No 1: Four 24-pounders intended to enfilade the batteries of the enemy which might open on our breaching battery and oppose, in front, a battery he had erected for 10 or 12 guns in front of the old castle.

---

†Deputy Assistant Quartermaster General.

No 2: Four 24-pounders against Fort San Cristobel
No 3: Four 24-pounders against San Cristobel
No 4: Four 16-pounders, to 10-inch howitzers, against San Cristobel and to enfilade the bridge. In reserve, four 24-pounders.

The breaching battery was considered by the Engineers to be 600 yards from the work but it is not less than 750 and, I think, too far to be effectual. By a flank view I got of the wall to be breached it appears to me to have a mass of earth behind it. About 1,500 men were at work last night.

At 8am the batteries opened. The practice was not good. The balls were Spanish, English and Portuguese and did not fit the guns. The enemy answered the fire fairly. One howitzer only opened from San Cristobel. This fort is of consequence for it will enfilade the right of our approaches as we proceed. There is an advanced bastion called the Picurina which will likewise annoy us on the left. As Picurina is beyond the covered way and has only field guns we have directed no fire against it.

This day the breach was begun but the hill on which the wall was erected was so steep that a great part of the earth slipped down it. The wall appeared strong. A battery of 2 guns erected just above the point breaching was dismounted and one gun brought down. A breach was likewise commenced in Cristobel and the defences there very much ruined. About twenty English artillerymen were on duty and the remainder were 120 Portuguese. Colonel Framingham commanded and Major Dickson commanded the Portuguese. One English artilleryman was put to each gun; this is a bad plan, the Portuguese officers do not feel such pride in their practice and the single Englishman, not understanding Portuguese, is of little use. The artillery are relieved every 24 hours at 7pm.

About 800 workmen are on duty every night to work by two reliefs; all this applies only to General Picton's attack. The trenches are in general nine feet wide by $3\frac{1}{2}$ deep.

I know not what to make of the place where we are breaching. It appears to me that the hill rises solidly behind it, and consequently all idea of battering through the wall is out of the question, all we can do is to form an accessible ramp.

> John Somers, meanwhile, was also at Elvas with Sir Stapleton and the following is a letter written to Thomas at this time.

4 June, Elvas. From Captain The Hon. John Somers Cocks to Thomas Somers Cocks, Esq:

Dear Thomas,

... I have been particularly fortunate in having seen a great deal of the country considering the short time that I have been in it. Everything being perfectly quiet on the Agueda, my general† obtained leave to join the army in this neighbourhood, and the same day that he got it he heard of the tremendous battle which took place before Badajoz on the 16th. We left Cesmiro on the 29th of last month and arrived here on the 1st. Charles accompanied us as acting DA Quarter Master General, Campbell being detained. On the 2nd we rode to the

---

†Stapleton Cotton.

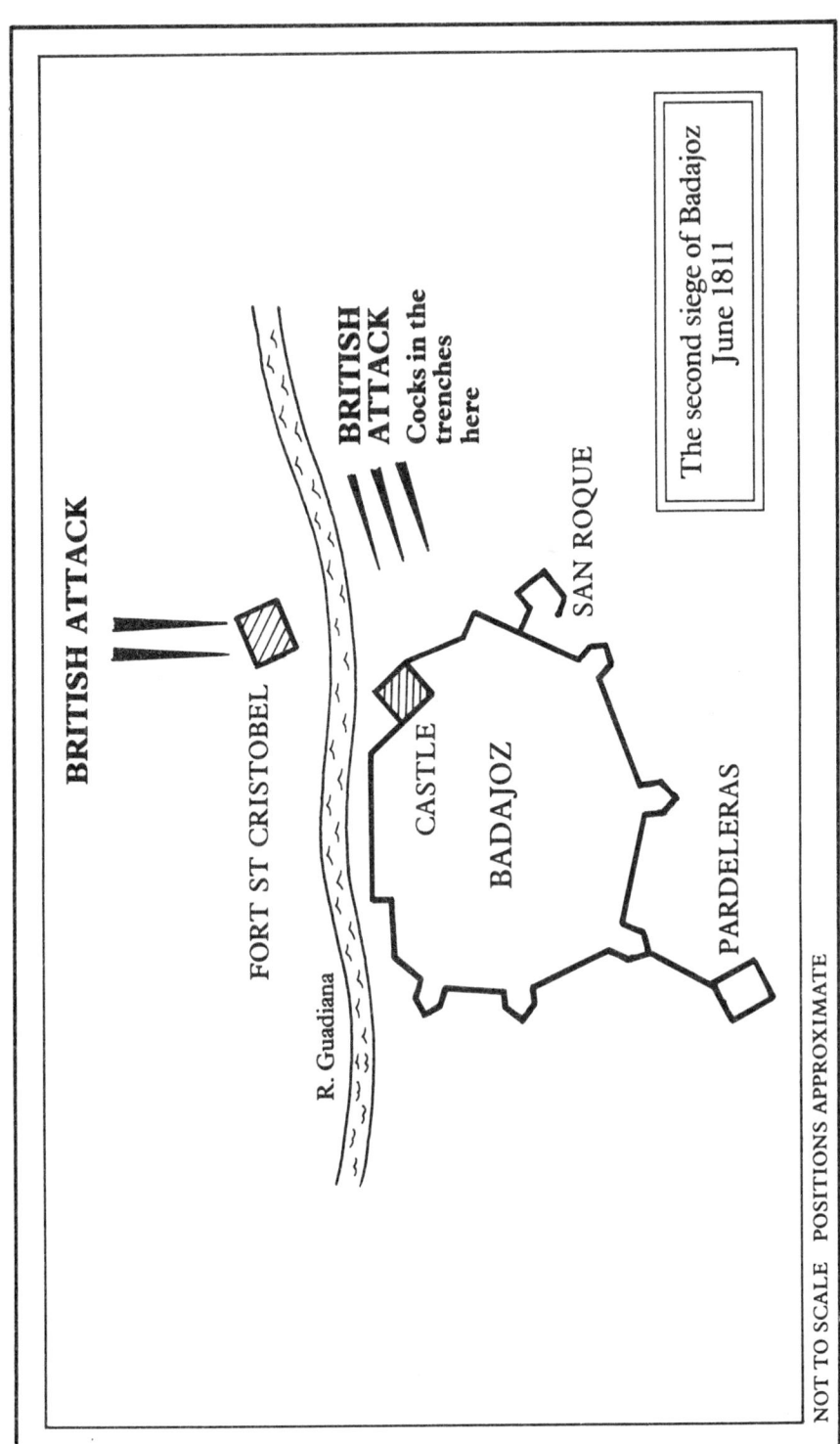

neighbourhood of Badajoz to view our batteries which opened before the town about ten o'clock yesterday morning and have continued firing ever since, it is hoped and supposed that the town must fall in the course of three or four days. Charles is in the trenches but he is to join us again today as we proceed tomorrow to Villa Franca which is clear fifty miles in front and of course where the Cavalry and the greater part of the army is stationed. You have heard quite enough probably of the battle of the 16th, it certainly was the most desperate thing that has been done this war, we lost two-thirds of the British troops that were engaged and I am sorry to say five stand of Colours, which I understand the Marshal has not mentioned in his despatch; surely he was wrong in not stating the case fairly for we shall hear enough of it from Paris . . . I cannot help feeling a good deal pleased that the tone is entirely changed with regard to the Heavy Dragoons, they are now as much praised as they have been abused, the enemy acknowledge a decided dread of what they call, the moveable *houses* with *red* tiles. What we shall do after taking Badajoz we do not exactly know but I should suppose that we shall pay our respects to Ciudad Rodrigo . . .

Charles now takes up the story of the siege

4 June Last night 1,000 men were employed to commence a new breaching battery of 7 embrasures to the right and nearer the town. A royal salute was fired at daybreak and mid day.† The enemy opened four new embrasures near the old castle. They likewise fired from an advanced ravelin to the left; they fired sharply.

This day two men were killed, four wounded, and one gun was rendered useless, the bushes being blown up. All the guns, being brass, got very hot and did not seem inclined to stand. The practice was much better but the firing wild, especially the mortars. Lord Wellington had directed that no shot should be sent against the town but the order was often evaded and at one time today Badajoz was on fire in two places for a short time.

The enfilading battery number one appeared to annoy the enemy very little; numbers two and three often missed the fort and threw their shot into the river. For two or three hours the question of firing was changed by order of Col Fletcher – Chief Engineer – which occasioned delay.

5 June The new seven-gun battery was not ready till 10 o'clock when it opened, the guns being brought from the old battery. The trench of communication is badly directed, being enfiladed from Cristobel. This was occasioned by the wish of the engineers to avoid the turns which embarrass the passage of artillery, but there ought to be a second trench or rather parallel to the rear for the covering parties to be in. The practice today was very bad, not above one shot hit the breach in six or seven but the guns were very hot and perhaps it could not be avoided. The breach, however, appears considerably improved. Four guns are disabled, one by the enemy's fire, one muzzle dropped and two bushes blown out. One mortar carriage disabled.

Today some 5½-inch shells were thrown from the 24-pounders in the hopes

---

†It was the King's birthday.

they would stick in the breach and have the effect of small mines. To succeed in this it is not only necessary to have long fuses but to wad the guns, otherwise the composition melts and the shells explode too soon. This being neglected, very few shells reached the breach and these did not stick in. I have better hopes of the breach. I can distinguish the roof of a house just behind it which proves there is a fall there and that the rampart is not supported by a solid hill.

Lord Wellington said today to Major Dickson, 'If we succeed with the means we have it will be a wonder.'

6 June Last night a new battery was commenced to the right, nearer the river and 120 yards in advance of the seven-gun battery. It will be completed for ten guns. The manner of tracing is by sandbags, three together and marking two lines for the outside and inside of the battery. Two lines of workmen begin at the same time, each throwing the earth inward. The workmen should have alternatively a spade and pickaxe. The soil of this new battery is not so good as the others, being very strong. The weather continues fine and the night light.

Last night the four disabled guns were removed, we lost 15 or 20 men of the covering and working parties by the enemy's grape. Another gun and another howitzer are disabled. An officer of artillery, Lt Hawker, was killed this morning beyond the river and 15 to 20 men killed and wounded here.

St Cristobel is very annoying. I went to Almendralejo, eight leagues, and got leave from Sir Stapleton to remain at the siege.

There is a rivulet in front of the breach at the bottom of the hill, fordable only in particular places. An engineer went last night to discover the ford and found several but, not noting them sufficiently, could not recollect in the morning where they were.

6 June, Trenches before Badajoz. To his mother:

Dearest Madam,

Both Somers and myself have had plenty of locomotion since our arrival in Portugal as, after things were settled in the north, his general was ordered to take command of the cavalry of the south and my regiment, being sent into cantonments, I got appointed Assistant Quartermaster General to the cavalry; this has brought us both into Estramadura.

For the last four or five days I have been a volunteer with the artillery at the siege of Badajoz, but today I am obliged to go away as General Cotton has gone up to the outposts on the road to Sevilla. Lord Wellington, some weeks ago, received permission to recommend twelve captains for the brevet rank of major. He was so kind as to send in my name without saying anything to me or any application on my part whatever. Nothing could be handsomer than this so I almost flatter myself you may have seen my name in the gazette before you receive this letter.

The affair of Fuentes was a good breaking in for Somers, his horses have arrived sometime in high order and he seems to like his situation. The siege of Badajoz does not go on so fast as was expected, I think it will still hold out some days. Our loss has been nothing till last night and this morning when I believe it amounts to 25 or 30. Albuera was a bloody business; fortunately all our prisoners, except 40 or 50, have escaped, which reduces our loss – British – to 3,500, of whom 1,500 are daily joining. The victory has enabled us to recommence the siege of Badajoz . . .†

7 June Returned to the trenches. Two guns and a howitzer have been got into the new battery so the state of the artillery this side [of] the water is:
Ten-gun battery: Two 24-pounders and one howitzer.
Seven-gun battery: Six 24-pounders.
Old battery: One 24-pounder and three howitzers.
Disabled: Five 24-pounders and two howitzers.

The breach of San Cristobel being considered perfect, an assault was made last night. The storming party: fifty – 51st and 95th – supporting party 200. Lt Foster and four men got up but the rest, instead of making for the breach, tried to escalade by the gorge, failed and gave way. Poor Foster was obliged to return and was mortally wounded. Four men killed, 76 wounded by musketry and hand grenade. I have heard no other particulars so God knows where the fault lies. This is bad work, we cannot get on without Cristobel.

The breach improved slowly, the Portuguese artillery are capital fellows, especially number three company. The communication with the new battery is by short zigzags, secure from Cristobel. The battery itself is likewise safe except the farthestmost corner, this battery is about 480 yards from the breach. Six iron guns are coming from Elvas. Our loss this side [of] the water has been trifling, about 10 killed and 25 badly wounded, and 35 slightly.

8 June Last night four iron guns arrived. The new battery is completed to seven guns from the seven-gun battery and a howitzer. There were two guns in the seven-gun battery and three howitzers in the old battery. The iron guns were not brought into action but two more arrived before night, with one brass gun from the other side [of] the water. I think the garrison of Cristobel spiked theirs when attacked the other night for they have never fired mortars since, and only one 24-pounder occasionally, and probably this they unspiked.

It seems a general opinion that it is absolutely necessary to make a lodgement here previous to assaulting the town. It is impossible to push our approaches nearer the town without possession of it as they would be completely overlooked. *Note A* If one breach were practicable and we assaulted from our present parallel our supporting columns would be dreadfully exposed to the flanking fire of the fort, even in the night. To carry it by assault would have the best effect in the spirits of both parties.

Case shot was fired last night on the breach but the enemy took advantage of short cessation to clear it partially away. Our case is very bad, it is Portuguese metal [?] and comprised of $\frac{1}{2}$-oz balls which do not carry home. The French fire half-pound balls which whistle over our heads. The practice today was very good and we all began to have hopes of the breach, in the centre all the tapis work was quite gone, and the earth behind it does not come off in perpendicular flakes as it did but slides down in great quantities. It is easily distinguishable, being a black mould, whereas the tapis work looks white and flies about, when struck, in dust.

---

†Weller gives the Allied losses as 5,916.

There is a communication tonight between the upper and lower slope and I think a man might get up but there is no doubt that the rampart is supported almost to its top by a solid hill and consequently we may consider ourselves as breaching a full bastion. The framework of the platform, on which the two guns were, holds the breach at present a good deal together.

Note B I fear we have mistaken the point of attack. The reasons for selecting it probably were that there is here no direct flanking fire on the breach but there was no glacis to prevent your beginning to breach at once, no ditch to impede your advance to the breach and the wall was considered as an old crumbling one, easily beat down.

The objections to the point were that the flanking fire from Cristobel and Picurina and the advanced redoubt are very annoying to the approaches, and that it was unlikely a wall should be left uncovered by glacis unless it was known to be strong. Besides this, the steepness of the hill renders it more difficult to form a breach and will considerably add to the difficulty of storming after it is made. The reason why the enemy did not expect us is that he knew it was the strongest part.

The faults in the conduct of the siege are that the breaching batteries are too far off and the enfilading fire has little effect. I look upon these as the two great points to attend to in a siege. Overwhelm and silence your adversary's flanking fire and then clasp your breaching battery close to him. I think we should have done better had we made sure of Cristobel first and then begun our first breaching battery where our last now is. It is even said from the state of the fortification we should have done better still had we attacked on the other side of the town, with our left to the river. As it is, instead of opening the place in 36 hours we have been pommelling away for six days and all we have done is to form a slope at an angle of 60°, and to get at this we must brave the flank fire of Picurina and Cristobel, cross a brook we do not know where to ford, ascend a hill too steep to run up, scramble up a breach 30 feet high, and when we get to the top we shall be open to the fire of the retrenchments which will still have to be stormed, with their ditch 5 toises in breadth.

9 June Our [?] was so bad that the enemy worked a little at the breach tonight but has not done much mischief. We have now got up some 1lb and 3lb balls which I hope will keep him in better order.

> The state of our artillery is:
> Ten-gun battery: brass 8; iron 2; howitzer 1.
> Seven-gun battery: brass 2; iron 4.
> Old battery: 3 howitzers.

Making a total of 10 brass, 6 iron and 4 howitzers but the two 10-inch howitzers on mortar frames are nearly useless and the iron guns, being mounted on lower carriages than the brass ones, require an alteration in embrasures which was not observed till daybreak, and the consequence was they never got into action until midday. After this their practice was better than the brass guns. Our casualties were trifling, one man was killed by a shot from Cristobel and a few wounded. The shells do not do so much mischief as I should have expected. The breach improves but is still very narrow and by no means practicable. The English artillerymen man as many guns as they are able and the rest are left wholly to the Portuguese. The ten-gun battery is supported by a second parallel.

10 June We assaulted Fort Cristobel again last night. From the second parallel we could distinguish every flash and hear every shout. The assault commenced at half past nine and the firing lasted three quarters of an hour though, I believe, the actual assault did not take many minutes. The interval was painfully anxious. We were beat off but our troops, by all account, behaved well. Major M'Greachy and Hunt of the Engineers were killed, the breach was impracticable and the French fought too well to allow escalade. In the main breach the slope is complete from top to bottom in the centre and perhaps four or five men might go abreast, but I should think it forms an angle of 55–60° with the [?] and I believe it is now ascertained that the garrison, for sure, has cut the breach off by a retrenchment with chevaux de frise. 10 o'clock am: Lord Wellington has determined to ruin the siege. Soult is probably in motion. I could cut my nails for vexation. I shall go instantly and join my general at Villafranca.

11pm Almandralejo: 8 leagues. The alarm of Soult is false. Lord Wellington cannot mean to raise the siege, perhaps he means to give up the first point of attack. If we should not be too exposed to the fire of the tête du pont I should prefer the front next the river, on the west, otherwise I should take Pardeleras first and then the town would fall en regle.

I am at Almandralejo. General Hill is here with between two and three divisions . . .

11 June Villafranca: 2 leagues. I joined Sir Stapleton Cotton as DAQMG. The general instructions of the covering corps are to remain as long as the enemy occupies Llerena and Usagre, with the infantry one day's march and the cavalry two from Albuera, where we are to fight again. Should the enemy fall farther back, then we may spread for more convenient quarters but, at all events, the infantry must be only two days' march and the cavalry three from Albuera. The cavalry is to watch the road from Llerena by Usagre and Bienvenida.

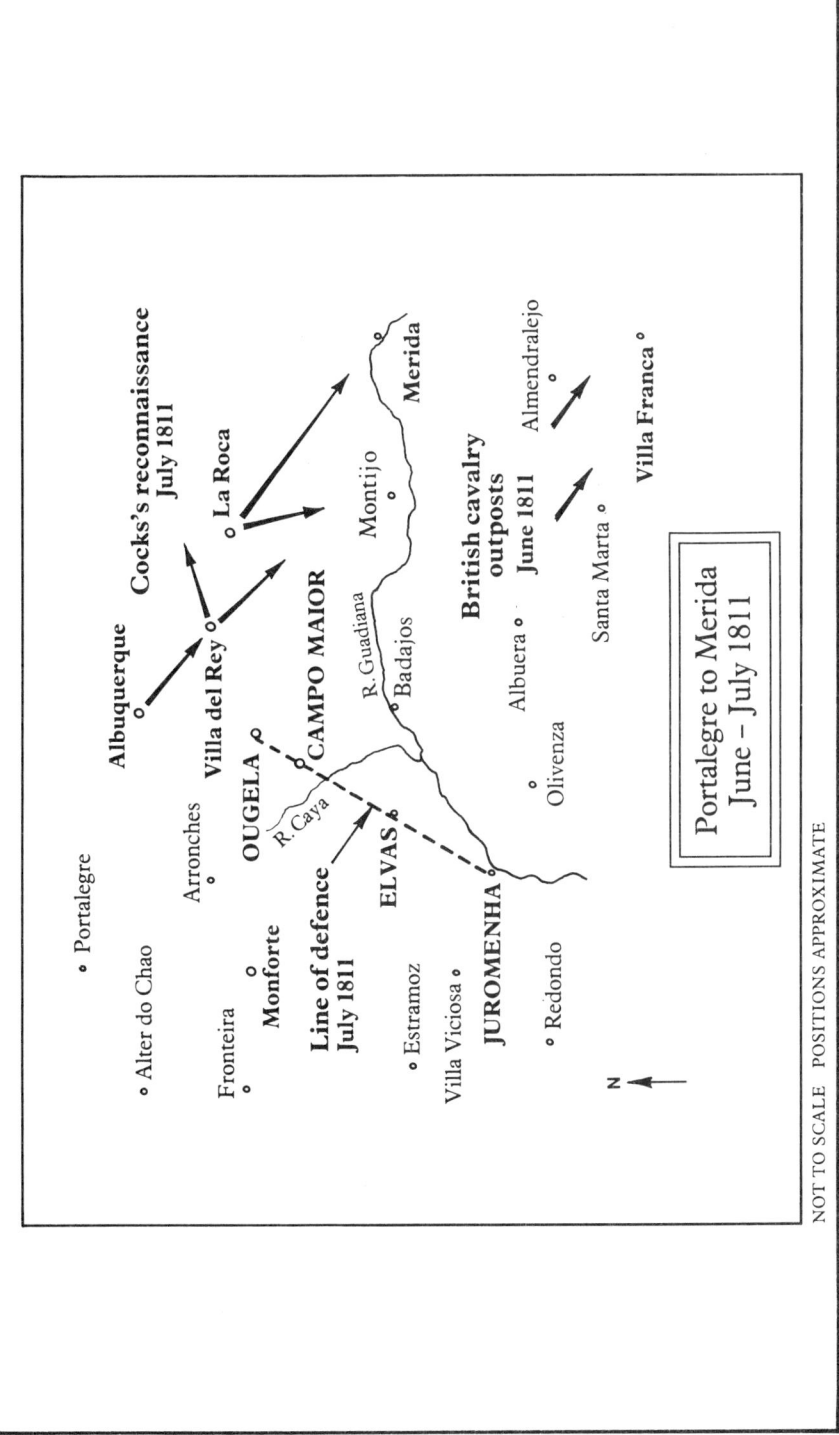

CHAPTER THIRTEEN
Reflections
16 June – 9 July 1811

COCKS'S FIRST SURMISE was correct, Wellington had learned that Soult and Marmont, Massena's successor, were expecting to form a junction close to Badajoz on about the 18th and, being unable to match their combined corps, gradually withdrew behind the Guadiana, taking up a strong, defensive position along the frontier from Ougela, through fortified Campo Maior, down to Elvas. The cavalry played its usual role during this rearrangement and for five days Cocks was fully engaged. Meanwhile, much needed reinforcements to make up the numbers lost at Fuentes d'Onoro and Albuera were on their march from Lisbon.

* * *

16 June Arrangements are made for the retreat of all the troops on this side the river. It is now clear that Lord Wellington has no intention of again fighting for Badajoz. The plan of our general has always been to run no risks that were not absolutely necessary and to harrass the enemy by placing him in situations where he must unavoidably suffer by privation and fatigue ...

17 June This day the investment of Badajoz was broken up and the whole of the army crossed the Guadiana. The movements commenced at 2 am when the moon rose. The 3rd Division, with Madden's cavalry, having passed the river by the ford above Badajoz, joined the 7th Division and whole fell back to Campo Maior. General Hill's infantry crossed at Puerto de Chica, a league below Badajoz. General Hamilton's Division of Portuguese infantry crossed by a ford nearer the town. General Hill and General Hamilton afterwards crossed the Caya and encamped in the olive groves near Fort Santa Lucia. The cavalry crossed by the Puerto de Chica and fell back to the olive groves on the right of the infantry. The Spaniards, under Blake and Loy, fell back to Juramenha, with their advance in Olivenza. A chain of cavalry outposts were established behind the Caya, communicating on the right with the Spaniards and on the left with Madden on Campo Maior.

18 June The army halted. Three squadrons of the 11th Light Dragoons have arrived at Elvas and the others will be there tomorrow. They are 600 strong and, by all I can learn, in capital order. They are brigaded with the 2nd Hussars under Long; the 13th go to Slade's brigade.

19 June ... The 2nd Hussars and the 11th Light Dragoons take the outposts in front of Elvas, and Madden's continues to furnish them in front of Campo Maior ...

21 June Went to Campo Maior ... General Madden's outposts are very well arranged. He has only 28 men on duty by day. In this country, which is perfectly open and full of commanding heights, very few vedettes are necessary while it is light. The most commanding spots are marked out to your hand by old watch towers erected during the wars of Spain and Portugal. By night there is no security except from frequent patrols.

Piquets may be established for two purposes and it should be always clearly understood which is the object in view, whether to watch the enemy or check him. If the first, a few men can be employed and these should be considerably advanced. In an open country eight or ten men cannot think of fighting and can always gallop away, whereas stronger piquets do not think it honourable to retreat without at least skirmishing with the enemy's advanced guard. Then they get men and horses wounded and, on trying to bring them off, the whole get into a scrape.

If piquets are intended to check an enemy's line the most advanced should be very small but immediately handy to these should be several squadrons forming a reserve, constantly saddled and accoutred. The small advance piquets should be posted with a view to looking out only, the reserve squadrons with a view to the strength and defensibility of the ground.

The object of all piquets is to enable the cavalry in camp to rest itself. The instant, therefore, it is clear the enemy is advancing in sufficient force, and sufficiently near to oblige the cavalry in the rear to turn out and load its baggage, they cease to be useful and should always fall back rather than run the least risk of being cut off.

1,500 French cavalry arrived this evening at Badajoz.

22 June The enemy occupied Olivenza this morning with 4,000 infantry and made a reconnaissance forcé all along our front. From twelve to eighteen squadrons crossed at Puerto de Chico and appeared in front of Elvas by the high road, the remainder went direct for the olive groves.

The 11th made an unlucky beginning. They contrived to lose three piquets, Capt Lutchens, another officer, and 60 or 70 men and horses were taken prisoners, and 10 or 12 killed and wounded.

Note It is said he was posted and remained near the Casa Comineda [?] in a sort of punch bowl, that the cavalry which moved from the Puerte de Chico amused him in front while the remainder gained his flank and rear. I am unable to conceive how this could have happened in such a plain. It is said that Lutchens fell back on a column of dust, supposing it English and it was French. But how could an officer allow a column to pass his right without seeing them? How could he fall back on dust without sending to ascertain what it was? How could the whole piquet surrender, one officer only having escaped? Had they either dispersed or endeavoured to make their way through in a body, many must have escaped.

The 2nd Hussars were also engaged in bringing off General Long and his baggage. They charged three squadrons of lancers, took an officer and 18 or 20 men but, being overpowered, were obliged to retreat, losing 15 or 16 killed or wounded and 35 prisoners. Our total loss in horses is 7 officers' horses and 125 privates', 119 in the hands of the enemy. This is the worst affront British cavalry has received in this country.

On the side of Campo Maior the enemy advanced 15 or 16 squadrons with 3 guns and a howitzer. The Portuguese had a good deal of skirmishing but a very few men and horses were wounded. The enemy advanced on one side of the town, but I think he got no further information than that we had infantry in the neighbourhood of Campo Maior. The Heavies were brought up but the Great Men did not think the enemy had committed himself sufficiently to take advantage of.

The Portuguese are very excellent outpost troops and skirmish very well. Their great fault is the little care they take of their horses; they should be made to save our Heavy regiments . . .

23 June All was quiet this morning . . .

24 June, Camp of Torre de Montao. To Thomas Somers Cocks, Esq:
My dear Thomas,

I enclose a letter for Stanhope,† I believe there is little doubt that he is anxious to exchange and might be induced to do so to Infantry. I have received a hint from Lord Wellington that he should be well satisfied to see me in Stanhope's place and would forward it as far as he could, and as the Duke‡, is now Commander-in-Chief I think the thing is practicable. The difficulties would be cash and the obtaining an Infantry majority. With regard to the first, the thing would be so very much consequence to me that I would mortgage or sell ⅔ of my estate and live on bread and water rather than it should fail that way, and I trust to the *Squire*,§ with old codger Price,†† to produce the sum which may be required.

In my letter to Stanhope I have said that you were commissioned to act for me and would call on him whenever he requested it, should you be so kind as [to] accept this offer of minister plenipotentiary.

Till I know whether Stanhope is ready to exchange and, if he is, that he has not already made his bargain, in short till I hear from you I can do nothing in the business here. I shall therefore wait your answer to this letter most anxiously.

Since my last letter I have been acting Quartermaster General to the Cavalry of Alemtejo but, the whole army being now collected near Campo Maior, I return to my Regiment. Our operations have been too active to give a detailed account of them. I can only say that Lord Wellington has acted in a manner perfectly consistent to the plan he has long laid down; and although the failure of the siege of Badajoz may be grating to our pride, it was no more than Lord W expected. The ends he had in view when he sat down before the place have been answered, upon the whole.

Had we fought in front of Badajoz we must have harrassed the army at a time of year and in a part of the country the most unhealthy. It is possible some of the troops would not have come up in time. I doubt whether under any circumstance we could have prevented the enemy from throwing succour into Badajoz. At any rate for this purpose we must have weakened our army too much.

---

†The Hon. Lincoln Stanhope, Major in the 16th Light Dragoons.
‡of York.
§Thomas himself.
††Probably a lawyer.

The only thing to be regretted is the loss before Cristobel, Lord W was deceived by the Engineers. He thought he could have taken it and it would have materially facilitated any future siege to have destroyed this Fort.

It now remains to be seen whether Soult will advance over the Guadiana and fight us. I think certainly not. Perhaps when he has put Badajoz in a proper state of defence he may make a movement on his left and draw contributions from the neighbourhood of Evora. But I think he will then retreat. In this case we shall probably go into summer quarters.

Blake and the Spaniards have marched from Sevilla where the enemy is said to have left nothing. Freire is also advancing on that point by Cordoba, where Sebastiani is supposed not to have above 2 or 3,000. These diversions, if well executed, are most important. By Lord Wellington's able manoeuvres the whole of the French force in Castile, Leon, Estramadura, La Mancha and Andalusia, - except 3,000 at Cordoba and 5,000-8,000 entrenched at Cadiz - is now drawn together before Badajoz and there kept in check. What a moment for Spain!

I congratulate you and your whole family on Maria's marriage . . .†

During the siege of Badajoz I was living with a friend of yours, Saunders of the Horse Artillery. I have not sealed Stanhope's letter that you may read it.

25 June 1,500 French cavalry again occupied the wood‡ this evening. Troops have been likewise in motion between Olivenza and Badajoz, I believe falling back.

In looking at dust it is sometimes very difficult to distinguish it from smoke, one naturally never expects to see the latter go against the wind but it sometimes happens that a stubble field catches fire at the lee end and then the smoke goes against the wind. Smoke rises higher than dust. Lord Wellington expects a reconnaissance tomorrow in consequence of the move of the French cavalry.

29 June Lord Wellington appears to me to have two principles in his formations. He likes to present a salient angle with his general front and he endeavours to secure his flanks by detached corps placed in echelon. He selects strong ground for the point of angle. This system enables us always to move flank to flank in less distance than the enemy can. If he attacks our centre he takes the bull by the horns, if he endeavours to turn either flank he is, himself, exposed to a flank attack from the corps posted in the centre, which is more advanced to the front than the flanks.

On the other hand, if our whole line is driven, it falls back concentrically, the worst of all retreats, but it also enables the enemy to act concentrically; thus if we want to reinforce one flank from another we have only to move on the right line $a\ d$, while the enemy would have to move on arc $f\ g\ h$, or even still further if he aimed at turning our flanks.

If the enemy attacks c it is naturally strong, if a or b he is taken in flank by c where there is a great deal of artillery. If the enemy pushes d it is reinforced by a [?] while b advances round c on the left of the enemy. Should our line, however, be

---

†To Admiral Sir William Hargood, RN.
‡Near La Roca.

driven in confusion it will be crowded together on *E* where it will be taken in flank, both right and left, by the concentric columns of the enemy.

The system to oppose such a formation is that pursued by the French at Talavera where they endeavoured to occupy the corps in the centre while they broke the left flank.

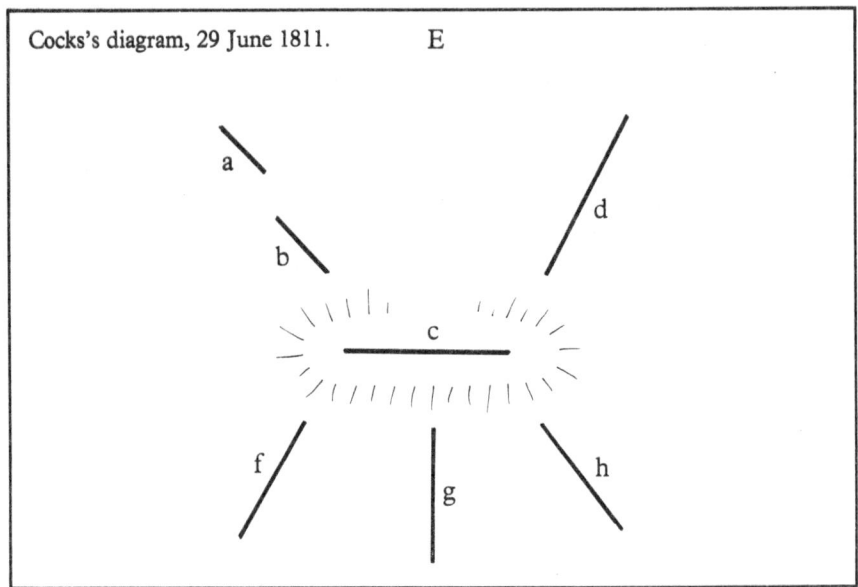

Cocks's diagram, 29 June 1811.

30 June It seems the general idea that the enemy is falling back. We have very few patrols, probably the minor information gained in this way is not wanted as an attack is not expected. Lord Wellington, having Spanish information of all the enemy's great movements, wishes to spare his cavalry.

30 June, Camp of Torre de Montao. To The Hon. Miss Margaret Maria Cocks:†
  My dear Sister,
    ... Since the siege of Badajoz which, though unsuccessful, fully answered the principal objects which the operation had in view, we have been quietly encamped here between Elvas and Campo Maior and scarcely see anything of the enemy; indeed, I believe the greater part of his force has already been drawn off from our front and that the remainder will go as soon as Badajoz is victualled. In this case it is said we shall go into cantonments during the unhealthy season. I have rejoined my regiment some days and must confess I am very glad of it, I never feel so independent or so much at home as among my old comrades. They talk of Estramoz and Villa Vicosa for our cantonments; if so I shall get some more deer shooting.

---

†He appears to have written the copy of this letter on the 30 June but not sent it before 9 July, writing the latter date on the actual letter.

The 11th Dragoons have made a bad business of it. This it is to teach soldiers at home nothing but the fiddlestick duties of parade. John Bull, in his growling humour, sometimes talks of the great risk of keeping thirty or forty thousand troops abroad in case the enemy should attack him at home, but either we are to have an army or we are not. If we are, that army – officers, soldiers, generals and all – must learn their business among swords and bayonets or they will be no better than so many citizens. I believe the enemy will never be able to invade England or Britain but if he should, with a respectable army, a pretty business we should make of it if we had nothing to oppose but armies made of men like so many volunteers. To be sure, it is very provoking to lose 125 men of the 11th Dragoons and 2nd Hussars but still I comfort myself that it will have its use by proving the necessity of training our troops in war itself, and altering our system at home to make it as like war as circumstances will admit. Barracks are the ruin of cavalry and the making of infantry.

I have plenty of books but very little leisure. St Pierre's *Theory of the Tides* is very interesting but not quite convincing, *Les Memoires de Prince Eugene* are delightful, Hammond's *Love Elegies* are written with great tenderness and purity of style, both in sentiment and expression, but rather too formal for the expression of an ardent passion . . . We are too idle here, I think the army will get sickly, but we are perfectly supplied and Anson's Brigade, the 16th and 1st Hussars are in good condition. My horses are all well . . .

9 July, Albuquerque. To The Hon. James Somers Cocks:
My dear James,
     As our operations have of late been principally carried on in Spain I have had opporunities of remarking the disposition of the people . . .

The character of the Spaniard and the nature of his country are well adapted for guerrillas, that is flying parties from 100 to 1,500 men, and as long as there is a pretext such parties will exist, particularly if those who compose them are allowed to plunder and have an opportunity of boasting. Also, as they fight no pitched battles and only attack when superior in number, and by surprise, they run no risk. The other qualities necessary for such partizans, such as patience under fatigue, hardship, knowledge of country, watchfulness, a Spaniard is generally provided with, and these parties are of great utility as long as there is also a regular army such as ours in the Peninsula. But it is one thing to possess a country in a military sense, and another in a civil.

If an army is unopposed, can march where it will and draw supplies from all parts, the country is militarily conquered, but not civilly unless the resources of every description are at the disposal of the governor and the individuals can pass freely. The guerrillas prevent this. Individuals and even small parties are not safe, convoys require strong escorts and the number of French required in Spain is inconceivably multiplied and Spaniards are kept out of the French service. If there was no regular army in the Peninsula the French could afford sufficient men to root out two or three of the principal guerrillas and then the rest would get frightened.

The war with the Spaniards should often be thought of by Englishmen. At the beginning of the contest the Spaniards possessed a regular army of 35–40,000 – not bad except that it had seen no service – and also a large population of peasantry filled with enthusiasm and only requiring instruction and chiefs; yet all these materials were overwhelmed. Spain was on the point of falling when an army of 30,000 English mercenaries, many of them disliking the Spaniards, has restored the affair and almost turned the scale. It signifies very little where the point of contest is, but Soult, at this moment, commands all the disposable French force in Spain and if he is beat, half Spain must be given up.

England should learn from this, that if she wishes to be independent and respectable she must always keep an army of soldiers and not merely of men in regimentals; besides, how is she to have generals? A commander should have talent improved by experience and all the generals should have commonsense improved by experience. Experienced stupidity I have sometimes seen do better than rare talent. I believe we cannot be invaded at present but our naval superiority may not last for ever and, put the case we are, and that the invading army is fairly reinforced and that we have not officers formed in war, as was the case four years ago, I believe we should be conquered. Before our new levies could learn their duty the enemy would have overrun so much of the country that there would be no means to assemble an army. I do not think we should remain conquered but we should be overrun for a time. When we came from England had we been the army Lord Wellington has made us God knows what we might not have done, but it is a hard task for a man to teach at once, soldiers, officers, commissaries, staff, generals, and last of all himself. This, however, he has done and Lord Wellington is worth fifty Sir Arthur Wellesleys.

Your ever affectionate brother,
E. Charles Cocks

CHAPTER FOURTEEN
More Reflections

1 July – 8 August 1811

ON 1 JULY Wellington sent Cocks out on yet another special duty, this time to patrol the country around Albuquerque, La Roca and Villa del Rey in enemy dominated no man's land. Soult had already retired to Andalusia and it was thought Marmont would also depart but he proved suspiciously slow in moving off. 'I shall only take twenty men and keep snug in the sierra,'† Charles wrote. 'I will get information through the peasants and spies and not patrol far until I think the enemy is in motion. In Spain you must get information in a way different from Portugal. As there are scarce any supplies except near great towns, the points by which the enemy will move are more marked. At the same time patrols can do little as the distances between towns are considerable; strong patrols harrass cavalry too much, small patrols are not safe in this open country. You get pretty good information through the peasants, only Spanish peasants sometimes give their guesses for facts and have always some absurd story about artillery.'[1]

They were out a fortnight and, until Marmont began to withdraw, the work was arduous. On the 8th Cocks noted: 'I slept for the night in a little garden near the town, I was heartily tired. For the last forty hours I have been almost constantly on my horse and have not closed my eyes above one hour.'[2] But at last the country was clear of the enemy and he was even able to ride into Merida and visit his acquaintances of 1809. 'I saw them all and they were delighted to see an old friend,' he told his mother, 'especially as their new friends Messrs Marmont & Co had only left them a few hours.'[3]

★   ★   ★

12 July, Camp near Albuquerque. To Thomas Somers Cocks, Esq:
My dear Thomas,
    I enclose a letter for Boverick‡ giving some directions as to the manner in which I wish some new cantiens to be constructed and also two new saddles ditto. Willie Hay§ has got a company and gone to England, I do not think he will return. He wishes to have Boverick as a servant and I think if he has not made an arrangement this would suit master and man.
    By the by, I always forgot to mention that the sword you sent me broke to pieces the first time I had it in my hand and I discovered a flaw about 22 inches from the handle. In other respects it was a well balanced sabre for cutting but too

---
†Wellington increased the number shortly afterwards.
‡Boverick's health had collapsed and he had returned home.
§Lt William Hay of the 16th.

broad at the point even to be useful if used in that way. All the commissions I had given I found executed with perfect punctuality.

I have a party of observation of 45 men. Dekin of the Hussars is with me. The enemy is dispersed in quarters from Badajoz to Truxillo. It has been for some time expected that they would all fall back and go behind the Tagus. They are very busy in strengthening and supplying Badajoz. The two or three next months will probably be quiet but I suspect it will blow a hurricane in October, November and December. The Cavalry now forms two Divisions – Sir William Erskine has one, Sir S. Cotton the other; both however reporting to the latter as senior officer.

I wish some move would take place. Nothing is more lively than a party of observation when the enemy is in motion but it becomes dull when you have nothing to report. I believe if the enemy were to go to the Tagus we should all go somewhere into Quarters.

I have not seen Soṁers this fortnight. He was beginning to acquire a respectable brown. He is throwing off the *despairing town* and country gentleman and commencing his career.† We live pretty well – lots of pretty girls, espanolitas, and we pass our time here very fairly – vive la guerre et la bagatelle . . .‡

19 July, Albuquerque. To The Hon. James Soṁers Cocks:
My dear James,

I received your letter the day before yesterday. Accept my thanks for the trouble you have taken . . . At present it is said we are going into cantonments and are to be quiet during the hot months; this, however, has been said so often before that I never expect it will be true . . .

Nothing could be a greater surprise to me than my promotion. I heard of it when dining at Lord Wellington's six weeks ago. Thomas has long ago communicated to you the content of my letter about purchasing Stanhope's majority. This is the greatest of objects to me and I am anxiously awaiting Thomas's answer. My present majority gives me no command nor does it facilitate my obtaining a lt colonelcy otherwise than that the time I must be major will begin reckoning from the date of my first commission in that rank . . .

> His surmise that the army would go into cantonments during the warm weather was correct and he rejoined the 16th shortly after sending this letter. The significance of the cavalry being placed in two divisions was that the regiments were re-brigaded and the 16th lost their old friends the 1st Hussars, 'which I regret most heartily,' he wrote. 'Never have two regiments been more united. We have been like one corps.'[4]
>
> With the break from active operations he began his most concentrated period of writing in the journal. Everything he had heard, read, experienced and pondered over was used to draw conclusions on the various subjects under discussion.

22 July I have now served 3 campaigns and I certainly think there is much less

---

†John Soṁers lacked his brother's intense dedication to the army!
‡All the same, during this period Wellington mentioned Cocks's work three times in his Despatches home. On 8, 11 and 26 July. See Vol 8 of the Despatches.

Above:
1. Edward Charles Cocks.
From a miniature by
J. C. D. Engleheart c1808
at Eastnor Castle,
Herefordshire.
(The Hon. Mrs B. A. F.
Hervey-Bathurst)

Right:
2. Thomas Somers Cocks.
From a miniature by
W. J. Thomson.
(J. V. Somers Cocks, Esq.)

3. The Duke of Wellington by Goya. Painted after the capture of Madrid, 1812. (Apsley House)

4. Reigate Priory today.

5. Oporto, looking up river from the Serra Convent. The old seminary where the troops landed is beyond the curve in the river.

6. The River Coa at Castel Mendo where Cocks and his party helped the peasants destroy the mills in August 1810.

7. Wellington's Headquarters at Pero Negro in the Lines of Torres Vedras.

8. View from Santarem towards Malhaquejo where Cocks harrassed Massena's forging parties in November 1810.

9. Obidos, from whence Cocks waged war on the enemy, January – February 1811.

10. Fuentes d'Onoro. The battle raged within its streets in May 1811. Camille Siego owned a house here.

11. Almeida. This fortress was abandoned by Brennier in May 1811, after the battle of Fuentes d'Onoro.

12. Frenada. A village between the Coa and the Agueda and Wellington's headquarters for a while.

13. Villa Velha. The crossing point over the Tagus used continually by the army.

14. Salamanca today.

15. Tordesillas today, showing the remains of the old bridge.

16. The Escurial Palace outside Madrid. Cocks and the 79th were billeted here.

17. Peninsular War c1812. Light Dragoons: *A Glimpse of the Army*.
(National Army Museum)

real courage than I once fancied and, what is still more mortifying, I think more splendid acts have been performed by soldiers than officers in our service. Real intrepidity is founded on a distinct sense of honour, a consciousness of virtue and confidence of hereafter.

There are in the army a few brilliant examples of this feeling, what should we not effect if we had only such men as Hervey, Krauchenberg and the Napiers. Another sort of courage, more common, is founded on strong nerves, a consciousness of personal power and a wish to do one's duty. This is all that can be expected in an uneducated soldier. Its effects are sometimes equal to the former species but it is not so valuable a quality, a headache, the want of a day's rations, a false report, is sometimes sufficient to overturn it; it is, besides, only constant in action and is not the feeling which enables a man to take daring resolutions or which support him when things are going wrong.

The first of these sentiments is only to be found in men habituated to danger and who have often reflected on it. I think this is less the case with English and Irish men than any other northern nations, their courage is more corporeal and results from a sort of prepossession that they are superior to every other nation. This feeling is more proper to the soldier than the officer and hence I think our soldiers are proportionally braver than our officers.

If Englishmen are beat I always suspect the officers. No nation is so liable to absurd fancies; when the enemy is far off they are alarmed but their spirit rises with his approach.

A French officer is different. He is familiarised to danger and wounds; his fame, his promotion, his future depends on his courage, wounds are the passports to ease; he, therefore, does not care about them. This is a great thing, let a man go into any situation and however dangerous, the chances are three or four to one that he is only wounded and not killed. If he can make up his mind to be wounded he is almost quit of fear. I think French officers reason in this way. Their soldiers are brave from vanitory and military esprit that require aqua vitae.

Germans have something of the French officers' feeling but do not carry it so far and they have also a pride from the high consideration a soldier enjoys in Germany. Usually ill-educated, their minds are confined to their profession, they are not liable to false alarms, but they know too much how to estimate the dangers of their situation and sometimes discover disheartening difficulties which might be concealed from other troops. They make capital subalterns and captains, but know too much for power and their views are not sufficiently enlarged for high command.

The southern natives have a distinct sort of courage, lively and vain, they are capable of high enthusiasm, their courage is wholly corporeal and requires to be directed by heads of a different description.

The Portuguese are a most affectionate people when well used by their officers, to which they have not been accustomed, this feeling alone makes them despise death, they possess great emulation and from their natural habits of perfect temperance are not easily distressed by privation. It is easy to see that this sort of character must be well directed to be effective; if they begin to despond they fly en masse.

24 July Marched to Monforte where I joined my squadron . . . the whole army is in cantonments . . .

27 July I am putting down different military ideas which have occurred to me at various times.

(1) *Retreats* should commence eccentrically and conclude concentrically.
Note An army that retreats eccentrically prevents its opponent from following with a corps only and, as it retreats itself by corps, it ought to outstrip its adversary. At the same time, if it has not the means of ultimately uniting it will be unable to oppose the mass advancing in its rear, whenever it comes.

(2) Rivers afford positions either by covering the front or the flank of an army. Of the two I prefer the latter, for most positions covered in front by one river require too great a division of force and even then are liable to be turned; they, besides, impede advance. Positions appuying one flank on a navigable river are often very good especially if our own country is down the river, supplies are then secure, the flank next the river may often be protected by batteries on the other side, placed in potince. Chains of mountains are generally parallel to the sea coast and navigable rivers perpendicular, therefore it often happens that a position with its flank on a great river can dispose its front along heights and perhaps cover it by some smaller stream running along the valleys of the heights and falling into the larger. Positions appuying a flank on an unnavigable river are usually very inferior because such rivers run parallel to the heights and afford no means of supplies; they are likewise, for the most part, easily turned.

(3) It has been said no army can turn without being turned but this maxim is not general, an army with two lines of operations forming a sufficient angle may always turn one with a single line of operation. The movement will cut off your adversary from all his resources, etc and only separates yourself from a part of your own.

(4) An advantageous situation of a fortress is a little in rear of a barren country because the invader's line of operation must necessarily extend beyond this country, and consequently be long and easily menaced. If the fortress be placed at the confluence of two rivers, facing outwards, its site is still more perfect, it cannot be masked except by a very superior corps. Abrantes unites all these advantages and is besides very centrical to the roads in the neighbourhood, it should be made a place of the first order.

(5) It is not necessary that a base should consist of fortresses, a tract of country producing requisite supplies will form a base.

(6) More generals are frightened into failure than beat into it. In general it is not hard to place an army in a situation in which, if beat, the risk is great though the chances of being beat are small. In such cases few men have resolution to stand their ground.

(7) C'est un maxim reconnu pour l'etablissement des ordres de bataille que toutes les parties doivent en être liées et présenter un ensemble qui fait toute bien force – It is a recognised maxim for establishing orders of battle that all involved parties must be in contact and present a united front.

(8) I think it is a wise maxim when you have once determined on your object to follow that with perseverence and not allow yourself to be drawn aside, even by

delusive hopes of greater success. Change your means according to circumstances but never lose sight of your end.

(9) Il ne faut jamais placer un corps de troupes dans une vallée sans etre maître des montagnes, on doit au moins occuper un des côtes si l'on ne peut garder tous les deux – One should never place corps of troops in a valley without having the mastery of the mountains, one ought to occupy one side, at least, even if one cannot hold both. If the mountains are very rugged it may suffice to occupy them with tirailleurs.

(10) I prefer an order of battle broken into corps and where part of an army is in column to one where the line is continued; this however, must depend on the ground not in your choice. If the ground is a flat or a continued and gradual slope the line must be continued supported by columns. If the ground is broken by deep ravines it is sufficient to occupy the heights.

(11) At the battle of Prague the fault of Prince Charles lay in neglecting to occupy the salient angle between Kolin and Aloupetin [?] in sufficient force. It was the keystone of his position and while he kept it the Prussians could not have overturned his line because the artillery there would have enfiladed the line as it advanced.

(12) In order of battle the salient angle of the flank not attacked should always endeavour to turn that of the enemy.

(13) When there are villages in front of the line but not wholly commanded from it they must be occupied, but it is necessary that the line be so near that the enemy cannot turn them, mask them or attack the line beyond them.

(14) If there be a village in front of the line commanded from it, it need not be occupied, and in this case it is probable that the enemy will use it as a rallying point for his troops, and, if repulsed, will fill it with infantry to cover his retreat. I would therefore previously dispose some guns, especially howitzers, so as to rake it well.

(15) The best columns of march near an enemy are parallel open columns, each line forming a column. If your enemy is opposite your front, march to his right or left, according to the country of the flank you have in front, then bring your right or left shoulders forward and you are ready to form parallel lines to manoeuvre on one flank after having demonstrated on the other, or take up a position refusing your own flank. It is true you cannot attempt this in a plain when your enemy can act freely but it may be used when he has taken a position behind enclosures and on the top of heights from which he cannot descend in line.

> Between 28-30 July Cocks compared the Peninsular campaigns with those of Frederick the Great in the Seven Years War, using Lloyd's History as his guide, and his arguments cover page after page, many almost indecipherable, as he sought to draw conclusions.

31 July A general move is taking place in the army to the left. Headquarters moved from Portalegre today and go to Castel Branco, the 1st Division likewise march from Portalegre and the 7th from Niza. We march tomorrow. I went onto Crato, five leagues, to take leave of my old friends the Hussars.
1 August Marched to Assumar and encamped.
2 August Portalegre: 3 leagues. It is said that Ney has arrived from France to the

neighbourhood of Salamanca with 30,000 men, this number will not do more than place the French army on the footing of last year; however, as Tarragona has surrendered perhaps a greater proportion may be employed against us. If they mean again to act offensively in Portugal it is probable they will establish magazines at Ciudad Rodrigo and Plasencia as they have already done at Badajoz. At the former place the harvest is nearly ripe and at the latter most part is already got in.

3 August Alpanhao: 3 leagues.

5 August After halting a day in Alpenhao, marched to Niza: 2 leagues.

6 August Villa Velha: $2\frac{1}{2}$ leagues. We bivouacked here. The bridge is finished and there are pontoons lying here sufficient to construct another.

7 August Castel Branco: $4\frac{1}{2}$ leagues. The 4th Division having marched into the town we again bivouacked. It is now reported that Bessières is between Salamanca and Ciudad Rodrigo and that his cavalry has made some incursions over the Coa; it is also said that Marmont's Headquarters are to be established at Plasencia, our Headquarters are today at Pedrogao.

8 August Loiza: $2\frac{1}{2}$ leagues. This is a miserable village. The first squadron is detached to Ladoueira to observe the Plasencia road. Headquarters are, I believe, today at Sabugal.

Note When your enemy cannot pass you but succeeds by manoeuvring against your lines of operation in compelling you to change your position, it is better to retreat parallel to your base and establish new lines of operation than make a retrograde movement to regain the old ones. This is beautifully exemplified by Frederick's march on Bohemia in 1758.

Honour should be the soldier's principle but generals should only fight for advantage. It is absurd, therefore, for them to sacrifice men for guns when the latter can be replaced.

When guns are abandoned the artillery officers should bring off the limbers and horses, the guns thus left without ammunition might become useless to the enemy and if the day should turn may be recovered. Partial defeat may occur in a day ending in complete victory; neither the loss of guns, colours or prisoners are therefore a test of conquest.

CHAPTER FIFTEEN
Catching up on Correspondence
12 – 31 August 1811

THE WRITING continued all August, even when the regiment was on the march and, along with the rest of the theories debated over the following months, can be found in the appendices of this book. They show his total absorption in learning the business of soldiering and improving the current training, and one has to remember that, in his own early days in the army, if he was taught to think militarily at all it would have been at a very superficial level and probably by men who may not have seen active service themselves. Nor would staff college, had he attended, have delved as deeply as he did himself. Only his lively personality kept him from being labelled eccentric by his brother officers, few of whom can have read the books in his library.† In fact he was both mentally and physically hyperactive and packed more into twenty-four hours than most into twenty-four weeks or even months.

★ ★ ★

12 August, Loiza. To Thomas Somers Cocks, Esq:
My dear Thomas,
    . . . I should be much obliged to you to send me out from Faden a set of the best *ancient* and modern maps of Europe; including Chambard's Julien & Fereares *Carte de la Belgique*, if to be had. These maps should be made to roll within one another and be strengthened at the back by linen and pasted on. They had better also be sent out together in a tin cylindrical case with a lock and key. The case must not exceed a yard in length . . .

12 August, Loiza. To the Hon. Miss Margaret Maria Cocks:
My dear Margaret,
    Just when we fancied we were quietly settled in our cantonments at Monforte an order suddenly transported us, in common with most of the army, over the Tagus. The motive of this change is not known. Lord Wellington either expected or pretended to expect to have remained sometime in the south for he was whitewashing his quarters at Portalegre. General Stewart was building stables, etc. etc.‡ We have changed for the worse in point of cantonments but they say this country is healthier. I do not think, however, place makes much difference, an idle army is generally less healthy than one on the move if the latter is well fed.

---

†A list of his books is in the appendix.
‡It was probably a ploy, with Wellington trying to conceal his true movements.

133

I have not seen Somers for a fortnight nor do I know exactly where the cavalry headquarters will be stationed. Como va el Espanol? ...

Margaret Maria was learning Spanish.

19 August, Loiza. To his mother:
Dearest Madam,
   I only received your letter dated 29th June a few days ago; it was delayed in consequence of being directed to Somers, who is in the north with Sir Stapleton. We have been cantoned upwards a fortnight in this village; it is rather a bad one and not well supplied, chickens are one pound a couple and onions not to be had. I wish we were in motion again. By the quantity of cavalry which is daily disembarking I think an active campaign must be expected after the unhealthy season has passed, that is in October. The 11th are making a bad business of it, they have allowed another officer and some men to be surprised and taken.
   My acceptation of the situation on the Quatermaster General's Staff was merely temporary and with a view to see the siege of Badajoz and the operations of the army of the south. I gave up my situation when my regiment formed part of that army and I was sent to the neighbourhood of Albuqerque with a party of observation. I have been reading *The Secret Cabinet* by Buonaparte. I never read such trash ...

28 August, Loiza. To his father:
My dearest Lord,
   So few events of importance have taken place lately that they scarcely furnish materials for a letter. Even reports have been scarce. Officers exposed themselves so much last year by the absurdity of their conjectures that they have become more cautious this campaign. It appears probable that this state of quiet will last some weeks longer, the enemy is at present too weak to attempt anything against us and I do not expect we shall do anything against him till it is ascertained whether he expects any, and how many, reinforcements, until the unhealthy season is over. Even if, at the beginning of autumn, the enemy should be superior to us I have no idea he will invade Portugal this year. He is probably convinced that force will not expel us and that his only chance is to possess himself, step by step, of the resources of the country, establishing magazines as he goes for his own subsistence and obliging us to draw our supplies from England. But this year there will scarcely be any wheat harvest in Portuguese Estramadura or the great part of Beira because the French were in possession of the country at the sowing season. He would find great difficulty in establishing sufficient magazines for the country and it is remarkable how great an aversion the French have to maize bread and how little use they make of it.
   If we shall find ourselves stronger than the enemy, the most likely enterprise is the siege of Ciudad Rodrigo. I almost doubt whether the French could unite all their force to relieve it as they did at Badajoz, for I think Soult is more tied down to the south than Marmont was to the north and without Soult or reinforcements from France it is probable we could take the place in spite of Marmont.
   The Spanish guerrillas have annoyed the enemy very much; they are very

useful because they oblige the enemy to form so many detachments in order to secure his communication and command in some measure the resources of the country. There will never be any want of these guerrillas, a Spaniard is very vain and fond of an irregular plundering life, he does not care for hardship the least, but cannot bear continual labour. This is just the character for a guerrilla, the Miguelets of Catalonia have been distinguished in all the wars of France and Spain for the last one hundred and fifty years.

As for the rest of the inhabitants, the landowners, the great farmers and the towns people, they are heartily tired of the war and would be very glad to put an end to it in any way. The Spaniards do not possess the inexhaustible patience of the Portuguese. This nation, which in personal appearance and manners is very inferior to the Castilians, in essential qualities is much the superior. I have been astonished that we have not had Spaniards in our pay, once open the door to them and I feel assured officers and men, or men *without* officers, would flock to our standard.

I have been often told that in mountains between Castile and Leon there are 20,000 Spaniards belonging to different corps that have been dispersed during the war, leading an uncertain life, and that would be glad to join any army that would pay and feed them. Led by British or German officers they would make excellent infantry.

The generals and the government of Spain, of course, set their faces against anything of this sort because it goes to lessen their consequence and give us a greater influence in the country than they like, but I do not see why we should attend to their objection or why their veto should prevent our enlisting Spaniards who choose to volunteer. An excellent opportunity presented itself the other day of forming Spanish regiments with British officers without any seeming unfairness.

Several of the regiments which suffered at Albuera had their second battalions in this country. The men were drafted from these to the first battalion so as to make these complete and the skeletons of the second battalions were sent home to recruit. Why should not these skeletons have been filled up with Spaniards?

Headquarters are still in Spain, at Fuenteguinaldo...

30 August, Loiza. To his uncle, The Rev Philip Yorke:
My dear Uncle,
Many thanks for your letter and for the trouble you have taken in copying the plan.† Believe me, I fully and heartily appreciate the sincerity with which you wrote and though I do not agree with all you say I am not the less aware of the advantages to be derived from a consideration of opinion differing from one's own.

I believe less profit is derived from the study of battles than might naturally be supposed. No battle, perhaps not a combat, has yet taken place in describing which, even those of the same side and with the same situation, have agreed. You cannot therefore depend on accounts and much less on places. Principles deduced

---

†Yorke had sent him a detailed plan for approval concerning an education for his son whom he wished to join the army.

from mistaken facts lead to error. In fact, after the fighting once begins, the calm of the troops, the intelligence of Generals of Brigade and Divisions, a thousand accidents usually decide the result. The skill of the Commander-in-Chief is shewn in the arrangements preceding the battle, these can be accurately explained and therefore may be studied and reflected on with effect.

As to religion, I believe heartily and without difficulty in God because I every moment see we are surrounded by a system of beneficent order, which, the more we understand the more we admire. I try all I can to love virtue and obey her dictates and this independent of any advantage to be derived from her. In this study, however, I find it very difficult to be disinterested because to follow virtue closely, appears to me, the same as commencing a diligent pursuit after happiness, and though when swayed by passion I sometimes depart from the rules of my cool understanding, yet I am afterwards inclined to blame myself on the score of folly as well as that of vice.

To love virtue is to love God, because he is the essence of it. To love virtue is to love the doctrines of Jesus Christ, because they contain a system of morality more than human. It is true I cannot consider him as God because he tells us he was not.

The old argument against all this is that it argues presumption to trust the understanding as a mere guide. But this argument, like most that have been handed down from generation to generation, appears not applicable because the understanding is directed by the simple rules of Christ, easily comprehended and easily remembered.

Love thy neighbour as thyself, and lest prejudice mislead us when you doubt, decide against yourself. The simplicity of such precepts renders them at once sublime and useful, virtue does not appear beyond our reach and we are constantly encouraged to follow her. After all, it is beyond man's power always to discern right from wrong. Will not God judge us by our endeavours?

I cannot believe upon trust. If I once begin I know not when to stop. If I am to adopt tenets blindfold because wise men have already adopted and recommended them, I must proceed arithmetically and should perhaps choose the Roman Catholic religion because it has most followers. This is a very useful church to the lower orders of people. Constantly instilling the principle of pious resignation, it gives the common people confidence and even cheerfulness in misery. I cannot distinguish what is the effect of natural disposition and what of their religion, but certainly the inhabitants of this country submit to the dispensations of Providence with extraordinary patience. Looking round on harvests destroyed, homes burnt and friends dead they perhaps drop a tear but they tell you it is the will of God, the due chastisement for their offences and all for their good.

You speak of Bibles – do you know, I am sure I did not know till I came here that the whole of the scriptures is in common circulation in the native language of their countries. Almost everyone who has any books has a Spanish or Portuguese Bible. In the catechism books for children the Latin prayers are on one side and the translations on the other. Altogether, even with us, I believe it is seldom that a congregation follows the sense of the prayers. If the church service reminds man of his creator and disposes him to pray in his own way it is perhaps as much as can be expected.

We have very little news here. Lord Wellington has made repeated reconnaissances round Ciudad Rodrigo and towards Salamanca. Heavy artillery has been sent in that direction and though some say it is sent up for Almeida I think it more probable it is with a view to besiege Rodrigo. I think we shall undertake this siege if we find ourselves stronger than the enemy after the hot weather, but this will depend on the number of reinforcements each army will receive, on the degree of loss by sickness, and in the occupation the Spaniards will give the French.

It is commonly said that we cannot advance towards Madrid even if we had Ciudad Rodrigo because Soult could, in that case, penetrate with a corps to Lisbon. It might be so but this would be feared rather in a political than a military point of view. He might create great confusion there but he could never dare wait for us, it is contrary to all the principles of war for an enemy, whose whole force is scarcely your superior, to divide and allow himself to be bent in isolated corps. Let us recollect too, that in the Seven Years War Austrian Corps were twice in possession of Berlin without producing any ill effects.

I was much gratified by the siege of Badajoz, though unsuccessful. It was a branch of war in practice quite new to me. I had an opportunity of viewing all the operations as I remained with the artillery on the south side from the beginning to the end. Our Engineers were very brave, but it is whispered that they made a trifling mistake or two; for my part, I am apt to believe it.

You probably know my situation on the QMG staff was merely temporary. I only accepted it to gain opportunity of leaving my Regiment, which was then idle, in order to see the siege and the operations of the South. Regimental service is, in my opinion, always preferable to staff employments. Recollect that a staff man shirks all hardship, and while his comrades are snoring in their cloaks under the canopy of the sky or perhaps on piquet, not daring to sleep for twenty-four or forty-eight hours together, my friend on the staff is undressed and lying snug between sheets. This particularly applies to Cavalry. A Staff man never has a command whereas an officer commanding a Squadron of Light Cavalry need not envy a Brigadier of Infantry. And to conclude, a Staff man is not much with secret till he gets pretty high in his department. Colonel Murray[†] may have the key to the great strategic movements of the campaign but your Deputy Assistants have little more to do than to look out for encampments with regard water and forage, and chalk doors for General officers. Certainly had I been inclined to remain I could not have been more tempted than by the situation of QMG to the Cavalry and I certainly got some information as to routine and detail during the short time I did that duty.

With kindest remembrances to your uncle,
Believe me, My dear Uncle,
   Your dutiful and affectionate nephew,
      E. Charles Cocks

---

†Colonel Murray was Wellington's Quartermaster General.

Coimbra
29 April 1809

My dear Somers

For the last fortnight or three weeks I have been so hurried that I have scarce had time to write to any one. You probably heard of my being in Granada. I there bought two horses, & proceeded to join Cuesta's army, where I intended serving as volunteer. my route was by Arched... ... Peiga, & Constantina, the country was most romantically beautiful, being the wildest part of the Sierra Morena. I met with no other adventure than being detained at Lerena as a French spy. I was the 2d stranger that had ever appeared here since the war 'whom'. the 1st had correct passports but afterwards turned out a spy. the Magistrate of the place was a most sagacious blockhead & had inferred from this circumstance that correct passports are a suspicious appearance. on this ground he detained me, unfortunately on examining my portmanteau, he found some receipts of my groom for hay & corn at Falmouth, which being written very ill, he with great gravity pronounced to be memorandum Cyphers. the business began to be serious, as the mob in their zeal for England seemed inclined to insult me. There were a number of ridiculous mistakes occurred, but I have

Part of Cocks's letter to his brother John Somers, describing his first weeks in Spain, 29 April 1809.

CHAPTER SIXTEEN
Heartache

1 September – 2 October 1811

AT THE BEGINNING of September Wellington moved his whole army, bar Hill's force in the south, back to their familiar stamping ground on the Agueda, and Cocks found himself in quick succession in Richioso, Monte Perebolio and Cesmiro, the latter's name intriguing him: 'The old people of the village told me that a certain goatherd of the place had a favourite goat which kidded, and lo! the kid was of gold. He took it to the King who immediately exclaimed, as well he might, "Es cest miro!" ("This is a wonder!") Hence Cesmiro.'[1]

Wellington and Marmont, meanwhile, were about to test each other's strength, the latter determined to re-victual Ciudad Rodrigo and the former equally resolved to prevent it, and amid all the manoeuvring one would have thought Charles had more than enough to occupy him without falling in love, but the heart is never a respecter of situations. Because the Peninsular army was, mainly, cantoned in the country, both officers and men looked to the villages for entertainment, getting up dances in the barns very much as they would today, and since the girls came unchaperoned, the freedom they enjoyed has quite a modern air. Charles, who flung himself into anything social, was always one of the prime organisers of the evenings: 'I borrow two or three clarinets, an octave and a tambourin from some neighbouring infantry regiment and set the girls dancing all night,'[2] he wrote, and it was one of these local maidens, albeit perhaps a little more refined than most, who proved his undoing.†

She was possibly Josepha Siego and her father, Camillo, a wealthy peasant farmer, owned property in Fuentes d'Onoro. He also leased to the military his large quinta, or farmhouse, at nearby Aquila, and everyone from Wellington down was acquainted with him. Besides Josepha he had several sons who were members of Don Julian's guerrilla band.

The year before, presumably for safety, Josepha had been sent to Lagiosa, down the Mondego valley, where she attracted the notice of every officer for miles around, but sometime in the late spring of 1811 she returned home, taking up her former role of belle of the countryside and falling a little in love with Augustus Schaumann, an amoral, mischievous rascal and commissary to the 1st Hussars. He described her as an 'extraordinarily cultivated girl, full of feeling and tender', with a 'steadfast, enterprising, passionate, severe but also faithful character'. In

---

†The evidence is taken from Augustus Schaumann's account of Josepha in his book *On the road with Wellington*, and Cocks's own journal and letters. I am supposing they speak of the same girl; certainly the dates and events match and there cannot have been so many Josephas, similarly placed, in that sparsely populated area.

139

looks she was 'gorgeous, her gait that of a queen', while her body 'overflowed with vitality and good health', and if this was not enough, her figure was 'wonderfully built'.³ All of which must have appeared as a gift from the gods to Charles, wearied from a summer of hard campaigning both in the field and the journal, and he fell headlong for her. His picture of her charms is as lyrical as Schaumann's. Writing to Thomas on the state of the army's health, he said: 'Thank heaven I remain quite well, which I believe is partly owing to the kind exertions of a little Portuguese 16 years old, with eyes black as jet, lips ripe as peaches, and teeth white as ivory and limbs for the Venus de Medici.'⁴

However, this Venus had problems. Her father had affianced her to Don Julian. 'Son brutos,' Josepha described him to Schaumann, eyes flashing. In order to escape her fate she may have decided to ensnare one of the personable young officers instead, her association with Charles being a last frantic bid for freedom, seeing in him, given his ardour and obvious means, a most acceptable alternative. But time ran out. Marriage was the last thing in Charles's mind and her hints of matrimony fell on uncomprehending ears. 'She regarded me her husband,'⁵ he wrote, with more naivety than one would have expected in so worldly a man, and Josepha, in desperation, flung herself on the commissary instead. Nothing delighted Augustus more than an emotional intrigue and, with great aplomb, he spirited her away to live with a respectable family in Cea, adroitly avoiding matrimony as well.⁶

Charles must have been aware of her betrothal. It may even, initially, have added spice to the affair, but he clearly never imagined being supplanted and when, in a flurry of tears and unable to give the true reason, she announced precipitately she was returning to a former lover, he assumed he had been weighed up and found wanting, and the combination of shock and fallen pride drove him into a state of frustrated fury which he poured into the journal, later scoring it through, hence the gaps, although the meaning remains clear.

'September 14 Josepha has left me. Though she loved me it was deluded for the love . . . she would not refuse to go . . . when at a word by the man with whom she had lived one year, poor girl. She regarded me her husband. Her departure has aroused feelings I thought my emotions had forgot, I could kill her myself and everyone I meet. Heaven bless her, poor girl, wherever she is. She deserved a better fate than will now be her lot. Had I seen her a year ago at Lagiosa how few should I envy. I dare not go now. My bed, the scene of so much pleasure, I left on the ground. When she went I shed the first little tears that have wet my eyes since I parted with – I thought I had forgotten this weakness.

Teutio tanta peur; mus he preciro, par forca vai ne embora. I shall not easily forget her.'⁷

And nor, considering the furore her flight caused, could anyone else. Schaumann came under suspicion at once but when the Commissary General sent for him, without disclosing the reason, the wily fellow pleaded an illness and despatched his deputy. This may have delayed matters a little but Siego was not to be put off, going straight to Wellington, and Augustus was forced to return her, impudently assuring the enraged parent that 'she was as pure as she had been when she came to me'.⁸

In the meanwhile Charles was inconsolable: 'Since Josepha left me I could cut throats with pleasure,' he savaged on the 16th. But by 2 October, presumably so dishonoured, the family had given her up, she was back living full-time with him although clearly very unwell. 'I am not quite so gay as when I wrote last,' he told Thomas. 'Josepha, my beautiful girl, is lying a few yards from me, scarcely knowing me from fever. I have been separated once from her but ultimately succeeded in securing her. This letter has been often interrupted by her crying for water and I can even now scarcely proceed while I listen to her heavy and painful respiration.'⁹

And that is the last we hear, although Schaumann tells of her becoming a legend for her beauty and sadness. She seems not to have married Don Julian and may have paid a high price for the weeks of passion.

The day following her abrupt departure Charles wrote to his father. He had been coming under pressure again to give up the army and resume his political life and it was time to scotch the idea once and for all. His words may have been partly chosen with this in view but also influenced by his state of mind, emotions along with politics had no room in a dedicated mind.

* * *

15 September, Cesmiro. To his father:
My dearest Lord,
Everyone appears to think that dissolution of Parliament may speedily be expected. I therefore take this opportunity of begging you will dispose of the seat at Reygate in anyway most agreeable to your views. It is too valuable a gift to be thrown away on me, who derive neither use nor amusement from it. If you thought that being in Parliament would be useful to James's views in life, I beg leave to be understood permanently to resign all wish to be in Parliament. I wish to be a soldier and all a soldier and only a soldier. Happy shall I ever think myself in having selected a profession so congenial to my disposition and ever grateful shall I be to you that you threw no obstacles in the way of my entering it . . .

<small>Militarily, of course, September saw the engagement at El Boden and Charles's letters describe the situation, along with some army gossip, and the continuing problem of his promotion.</small>

10 September, Cesmiro. To Thomas Somers Cocks, Esq:
My dear Thomas,
I believe your letter with Stanhope's inclosure arrived since I last wrote. I agree with you that nothing can be done at present – at least for the moment. But Pelly's† in such a state of health that I think he is going home and altogether I feel nearly certain that some change will take place in the 16 soon, for the command of the Regiment will never be left to the 2nd captain Hay, Murray being at home. I feel the more confident of this as the singular awkwardness will arise of my taking the command of Hay when in the field with other troops and then having to resign it when we separate from them. On the whole therefore I would not let any

---

†Major Pelly of the 16th.

Majority slip through my fingers as I am nearly certain I could arrange to stay here.

Since my last we have been moved up to the neighbourhood of Ciudad Rodrigo. But I am sorry to tell you there is no appearance of a siege, in fact the place is hardly blockaded. Lord Wellington's object has been to annoy the French by making them always be on the move and in this he has succeeded for they must have been obliged to break up from Talavera and draw more in this direction . . .

The 11th continue to expend their men and horses. It is melancholy for anyone who regards the honour of his country or his profession to observe the deplorable ignorance and want of spirit which pervades our Cavalry officers on their first arrival from England. Can you conceive a Gentleman reporting officially 'that the French army had gone to *Castile*', which he conceived must be a *very large town* though he 'could not find it *in the map*, for it held the whole army'. An Englishman by national character is so vain and so much accustomed to underrate the military profession that he thinks if he knows a few manoeuvres he is fully qualified to perform his duty. His own courage he never doubts; till when at length placed in situations of responsibility he finds to his cost that the intrepidity which enables a man to use the powers of his mind in danger is but a rare gift of nature and usually requires an habitual acquaintance with an enemy not to be acquired in the heath of Newmarket and the Purlieus of Covent Garden, nor even Jackson's School.†

The affair of Lt Wood is the more mortifying because the Hussars cut their way through, though he actually called to them from the window: 'Give up my boys, give up. You'll be all killed.' This officer had the same opportunity of escape they had, but dared not make use of it. In his pouch belt was written: 'This belongs to Lt Wood, who came all the way from Ireland with Paddy O'Toole, to tear the Eagles from the French Legions.‡

Living is horribly expensive here, every article has become so dear. A quartillo of wine which used to be 3 or 4 halfpence is now 9d or 1/-, of coarse quality. Colonel Cochrane of the 36 – brother of Lord Cochrane – has got into a scrape, he is in the 6th Division, commanded by Campbell. At the affair of Almeida where, if you recollect, instead of a whole garrison we got only a few hundred men,§ Campbell, at first, was so pleased that he thanked Colonel Cochrane. Afterwards, when Campbell got rowed by Lord Wellington, he, in turn, rowed Cochrane – *I*

---

†A school of pugilism.

‡On 21 August Cocks recorded: 'The 11th Dragoons had a party of observation in the Sierra de Gata, consisting of Wood and eight men, together with one serjeant and eight of the Hussars. Wood was in his walking dress and the horses of his men grazing when 100 French infantry entered the town by a by-road and just as he got a report from the peasants that all was quiet. I believe all the Hussars got to their horses, but two were shot and fell. Three of their horses also fell but the serjeant and six got off, with one of the 11th and five horses. Three Hussars were wounded, one mortally. Wood, seven of the 11th and ten horses captured. Such a mixture of folly and negligence is very melancholy.'

§This refers to the escape of Almeida's garrison after Fuentes d'Onoro. Campbell is General Alexander Campbell who had not posted his piquets very wisely.

believe with reason. Cochrane was nettled at being first praised, and then rowed, and wrote an insolent letter. Campbell sent to him that he must retract it or stand the consequence. He refused to retract and has been reprimanded by sentence of Court Martial at *the head of the 6th Division*. Officers are usually reprimanded in private.

Poor Cavendish Square! I have long ago determined to be neither surprised nor mortified at anything that may be done by a certain relation. I have isolated my own character and my own fame and will either make them by my own exertions or lose them by my own fault.†

> Following Josepha's disappearance, Cocks resolutely returned to his studies and began a 'Sketch of the System of Supply adopted by the Prussians in the Seven Years War, by Tempelhoff', and succeeded it by a résumé of 'Colonel Jomini's modifications of these arrangements', but the fighting caused by Marmont's introduction of a convoy into Ciudad Rodrigo interrupted things. Meanwhile Wellington suffered a blow in the capture of one of his other intelligence officers. 'Poor Grant is taken,' Charles recorded on 20 September. Colquhoun Grant had been a most daring operator.
>
> El Boden saw Charles's old comrades in the Hussars severely mauled and he wrote on the 25th: 'Poor Hussars! I have scarcely a friend left in the regiment. Bergmann dead, Krokenberg dying, Lewis and Krauchenberg and Poten maimed for life, Dekin and Linsingen on the staff. Ernst Poten has likewise lost his arm. These are men not to be replaced.'

2 October, Freixedas. To Thomas Soṁers Cocks, Esq:
My dear Thomas,

Your last letter complained of the stupidity of our operations here. I conclude you communicated these ideas to our Chief and Marmont and that they arranged the manoeuvres of last week in consequence.

To speak seriously, I believe the inactivity of this campaign may be principally attributed to our sickness. Upward of 25,000 on the sick list have obliged our

---

†Lord Soṁers seems to have been going through what one might today term the male menopause. A letter from his wife written about this time shows she was finding life with him very difficult. Charles, for his part, was constantly fending off pressure to give up the army and return to politics, while John Soṁers had told Thomas in July 1811: 'I must say that my father's conduct towards me before I left London and indeed altogether has annoyed me much more than anything else, but I flatter myself that I shall be able to drive even that out of my head shortly, you know a trifle will not make me down in the mouth and having a queer Sire is nothing very uncommon.' By this he was using 'queer' in the sense of being odd. Meantime, all their childhood homes were fast disappearing. Castleditch was to be replaced by something much grander; the family town house in London, in Cavendish Square, was already sold and a smaller one, 22 Great George Street purchased from Thomas Creevey; and the brothers feared Reigate Priory would also go. However, in no way did the disagreements divide the family, their affections remained and all the parties simply accepted each other as they were. It may be that ambition lay at the root of the difficulty. Lord Soṁers wished his sons to make their marks in Parliament, as had, of course, the Lord Chancellor and successive Cockses; this was the road to influence, not through the army, and John Soṁers' departure for the Peninsula too, may have been the last straw.

general to confine his plans to annoying the enemy by never allowing him to be quiet. Too weak to fight the main force of the French, we have been too strong for any isolated army and they have been always compelled to drop every other object and concentrate whenever our demonstrations have alarmed them. How much this was contrary to their wishes may be collected from Massena's orders previous to the affair of Fuentes, where he promised his troops rest and allowed the necessity of it when the immediate operations were concluded.

Lord W blockaded Ciudad Rodrigo the beginning of August. The blockade was sufficiently close to prevent any convoy of importance from entering. Tho' I do not know the exact state of the garrison I have little doubt they would have been reduced to considerable strengths by the end of this month. It was necessary to introduce supplies but we had the 1st, 3rd, 4th, 5th, 6th, 7th and Light Division, with four Brigades of Cavalry, making 40,000 within a day or two's march of the place.

Two convoys were formed at Salamanca and below the Puerto de Baños, Bessières, Suchet – I believe – and Marmont assembled from 50 to 80,000 men to escort them.† Moving concentrically they united four or six leagues to the NE of Ciudad Rodrigo.

Lord Wellington had previously reconnoitred the ground beyond Rodrigo but water and forage was so scarce it was useless to occupy a position which we could not maintain and where our enemy, had he feared to fight us, need only have waited a day or two to have seen us retreat.

He determined, however, to give the enemy trouble. The 3rd, 4th and Light Division occupied Martiago, El Boden and Fuente Guinaldo with Alten's Brigade – the 11th and Hussars. The rest of the army was so near that no one could tell whether it was intended to bring them up or fall back. Marmont was grossly ill-informed. He had not an idea we were so near him in force. The greater part of his army reached the vicinity of Rodrigo the 23rd and 24th, on which days we took the field. The 24th part of the French force was brought over the Agueda by the Bdge of Rodrigo.

The 25th was destined to introduce the convoy; 2,500 French cavalry with two brigades of H. Artillery – 8 prs – were sent to occupy the heights of El Boden to the left of the French, while from 1,500 and 2,000 more with one gun and one howitzer advanced towards Carpio and Espeja.

On the heights of El Boden the French fell in with 5th and 87th and another Regiment of Infantry, 3 Squadrons of the 11th Dns and 3 of the 1st Hussars, under Lord Wellington in person. By universal and uncontradicted accounts the affair was most brilliant. We had a brigade of Portuguese artillery – 9 prs. The French Cavalry charged it and, were in possession of most of the guns. The 5th Regiment were lying down a little distance in the rear. The commanding officer would not allow them to get up till the enemy was close to them. At the distance of a few yards this little Regiment poured a volley into the enemy and, dashing on thro' the smoke with the bayonet, charged the French Cavalry, drove them and retook the guns. Thus foiled in part, the French tried a double attack on our flank.

---

†Weller says that Wellington had intelligence of 60,000.

But as often as he advanced he received a fire from our Infantry and was instantly charged by our Cavalry. He never broke them. Lord Wellington brought off the detachment formed after destroying numbers. I am told 1,000 wounded entered Rodrigo.

On the left we had less to do. Between Carpio and Espeja is a wood. When our piquets were driven from the line of the former I was ordered to support them in the wood with 2 small Squadrons. They advanced with 500 men, leaving the rest in support. I kept them in check a little but was obliged to retire thro' the wood, as they attempted to surround me. On getting through the wood I found three more squadrons formed. I made my arrangements and the instant the head of the enemy column had cleared the wood and begun to deploy, Hay, who had come up with one Squadron, myself and *Brotherton* of the 14th charged with complete success. The enemy – pikemen and chasseurs – scarcely awaited the shock and we drove them to their supper.

Our men were broke; but they are no longer ignorant barrack soldiers and they reformed constantly. We retired, again drawing on the enemy to the top of the wood. He had the imprudence again to come through. He got a volley from the light company of the 11th which had by this time come up and was again charged by us. We drove him all way through the wood and he never afterward advanced but, after waiting till evening near Carpio, returned to Rodrigo.

I was only personally engaged once with a Chasseur and had the fortune to kill him the first blow. We had 8 men of the 16th wounded and some horses killed; the 14th had an Officer and a Dragoon wounded. It is difficult to judge the loss of the enemy because as fast as his men were cut down, if not quite dead they crawled into the thickets and could not be found. We took up a chef d'escadron and 15 men, all wounded. Eight or more lay dead on the road and we afterwards learnt that 21, including four Officers, were brought back to Carpio in blankets unable to sit on their horses. The total loss in killed, prisoners and badly wounded was probably 70 or 80 men. Col O'Fin who commanded the party was killed on the spot. He is an Irishman, a Cork man, and took a conspicuous part in the rebellion. This affair was pleasing, as it is the first time we have had anything to say to the lancers.

Marmont was provoked. He brought his whole army over the Agueda. From 10 in the morning till night on the 26th, I watched a Column near four leagues long which I could see by intervals wending among the hills and concentrating between El Boden and Guinaldo. Marmont knew the position of Guinaldo was bad and only occupied by part of our force. He hoped to strike a blow. But Lord Wellington, having given his adversary all the trouble he could, retired in the night of the 27th. We occupied the position of Alfayates where, from the general to the drummer boy, we looked for nothing more than to be attacked. But Marmont knew better. He had introduced his convoy and after a skirmish in Aldea de Ponte he went back to his quarters and we have taken up ours for the present behind the Agueda and Coa.

Gordon – Lord W's ADC – went with a flag of truce to the French camp and was detained there a few days. Marmont spoke in the highest terms of our Cavalry but complained they gave no quarter. This is not true; we never kill prisoners if it is possible otherwise to secure them. The current report among the French was that two armies are to be formed against Portugal – one in the North under Audinot and one of the south under Marmont. And before operations commence the army of the North is to reduce the Spanish army of Galicia. What is very remarkable, all the French officers, Montbrun was particularly mentioned, positively said that if they did not expel us in a twelve-month, they should never try again.

Other reports are in circulation but they are scarce worth mention . . .

God bless you,
   Your affectionate cousin,
      E. Charles Cocks

CHAPTER SEVENTEEN
Autumn Activities

11 October - 20 December 1811

IT IS POSSIBLE Josepha's illness grew so serious that she had to return home but certainly by the 11th October Cocks was anxious to get away from the army for a while. Everyone was going into winter quarters and there seemed nothing to keep him.

★ ★ ★

11 October Having obtained a fortnight's leave for Oporto I went today to Leomil, leaving Trancoso a little to my right and Celorico to my left. This was about 10 leagues and some part a very bad road. The scenery in general was wild and romantic. The last 3 or 4 leagues I observed all valleys carefully cultivated in Indian corn, there were likewise a few vines.

12 October Lamego: 4 leagues. This stage brought us to the heart of the wine country. All the hills are laid out in terraces and every inch of ground is planted in vines. Lamego is a very good town and was at present our principal depot for supplies; there is a very good road from Leomil to Lamego. From Lamego we descended by a superb cabrazada to the Douro, where we embarked, sending our horses round by Amarante and Tenafil. The navigation of the Douro is a singular one. You are principally impelled by the stream which is very fast, especially in particular points where the falls of the river are very great. The vessels are guided by a large oar fixed to their stern in lieu of a rudder. In going down one of the falls we ran foul of a vessel coming up. This threw the head of our boat so completely out of its direction that it went against the rocks on the other side and we were obliged to be carried stern first almost down the fall. The spot was an unlucky one, being the very same where a boat with General Cameron's sick was swamped in 1808, but we saw the use of the moveable rudder, which continued to guide us even stern foremost. We made about four leagues this day along the river.

13 October Oporto: 10 leagues. We were twelve hours about these ten leagues, the wind was against us and though our men worked well at our two oars, three men to each, yet we got on but slowly.

The novelty of travelling is worn off with me.

Three years ago I should have seen all the churches and all the hospitals and all the conundrums and should have studied very hard the history of the town. I was then like a child coming to a great town for the first time in its life, everything was an object of curiosity. There is nothing particularly worth seeing in Oporto, at least I found nothing out. The town contains 80-90,000 souls and is situated on a steep hill over the Douro. The streets are more regular and the principal ones cleaner than at Lisbon; the houses are furnished more à la anglais but instead of solemn churches and musty tombs I came to Oporto to seek laughing dames and spritely lasses to enliven the dull campaign which had just closed. But I was unlucky in the time I chose, all the best families of Oporto were at the watering places and had not returned to the city for the winter. There were no balls, no concerts, no frolics, I dined sometimes with the English merchants who gave me a quantity of hot port, very good perhaps, but as strong as the port in England. I was not used to it and it got into my head, which I did not at all approve of. Trant is state governor of Oporto with the rank of Brigadier General. The garrison made a respectable appearance on the Sunday parade, two very fine regiments of Militia, one of Volunteers, a company of police guard and two new raised regiments of Caçadores, the 10th and 11th. The theatre of Oporto is very good but the performance detestable; the Portuguese have no delicacy of taste.

26 October Freixedas: 10 leagues. When I joined my squadron I passed by Villa de Ponte, four leagues from Lamego where our heavy train of artillery is, but whether to form the siege of Ciudad Rodrigo in the spring or to throw into Almeida appears doubtful. Nothing new had occurred at the army during my absence except that General Reynaud, governor of Ciudad Rodrigo, coming out from his garrison to see after his cattle, was attacked by Julian's guerrillas and taken with fifteen men. This is a fine hoax against the enemy. He says the next campaign will be a bloody one if Lord Wellington chooses, by which I suppose he means Buonaparte will again attempt to drive us from Portugal. Vain enterprise!

A Russian war is confidently talked of, some think Buonaparte wants an excuse to draw his people from here. I wish the Russians were at peace with the Turks. Probably the French can march to Petersburg if they choose, but the fate of Russia is not involved in that of Petersburg. If Alexander has the magnaminity to give up his capital and fight without a faible†, drawing on the French army into his immense [?] lines, he will play a sure and successful game. If he fights for Petersburg all will turn on a battle, which he will very likely lose.

Grant has escaped from the enemy.

Those unused to war consider soldiers as ferocious characters because they always figure them to themselves such as they are in the moment of action, and constantly associate with their idea that of the destruction of the enemy. But such men should recollect that a soldier only meets his enemy thrice or four or, at the most, a dozen times a year while every day he is called upon to do some friendly office for his comrade, for mutual necessity always makes friends. An officer's usual occupation is to preserve his people in health, in heart and in comfort. Are these occupations unworthy of a mind replete with the most humane and tender sentiments? Even in action it often happens that an officer has to think more how to preserve his own people than how to destroy his opponent although, on certain occasions it is true, that disregarding all ideas of safety for others and for himself, he must think only of gaining the object which his general has in view and is considered necessary for the interest of the army.

14 November Lord Wellington himself told me that had we stood our ground at El Boden on the morning of the 27th the enemy would have retreated. He came to the knowledge of this first through Renant, governor of Rodrigo, who told him

---

†A military and sometimes politically sensitive point.

that on the 26th he was in the rear of the army when an order came to him to serve out brandy from the stores. 'Such an order,' said he, 'with us Frenchmen always precludes an attack.' The brandy was served out at noon. At midnight, to his great surprise, back came two divisions of the Imperial Guard who had been ordered up in the morning. 'The officers,' continued Renant, 'told me that Marmont was convinced he could beat Lord Wellington at Guinaldo but as he expected to lose a great many men, and could not follow up his victory, he had determined not to risk a battle.' Afterwards, however, when he learnt that Lord W had retreated, he brought up his troops again.

24 November, La Puebla de Azava. To his mother:
Dearest Madam,

We have been an unparallelled time, 57 days, without mail from England when the arrival of three was announced. Everyone was on the alert for their letters and papers, when, alas! the dragoon who was conveying the bag for the cavalry fell in the night, lost his horse and lost his bag. I beg you will observe he did not belong to the 16th, who are not in the habit of such accidents. For some days we gave up all hopes of recovering the mail but I believe nearly the whole has since been found, though how I do not know. Among other letters I received one from you dated September 28th.

The whole army in this neighbourhood was yesterday put in motion.

... I hear the object is to intercept a convoy the enemy want to throw into Ciudad Rodrigo; we have received no orders for today and shall not, perhaps, again move until tomorrow.

This alert has put a stop to our gaieties which we are rather proud of. Lord Wellington keeps foxhounds which hunt twice a week and have already killed three foxes. Several theatres have been established. At the Guinaldo theatre, set on foot by the Light Division, I saw Henry IV the other night, got up very respectably. We are now taking our turn at the outposts and are cantoned between the Agueda and the Coa. We relieved Slade's brigade and expect ourselves relieved about the 20 December when it is said we shall go to Covilha, one of the best towns on the frontiers of Portugal. No military operations of consequence are expected for some time.

The last pound of tobacco you sent me was incomparable. I regularly in and exhale it after breakfast and dinner. We are living pretty well but necessaries are dear, we have been of late very badly off for forage and I never saw my own horses so low. It is currently said Lord Charles Manners is likely to command us as an exchange is on foot between him and Colonel Archer†. I hope it may be true.

Somers was very unlucky in failing as to the majority of the 3rd Dragoon Guards, though perhaps there are more eligible regiments, yet it was a great object being in this country. I have just heard Headquarters moved this morning to Fuenteguinaldo. The weather is extremely cold but fine, very hard frosts every

---

†Clement Archer, currently commanding the 16th. Cocks had known him since 1803. He was plagued by the gout and finally died in 1817 and a plaque commemorates him in Boughton Monchelsea church in Kent.

morning, indeed for the time of year full as cold as in England...

27 November ... In cantoning cavalry in villages men of the same mess should always be put together and I like to see the men live and sleep in the same stable with the horses; their accoutrements are not so liable to be stolen, they are more handy for a turn out and they grow fonder of their horses by being constantly with them. The Arabs, who love their horses, always keep them in the same tent with themselves. In general it should be a rule to save the health of your men in preference to that of your horses. When a man feels hearty and strong he will work to find forage for his horse and otherwise provide for his comfort. I lay down this rule as much in motives of interest as unanimity. On wet or cold days I would always march an extra league or two to get my dragoons under cover. Infantry who have nothing to do at the end of the march but provide for their own comfort do not require to be nursed like cavalry. I would always put the latter in cantonments first.

29 November The army is ordered back to its former cantonments, my squadron marched to Ituero... We are feeding our horses on acorns, those of Spain are all from the holm oak, sweet and rather pleasant to the taste, they make pigs fat and why not horses? Perhaps they would not do for hard work but we have scarce any duty.

> John Somers, all this time, was still with Stapleton Cotton but his stay in the Peninsula was drawing to a close. The following is written by him from Lisbon.

December, Lisbon. From Captain The Hon. John Somers Cocks to Thomas Somers Cocks, Esq:

My dear Thomas,

Owing to unpropitious winds your letter of 1st October did not reach me till the latter end of last month, since which time I have been so much on the move, as you will perceive by the date of this, that I have not had much opportunity of writing. From Alverca we marched on 24 October nominally in guard of a convoy but in my humble opinion our Great Man thought proper once more to collect his army in the neighbourhood of Ciudad Rodrigo for some purpose which did not enter our wise heads. On the 29th we marched towards Covilha, a most beautiful town, at least for Portugal, and more beautifully situated than any town I ever saw before.

Sir Stapleton only remained there two days which he employed in inspecting the 11th Light Dragoons and 1st Hussars and also in attending a most gay Ball given by the latter regiment. The room abounded in *Diamonds* and other precious stones, and some fair faces. We danced upwards of 20 couples and many jealous husbands prevented their wives from dancing.

On the 4th we proceeded to inspect General Le Marchant's brigade, consisting of the 4th and 5th Dragoon Guards and 3rd ditto, my friend and brother Captain, Gabriel, is Le Marchant's ADC. The 5th Dragoon Guards being quartered only 80 miles from here, we pushed for a fortnight's holiday here. Three marches have nearly put out of my head the inclination to disappointment I must acknowledge that I felt at my failing in my attempt at the Majority of the 3rd Dragoons Guards.

However, it is not for mortals to command success and I certainly do not deserve it. Many thanks are due from me to you and those friends who exerted themselves for me. I do not approve of wasting one's strength without sufficient grounds, I therefore shall remain quiet till I can see or hear of another fair opportunity of promotion. I heard of your joining the Merry party at Castleditch, and that you have since returned to the Metropolis where I do not think it very improbable we may meet before the month of April . . .

> With the long winter days before him his brother Charles returned to his journal and correspondence. He wrote a long comparision between Frederick the Great's campaigns and those of revolutionary France in 1792/3/4 and then began a treatise on 'Hints for a Patrol', and this last can be found in the Appendix. He was as disappointed as John Soṁers with regard to promotion because the hopes of obtaining Stanhope's majority seemed to have disappeared, that gentleman having gone back on the agreement, and he had to start all over again.

5 December, Ituero. To Thomas Soṁers Cocks, Esq:
Dear Thomas,

Tomkinson of the 16th has got his brother to purchase two horses for me in the spring. Shall you therefore be so good to answer his drafts to 250 guineas. I enclose a letter for Tommy Nickolls† who can bring them out to me as also any parcels.

I have written to you since your last letter to me and have therefore no news to send you. Stanhope's conduct is unaccountable but I have some hopes of a Majority in a Light Dragoons Regiment out here. Will you send by Nickolls 3lb of Tobacco and 1 of Snuff, not scented . . .

> The 'Merry party' at Castleditch, which John Soṁers mentioned, had occasioned Margaret Maria and her cousins to make a giant pudding and afterwards she had sent Charles a long poem describing the event. With time hanging heavy, he wrote one in return and it is a good indication as to how he spent his evenings.

6 December, Ituero. To The Hon. Miss Cocks, Miss Jane Cocks, Miss Harriet Carew:
My dear Sister and my dear Cousins,
Don't talk to me of puddings!!! Here we do nothing but dance:
It would really do your heart good to see the Spanish lasses prance,
And all our merry boys find in it such amusement
That paisanas, young and old, there's none but they manage to use 'em in it.
If you could see the dress they come in you really would stare

---

†Nickolls was one of his servants. Originally Charles brought out John Day but, after the Oporto campaign, had been forced to send him home, the reference declaring: 'He leaves me in consequence of the state of his health which renders him unequal to the fatigues and privations of service,' adding: 'He is perfectly honest, attentive, clean, good-tempered and remarkably sober . . .'[1] Boverick followed, but he, too, collapsed under the strain and Nickolls, about to arrive, had already been out once and was then returned to England because he could not cope and was more of a liability than a help. In general, Charles found the best servants were either locals or, on one occasion, a man who had just left the French service!

Their shoes are like our great-grandfathers, with the toes almost square.
Their petticoats are made of a dark brown stuff
And though rather homely, yet it's better than coming in buff.
Their stockings are mostly blue, with red and white clocks
Always pretty coarse, as indeed are likewise their smocks;
They are, however, mighty clean with little cuffs round the wrists and neck
And so nice in their linen you can never discern a speck.
Besides this, they wear a little cloth jacket of black or green
It fits the body quite close and discovers whether they are fat or lean.
The colour of their garters I leave to the knowing in such matters
You know the old proverb about the man who kisses and chatters.
I shall only tell you to make my account more complete,
That, take their dress all in all, and I think it very neat.
About seven or eight at night when we've done smoking
We make the music strike up and in they all come flocking.
Our music, by the by, we get from some neighbouring cantonment
For there's scarce a village near us but what has a regiment in it –
We borrow clarinets or a fiddle or perhaps a drum or fife –
So you see, for quiet comfort, there's nothing like a soldier's life.
Well, we get eighteen or twenty girls, good ones and bad ones,
And we all fall a-capering just like so many mad ones.
The rooms here are never boarded and they are mostly of clay
So you may easily conceive what a dust flies in every way.
When we've kicked our heels, until saving your presence
We're rather hot,
We sit down on the benches just with the partners we happen to have got,
And you must plainly understand we've no senhoras or splashers
For the little villages we're in don't boast such grand dashers.
Ours are honest peasant girls who make pork sausages all day
And at night divert themselves in their own quiet way.
When we sit down some of the natives come forth,
They always sing and dance together as a matter of course.
Their instruments are only a key and a pewter platter
It's no great music but it makes the devil of a clatter,
And they keep such time to their fandangoes and Malbrook
That faith, they sometimes jig till the very walls have shook.
Well, you know it would not do to send the girls off without eating
Particularly after such determined fagging and sweating,
So we generally give them some light things for supper,
Fried pork steaks at the lower end and garlic sausages at the upper.
We wash this down with vino, which we let them drink at will,
And then send them home contented when they've had their fill.
And so, God bless our noble King and the Army of Portugal and Spain,
And grant we all may meet to dance at Castleditch again . . .
   Your affectionate brother and cousin,
      E. Charles Cocks

About 20 December he drafted a letter to his uncle, the Rev Philip Yorke, but failed to despatch it until he reached Cea in January. It is in answer to a further one from Yorke on his son's education:

My dear Uncle,

There is no part of your letter I feel more inclined to answer than that where you mention you wish to educate your son Philip as a soldier. Perhaps you will give no credit to the ideas of six and twenty on education but if you find nothing worth attending to, you can at least burn my letter. If you think it may be worth a second thought keep it, as I will a copy, and should I hereafter find reason to change any opinion I may now express I will write you word that I have so.

An education founded on Military views is now more necessary to an Englishman than to any nation I know, because the habits and ideas he learns at home are less assimilated to a soldier's life than in most countries, while, at the same time there is nowhere where it is less understood. A mind free from prejudices, impressed with liberal and philanthropic ideas, love of his profession and emulation in it, with a sufficient ease of behaviour to render him at home in society which is strange to him, will enable a young man to distinguish himself in the army much sooner than having Dundas and even Tempelhoff by heart.

Philip's delicacy of temperament I consider no objection now, look at the weak boys who fill the ranks of our battalions, see how well most of them get on and you will easily imagine, with the superior luxuries an officer possesses, our hardships are in general more imaginary than real.

A plethoric robust habit is more liable to disease than a spare one, and for one who falls sick for want, a dozen die from the gross habits of eating and drinking which they have formed amid the plenty of England.

Another cause of illness is our national stupidity which renders us averse to conform our habits to those which are necessary in foreign countries. I daily see men pining for home comforts and neglecting those and amusements which are within their reach. The novelty of a soldier's life renders a young man on first joining his regiment very anxious, if well disposed, to learn the details of his profession. Six months suffice to teach him right face and left face, I therefore would not bother or tire him on this subject before he joins, it is throwing away precious time.

I like to see a young man on first joining his regiment with the air of a gentleman and not of a serjeant-major. For this reason I dislike Marlow. Boys there either become disgusted with duty and on joining break loose into all manner of idleness and extravagence of behaviour, or they learn to be military pedants and to despise the advice of those who, though they do not step just 30 inches every pace, know how to fight their enemy when they meet him in the field.

What I am saying and going to say, must, however, be taken with this caution, that the different branches of the profession require a degree of difference in education. The service of light cavalry to which I have been always bred is nowhere taught in England and, beyond a few general rules, can only be learned on service and by a reflection and observation in the field. The service of the line requires more routine but I think this routine is better gained after a man joins than before it. For the artillery and engineers, previous theoretical knowledge is certainly necessary but I conclude your son is not destined either to the one or the other.

A soldier, to be a good one, must love his profession, should know how to amuse himself within himself, and should have that sort of spirit which does not like to be outdone and yet is sufficiently restrained not to attempt distinction by any of those fashionable absurdities so much the vogue in England.

Everyone says history is useful to a soldier – very true. But it is not a dry knowledge of chronological facts but a familiar intimacy with the great military characters of ancient and modern days, and a sufficient acquaintance with the history of the last two centuries and a half to understand what is said by others on the military interest and power of states, and sometimes to speak himself without fear or danger of exposure.

Memoirs of heroes and military anecdotes easily rouse boyish enthusiasm and teach the young spirit those principles of courage, patriotism and ambition which have formed and guided great men. A man never reaches the summit of his ambition but his progress in the world is usually in a ratio compounded of his talents and the extent of his views. The latter depends on himself and he cannot therefore raise them too high. With a little assistance from older and wiser heads the young soldier will learn not to expect fame at once, but to wait with patience and forward with industry the happy moment when glory will reward him. Most of our young Englishmen are so anxious to distinguish themselves at sixteen that, being able to excel in nothing else, they mount a mail coach to astonish the natives. They drive with éclat to twenty-five thinking they have gained their point, but what the world laughs at in a boy it despises in a man. At twenty-five, with habits too formed to change, they dwindle into insignificance and gradually become so many Pogy Powells. Alexander and Caesar learned how to act before they began to act.

I need not mention the necessity of modern languages; French is indispensable, I cannot speak it fluently and there is not a day I do not feel the loss. Latin so completely includes the principles of European tongues that I esteem it highly useful. At the same time I lament that our Latin grammars are so pedantically written. This language is much more like Spanish/Portuguese and Italian than anyone would suspect who had only considered it in the light it is taught at Eton and Westminster and, if taught in the way they are taught, would be much more useful in facilitating their acquirement.

In Germany, statics is a regular branch of education. I wish it was the case with us. Under this head I include the Geography, Resources and Population of States, the Principles on which they are governed, how their military force is produced, etc, etc. There have of late been some very good travels written on this subject which it would be very well for a young soldier to peruse.

A general acquaintance with the Seven Years War to be learned from Lloyd, Tempelhoff and the King of Prussia's works and a tolerably correct knowledge of the late war from the year 1792 is highly desirable. It is however, sufficient to be at home with the locality of the campaign, the numbers employed and lost and the general causes usually assigned for the failure and success of the respected operations. A young man who has not served should not attempt to learn more, he cannot comprehend the grand principles on which tactics and, above all, strategies are founded.

To complete this theoretic education, I would add that sort of arithmetic which is taught in Dalby's Course of Mathematics, Geometry as far as the first six books of Euclid, plain Trigonometry, the first principles of Natural Philosophy and the mechanic powers; Algebra as far as quadratic equations inclusive, with the Principles of Fortification as taught in the two first books of *Essai Generale de Fortification*.

Perhaps you will be surprised at what I am now going to add, but I must highly recommend a knowledge of music, dancing and drawing, or *at least* some two of these accomplishments. Fencing, too, is a capital exercise. When once a soldier becomes a prey to ennui it is all over with him, he is first sorrowful and then sick, but a man will always get ennui unless he has the power of amusing himself for we cannot think for ever, especially at nineteen; a soldier is continually changing his society and sometimes left without any. Put a man among strangers and they cannot know his sterling virtues, they can only judge of him by his manners and appearance. If he can sing and dance he makes nine out of ten his friends, he passes his evenings gaily and pleasantly, picks up perhaps some useful information and rises in the morning with a light heart and a clear head, ready to set to work at his duty; while his unharmonious comrade avoids society because he cannot excel in it, perhaps gets drunk for want of something to do, collects a quantity of black bile and turns out in the morning with a gloomy face and a grumbling air, enough to frighten the very sun behind a cloud. It is worse when a man is left by himself without much duty, as sometimes happens, especially in light cavalry. You think we have a great deal to do but I can assure you there is nothing we really dread except having nothing to do. On these occasions some, especially the new hands from England, give the matter up, go to bed, report themselves sick, or disgrace themselves by selling out in disgust, others call literature and fiddling, mathematics and dancing, in a word sense and nonsense, to their aid and get through the business cheerfully and well.

Sterne's 'Gascoigne Roundelay' should be a soldier's motto: Viva la joia, fedom la tristesse. Thus I think of the sort of education previous to joining which is most likely to form a proper spirit and to give the young soldier both the will and the power to make himself happy and distinguished in his profession.

The more he is accustomed to content himself with two meals a day and take his rest with his clothes on, the less, of course, he will feel these things when obliged to practise them. Such habits are only hardships to those who have formed others; the Spanish peasant would be astonished at the idea of undressing in order to sleep. But it is easier to say what should be learned than to point out the means of how it is to be learned. Few useful things are taught at a public school yet it is a great disadvantage not to have been at one because then a young man sets out in the world without any friends of his own standing. For my part, I should send a boy there from twelve to fourteen if merely with these views. Previous to twelve and from fourteen till he joins it certainly is of the utmost importance that he should imbibe proper ideas and should ground himself in useful military knowledge.

When he enters the army he cannot go abroad too soon and then, though he may have plenty of time on his hands, yet he will not be able to carry many books with him and his unsettled life will not be favourable to habits of study and mental requirement. I am the more convinced of the necessity of previous preparation in order to form a good soldier because, amid the many hundred young men of spirit who compose the officers of our army, I meet with very few who are soldiers in their heart. Thank God, however, that number is fast increasing for those who have come out boys have grown up in the military habit.

A soldier must regard his regiment – or if on the staff, his military station – as his home. He must sigh after no particular spot and no particular country. If allowed leave to visit his family he must call it *going out* on pleasure. Years must elapse before Philip can hold a commission, circumstances so change in the interval that it is impossible *now* to say what will *then* be the military line most eligible.

One word more generally on the profession. Few regard soldiers in their true light, that is as a body of men giving up many individual pleasures and comforts for a general national advantage, coupled certainly with the hope of personal fame and at the same time preserving more individual independence than any class of men. Englishmen cannot comprehend this because they confound a selfish love of individual licence of action with patriotism, but love of liberty if applied only to self is an interested and consequently base feeling. A man only deserves honour for jealousy as to the freedom of society at large, considering himself not more than his neighbour. Men unused to war and ignorant of its ways regard soldiers as pernicious characters because they always figure them as intent on the destruction of their enemy, but a soldier only meets his foe now and then and he is every day engaged in reciprocal offices of kindness with his comrades.

The officer is more employed in thinking how to make his own people comfortable than to kill his adversary; for my part I think there is much less ferocity in putting your foe to death when you see him aiming at your life, than in coolly rejoicing in your cabinet at home at successes purchased by the blood of thousands.

Your dutiful and affectionate nephew,
E. Charles Cocks†

---

†Whether Yorke followed his advice or not is unknown but young Philip James, 1799–1874, became a colonel in the army as well as a Fellow of the Royal Society.

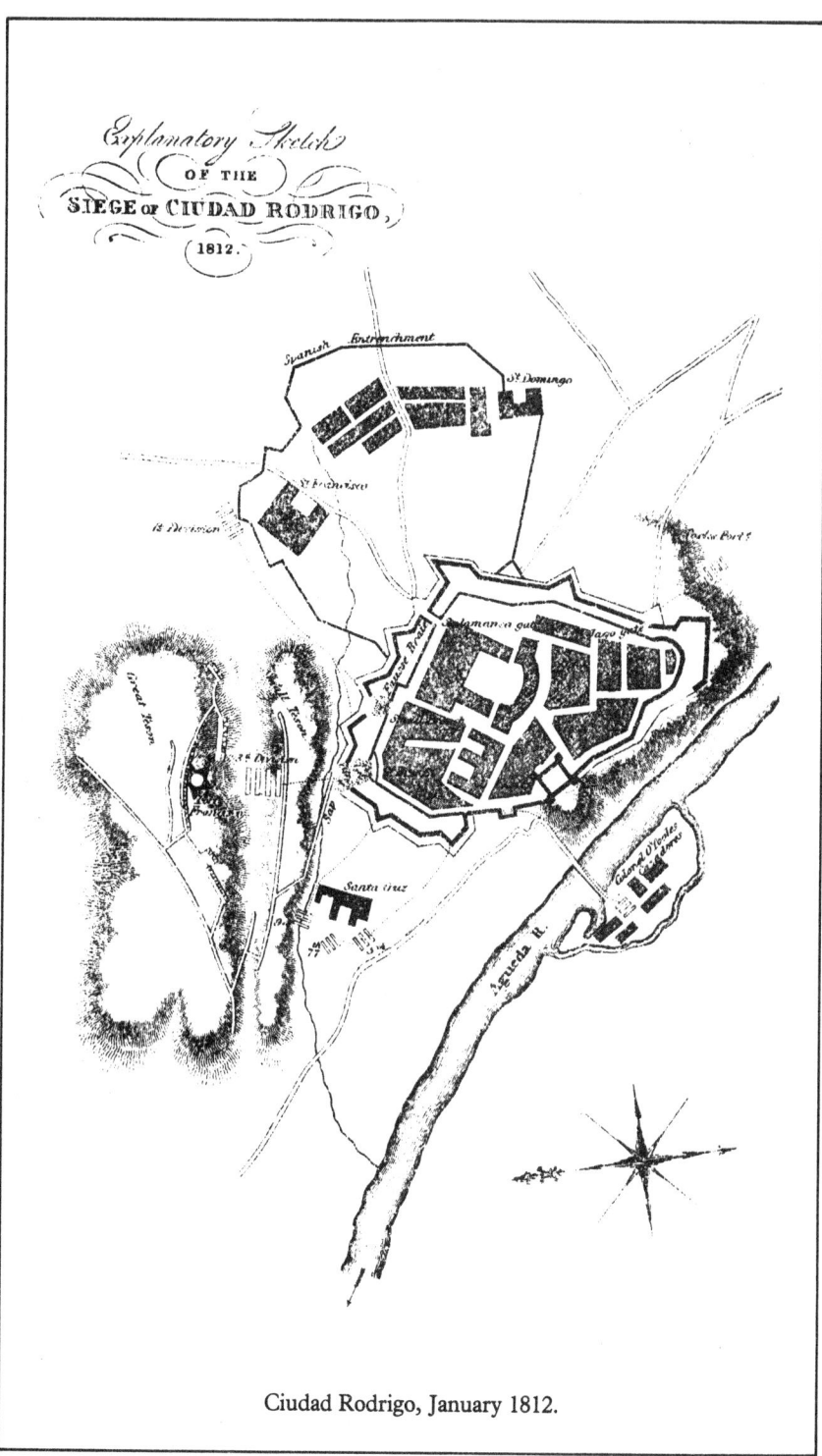

Ciudad Rodrigo, January 1812.

CHAPTER EIGHTEEN
Ciudad Rodrigo

27 December 1811 - 30 January 1812

WELLINGTON FULLY INTENDED besieging Ciudad Rodrigo in midwinter and once the heavy guns had arrived from Oporto, so disastrously lacking at Badajoz in June, he began the final preparations. Meanwhile, possibly both to deceive the enemy and to procure more forage, the 16th set out from Ituero on New Year's Day for the Mondego valley, marching in the worst weather Cocks had known. However, a week after their arrival orders came for them to retrace their steps back to the frontier and, with the siege commencing, Cocks obtained permission to watch it, along with Felton Hervey and William Tomkinson.

★ ★ ★

27 December We are making a bridge over the Agueda at Mollino de Flores and Major Sturgeon† has the direction of it. It is a planked one supported on trellises and will be finished the first week in January; half the army is employed in making fascines, gabions, etc. We are rapidly getting over our sickness. The engineers have orders to hold everything in readiness to besiege Rodrigo in a fortnight... The Corregidor escaped from thence the other day and he says the garrison receives only two ounces of meat and half a pound of bread as the daily ration. They have pulled down a great many houses in search of corn. Our cavalry is very badly foraged, we get scarce any corn and live on the miserable sour, dry grass we cut ourselves and have, in consequence, lost several horses. Since July our brigade has lost upwards of 130 of which the 16th have furnished above half...

31 December, Ituero. To Thomas Somers Cocks, Esq:
My dear Thomas,
There is no pleasure I enjoy so purely as increase of happiness to my friends ... I wish you and Agneta a thousand happinesses. Now, if you love as you ought to do, you will thank me more for the last 1000 than the first.‡

I sent down a mule a month ago for my cantiens but they are not to be heard of yet at Lisbon... If we have a dull campaign next year as we had last I shall have

---

†Sturgeon was an engineer and a specialist in bridge-building. In private life he had married the fiancée of the luckless Robert Emmet, the Irish rebel, and her early death in 1808 had shattered him.

‡Thomas's engagement may have woken an old memory. Back in February 1808 five of them had dined one evening at Jacquier's Hotel in Bond Street and composed the following.

'Whoever of the present company first enters into the holy and honourable state of

time to read through the Bodleian Library; I will therefore thank you to order the following books. Books are never thrown away, as when you have read them yourself they make most acceptable presents.

> Ferguson, *Lectures*
> Rousseau's *Nouvelle Eloise*   These books are in my library
> *Essai General de Fortification*   and may be sent from there.
> Adye's pocket *Bombardier*
> Blair's *Lectures*

With anything new you may recommend. NB: Tobacco will always be acceptable.

I had a letter from Somers last night and from the contents judge you have seen him before you will this. I am sorry he has gone home.

10 January 1812, Cea. To his father:
My dearest Lord,

I thank you most heartily for the friendly kindness with which you have applied to the Commander-in-Chief† for my majority. This step is, at present, my main object and as I have now served nine years within three months and as seven years only are required, I feel very great hopes that your application will perfectly succeed. Indeed, it would be very hard if my brevet rank should check my obtaining regimental rank as, in that case, so far from being of advantage it would be of considerable disservice to me. I know that Lord Wellington has just recommended me for the purchase of a majority. If therefore your lordship's application should as yet not be wholly successful his letter, which will arrive by the same post as this, will probably assist in smoothing difficulties.

General Anson, too, has gone to England and will, I am sure, be ready to recommend me any way that will appear most desirable . . .

We are now all occupied in preparation for the siege of Ciudad Rodrigo. Marmont has gone to Valencia to assist Suchet against Blake and if what I hear be true, is too far off to interrupt us. He probably presumed that we should not attempt a siege at this season of the year but the rains have not yet set in and at present we shall suffer nothing except from the cold . . . My own squadron has nothing to do with it but I have obtained leave to attend as a volunteer. If ground is broke tonight as is expected, we may hope, according to common chances, that the place will fall by the beginning of February. The garrison is said to have been reduced by sickness to 1,000, composed, with the exception of three companies of

---

Matrimoney shall give the rest a dinner to be considered according to its goodness as the criterion of his satisfaction in the marriage State within one year from the day of the ceremony.

> Jacquier's Hotel,   E. Charles Cocks
> Bond Street,   H. G. Clive
> Tuesday evening   G. C. Agar
> 9th feby 1808   T. Somers Cocks
>   John Craufurd.'

Thomas subsequently took this home for safe keeping and it is still in his family.[1]
†The Duke of York.

Jacquier's Hotel matrimonial declaration, February 1808.

good artillery, of troops of an inferior description. The governor's name is Barrier, I never heard that he has distinguished himself. When the siege begins it will probably be carried on with spirit as the engineers and artillery were not a little piqued by their ill success at Badajoz last summer. There, however, they had an insufficiency of artillery and what they had was very bad. Now we have a most beautiful train of English iron guns . . .

13 January Last night a route arrived for the brigade to march to Alverca and Freixedas, we halted at Sanpayo and Villa Cortes . . . The siege has commenced, Hervey and myself set out for it tomorrow.

15 January Arrived at Gallegos where we found headquarters established. The snow which fell on the first and second of this month only delayed the siege one day, everything was ready by the 8th. Since that day the weather has been perfectly favourable, clear, sunshiny, frosty days, the night rather dark but not so much as to impede working, the moon in her first quarter. Though the frost appears above ground as hard as in England, yet it does not sink so far into the ground and render it too hard to dig. Though the governor, General de Barrier must have had information of the fascines and gabions which we were making, yet it appears that he considered them only as demonstrations to deceive Marmont and had no idea we really intended to besiege the place.

Ciudad Rodrigo is situated on a rising ground close to the river Agueda which runs at the foot of the hill on which the rampart is situated on the south side. It is surrounded by a strong Moorish wall about twenty feet, forming an irregular oblong without bastions and with very few towers. The ditch is seven feet deep. On three sides which are not covered by the river a fausse braie has been erected of masonry, nine feet high, with ravelins at intervals which afford a very imperfect flank fire. There is a ditch in front of the fausse braie and beyond is a glacis with a counter scarp of masonry but no covert way.

Three hundred yards from the western front is the Convent of Santa Cruz and four hundred and fifty yards from the northern front, opposite the Salamanca gate, is the Convent of San Francisco. To the east of the convent are the suburbs, separated from the glacis by an esplanade of three hundred or four hundred yards. Opposite the north-west angle is a hill called the Tero de San Francisco, distant six hundred to seven hundred yards. This hill commands the town. There is another small hill between the Tero de San Francisco and a glacis, lower than each. All the gates had been closed up except the Salamanca, to the left of this was a small ravelin in front of the fausse braie. Opposite the north-west angle the fausse braie formed a small re-entering angle which was completely a dead angle. Over the Agueda was a stone bridge.

On the Tero de San Francisco the enemy had erected a sod redoubt, forming two faces to the front with the ditch pallisaded; behind it was open to the fire of the place and its gorge only closed by pallisades and chevaux de frise. He had calculated that this would require five days to reduce, probably thinking it must be shelled. The garrison consisted of a French regiment, a German and Italian one forming 1,400 or 1,500 effectives, with 160–200 excellent artillerymen.

On our side the 1st, 3rd, 4th, and Light Divisions were destined for the siege, each taking the duty for twenty-four hours and finding everything for that period as well as working as covering parties. Five hundred men were, on the average, constantly at work. The remainder of the army was closed up to within three days' march and General Hill's corps [?] the Tagus in order to join, should the concentration of the enemy's force render it necessary.

Thirty-five 24-pounders and three 18-pounders, all beautiful iron guns belonging to our battering train, had been brought up. We had two companies British artillery, some German artillery and the Portuguese regiment of artillery number 4. The artillery was under the direction of Major Dickson of the Portuguese service; Col Fletcher was Chief Engineer.

The advantage of approaching within seven or eight hundred yards under cover was so great as to decide Lord Wellington on attacking the place from the Tero de San Francisco. This was the side in which the French attacked it and it was to be expected that the new wall, built where they had breached, would not be so strong as the old one. Lord Wellington was said to direct the works. It is a principle of his to avoid the use of mortars: 'The way to take a place,' I heard him say, 'is to make a hole in the wall by which the troops can get in and mortars never do this, they are not worth the expenditure of transport they require.' Well, this is very well against such a place as Ciudad Rodrigo, but it would sacrifice men against a more respectable fortress.

On the 8th the place was invested and the Light Division came first on duty. A party of volunteers from the 1st Division, headed by Col Colborne and Major Gibbs, attacked the fort by surprise and carried it an hour after dark. Finding their ladders rotten, they stuck bayonets in the sod and ascended it in this way. An officer of the name of Mayne was the first who got in. The French made a feeble resistance. Two were killed and forty-seven, with several officers, made prisoners. One man only escaped. The garrison, on first hearing the fire, almost all came out of the place and finding by the huzzas of our people that the thing was done, they returned. Our party lost three killed and twenty wounded.

It was so little expected that the place would be invested or carried with so much vivacity that no preparation was made in the town for opening a fire, which enabled our warring parties to get on well. They were only annoyed by a 9-pounder and a small mortar in the convent of San Francisco which, as well as Santa Cruz, was occupied by the enemy.

The first parallel was completed this night, above 700 yards from the glacis. Poor Ross of the Engineers was killed.

On the night of the 10th Santa Cruz was carried by the Germans of the Legion, the garrison escaped.

On the night of the 11th, the 40th Regiment drove the enemy out of San Francisco and the [?], they were ordered to keep possession of this convent for the remainder of the siege.

The divisions took the duty in the following order: Light, 1st, 4th, 3rd, under Generals, Craufurd, Graham, Colville and Picton. The divisions when off duty returned to their cantonments and as they had a good way to come and go the relief took place at midday. The day on duty they had an extra ration of rum.

On the 14th the enemy made a sortie on our works, they were repulsed by the 42nd, who were just going off duty, with trifling loss on both sides. Our average loss had hitherto been fifty per night. In the afternoon of this day the batteries opened, one was in the first parallel, the other two in front of it. They contained 26 guns of 24. Their fire was directed principally at the north-west angle and the dead angle of the fausse braie opposite to it. In the course of the 15th most of the enemy's heavy guns were silenced but he continued a very brisk fire from the mortars and some light guns in the fausse braie and different parts of the rampart. A breach was commenced to our right of the north-west angle, close to it and almost including it.

16 January It was so foggy the greater part of this day that the breach could not be seen from our batteries; this, however, was the less consequence as we were rather short of ammunition.

The fog enabled our sappers to work boldly, they got on well with the second parallel, 400 yards from the place, and commenced a fourth battery in front of the first parallel, 500 yards from the place to our left of the other batteries, and much nearer the convent of San Francisco.

17 January The breach continued to improve notwithstanding the enemy had partially cleared it in the night. We had a few sharpshooters buried in holes to fire at the embrasures but they did little good. One of our guns burst today and occasioned some casualties, it had been struck by a shell yesterday which perhaps caused this accident. Another cause was also assigned: we had 8,000 Portuguese balls, the calibre of which are probably larger than ours, but these 8,000 had been picked out as the smallest from a great number and had been thought not too large for our guns. Perhaps one had accidentally been brought which would not ram home.

18 January Our guns were got into the fourth battery tonight and it opened this morning. The fire was directed along the ditch of the small ravelin near the Salamanca gate. By this means it ran the fausse braie to the very foot. Last night the field howitzer and the 9-pounder threw shells and case on the breach. By night the main breach was practicable and the breach of the fausse braie was practicable to the left.

19 January Both breaches were shelled and cleared by case from field howitzers and guns. A good deal of our fire was directed against the defences; the enemy's fire was infinitely less brisk.

It being evident early in the day that both breaches would be practicable by night, Lord Wellington determined to storm at 7pm, that is an hour after dark. The main breach was allotted to the 3rd Division which was on duty. The left breach to the Light Division, the next for duty. Four attacks were made. The 5th Regiment under Major Ridge had orders to assemble between the Convent of Santa Cruz and the river. At ten minutes before seven they were to advance to the point where the fausse braie joins the main wall, in order to escalade the fausse braie and from thence proceed by the main ditch and join General McKinnon's brigade at the breach. They were provided with, I think, six ladders of twelve feet, they were supported by the 74th.

General McKinnon's brigade, 88th and 45th, were to storm by the main breach, they were to move at seven, had ladders 24 feet long and were preceded by their flank companies as a storming party.

Storming of Ciudad Rodrigo, 19 January 1812.

The Light Division, 52nd, 43rd, 95th and 3rd Caçadores, were to move at ten minutes after seven and storm by the breach near the Salamanca gate. They were preceded by a storming party of 300 under Major Napier, who were picked from 600 volunteers.

General Vandeleur's brigade followed the storming party.

General Pack's brigade, 1st and 16th Portuguese, were to make a false attack by escalade on the west. Each ladder was carried by three men without arms, the different columns had orders to separate to the right and left along the rampart after reaching the top of the breach. Parties of tirailleurs were ordered to fire on the embrasures but the storming parties were to use the bayonet. The main breach was near thirty feet wide, its slope formed an angle of 50°, comprised of crumbling earth. The left breach was not above ten feet wide, steeper, and comprised of large stones which gave a good foothold, it had, however, this inconvenience that the breach on the rampart was not opposite the breach on the fausse braie.

The parties moved forward at the hour appointed, the 5th got to the breach first, destroying in their way some guns which might have taken the 3rd Division in flank. The enemy kept a fire of musketry upon them but threw few or no grenades and fled when the party had nearly gained the summit.

The 5th, joined by the 88th and 45th, possessed themselves of the breach but their work was not done. The enemy, by traverses, had separated the breach from the rest of the rampart, the column could not proceed, it remained opposed to the heavy fire of the musketry.

Meantime the Light Division stormed their breach. After some little delay in looking for the breach of the main wall, the 95th turned to the right, the 52nd to the left; the enemy in the houses opposite the main breach, finding the 95th in their rear, abandoned the houses and all resistance ceased.

At this moment the commandant of artillery sprung in train a skit communicating with a [?] magazine in the rampart, which exploded destroying French and English. General McKinnon was killed. The Governor, if ever he was on the breach, had by this time left and concealed himself in his home. He was made prisoner by an officer of the 95th, who took him to Lord Wellington who had now entered the town. The Governor wished to surrender his sword to Lord Wellington but he directed the officer to take it, 'Keep it,' said he, 'for you deserve it.' This officer had led the forlorn hope, his name was Gurwood.

All resistance was over. Our men were not bloodthirsty and gave quarter almost in the breach. Maj-Gen Craufurd and Vandaleur were wounded; Major Napier lost an arm. 450 men were killed and wounded.

Considerable confusion ensued in the town. Our fellows plundered most of the night but I am afraid they got very little. There were very few Spaniards in the place. Some accidents occurred from our people firing at the windows under the idea that the houses were occupied by the Frenchmen.

We made about 1,300 prisoners. General Pack's people had escaladed the fausse braie and afterwards got into the breach. The town got on fire by accident and many houses were burnt, it is in a wretched state.

20 January The 3rd and Light Divisions returned to their cantonments, the 5th

Division was brought into the town and instantly set to work destroying our works and repairing the breaches.

Last night was a proud one for our infantry; altogether the siege of Ciudad Rodrigo reflects the greatest credit on Lord Wellington and all engaged. In eleven days we have effected what employed the French nearly 25 when the town was not so strong. Lord Wellington's correctness in choosing this moment for the siege proves the exactness of his calculations. I would not be Marmont's aide de camp to report the event for a year's allowance.

22 January Left Gallegos . . . and went to Fuentes.

23 January Almeida. This place is still in a miserable state . . .

24 January Rejoined my regiment at Freixedas. We have been tolerably off for corn but have had to go five leagues for forage.

26 January Received orders to hold ourselves in readiness to march at a moment's notice. Poor Craufurd is dead. He was a zealous, hardy and indefatigable officer who had studied his profession thoroughly and was fond of it. But he was obstinate, violent and sometimes peevish though his personal courage was unquestionable. He was confused in action but altogether, considering what some of our generals of division are, he is a loss to the army. I am sure he will be regretted by the soldiers of his division for no man had his troops so well supplied.

30 January At ten o'clock am we received a route to march to our old cantonments near Cea . . . Our means of transport have of late been so deficient that it has been impossible to get up the articles of camp equipment necessary before we can again take the field. The troops therefore will be drawn back towards the Tagus and the Douro in order to fit themselves out from the depots which have been established on the rivers. The troops on the Tagus will be ready to assemble in the spring in the Alemtejo for the siege of Badajoz.

CHAPTER NINETEEN
Winter Letters

1 February – 15 March 1812

A PERIOD OF QUIET followed and Cocks returned to his writing, completing treatises on Piquets and Chains of Posts before returning to his study of Frederick the Great's campaigns and then reviewing Vestot's *Revolutions de la Republique Roman*. On the social side he found Portuguese friends aplenty, the widow on whom he was billeted in Cea got up musical evenings, and in a village near Santa Marinha he, 'met with a singular character who was a desembargada, a judge I believe, of Oporto. Without having been out of Portugal except once, as far as Salamanca, he spoke French perfectly and understood English virtually well. He translated offhand some of the most difficult passages in Shakespeare and *Hudibras*† One word in Brutus's speech at the beginning of Julius Caesar which I did not think English he was able to explain, to his great delight; and in referring to Johnson‡, he was right. He had a good collection of the best English and French authors which he told me formed part of a very large library he had at Lisbon. He was evidently a man who had read a great deal and who possessed quickness to understand, and memory to retain what he perused. But he had studied principally without object and consequently without system. There was a good deal of miscellaneous information to be collected from his diversity but he flew from idea to idea faster than I could follow him.'[1]

In the middle of February Sir Stapleton Cotton gave a ball at Covilha and a group of them walked part of the way over the mountains to attend, according to Tomkinson, 'over the steepest and highest hills I ever passed.'[2] But an orderly caught up with them, en route, taking to Frederick Ponsonby, commanding the brigade in Anson's absence, orders to commence the march to Badajoz, and the next day they had to retrace their steps.

On the family side James was preparing to make an extended visit, touring the unoccupied parts of the Peninsula, and letters flew between Charles and him over the next few months.

Tomkinson, too, had good news in February when he was appointed to command a troop and left Cocks's. 'I before refused the command of a troop out of his squadron,' he wrote, 'and would not have taken this had it been out of the one under his command.'[3]

* * *

---

†The Rev Nash had published a new edition of Butler's *Hudibras* in 1793. Cocks would have been very familiar with the work.
‡Samuel Johnson's dictionary.

2 February, Santa Marinha. To The Hon. James Somers Cocks:
My dear James,

Your last letter gave me very great pleasure and I will give you every hint I can to render your tour as little troublesome and inconvenient as possible.

In the first place you are perfectly welcome to use my name in any way you like for security as to the £500. For your dress I recommend you not to bring your Yeomanry uniform, at the same time a military dress of some sort is necessary and you had better get the following articles. A pelisse with black lace lined with fur or something warm. Nothing looks so bad as an ill-made pelisse; get it, therefore, made by Schultz, a German tailor, or Chambers; do not employ Somers's tailor or mine. There is hardly any tailor in London who can make them and when ill-made they make a man look most ungentlemanly and ridiculous. A blue great coat, a blue cashmir waistcoat and another of buff. Two pairs of blue or grey loose trousers, they are cool for summer and in cold weather you can wear any number of drawers you like under them. Two pairs of boots, either laced or strapped. One pair of shoes. Six changes of linen, if you are in the habit of wearing flannel, of course you will continue it. Instead of neckcloths I should recommend a black stock of velour or leather. A cocked hat, rather low than otherwise, a cap for common use from Bicknell, the corner of Bond Street and Piccadilly, the same as the one I had from him when in town last. You will, of course, bring a sword, your Yeomanry one will do, with *black* belt and *sabretache*. A brace of pistols. Two English saddles, one for yourself with holsters and a small military valise fitted behind. Recollect that nothing will plague you so much as sore backs, therefore take care that your saddles are well stuffed, strong and very high over the withers so as not to press on any horse's shoulders. The pad which supports the valise should be large, forming one with the pommel of the saddle. The valise should on no account be stiff but made of cloth and be flexible; a small piece of oil skin will keep it dry. Your other saddle should be contrived to carry a common-sized pair of saddle bags behind. Cuff or Gibson will be the best saddler to have these things from. Two military bridles. Two good blankets to put under your saddles when travelling and to sleep in at night. A large cloak made of *cloth* and lined with baize to come well up about your throat and cover your feet when riding. A small dressing case, rolling up, holding two razors, a penknife, a pair of scissors, a corkscrew and your tooth brushes. A similar rolling case holding a knife, fork, spoon and teaspoon to go always in your sabretache. A small canteen to sling on your shoulder holding about a pint or a pint and a half; another for your servant holding somewhat more. Two or three small tins to fit one into the other in which you may boil tea or coffee or make a stew, to be tied to the side of your servant's mule. A small frying pan, a silver cup for yourself, holding near half a pint. This cup, your dressing case and two changes of linen and your shoes, you had better always carry in your own valise behind you, together with your cap, which will serve as a night cap.

I will write to Casamajor, Secretary of Legation at Lisbon, begging him to show you any civilities in his power. I likewise enclose a letter for him which you may personally deliver. I will likewise write to Capt Walton, 4th Dragoons, who commands the cavalry depot at Belem, three miles from Lisbon, to the same effect and I likewise send you a letter to him. The packets generally anchor off Belem, in which case perhaps it will be best to go at once to him, to the Cavalry Barracks at Belem. I am sure he will do everything he can to be of use to you. Enquire likewise for Serjeant Drawbridge, 16th Light Dragoons. He will perhaps be useful in getting anything you may want. It will be a good thing to get a letter to Mr Stuart, our Minister at Lisbon. It is said he is going to the Brazils and that someone else is to be Chargé d'Affaires in his absence. You had better enquire about this and, if it is true, get the letter for the Chargé d'Affaires, whoever it may be.

Arriving at Lisbon you had better purchase a good Portuguese or English horse, I should think a Portuguese should answer your purpose best and you might get it for about 200$. Likewise, a very strong mule, a macho or he mule is preferable, to carry your servant and baggage. This you can get for 120 or 125$; recollect that your horse and mule must be of the same *sex* or you will have great trouble.

You can very well amuse yourself in Lisbon while you are making these purchases. Bear in mind that the girls are very hot for anyone who does not know the town. It will be a great convenience if you can come up with some officer, which you may easily manage as some such or other is continually coming up from Lisbon to the army. By this means you will be enabled to draw rations with him. Consult on this subject with Capt Walton. Wine in Portugal is carried in skins, you had better buy a small skin holding about six or eight quartillos, or half pints, to carry with you; a new skin usually gives the wine a disagreeable taste, a seasoned one is much better, but mind that there are no holes in it.

When you leave Lisbon carry with you a pound of tea or coffee, some sugar and pepper and a little brandy. I would recommend you to put a spoonful or so of brandy in the wine you get in the country as it sometimes affects the bowels of those not used to it. Dollars in Lisbon cost 5/6 though in the army they only go for 4/6. It would therefore be a good plan to purchase as much Portugal gold in London as you can. Take care not to get Spanish gold which does not pass in Portugal and take care that it is full weight, there is great cheating on this subject.

Immediately on your arrival if you will write to me stating any difficulties etc, I shall perhaps be able to give you some further hints; you had better not leave Lisbon till you have my answer. When there, I usually go to La Tour's Hotel, he is a Frenchman, but there are others kept by Englishmen, you have probably seen Somers before this, he has been more in Lisbon than I have and can therefore tell you more about it. At Belem, Barnes's hotel is one of the best. I conclude you bring your servant with you, he has been a groom and of course will have no objection to taking care of horses, a servant who would not take care of horses would be only an encumbrance. Very little grooming is necessary, the great thing is get them plenty to eat. An oil skin cloak, in addition to your other, is no bad thing, it keeps out the rain and renders it unnecessary to put on your other cloak, by which means you have that dry at night to sleep in. Your servant should have a cloak . . .

11 February, Villa Nova. To his father:
My dearest Lord,
 . . . I wrote to Bromley [unidentified] last post in answer to his letter. Lord Wellington recommended me six weeks ago. Some fine day I shall hope to see my

name in the gazette, I have very nearly served my time for a lieut colonelcy and that rank, once obtained, I am settled as promotion afterward goes by seniority and nothing except occasionally a piece of good fortune can forward or impede it . . .

Currently our quarters are good and we have here some society out of the army. The Portuguese are not so gay and lively as the Spaniards but they are fond of music and singing, which amuses our evenings.

Barrier, the late governor of Rodrigo, was apparently a man of little talent. I dined one day in company with him at Lord Wellington's and he had the indelicacy and folly to take advantage of the liberty allowed him as a guest to abuse the Spaniards, calling them Des Geaux† and to justify the conduct of the French in the Peninsula. Lord Wellington gave him a hint to be silent, 'N'en parlons plus, monsieur,' but perceiving this had no effect he was obliged to say: 'Monsieur, je vous ai dit n'en parlons plus, voulez vous parler encore quand j'ai dit, n'en parlons plus;'‡ there were several Spanish officers at table. Headquarters are still at Frenada but they will probably soon move to Castel Branco and from thence to Elvas.

> On 18 February the brigade began its march south to Elvas and the forthcoming siege of Badajoz. With Ciudad Rodrigo in his pocket, Wellington aimed to capture this second fortress, and gateway into Spain, in the spring, but to conceal his intentions he sent the regiments on a very roundabout route.

26 February Torres Novas: 3 long leagues . . . The army is stealing imperceptively into the Alemtejo, and probably in order to keep up the farce Headquarters will not move until the whole is ready to assemble. The directions in which the divisions first moved after the siege of Rodrigo would have left the enemy to suppose the army was separating in all directions for winter quarters. One division I believe moved on Oporto. No general understands the art of unexpectedly assembling his army on a given point better than Lord Wellington . . .

7 March, Aviz. To Thomas Somers Cocks, Esq:
My dear Thomas,

Since there has been a British army in the Peninsula there has been perhaps but one occasion more anxious than the present one, namely those few days which succeeded our retreat to the Lines during which it was uncertain whether or not Massena would attack us in them.

I believe the whole army is now south of the Tagus or crossing it. I can hear of no troops left behind, except that it is reported there is a brigade of the 5th Division still in Rodrigo. The Light Division, which is the last in order of march, is to arrive at Niza today or tomorrow. I believe Headquarters leave Frenada tomorrow and are to be at Elvas the 11th. Lord Wellington has kept them quiet as long as possible, probably to withdraw the attention of the enemy from the movement of the troops and to induce him to believe our preparations were not so forward as they really were . . .

---

†He probably meant 'dago', the derogatory term for a Spaniard, derived from 'diego'.
‡Wellington asked him to be silent.

I am ignorant where our battering train is, mortars and block carriages for guns have, I know, been sent some time back from the north, but I know nothing certain as to the guns themselves . . . I expect that Badajoz will be invested soon after the 12th and I calculate that it will hold out four and twenty days from the night we break ground, exclusive of interruptions from the enemy . . . If a general action is fought in the neighbourhood . . . and we have the good fortune to gain a victory, the most magnificent prospects are opened to us. The common idea in the army is that we should make a movement on Sevilla and endeavour to clear Andalusia and raise the siege of Cadiz. I do not believe it. I believe we shall march on Madrid. My squadron is in good order – fatter, of course, when green forage shall come in – my own horses in excellent condition. I have a good stack of health and since I have been in the country never felt more sanguine as to what is to be hoped from the approaching operations.

We are about ten leagues in rear of Elvas, in a very pretty village. We have been almost constantly on march since the 18th when we left Cea . . . We arrived here yesterday. I am very anxious to hear from England and learn what effect Lord Wellington's recommendation of me has produced. You see Stanhope is rewarded for his eminent services by a lieut colonelcy, probably he was glad to be excused again facing his old comrades. Hay has got the majority, he was unlucky enough to break his arm yesterday.

The officers of the 16th are very anxious to present a meerschaum pipe to our old trumpet major, John Dyter, and have deputed me to order it. Perhaps you would undertake the commission. The value is to be twenty guineas. Perhaps Eliot, silversmith to the regiment in Oxford Street, somewhere near Margaret Street, would execute the commission well but it is left to you to choose this. The tube should be a short, plain one and the ornament should bear an inscription to this effect:

> To John DYTER, Trumpet Major and Serjeant,
> 16th Queen's Light Dragoons.
> After 30 years service, the officers of his
> regiment presented this pipe in token of
> their esteem for his character as a man and
> as a soldier.

We are very anxious that the pipe should arrive safe, etc . . .

15 March, Aviez. To Thomas Somers Cocks, Esq:
My dear Thomas,

The last night we got our letters and papers to the 26 Feb by which I find I am a Major in the 79th or Cameron Highlanders. The 2nd battalion to which I conclude I belong is in England. I shall go to Headquarters the day after tomorrow to arrange my staying in this country. If I could manage it, I should prefer doing duty with the 16th for the pending operations. I am now looking forward to a lieut colonelcy, for which I have served my time.

I have little news to add to my letter of the 7th. Headquarters arrived at Elvas the 11th and are I believe still there. The whole army is in the neighbourhood. I still have not heard that Badajoz has as yet been invested, though it may be considered as blockaded, two divisions with some cavalry being in front of it. Cavalry headquarters are at Olivenza. We march tomorrow for Villa Viciosa, it is said the enemy is concentrating at Llerena. If this latter piece of news be true it may delay the commencement of the siege. The enemy can only be concentrating with an intention to fight us and endeavour, by a victory, to put Badajoz in security. This must be his object for he cannot long remain concentrated. Want of supplies and a necessity of acting in other quarters would soon oblige him to disperse. But if an opportunity offers of fighting the army before the siege, it will be our interest to profit by it rather than fight him after beginning the siege. We shall be able to bring the whole of our force into the field and shall not be embarrassed to provide for the security of our heavy train, etc. It is said that the garrison consists of four thousand men, badly off in all respects. If they are short of provisions this will give us the option of a battle.

I have always forgot to mention that Trumpeter Gorse died of a fever while I was in England, being absent I know nothing of his effects, but I have since got £4.13.6 prize money due to him which I will be much obliged to you to remit to the widow.†

I have received my canteen, saddles, etc perfectly safe and am very highly pleased with them. I have as yet heard nothing of the maps.

Believe me, dear Thomas, Ever most affectionately yours,
E. Charles Cocks

---

†Gorse was his trumpeter. On 17 Jan 1811 Cocks had written to Thomas, 'The bearer whose name is Gorse is wife to my black trumpeter. Will you be so good as to allow her 16 shillings on my account.'

CHAPTER TWENTY
All Points of the Compass

4 April – 23 May 1812

Preparations for the siege of Badajoz began on 18 March and, acting once again as a volunteer, Cocks remained in the trenches until 3 April when the French advance to its relief required the cavalry to fight on the outposts. Aficionados of sieges can find his daily account in the appendix. He missed the storm, of course, and instead his journal gives the lively cavalry engagements. Gone, however, were the days when the 16th, 14th and 1st Hussars alone kept the enemy at bay; the army was now much larger and operations were so involved that his descriptions, in the main, can only cover his local view. Meanwhile, James had arrived in Lisbon and one or two of his letters give another picture of Portugal in the middle of this war.

★ ★ ★

4 April, Lisbon. From The Hon. James Somers Cocks to his mother:
My dearest Madam,
   We are in daily expectation of a packet from England, the arrival of which I am looking forward to with great pleasure. My balcony offers a beautiful prospect of the mouth of the Tagus, from whence I take a view of the vessels sailing backwards and forwards with my telescope. I am the more anxious for it to arrive as I shall set out very soon on my visit to Charles. The French have been good enough to retire so that if they persist a little longer in this retrograde course they will leave me a large part of Spain to explore; there is no further news than I mentioned in my last letter; I have not heard from Charles again and do not expect to do so as he is in the outposts and could hardly have time I should think to answer my letter before I should set out from Lisbon.
   I have been so much taken up since I came that I have not been able to explore the country much but the views about the town are very beautiful; I have bought a mule and a pony besides my own horse. I was told my baggage was too heavy for one animal so that I have been obliged to get a pony in addition and a Portuguese lad whose name is Luis, who understands English, Spanish and Portuguese; when I reach the army I shall probably be able to disencumber myself of part of my equipage. I have received great civilities here and have dined with Mr Stuart and Admiral Berkeley whenever I chose; General Peacock† has also been very civil; he has been very useful to me in procuring me an order for drawing rations and a route; I dined with him the other day; I went last Tuesday to the opera which is in fact a play; it concludes with a ballet and a musical farce; the farce was

---

†Commandant of Lisbon.

the most entertaining part; comic humour seems best adapted to the talents of the Portuguese; I quite longed to be able to understand what was said; the theatre is uncommonly handsome tho', like the Portuguese themselves, dirty and dingy; it was ill-lighted and the performance I thought poor, particularly in the dancing. However, it certainly has the advantage of our English theatres in the good order and regularity which is maintained in it.

It was a new sight to me when I went last week to the Church of San Domingo, to see the aisle of the church lined with soldiers who were posted at stated distances; tho' every corner of this immense Church was full nobody was crowded; nobody was allowed to go far up the church who was not decently habited; yet all were satisfied and probably everybody heard better than he would have done in an indiscriminate crowd.

Last Saturday was the end of Lent and I heard nothing could be more ridiculous than the grand preparations which they were making for a supper at night; not a moment was to be lost; but at twelve o'clock at night they were to repay themselves for their long abstinence . . . I have just had a letter from Charles dated 1st April . . .

> The same day that James wrote home his brother moved up to the outposts beyond Badajoz carrying permission to act as a Major with the 16th for the coming operations. Charles's next letter is to his mother, written after Badajoz had fallen and the French had retreated.

15 April, Ribeira. To his mother:

Dearest Madam,

Since my last letter the storm of Badajoz has added a new laurel to the Earl's brow. Ciudad Rodrigo is not to be compared with it, Philippon had a very different garrison and was a very different man to Barrier. A town has perhaps seldom been defended better or carried in a more daring manner.

We had a pretty affair with the enemy's cavalry the other day. Young Soult, brother to the Marshal, who commands their cavalry, wished to show Count d'Erlon how light he held us and waited for us with an immense body of cavalry between Villa Garcia and Llerena. We fortunately had two brigades up and drove him 2 or 3 miles over a plain till he got under the protection of his infantry and guns . . . I had no personal adventure except that in coming in contact with a French hussar we rolled over each other. I was on my legs first and with a coup de sabre invited him to surrender. But I lost the best dragoon in my old squadron, a man who loved me as if he had been bred up with me. He died of his wounds the next morning. I am at present attached to the 16th Dragoons but have, of late, had an independent command of two squadrons in charge of the avant poste. We are now on march for the north, our whole army is in the highest spirits and the enemy is in the most miserable state of despondency. If you have any commission for Madrid pray send it soon lest it should not arrive till we are on the other side . . .

> With both Ciudad Rodrigo and Badajoz in their hands, all appeared to be going well for the Allies at last, but Marmont still posed a threat to Rodrigo and during the coming weeks the army marched up and down the frontier, from south to north and back again,

Charles remarking on 3 May: 'In the last 32 days my horse and I have marched upwards of 500 miles with only two days' halt...'¹ James became unwell in Lisbon and so delayed his departure, while his brother, moving from village to village, got wind of some lieutenant colonelcies up for sale and wrote urgent letters to Thomas asking him to find the necessary cash, for purchase, by raising a mortgage on the estate Nash had left him. Well aware that his father would be appalled by such a decision, considering it throwing money away when he could have a political career for nothing, it had to be kept very quiet.

22 April, Niza. To Thomas Soṁers Cocks, Esq:
My dear Thomas,

I enclose an order on Collyer† to make over to you the amount of the sale of my troop. I have at present some very flattering views of promotion and therefore write to Price‡ that he must have something forthcoming in case I should want it. James has not joined me yet, therefore I do not know exactly what has been done about the mortgage.

I am very sorry you did not give Collyer more encouragement when he mentioned the lieut colonelcy of a Cavalry Regiment now in Portugal. It is always well to have two strings to my bow. The instant I was gazetted Major I applied to Earl Wellington§ about a lieut colonelcy and he is anxious to do everything he can, if I can make a bargain, to carry it through for me. I have a negotiation on the tapis but we have been so much on the move lately I have not been able to get a positive answer. I will write to Collyer by this post.

The storm of Badajoz cost us about 3,000 men. The Governor's precautions were admirable. Had it not been for the Escalade of the Castle, which was Earl Wellington's favourite idea but not relied on by the Engineers, I suspect it would have been an affair manquée. The obstinacy of the Light Division is admirable. The town was plundered for four-and-twenty hours and thoroughly sacked. I was obliged to leave the siege three days before the storm in consequence of the advance of Soult.

We had a pretty affair on the 11 at Llerena, with young Soult. General Perémond's Division of Cavalry got a great dressing ... Marmont has been pursuing the system of all generals who are conscious of their own weaknesses; attempting to draw us from important objects by a diversion against those of less consequence. This miserable system can only succeed against weak generals. We are now on our march northward to clear Beira of his plunderers. So many reports are in circulation that I know not what to credit, but my own opinion is that he will be off over the Agueda before we can bring him to action.

The future operations of the campaign depend so wholly on our means of supply that I cannot divine them as I have no means of knowing yet what magazines are in Almeida, at Elvas, or even at this place. If the Earl could subsist his army I should not be surprised at our advancing direct on Madrid through Plasencia; but I do not know the resources of that country. I do not think the

---

†Collyer was an army agent.
‡Price was probably a lawyer.
§Wellington had been made an earl after Ciudad Rodrigo.

enemy has been there since Xmas. Soult expected us to have followed him. I know not where he meant to have stood, but it was very evident he had no intention of defending the entrance of the Sierra Morena. His army diverged at Llerena by two routes: one column marching by Guadacanal and Constantina on Lora del Rio where is a flying Bdge over the Guadalquivir; the other column marched by Azuaga and les Pedroches de Cordoba, on that city, the keystone of Andalusia.

We have magnificent prospects before us. If the Wellington star shines bright and clear I shall win my hogshead of claret this year by marching into Madrid.

Ponsonby commands our Brigade, who with fair luck will make the best Cavalry General in our service. I am doing duty with the 16 as Major ...

This next letter is from James, who had started out from Lisbon and reached Abrantes.

26 April, Abrantes. From The Hon. James Somers Cocks to his mother:
My dearest Madam,
I am much obliged to you for your letter of the 29th March. I flatter myself that you have long ago heard from me; how many I may receive from you that come by the Portuguese post office I do not know as they are exposed to the examination of every person, and many, so I am informed, have the abominable impertinence to pay for other people's letters either through the curiosity of reading them as the hopes of finding money. If you envelope them as I did mention to you they will come by the English post office and will be more secure. The Portuguese are universally negligent of every public trust and duty. I believe this arises partly from indolence and partly from ignorance of public principle. Their sum of public virtue consists in implicit obedience, this renders them easy to be moulded into any form as long as they are considered as mere instruments, but whenever they have any responsible situation, whenever anything depends on their activity and attention, they do it ill. They talk incessantly but are very little inclined to exert themselves; I find them extremely civil at the houses where I am billeted, they appeared to consider me as a guest rather than an intruder; on my part I am always inclined both from interest and inclination to treat them, too, with particular civility; they have a comical mixture of pride and equality in their manners; they are uncommonly formal and make a great point of the little circumstances of etiquette; at the same time it is difficult to distinguish between the masters and servants, they are both equally mean and dirty in their appearance and seem equally deficient in respect towards each other. I am now speaking of the middling classes in the Country; the great men of the village, the Fidalgos, of course receive more respect.

When one is abroad, news from home is greedily received. I was very glad to hear an account of your parties at Ryegate ... I do not mention John Somers, because I flatter myself he has recovered of his aguish symptoms;† if he should not have left you before you receive this, pray tell him I have sent a brace of letters to York after him.

---

†John Somers was now home and on a posting to York. In 1809 he had taken part in the Walcheren expedition which, in common with many who served in the operation, left him a chronic sufferer from ague.

I have been pleased with all the other towns I have passed thro', but Abrantes is the most horrid, disagreeable place I ever was in; my days' journeys have been Sacavem, Villa Franca, Azambuja, Santarem, Gologao and this odious Abrantes. Yet it is finely situated on the summit of a gigantic hill; the country on every side of it is uncommonly bold and beautiful. I am looking anxiously forward to another cargo of letters ...

27 April, Headquarters, Fuenteguinaldo. To Thomas Somers Cocks, Esq:
My dear Thomas,
I have now an arrangement on the tapis in which if I succeed I shall have reason to consider myself a most fortunate man. But I fear a considerable sum of money will be required. It is of so much consequence that I do not scruple to tax your friendship – as James is out of England – to learn from Price what money he can produce. I write to him by this post, telling him that he must be answerable to produce £3,000 with security for £6,000 more immediately.

My profession is everything to me. Such an offer as I now have may never occur again. To obtain a lieut colonelcy at this moment when a brevet is expected would be most fortunate. Price must raise the money if he sells every acre of land I have.

I know not whether I shall be able to succeed although Lord W knows of my plan, approves of it and will do all he can to forward it. I have three people to manage and although all their interests are concerned in acquiescing yet some unaccountable obstinacy on one or other may occasion a difficulty. Two however I am pretty sure of. The 3rd I shall see the day after tomorrow.†

When I mention £9,000 I take the outside but £2,500 will certainly be wanted immediately. I conclude money arrangements to such extent will create considerable confusion in my affairs. I shall therefore endeavour to come home for a month the first opportunity afterwards.

Marmont has been making a most beggarly expedition. He partially invested Rodrigo March 31, plundered Covilhão and Castel Branco and ultimately retired on our advance before April 26 ...

The brothers finally met on 3 May at Aviz and for nine days sat in the sunshine exchanging news. Their father was about to lay the foundation stone of Eastnor Castle and James had brought the plans out with him to show Charles. Old, rambling Castleditch was to be demolished and a splendid replacement, designed in the Gothic style by Robert Smirke, would be built on rising ground to the west, its terrace facing south across to the Malverns where an obelisk had already been raised on one hill. 'I trust when finished it will answer your expectations in comfort and magnificence,' Charles wrote to his father. But even before completion his mother entertained reservations over the distance between the dining room and kitchen, foreseeing a lifetime of cold dinners for successive generations of the family.‡

---

†It is possible he hoped to buy the lieut colonelcy of the 16th.

‡A carved fireplace from Castleditch was taken to Reigate Priory where it still stands, incongruously, in a classroom.

Eastnor Castle in the 19th century.

The time was fast approaching for Cocks to join the 79th and, together with Tomkinson, he and James spent a week in Lisbon, ostensibly to kit up but they enjoyed themselves as well. Meanwhile, up on the frontier Wellington's plans were reaching maturity. He had resolved to cross the border and march on Salamanca, and in order to join the advance the trio in Lisbon broke up, with James setting out to see Setubal before rejoining his brother and the two officers riding post haste for their regiments. The following letter is written by Charles at the start of this mini-holiday.

22 May, Lisbon. To his mother:
Dearest Madam,
Here I am in the capital of Portugal diverting myself with sea-bathing, eating strawberries and visiting senhoras and going to balls. In a few days I join the 79th; it is a Highland Regiment and I assure you I make a very respectable figure with the bonnet and tartan. We look forward to something very active this year though we are still in suspense exactly what it will be. James is here and very well, he intends making a tour by Setubal and Evora and meeting me again in a fortnight . . .

22 May, Lisbon. To Thomas Somers Cocks, Esq:
My dear Thomas,
I enclose three orders on Collyer – as you desire – for my three commissions – Cornetcy, diff. to Lieutenancy and diff. to Troop. I cannot specify the sums for I do not know what they are – but if this should be necessary you had better send me the correct form of the orders . . . My immediate prospects of a lieut colonelcy have vanished but I expect to bring Major Lawrie round, who is the only obstacle to my obtaining the rank in my own regiment – All prospect of returning to my old regiment is at an end by old A—selling to P—y.†

I am now at Lisbon equipping for the Highlanders, having got leave to join the battalion here. I shall be with them in a week or so . . . I do not regret leaving the cavalry at this period, no man is fit to rise to command who does not know both arms. The cavalry is a fine service for subalterns and captains, affording most opportunity to this rank of officer to act individually and obtain individual reputation. But it loses these advantages as you rise higher and when not doing outpost duty it is often dull. It gives you less opportunity of society and knowing what is going on beyond your immediate sphere. Of course, since the cavalry has been so much increased, the regiments have had each less to be in advance. I am therefore glad to leave the arm. As for the division I have got into, it has done very little hitherto, but as the 2nd Division at Albuera, the 3rd at Rodrigo and Badajoz, the 4th at Albuera and Badajoz, the 5th at Badajoz and the Light everywhere, there is only the 1st (mine), the 6th and 7th to push forward. The 7th is a light division and not much esteemed, so I trust we shall no longer be in reserve if there is anything to be done. Sir Roland Hill with part of his corps, is marching on Almarez where the enemy has erected a fort on the other side the bridge and collected a depot. He has with him scaling ladders and a brigade of 5½-inch

---

†Almost certainly Lt-Col Archer and Major Pelly.

howitzers designed to throw 24-lb shot, a new idea of the Earl's. On the 15th he was a day's march from Truxillo, stores and artillery well up. Neither the peasants nor the enemy had an idea of his intentions, he hoped to reach Almarez the 20th and surprise the enemy.

I have shaved off my moustaches and most of my beard and turn out a smooth regular infantryman! ...

23 May, Lisbon. To Thomas Somers Cocks, Esq:
My dear Thomas

Since writing my other letter a strong report has reached this place that Sir Roland Hill has got possession of the tête de pont bridge and depot at Almarez, driving La Foix from thence. Hill has lost 100 killed and wounded; La Foix, 300. Drouet's corps, the 5th, is manoeuvring in the direction of Albuera and Villafranca and part of Graham's corps has, in consequence, moved up to the neighbourhood of Badajoz. Headquarters *were*, very lately, and *I believe* are still at Fuenteguinaldo where the Earl will wait till he has seen six months' supplies into Rodrigo ...

Yours most sincerely,
E. Charles Cocks

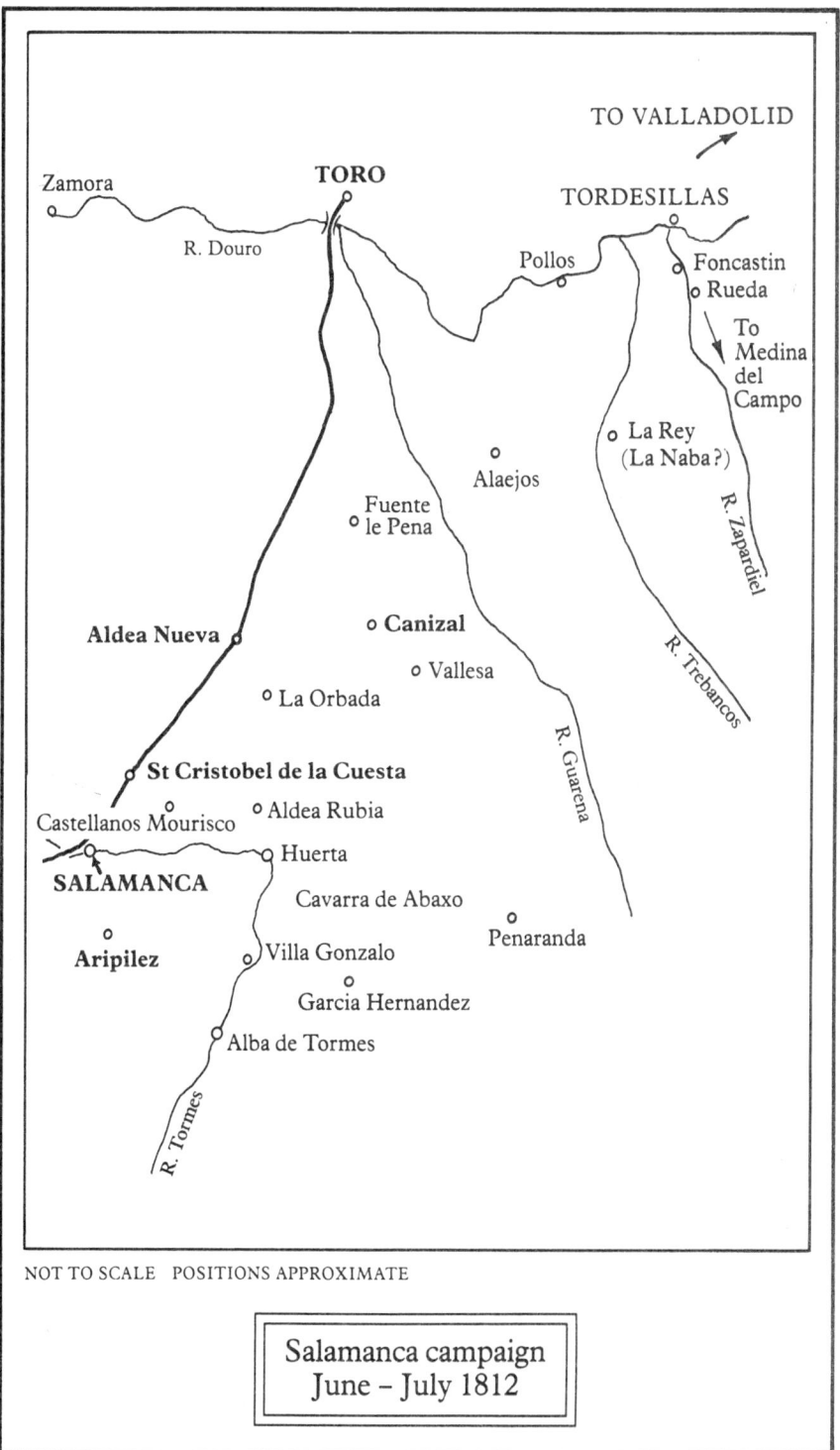

CHAPTER TWENTY-ONE

Salamanca

10 June – 6 August 1812

THE SALAMANCA CAMPAIGN was conducted during June and July across a wide plain and in the glare and heat of a Spanish midsummer. Cocks's journal gives a detailed account of each day's movements insofar as he could understand them from his place with the 79th in the line of march for, to some extent, gone were the times when he could ride off to cavalry headquarters and pick up the latest news; thus he had to fall back on conjecture. As might be expected, he took his new role of an infantry officer very seriously and, where before he had considered how to improve cavalry performance, he now began, hesitantly, to question that of the infantry. His regiment formed part of the 1st Division under General Thomas Graham and to his disgust played little part at the battle of Salamanca, 'My cursed division not engaged,' he wrote to Thomas, conducting mopping up operations not being his scene at all.

> James was with the army the whole time and the experience finally decided him on a career. He had already tried law and decided against it and one reason for the current trip was to help him choose between the army and the church. The following selection begins with a letter from Charles.

* * *

10 June, Camp near Puebla de Azava. To the Hon. Miss Margaret Maria Cocks:
My dear Sister,
 We are breaking James into a bivouac, yesterday he experienced that luxury for the first time. Expectation is on tiptoe as to the result of the pending operations, the army is assembling near Ciudad Rodrigo, I suppose we shall for some time be strangers to the inside of a house. I have become used to my bonnet and my petticoat soldiers; is it not a pity that field officers do not wear kilts?
 My regiment, the 79th, is in Major General Wheatley's brigade, a friend of my uncle Philip's.† I hope to have something worth writing about soon, there is a report that the Earl has prophesied a battle in the beginning of next month.
 I have taken a servant whom I like, his wife lives by washing in number 9, North Row, Park Lane. Her name is Churchill. If you can do anything for her in the way of getting her washing I will be obliged to you.

16 June Halted two leagues from Salamanca ... Its appearance is striking. The Tormes is more considerable than the Agueda and winds close to the town, it is crossed by a long, straight bridge ... The convent which the enemy has fortified

---

†This is Philip James Cocks, not Philip Yorke. Philip James was a colonel in the 1st Foot Guards and actually Charles's half uncle.

lies to our left of the bridge, on the river, with the south-west angle commanding the bridge but not enfilading it. The Earl did not think it advisable to attack this evening, it is a principle of his not to do that by force which can be done without it, unless when it is necessary as the commencement of a chain of operations with a view to the result. From his quiet, therefore, this evening, I conclude we are likely to remain at Salamanca a few days . . .

James described the army's entry into the city in a letter to his mother.

18 June, Salamanca. From The Hon. James Soṁers Cocks to his mother:
My dearest Madam,
   I have been very fortunate in the opportunity which the advance of the army has afforded me of seeing an interesting part of Spain. Salamanca is a fine town built entirely of stone with many striking buildings . . . Lord Wellington entered in triumph. We were received with strong expressions of joy and attachment. It has never seen English troops since the expedition of Sir John Moore. I was particularly struck with the delight of some of Don Julian's troops who perhaps revisited their native city when they were beginning to despair of doing so. The French have still left some troops who are in possession of the fort. This it is supposed impossible for them to hold out above a day or two . . .

Charles continued the description in his journal.

19 June . . . Salamanca has suffered considerably from the enemy. Most of the convents are in ruins, many houses have been destroyed in forming the esplanade of the fort. Marmont even talked of pulling down the tower of the cathedral lest we should erect a battery there, though God only knows how we could have got any guns there. The French officers individually appear to have behaved well. They say 300 married here. The town appears to have been completely divided into parties, the quarter part of those who favoured the French went off with them. Our friends, I mean principally the women, scarce ever associated with them. Many fled the neighbouring villages and have not returned.

25 June, Camp near Salamanca. To Thomas Soṁers Cocks, Esq:
My dear Thomas,
   Some very interesting movements have taken place since I wrote last. On the 11th the army assembled behind the Agueda forming three columns. The right under Sir Thomas Graham, including the 1st, 6th and 7th divisions, making 14,000 infantry and 3 squadrons; the centre, with Headquarters, including the 4th, 5th and Light Divisions, 11,000 infantry and 15 squadrons; the left under General Picton, including the 3rd Division with Pack and Bradford's brigade, 8,000 infantry and 12 squadrons.
   The 12th we halted. 13th passed the Agueda and bivouacked on the line of the river Gavillanos. 14th bivouacked on the Huebra; 15th ditto on the Matilla, 16th ditto two leagues from Salamanca. A skirmish in the morning put a few prisoners in our hands. James made his coup d'essai and behaved by every account perfectly well. I did not see him, being with my division, but his horse was wounded in two places by a ball and sabre cut. He charged with some of the 1st Hussars. The

enemy withdrew his outposts over the Tormes at night and retreated on Toro, leaving from 5-800 men in a convent which he had made into a very strong fort.

17th: the 6th Division occupied Salamanca and invested the fort and the army bivouacked but the enemy had only fallen back to Aldea Nieva, about six leagues off, where he was collecting troops.

18th: the 6th Division worked at batteries against the fort.

19th: the batteries opened – four 18-lb guns, two $5\frac{1}{2}$-inch howitzers with some field guns.

20th: the enemy advanced and we took up a position on the Toro road covering Salamanca. The enemy occupied the villages of Castillanas and Morisco. These were not about five hundred yards from the foot of the chain of rising grounds we occupied and the two armies were within cannon range of each other . . . a round shot, 8lbs, went very near Major Lawrie who stands in my way for promotion! This evening, by my eye, I should not have judged the enemy above 20,000 infantry and 25-30 squadrons. Our position was a good one comprising what I consider the three principle points:

(1) To discover the enemy's movements and conceal your own.

(2) To enable you to reinforce every point by a shorter route than the enemy could move troops to attack it.

(3) To give a fine glacis in front where fire would tell.

At this time it was evident we could have beat the enemy, for we had all the army up except General Bowes's brigade, eg. the 6th Division, but it was not our game to fight except with very manifest advantage, for the fort of Salamanca commanded the bridge and our communication with the rear was by a ford. We could not, therefore, have followed up our victory. Besides, Castanos with a Spanish army was advancing by Astorga on the enemy's rear and it is our interest to keep those in play till the other has got well forward. The enemy was, besides, partly covered by the two villages and had so timed his advance, about 5 pm, that nothing decisive could have taken place before dark.

21st: we looked at the enemy and he at us – some with glasses, some without. He received a reinforcement of 3 or 4,000.

22nd: we bullied the enemy out of a hill he wanted to occupy. This appeared to put him in a great fidget. The mess I belong to finished its last two bottles of champagne – we have nothing left but Bucellas and Claret.

23rd: the enemy walked off before daybreak to some heights three miles off. The 6th Division resumed the siege. The 1st and 7th were moved back to a wood on the right of the river above the town, opposite the ford and the village of Santa Marta. They were thus ready to act on either side.

After dark an attempt was made to storm the two detached forts, I believe it was ill managed; at least it failed, which to me is always damning proof. General Bowes was left behind, I suppose killed. His body was yesterday lying on the glacis, for the enemy would not carry it away or allow us to do so.

24th: the enemy made a strong demonstration on the left of the river by the Madrid and Arebalo road. The 1st and 7th Divisions, with part of the 6th, moved over the river, the siege was suspended, principally faute de poudre. Bock's brigade of Heavy German Cavalry behaved extremely well. The enemy might have three plans:

(1) By demonstrating on the left of the river to draw so much of our force there that he could attack us with advantage on the right.

(2) To advance with his whole army on the left of the river across our line of operation.

(3) To draw our army to the left of the river, then re-pass to the right and so open his communication with the fort before we could reoccupy our first position.

With any of these plans he can harrass us and gain time. He will not dare to attack us except with great advantage. Our object is not at present to fight, though we should fight with less convenience on the left bank than the right. At night the 1st Division recrossed the river.

25th: today, I believe the enemy has fallen back but the post is going!

The 7th Division has recrossed the river and I hear the 6th is going to resume the siege. King Jose† is with the army, it is said. Hill I believe, is going on as usual in Estramadura, Jack Slade had got into the devil of a scrape, allowing six squadrons of his brigade to be beat by some very inferior force of the enemy. He has lost 30 killed, 100 men and 120 horses taken.‡

I have not the least objection to borrow of Lord Beachamp or anybody else for I suppose they will demand as much for their convenience as I shall borrow for mine. As for going home at present it is out of the question, I should have no objection if a favourable opportunity occurred for a very short time but I doubt if I could as both the field officers of the 79th want leave and I should have no pretext unless unlucky enough to get wounded to go before them . . .

25 June A French captain who has deserted says Marmont will not fight us but wishes to prevent our getting the harvest. I think they won't have it. Nothing done against the fort, all at a stand for shot.

26 June . . . When the Earl was at Guinaldo a letter was brought him from Marmont which had been interrupted; in it, Marmont, after speaking very highly of the Earl and his army says they are both so little accustomed to offensive war that he shall be able with inferior force to measure up to their ability. It is said the Earl is now nettled at this as Marmont at least will say he has made good his word. He has, however, acted on the first principle of offensive war which forbids fighting until you are quite prepared to follow up your blow. The only question that can be raised is whether the tempting occasion would not have justified acting against principle.

Red-hot shot were fired against the fort this evening, from the howitzer battery and some 6-pounders, in the windows of the convent. Sturgeon has the merit of the idea. The process is very simple. An ordinary bellows will heat the furnace, from the furnace they are carried in iron crab claws and some good wads of turf are placed between them and the powder. In less than an hour the convent was partially on fire . . .

---

†Joseph Buonaparte whom Napoleon had made King of Spain.
‡General Slade, a cavalry commander with Hill, in the south.

James wrote to his mother a few days later. With more time on his hands his description is fuller and this letter from him comes next.

30 June. From The Hon. James Somers Cocks to his mother:
My dearest Madam,

How to date this letter I am somewhat at a loss as we are not near any town but in the midst of the richest and most extensive plains I ever saw. We left Salamanca yesterday, the fort having been at last taken with very little resistance; since that time we have passed over more open country with scarcely any wood but abounding with corn. This will not give you a mere picturesque idea of it, but at this time of year the appearance of richness and cultivation with a boundary of snowy mountains is really fine. The French are in full retreat and are not expected to make any serious stand here; I am in hopes of shortly visiting Tordesillas, Valladolid; this talking very modestly as we expect to be ere long at Madrid.

The evening before I left Salamanca I went to a play there; the theatre was very neat, but I cannot say much for the performance. John Bull is certainly a little fond of a row, particularly at a playhouse; you may imagine how petrified with astonishment the Dons must be to hear a glorious contest between clapping and hissing which took place the other night. In the middle of the performance, the musicians who were engaged to play at a ball in the town, marched off, consequently there could be no bolero, this excited great indignation and when the actors took their leave they seemed to skip off as if they were running for their lives.

The joy of the inhabitants upon the fall of the fort was very great, it certainly was not a pleasant thing to have shells every hour breaking over their heads; however, the town did not suffer much except in the immediate vicinity of the Fort, here the French burnt down a great many houses to clear the ground ... I was witness to a ridiculous scene which arose from a false report of the Fort having surrendered. The whole town was poured forth under its walls, English as well as Spaniards. Had the garrison been cowardly enough to take advantage of this some lives might have been lost, but they knew they were in our power ...

By the beginning of July James had settled the problem of his career. The next letters are from Charles.

12 July, Villa Verde. To Thomas Somers Cocks, Esq:
My dear Thomas,

James writes by this post ... As for Stanhope's offer or any other which would take me from this country, I would not accept it. I would not give money to exchange to Cavalry except to procure the command or a lieut colonelcy of a *light* regiment in the Peninsula.

My last letter was, I think, dated the 25th. You are already informed of the surrender of Salamanca fort. The red-hot shot were a lucky hit of Sturgeon's. The fort was too strong for escalade and we had not ammunition to breach it.

The 29th we were again in motion. The 1 July we reached Alaejos, when the enemy had at one time an idea of waiting for us. The 2 July we passed the Trebancos and the Zapardiel, two muddy rivulets. I believe the Earl expected from his interrupted information that the enemy would have taken up a position behind the Zapardiel. He, however, retired behind the Duero and Adaja. Thus we have remained ever since. We have received to ourselves the harvest of Leon, great part of old Castile, Asturias, and the enemy is reduced to this dilemma. Either he must remain en masse, in which case the harvest in his rear will be got in and secured by the peasantry without his being able to profit by it, or he must detach to secure the harvest and clear himself of the guerrillas hanging on him, in which case he will not be able to oppose us in front.

Our headquarters are at Rueda – our line of defence from Alayes to Medina del Campo and that of the enemy from Toro to the Puente de Duero. Each army near 40,000. The only reinforcement the enemy can hope for is a Brigade from Caffarelli in Buscay, we expect 5,000 . . . José is at Madrid in a great fright. We command the road from Madrid to Valladolid. But there is another road to Burgos by Aranda . . . James has determined on the church, I am glad of it; for a man who could ever hesitate between the army and the church could not have a decided turn for the former . . .

19 July, Canizal. To Thomas Soṁers Cocks, Esq:
My dear Thomas,
I enclose £100. I have always forgot to say I am delighted with the maps. The cases are hardly strong enough. John Dyter's pipe has come safe. Marmont has manouevred very well. He has obliged us to fall back from the Zapardiel to the Guarena; when our reinforcements join I think we ought to fight him. The first favourable opportunity very likely we shall . . .

19 July, Canizal. To The Hon. Miss Margaret Maria Cocks:
My dear Sister,
We have amused ourselves with plenty of marching lately, very little fighting but a good deal of chess-playing with the enemy. I expect the next fortnight will bring us to hard blows. The two armies are close to each other today, we get plenty of lemon ice-cream and I received yesterday a strong reinforcement of claret but am still badly off for champagne. Very little game or poultry is stirring. At Medina del Campo we were encamped eight days, we had a ball every evening . . .
PS: 23rd: Beat the enemy yesterday; in the action and pursuit took 5,000. Our loss 1,500 killed and wounded. Generals shot out of all proportion. The enemy retiring apparently towards Madrid. Marmont said to have lost an arm. We have taken 12 guns, 2 eagles and a general. We pursued by moonlight . . .

With his brother otherwise engaged, James sent home the main Cocks despatches on the event and the following two letters are from him.

23 July. From The Hon. James Soṁers Cocks to his mother:
My dearest Madam,
Charles is quite well, the French were completely defeated yesterday evening. They are flying and Lord W continues the pursuit today. Everyone is in high spirits; the loss of the French is great, ours comparatively small.
My decision is in favour of the Church as to my own profession . . .

2 August, Portillo. From The Hon. James Somers Cocks to his mother:
My dearest Madam,
   I wrote my last scrawl in so great a hurry I had only time to congratulate you on the late victory. You will see by the despatches that the 1st Division were scarcely engaged in the battle; Charles comforts himself that the 16th likewise scarcely sustained any loss. It will no longer be said that our victories are attended with all the consequences of a defeat. King Joseph has been forced from his lurking hole in Madrid but only dares to retire. The sudden advance of the army has induced me to remain longer with it than I intended. I have spent the last two mornings at Valladolid where the French were obliged to leave 600 or more of their sick. It is a larger town than Salamanca, but not equal in beauty, the houses are good but bending with age. The University, which formerly gave instruction to 4,000 persons, is still in existence; the French affect to protect the Seminaries of learning and to dissolve only superstitious communities. They have everywhere abolished the monasteries; the universities they have spared but as they have made them the objects of their rapacity they have fallen into decay and there are not now above fifty students at Valladolid; the masters however, continue to deliver lectures; I regret that this is a time of vacation as I should have liked to see the forms and systems which are in use here . . .

> And perhaps it should be left to the warrior to conclude the account of the Salamanca campaign, thus Charles, writing at length to his father, takes up the tale.

6 August, Camp near Remondo on the River Cega. To his father:
My dearest Lord,
   . . . Our prospects here are daily becoming more splendid . . . after obliging us, after advancing to Medina del Campo, to fall back to Salamanca, Marmont appears to have been so delighted with this success that his caution failed him, he mistook the Earl's prudence for timidity. On the heights of Arapiles he made an awkward attempt to turn our right but found to his astonishment that an army had learnt in its fifth campaign not only to fight better but to manoeuvre quicker than French troops. The 3rd Division turned Marmont's left and in less than two hours 45,000 men were in a state of complete rout. Marmont and ten generals, wildly endeavouring to restore order, were killed or wounded; one division under La Foix was so completely separated from the rest it did not rejoin the army till the next day. But for the darkness I believe the battle of Salamanca would have completely dispersed the enemy's army but night and darkness impeded our pursuit. Not a peasant could be met with for a guide, the enemy fled through woods where we blundered till midnight. However, the battle and its consequences has deprived the enemy of 17,000 men and 25 pieces of artillery, which we have taken or he has buried. He only got off his wounded by dismounting part of his cavalry and loading the carriages of his guns. This broke all Marmont's measures; his army, inferior in number, heartbroken, without stores, many regiments without officers and many individuals without arms, could no longer come near us. He never stopped till he had crossed the Duero. Eight grenadiers supported the unfortunate Marmont, once the favourite aide de camp of

Battle of Salamanca.

Buonaparte and the handsomest man in Paris, in a sort of litter they use in Spain for carrying corpses to interment . . .

We are with 40,000 men, in high spirits and tolerably healthy, twenty leagues north of Madrid. Hill has 20,000 watching Soult. General Maitland is daily expected to land in some part of Spain with 8,000 British troops and an army of Spaniards disciplined by Whittingham and other British officers. Madrid is at our mercy . . .

James is still with me but purposes going in a day or two towards Plasencia. As he has abandoned all idea of becoming a soldier, I am anxious he should not continue too long about the army but he is very desirous to see Madrid. He is in perfect health, as well as myself . . .

Believe me, my dearest Lord,
    Your most dutiful and affectionate son,
        E. Charles Cocks

CHAPTER TWENTY-TWO
Sweet Success

16 August – 26 September 1812

THEY MARCHED INTO the capital on 12 May and Charles who, back in 1809 after Talavera, had bet Frederick Ponsonby £100 and a hogshead of claret that, 'I shall yet be one of a victorious column of this army that will enter Madrid,'[1] triumphantly accepted his stake.

★   ★   ★

16 August, Madrid. To The Hon. Miss Margaret Maria Cocks:
My dear Margaret,
The Earl made his entry into this place the 12th. I think he could not have paid the Prince Regent a more noble compliment than in thus associating his birthday with an event so proud for England. Our arrival produced a joy far beyond description; indeed, anyone accustomed to the cold manners of England can scarcely conceive what on such an occasion a character so lively as the Spanish is capable of doing. I was never kissed by so many pretty girls in a day in all my life, or ever expect to be again. If we moved on horseback the animals were embraced and pulled one way and we were hauled and caressed the other. On foot it was impossible to make your way, this ebullition of enthusiasm was kept up until dark although the Earl did not remain in town but returned to Arevaca. The following day his headquarters were finally established here. We expected some trouble with a garrison of French left in the china manufactory but they surrendered, 2,000 strong, the day before yesterday. He got in this fort an immense depot. Unless the Emperor gets through the Russian war with perfect éclat the French must no longer think of acting south of the Ebro. The war will then assume a wholly different aspect and all will depend on the power with which we shall be entrusted with making the Spaniards what they are capable of being made. Drilled by us and led by us and mingled with us, no soldiers will be more formidable. Left to themselves they will afford more proofs that in this age and our present system of warfare, where heroism has little part, discipline is far superior to courage...

16 August, Madrid. To Thomas Soṁers Cocks, Esq:
Dear Thomas,
Imprimis: I enclose an order from James on you for £25. Secundo: I have this day sent an order on you against me to Bulkeley & Son, Lisbon for 150. Tercio: You may daily expect one hogshead best claret to be lodged in your hands for me, being a bet I won by our entry into Madrid. So much for business.
I have not time in this delicious paradisical place to detail all our operations;

suffice to say, that the red-hot shot at Salamanca seem to have produced an effect over Spain. I cannot otherwise account for our easy capture of 2,000 men here, especially as they had in their possession the main depot of the French artillery with 190 pieces of artillery, 26,000 stand of arms, 6,500 new French arms in beautiful order, clothes, hats, shoes, etc, in abundance.

The outline of the present situation of the armies is this: Within a short period the enemy will find himself so cramped in his communications and supplies that he must either make an effort to resume the offensive or retire towards the Ebro. Under either supposition the siege of Cadiz will be raised and Andalusia evacuated, with the exception, perhaps, of certain forts which he may garrison. If the enemy is not wholly heartbroken, the former plan will be adopted. If he does not adopt it, let no Frenchman presume again to call himself a soldier in Spain ...

> Towards the end of August the 79th was sent to Escurial, outside Madrid, and James wrote to his mother from there, just before he left Charles.

By inference August 1812. From The Hon. James Somers Cocks to his mother:
My dearest Madam,
    I continue to fill up my time without any great ennui by the assistance of divers balls, plays, promenades and, for John Bull must not forget himself in Spain, dinners. Madrid is a delightful town; we were to have had a masquerade but the government have voted it not religious and placed a prohibition against it. We have likewise been tantalised with a bull fight, but notwithstanding these disappointments I have spent my time very pleasantly ... Charles is very well and looks so but I think not particularly fat; as to myself my poor mule groans under the full weight of my portative laboratory ... I was very much disappointed with the Escurial, a palace so celebrated in history raises one's expectations; the Chapel is handsome and the Mausoleum, this last is a large room in the form of an alcove built entirely of the finest marble; there are marble shelves in which are deposited the sepulchres of many of the Kings and Queens of Spain beginning with Philip the Third. There is no window so you are obliged to descend with a lanthern down a marble staircase into this place of death ... How gay you seem to be at Castleditch, I should have liked much to have been at the fete. I could not help laughing at all the marriages you announce, I hope those in the family will all be celebrated in Eastnor Church on the same day, it will form an unexampled page in the Parish register ...

> Militarily, at this point Wellington decided to take full advantage of the French disarray and drive north to clear the country bordering the Duero and Ebro and, taking with him the 1st Division – including, of course, the 79th – left at the month's end.

8 September, Valladolid. To Thomas Somers Cocks, Esq:
My dear Thomas,
    Your letter dated July 7th only arrived the night before last ... Part of our army is now encamped here, from whence we expelled Clausel† yesterday. It is

---

†Marmont's successor.

probable we shall push our operations as far as Burgos or the Ebro and then turn by Aranda de Duero and meet Hill at Madrid in time to strike a blow against Soult who, having raised the siege of Cadiz the night of 25 August, is in march for the eastward and northward. Our army on the whole is very healthy and I trust we have now passed the most critical season of the year. We, of course, want Cavalry and dollars which you deal from England with a sparing hand . . . If we meet with no reverse and you send us *Dollars* mind, not bills but coin, I think the enemy will be behind the Ebro before Christmas, perhaps then an opportunity may occur for my coming home, which I well know is of considerable consequence for my individual interest . . .

12 September, Majaz. To his mother:
Dearest Madam,
I was very near dating this letter from the bottom of the Grand Canal at Palencia where I pitched my tent yesterday. Not, however, that I have become a frog but that the said canal holds no water. I received your letter August 22nd yesterday, in future I expect our communication with England will be very quick as the mail is establishing through Corunna.

We are now on the high road to Burgos which I expect to reach the 16th. I know not if we shall have to fight our way in, probably not, but beyond the town is a fort which we must take in order to leave the enemy nothing in this part of Spain without the Ebro. We shall then return to Madrid and, if things go on well, may have a chance of striking Soult such a blow that the scar shall remain for ever.

This month and the next one are the most critical of the campaign . . . I was quartered for ten days in the palace of Escurial, it would have angered old Philip could he have risen from the grave and seen 20,000 British and Portuguese – the two nations he most hated – at least latterly, coolly in possession of his favourite grid-iron palace. I could not make out the grid-iron unless it be a grid-iron with double crosses . . .

En route Wellington formed the light companies of the Highland Brigade into a separate battalion under Cocks. Clausel continued to retire and by mid-September the Allies were before Burgos. The castle stood a little apart from the town, its original old walls strongly reinforced by a second line of defences further up the slope and the whole crowned by a keep which housed a formidable battery. Yards away, and equally high, but separated by a deep ravine, rose St Michael's hill complete with hornwork and fleches.

Wellington reconnoitred the defences on the 18th and then directed that Charles and his party, on the following morning, should first capture the fleches on St Michael's hill and then, in the evening, provide a diversion on the gorge side of the hornwork whilst a full assault took place at the front. Accompanied by men from the 79th and 42nd, Cocks successfully seized both fleches although a small advanced post, discovered close in, gave them some trouble and only fell after Lt Hugh Grant valiantly stood his ground whilst waiting reinforcements, at the cost of his own life.

The evening attack was due to begin at 8 pm, the main assault being on the two demi bastions at the front while Charles, with 8 officers and 250 men, expecting to be reinforced by a further 300, were to occupy the enemy's attention at the back and prevent troops from the castle coming over to relieve their comrades. He described the place as

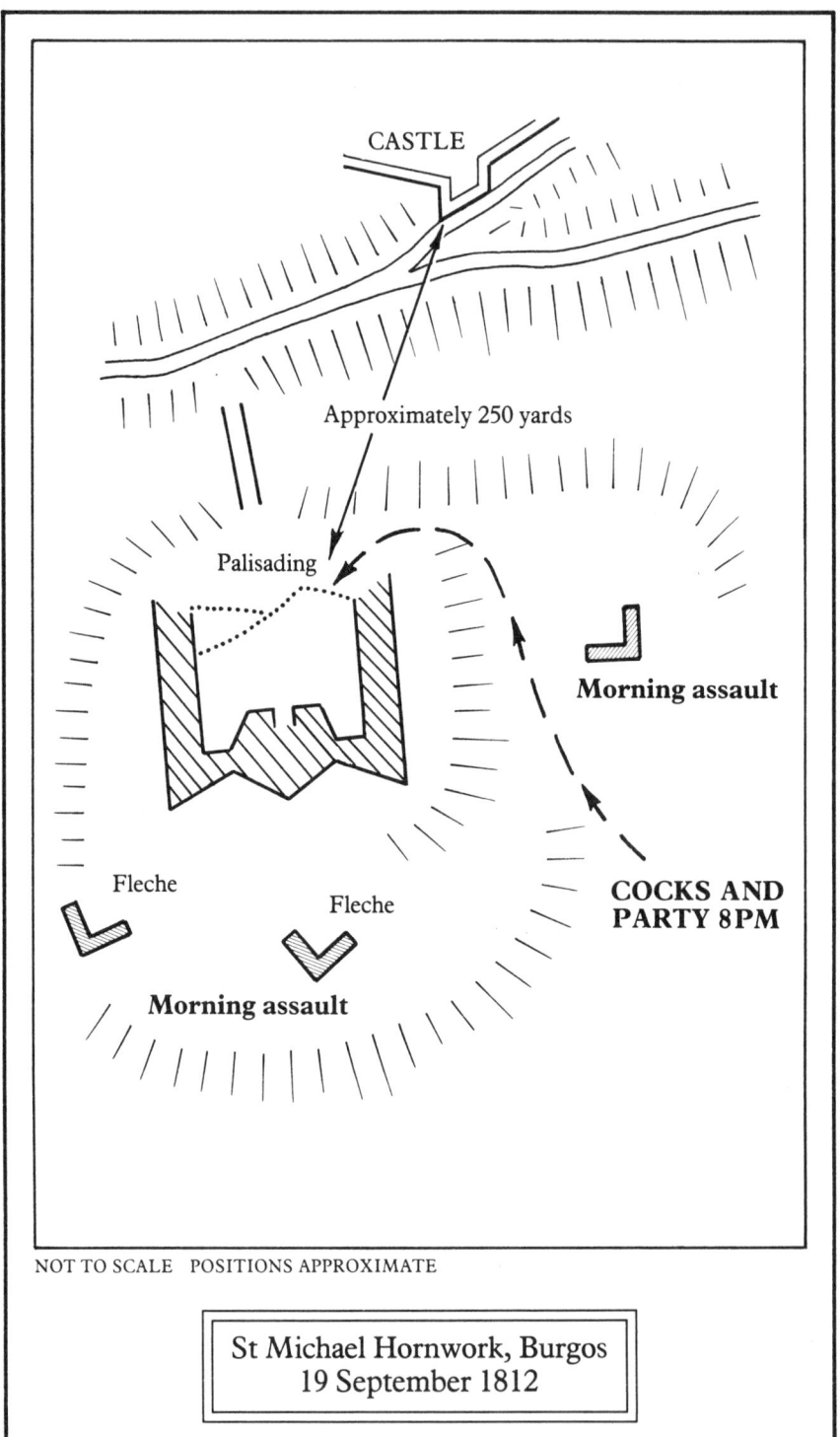

'resembling a square, three sides were enclosed by an earthen rampart 35 feet from the bottom of the ditch to the top, while the fourth side, next to the town, was left open' to enable the castle's guns to fire straight into the hornwork. 'This side,' he went on, 'was defended by a strong, pointed palisading seven feet high, placed on the top of the steep, earthen bank twelve feet high and the inside of the work was on a level with the top of the bank. This was the side I was ordered to attack.'

By eight o'clock all was ready and Cocks led his men out at the double, running along the hill from the right, heavy fire from both the castle and the hornwork mowing down many in the race for the palisading. With Serjeant John Mackenzie of the 79th close behind, he reached it first and, without bothering to wait for the ladders, the pair of them heaved each other up and over followed by the survivors of the dash. Serjeant Donald Mackenzie, whom at his own request was armed with his major's dress sabre, and Bugler Charles Bogie, 'a man of colour', were immediately sent to guard the only escape route to the castle while the rest, maintaining the momentum, rushed one of the doors, beginning a fierce hand-to-hand struggle.

Meanwhile, the frontal attack had failed but the defenders, panic-stricken by sounds of fighting in their rear, lost courage and fled the exit nearest the castle, literally trampling over Mackenzie's and Bogie's party, and minutes later it was all over and the hornwork in British hands. 'My party drove out the garrison,' Cocks told his father on the 26th, and this despite the fact the reinforcements failed to arrive.

The toll was high yet he wrote: 'It pleased God I should receive only a slight wound in the arm which, as it did not disable me, I have not returned.' Maybe his 'protecting genius', as Boverick had called it, was looking after him while a more mortal one, in the shape of Wellington, assisted even more. After assuring Cocks 'he had carried the fort and the affair was all his own',† the Commander put in a recommendation for a brevet lieut colonelcy.

26 September, Camp before Burgos. To Thomas Somers Cocks, Esq:
My dear Thomas,

Clausel, with the remains of Marmont's army, retired before us from Valladolid, abandoning Burgos, where he left 2,000 men in a strong fort under the orders of General de Brigade, de Bruton. A large outwork called the hornwork of San Miguel considerably added to the strength of this fort. The Marquis‡ resolved to assault it the night of the investment, the 19th, and I was entrusted with one attack with the light companies . . .

We tumbled the garrison out, bayoneting 70, taking 70, and wounding from 2 to 300. In consequence of this the Marquis recommended me for a brevet lieut colonelcy. But now we come to the main story. Three days after this an assault was ordered on another part of the work; Major Lawrie, 79th, commanded and was killed, leaving me first major for purchase. A few hours afterwards I concluded an arrangement with Lt-Col Fulton by which he leaves the regiment when the siege is over, resigning his lieut colonelcy in my favour. This will give me the permanent command of the 1st battalion, 79th.

I enclose a letter for Price. You see that it is absolutely necessary that he should instantly produce from £2,500 to 3,000. I have not at this moment any

---

†Captain Jameson in his *History of the 79th* gives a long description of the affair.
‡Wellington was now a Marquis.

memorandum of the exact sum. Part of it, viz. the *regulation* difference between a Majority and Lieut Colonelcy of Infantry I will thank you to lodge as soon as possible in the House of Lawrie & Co, Agents to the Regiment. I will write again respecting the disposal of the remainder of the sum, but if he sells everything he must produce the money . . . I tried to get my majority for Somers, there being no captain in the 79th who can purchase, but Lord Wellington gave me to understand he had a captain in his eye who had constantly served in this country.

I think Burgos will fall about the 5th October; part of the force employed here will then probably move towards Madrid. Soult has evacuated all Andalusia. He is now near Jaen and Baeza. The French chiefs have no union; Suchet absolutely refused to go out of his quarters at Valencia for Joseph who, in consequence, removed to [?]. Soult hates both. If things continue to look well in the north I do not think there will be a Frenchman on this side of the Ebro in January.

For heaven's sake don't let Price talk but make him produce the money. I enclose the letter, open, for you to seal. Pray answer this letter as soon as possible.

NB: If Price is slow perhaps Thong could manage to get as much money as would enable you to lodge the regulation in Lawrie & Co's hands. When that is done I shall be easy as I cannot be jockeyed.

Ever most affectionately yours,
    E. Charles Cocks

CHAPTER TWENTY-THREE

Siege of Burgos

September – 6 October 1812

ON 20 SEPTEMBER in a new, red leather-bound book he had obviously 'liberated' from a French commissary Cocks began his journal of the siege, but after Lawrie's death the entries were short, for the most part brief sentences and very much, one suspects, on the lines of his memorandum books, his mind being almost wholly occupied by the forthcoming promotion and the financial arrangements.

However, it was probably the worst of all sieges so far. Autumn had come swiftly with drenching rain and this, together with poor entrenching tools, too few guns and an unexpectedly fierce defence, lowered morale. With the exception of Charles, everyone from Wellington down was depressed by the daily worsening situation. The lack of a proper siege train, as well as a shortage of ammunition, plagued them from the start. On 18 September Cocks had noted that 'our 18lb guns are only provided with 300 round, the howitzers have only 60 round of shot and 40 round of shells',[1] and there were days when the artillery could not fire.

★   ★   ★

20 September A lodgement was formed in the hornwork.

The duties are arranged as follows: The working parties to relieve every 24 hours. The night reliefs 500 [men]. The day reliefs 250. The covering parties return every 12 hours and are 300. This brings the men on duty in the 1st Division and the two Portuguese Brigades in the proportion of one to five. The 6th Division found separate duties for the other attack. The engineers relieve every 8 hours, the artillery every 12; the field Officer of the trenches and adjutant of the day every 24.

22 September The approaches and Batteries were continued.

23 September The two approaches were connected but one of the branches wall is ill-traced and is enfiladed. It must be altered tonight. Two 18lb guns and three howitzers were got into Batteries Nos 1 and 2. A new Battery was traced in the hornwork behind the palisades of the gorge, it will be very much exposed.

At midnight the town wall was attacked. 200 of the 1st Division, supported by as many men, were to escalade in front while a Regiment of Caçadores, supported by two Portuguese companies of the line were to force the palisading which joined the left extremity of the wall with the other works. They would thus have cut off the troops defending the wall, as the only retreat of the latter to the lower enclosure was by a gate, near the point where the two Portuguese, if successful, should have entered. There was cover for both these parties to have assembled within 50 or 60 yards of the points to be attacked; nevertheless, they both failed. Perhaps they would have succeeded had they been stronger. During the day gratings were made for heating the balls. The 6th Division had established themselves under a bank 60 yards from the town wall.

24 September Zigzags were commenced, breaking off from Battery No 1 to connect with that of the 6th. A sap from this last attack approached the town wall. A new Battery was completed. The attack on the city wall having failed, it is resolved to open it by mine. A gallery was commenced from the attack sap of the 6th Division. The depressions [?] were 3 feet, 4 inch high by 3. 2 wide. The soil is so far favourable, that it does not fall in, and frames are therefore not required to support it; but rock occasionally turns the miner from his line.

The miners are formed into Brigades of 4 each. They have four reliefs each working four hours and relieving amongst themselves every half hour. This mode of attack will considerably lengthen the siege. The length of the gallery is calculated at 50 feet. This will at least require four days before the mine can be ready. The gallery is to pass under the ditch.

25 September A new Battery for two embrasures was begun last night to the left of the hornwork. The sap of the 6th Division approached within 12 yards of the wall. Another gallery was commenced 40 yards to the right of the first. The musketry fire of the 6th Division had nearly silenced that of the enemy. He could only keep some destructive marksmen in some little wooden towers formed of palisading and placed on the top of the only wall. A howitzer which opened failed in hitting them.

26 September The galleries continued. At the distance of 40 feet it was found difficult to make the candles burn. It was necessary continually to suspend the work, in order to allow the air within to purify itself. The two 18-lb guns were removed from No 2 to No 3 and replaced by howitzers.

27 September The galleries continued. The zigzag communication continued between, through the attacks of the 1st and 6th Division.

27 September, Camp before Burgos. To The Hon. Miss Margaret Maria Cocks:
My dear Margaret,

In what a different situation do I write and you read this letter. I am sitting in a very small bad tent – NB: I have a very good marqui on the road from Lisbon – on a box which feels very hard to the part applied to it. My table is rickety, one leg being too short, and whenever the stone slips away, which I shove under to keep it steady, down rolls the ink. The said table is covered by a blanket instead of green baize, which identical blanket, in the course of half an hour with an addition of a bear skin and a cloak will form my bed, bedstead and bedding. So much for the inside. Outside three mules belonging to my nearest neighbour are occasionally whinnying.

Note The whinny of mules is between the bray of an ass and the neigh of a horse, more unharmonious than either. A little further some drunken Portuguese have got some music and are singing, playing and huzzaing, much to their satisfaction. Further still is heard the continual firing of the siege and if I chance to look out, the chances are I see a shell or two in the air; all round are our camp fires.

The most magnificent part of my writing equipage is *my wax candle in a silver candlestick*. You will receive this in a room so closely shut that everything like free air, when it accidentally approaches you, is denominated a 'thorough draught', and voted dangerous being supposed impregnated with cold, rheumatics, etc. In this close room you will be further warmed by a large coal fire, there will be a dozen tables and *soft* chairs – these I envy you – your bed, instead of being handy and convenient, eighteen inches off, is God knows where, at the other side of the house and when you get to it you must be at the trouble of undressing instead of just laying down ready prepared for breakfast in the morning.

You will probably see by the papers that I was engaged in rather a sharp affair the other day; however, I got well out of it and it has got me a lieut colonelcy. Whenever I see my name in the gazette for that rank, which I hope you will about the time or soon after receiving this letter, I shall begin to feel settled as my promotion is then secure and cannot be accelerated except by some great piece of good fortune. As soon as I get the command of my regiment, which I expect to do in a few days, I shall be much more comfortable than I have been this campaign, which I have been obliged to spend in rather stupid society. However, it has turned out most fortunate for me that I have adopted the line I have. I received a slight wound by a musket ball the day of the storm but it was so trifling I did not return it. When will Thomas and Agneta be noosed? I was much pleased with *Childe Harold* though I must despise the prejudiced liberality of some of the sentiments.

An odd incident occurred to me; it was represented one night in the trenches, apparently from authority which left no doubt, that I was killed. Next morning it was my turn for duty. The first groups I met were of other regiments. 'What news, lords?' say I. 'Nothing sir, but Major Cocks is killed.' One man actually argued the matter with me. A little further were my own men and some of my friends, condoling over my fate. The surprise of their faces was very whimsical and it [was] not a little gratifying to observe how one's death took. The last of all was Colonel Guise, whom I was coming to relieve and who was the very man through whose mistake the report had originated. He had half a mind to run away and when he came to himself his stammering apology for killing me almost did kill me with laughing.

28 September The soil is very stiff and hard; and as the zigzags are now proceeding down the slope of S Miguel, opposite the Castle, it is necessary to make the trenches very deep. They get on therefore but slowly. The covering parties of the 1st Division are reduced to 200, the zigzag would render it difficult for the enemy to reach the Batteries.

29 September Rock has turned the miner of the first gallery so often from the straight line that a length of gallery is required considerably exceeding previous computation. It has now been extended to 60 feet and scarcely reached the bottom of the wall.

The communication was completed between the two attacks. The enemy brought down two small howitzers behind the only wall, immediately opposite that part to which the galleries were directed. Firing them with great elevations and small charges of a few ounces they threw the shells just in front of the walls. They however failed to break into the galleries and did not materially inconvenience the firing parties of the 6th Division.

30 September The first gallery having reached the wall, a chamber was formed loaded with 400lb of powder and exploded at midnight. It brought down the city wall for 8 or 10 yards but not the earth behind. The attack combined by a party of the 6th Division but ill-executed and failed.

The second gallery was continued to 60 feet and reached the bottom of the ditch. It had an inclination to the left. A zigzag was carried down the face of the hill in front of the hornwork. Its object was to form a parallel trench for musketry as near as possible to the fort but the fire was so heavy on the working party little progress was made.

At 10am the Marquis ordered Batteries Nos 1 and 2 to fire en échasse on the breach with the view to improve the slope. They destroyed one of the palisaded towers from whence we had been previously annoyed. The enemy was at work within the city walls.

1 October The new zigzag was completed. The three 18lb guns were removed by an extra working party of 200 men of the 1st Division from No 3 Battery to a new Battery 150 yards from the city walls, behind the firing party of the 1st Division and to the right of the breach. This Battery was placed within the line where the [?] and passing along the superior [?] of the enemy's works intersected the surface of the ground. Consequently no fire could be brought against it except from the city wall, as that work covered it from the fire of the other enclosures. As there were no guns on this line the Battery was thought secure, except against musketry, and accordingly only made one gabion thick. But when day broke the enemy threw so many shells so well from the little howitzers aforementioned that it was found impossible to open the Battery or get the guns away. All that could be done was to take them off their carriages and leave them on the ground. This gave the enemy time to bring another howitzer or two and a field gun against the Battery.

The working parties are reduced. The 1st Division took the whole of the covering party.

2 October A new attempt was made to re-establish the lower Battery but the enemy had arranged so superior a fire it was found impossible.

2 October, Camp before Burgos. To Thomas Soṁers Cocks, Esq:
My dear Thomas,

I wrote to you in such a hurry by the last mail, being afraid of losing it, that I had not time to state to you the particulars of my agreement with Lt-Col F— or the money which will be wanted to complete it.

I am to give him £1,500 above the regulation and take on myself the sale of his commissions. There is a doubt whether he will be allowed to sell his Majority. If he cannot, the loss falls on him. The sums to be provided therefore are as follows:

To be lodged immediately in the hands of A. Lawrie, Army Agent, Adelphi, London:	£900
To be paid under the [?] to a friend of Lt-Col F's as shall be hereafter mentioned:	£1,500
	£2,400
To be paid to Lt-Col F on account of his Company & Lieutenancy:	£1,500
To be paid as above in case he is allowed to sell his Majority:	£1,100
Total:	£5,000

These two latter sums, viz. £1,500 and £1,100, in case he is allowed to sell the Majority I shall only be out of till the commissions are filled up, which will be done immediately. The sum therefore that I shall have to pay is £2,400; I do most earnestly hope that Price will produce this money immediately. The £900 to be lodged with Lawrie is indisposable as the promotion might otherwise not go on.

I expect F will send in his resignation the day after tomorrow. I will then write again to you. Should Price be in any difficulty about the sum I think it might be procured from Lord Beauchamp.

We are getting on slowly in our siege. The Army continues very healthy. Soult is moving from Grenada toward Valencia; Drouet in a parallel direction from [?] on Valencia. Suchet seems moving from Valencia to meet Soult and Drouet, but it is reported that heavy baggage and King José have gone to Saragossa. Sir R. Hill is at Toledo where the three divisions left at [?], near Madrid, have joined him. Col Skerritt and General Cooke from Cadiz are likewise on their march by Almarez with the same intention. Clausel, with the remains of Marmont's army, is between Pancorvo and the Ebro . . .

3 October The 18lb guns were withdrawn last night and placed in Battery No 2. One gun is ruined, a trunnion being blown [?] off, another is very much injured. The howitzers in No 2 were removed to No 3. Forty barrels of powder arrived today. The siege has been at a standstill for the last four days.

4 October During the night four Batteries of field guns were passed to the W and SW of the castle. Partly covered by buildings and partly by natural [?] they were soon made secure. They consisted of two pieces each, making four howitzers and four 9lb guns and were destined to fire on the defences and the enemy's batteries in reverse.

At 9 am the gallery had passed the city wall seven feet. It had latterly taken a turn to the right, which brought it outside of the corner row of palisades where there was no earthen rampart against the wall. The chamber was filled with 1,000lb of powder and the miners proceeded to stop the mine. The line of least resistance was judged 15 feet, sloping toward the outside of the bank just below the bottom of the wall. As the gallery made a short turn or two it was not thought necessary to stop it much beyond the length of the line of least resistance.

By 3 pm the mine was reported ready and the old breach was much improved. The 24 Regt (200) had been ordered into the trenches, Lord Wellington having resolved the attack should take place just before dark, and by a corps, not, as heretofore, by detachments. All duties are better done by corps than by detachments.

As it was expected the mine would form a second efficient breach, two attacks were prepared; each consisted of a forlorn of a Sub and 20, and of a storming party of a Capt and 50. The remainder of the 24th and 150 men from the 6th Division formed a support to both. The whole assembled on the parallel, opposite the breaches. Strong working parties were ready. They were ordered to communicate as soon possible from one breach to the other, breaking away through the palisades. The storming parties were to lodge themselves under any cover they could find, especially in a loopholed Guardhouse between the points to be stormed and behind some piles of shot the enemy had left between the lower enclosure and the wall to be attacked.

At half past 5 pm all was ready. There was light enough to complete the storm, and the darkness which would immediately follow would enable the parties to work with security.

The signal was given. An anxious pause ensued, then a volume of flame arose immediately below the wall, followed by a column of black smoke. Immediately after, a portion of the wall behind was seen to vibrate backwards and forwards. The limestone crumbled. As the clouds of dust and smoke cleared away a breach was discernible. The forlorn hope rushed forward led by Lts Holmes and Frazer. The enemy appeared prepared to defend the first breach but wholly dismayed by the explosion and its effects. The 24th, commanded by Capt Heyderwick, behaved perfectly. A tremendous fire of artillery from all our pieces, two 18-lb and four 9-lb guns and nine $5\frac{1}{2}$-inch howitzers, and of musketry from the trenches, directed against the enemy's upper works, kept him in order. He abandoned the breaches. A false attack by some Portuguese from the Tower on the palisades near the lunette prevented his holding behind the palisades in front of the gates by their reverse fire. In half an hour the 24th had established themselves as they were ordered. They lost 10 killed, one officer and 57 wounded.

5 October Little work was done in the night. The enemy made a demonstration to sortie, which alarmed the working parties. Their arms had been piled at some distance from the work, which deprived them of confidence. The 24th had been relieved soon after dark by detachments as usual.

The artillery removed the two 18-lb guns and one howitzer to Batteries Nos 3 and 4. The remaining four howitzers were placed in No 2. A furnace was placed in No 1 for heating shot. It consisted only of large stones without mortar. There was a grating ready for the shot and the wood was to put under and round the grating. A bellows was erected on one side. During the day the working parties were employed in forming cover with boxes, etc and banquettes along the outside of the city wall for the musketry, thus making it a change front and becoming a parallel for us. The fraise and palisading was cut away and ramps formed at intervals to ascend. The hill was so steep that the whole space between the parallel and the wall was secure from the fire of the enemy's upper works.

At half past 5pm the enemy made a sortie en face. Our people were not prepared. The Portuguese gave way at the breach to the right, which enabled the enemy to gain the wall at that point and drive our parties from the whole line, flanking them by the right. They retired to the parallel. The enemy destroyed a sap we had commenced toward the town enclosure or fausse braie. They then retired and our parties were prevailed on to leave the parallel and reoccupy their former posts. The fire during this affair was very lively but the enemy lost more than we did.

6 October A sap was commenced from the left of the left breach to communicate with the piles of shot, but it was not completed. Two howitzers opened today from Battery No 2 on the palisades in the ditch of the fausse braie. The practice was bad, the soles of the embrasures being too full of earth. These guns fired 80 shot. Our casualties in the last 24 hours have been heavy.

CHAPTER TWENTY-FOUR

8 October 1812 and its Aftermath

IN POURING RAIN on the night of 7 October, Cocks took over as field officer in the trenches and, unlike most, immediately checked every subaltern's piquet and individual sentry, ensuring all understood their orders. A wise precaution because just after 3 am the enemy made a sortie and succeeded in driving both the workmen and the covering party to the foot of the breach. After reforming, he led the way back up the slope to regain the outer wall but had no sooner reached the top than one of the French, standing not five yards off, fired straight at him, and the ball entered 'between the 4th and 5th rib on the right side, passing through the main artery above the heart and so out at the left side, breaking an arm',[1] and killing him instantly. The men fought on until the enemy was pushed back into the covered way and when morning broke his body was returned under a flag of truce 'to be buried with military honours in compliment to his distinguished service'.[2]

Frederick Ponsonby was at his desk soon after dawn when Wellington suddenly walked into the room, but after pacing up and down in silence for a few moments he turned again to the door: 'Cocks is dead,'[3] he said abruptly as he left. Tomkinson heard a while later and was deeply shocked: 'In Cocks the army has lost one of its best officers, society a worthy member and I a sincere friend,' he grieved. 'He had always been so lucky in the heat of fire I fancied he would be preserved.'[4]

They buried him the next morning under a cork tree in the 79th's ground at Bellima. 'Lord Wellington, Sir Stapleton Cotton, Generals Pack and Anson and the whole of their staff and the officers of the 16th Light Dragoons and the 79th Regiment attended him to his grave,' Tomkinson continued. 'He is regretted by the whole army and in those regiments in which he has been, not a man can lament a brother more than they do him.'[5] 'He is on every ground the greatest loss we have yet sustained,' Wellington wrote to Beresford.[6] Burgos was proving to be one of his few military miscalculations and it was ironic that Cocks, dedicated to avoiding situations which cost needless lives should forfeit his own in just such an action and led by a commander whom, above all others, he respected. And possibly thoughts of this nature ran through Wellington's mind as he stood ashen-faced at the graveside that October morning, so remote none dared speak to him.

Tomkinson took over the responsibility of arranging all the affairs, giving most of his things away to his friends, but keeping the sword for himself, to treasure for the rest of his life, and that evening he wrote to John Somers, who had returned home the previous Christmas.

'My dear Somers,

I have been so distressed at the loss we have suffered that to you, Somers, I do not know how to break it, but as you must know the worst it is better to hear it through a friend than otherwise. Poor Charles was killed in the breach of the hornworks to the foot of Burgos when on duty on the night of the 7th, or rather yesterday morning, and in the act of leading his men to carry the breach the enemy had gained.

We have this day done our last duty to him and I derived what little satisfaction I could on so mournful an occasion by seeing Lord Wellington, the Prince,† and the whole Headquarters with a list of sorrowful friends attending the funeral. I have taken upon myself to settle his affairs, disposing of his favourite mare to the Prince, who wished to take her, not allowing any little thing to be sold, distributing them to his numerous friends and kept his journal and notes to proceed to you. Money matters I have placed in the hands of the Paymaster 79th; not allowing his clothes to be disposed of, giving to his servant; and when all is settled, which shall be as soon as possible, I will remit all to his bankers. I have acted as for my own brother and I hope you approve all I have done.'[7]

It took time to locate James but eventually a letter found him in Cadiz and his grief, coming on top of an illness, brought on a fever and he did not arrive home until well after Christmas.

The official notification arrived at Castleditch just after 11am on the 26th, accompanied by a letter from Wellington:

'*Villa Toro, 11 October 1812.*

My Lord,

As I have before had the honour of writing to you respecting your son I cannot allow my despatch to go to England with the melancholy account of the loss which you have sustained without addressing a few lines to you.

Your son fell, as he had lived, in the zealous and gallant discharge of his duty. He had already distinguished himself in the course of operations of the attack on the castle of Burgos and to such a degree as to induce me to recommend him for promotion; and I assure your Lordship that if Providence had spared him to you, he possessed acquirements, and was endowed with qualities to become one of the greatest ornaments of his profession and to continue an honour to his family and an advantage to his country.

I have no hopes that what I have above stated to your Lordship will at all tend to alleviate your affliction on this melancholy occasion but I could not deny myself the satisfaction of assuring you that I was highly sensible of the merits of your son and that I most sincerely lament his loss.'[8]

Tradition has it that the shadow of his death hung over the family for the rest of their lives. Lord Somers became an earl and Eastnor Castle rose in all its splendour but the star was missing. John Somers, a sincere, hardworking, worthy

---

†The Prince of Orange, one of Wellington's ADCs.

man, who married one of Hardwicke's daughters, could not match his brother's brilliance. James remained single and ended his days as a Prebendary of Hereford and Canon of Worcester. Margaret Maria did not marry either but continued to write poetry and in later years befriended a young Elizabeth Barratt (Browning). Thomas and Agneta were married the following year and it was their third son, another Charles, whom, whilst serving in the Crimea, heard of Owen and Rennie's meeting in Oporto.

His mother collected everything of his she could lay hands on, the childhood verses, essays of his teenage years, an old, rough history notebook and even the outline drawing of his foot her husband had taken to the trussmaker in London when the splint was being made. Friends and relatives sent any letters they still had† and once the castle was completed, together with the diaries, all were put in the muniment room.

'I cannot look back on the life and conduct of my beloved Charles,' she wrote in December, 'without the strongest assurance of his finding grace with God as he found favour with Men, for his merit is not to be known only by the Gazette or by the very expressive manner in which Lord Wellington speaks of him; his glorious military career is acknowledged in the most ample manner throughout the army. In private life he was the best of Sons, of brothers and of friends, the universal testimony at his loss ought to make us rejoice in his life rather than lament its early close.'

They made the obelisk his memorial, standing high in the Malvern hills above Eastnor, overlooking the patchwork of the Severn vale. Another may also have been erected: 'If we go into Spain again and should happen to reach Burgos it is my intention to cause a stone to be put on the grave of your poor brother,' Captain Robert Gabriel told John Someȓs, and a chance encounter with a soldier in 1815 confirmed a monument of some kind.[9]

However, possibly Wellington spoke the tribute Charles would have appreciated most: 'D'Urban,' he said at last, to the officer next to him at the funeral, 'had Cocks outlived the campaigns, which from the way he exposed himself was morally impossible, he would have become one of the first Generals in England.'[10]

---

†Thomas tactfully sent censored copies of those he felt would cause distress, particularly the ones in connection with the financial arrangements for promotion.

Appendix A

Gibraltar

THE ROCK OF GIBRALTAR is joined to the mainland by an isthmus of sand about 1,000 or 1,200 yards wide. It runs east/west; to the north is the bay, to the south the Mediterranean. Opposite to Gibraltar, on the other side of the straits, a distance of about 15 miles, is Ceuta.

The best history of Gibraltar is James's. A very accurate account of the siege in 1781-3 has been published by Drinkwater and there is also a Spanish history, tracing it to its earliest foundations.

Though the Rock, in general, exhibits but a very slender covering of earth, yet the efforts of vegetation which are discernible in every part are wonderful; fig trees appear, forcing their way through its crevices and the palm relieves the eye by its vivid green. Goats are perched on the boldest crevices while foxes and apes may be seen in the more retired corners, the last are particularly remarkable from there being no more in any other part of Spain.

The greater part of the Rock is perfectly inaccessible, on the north-east side the descent is most gradual and here is situated the town; it contains about 18,000 souls of all nations and all religions, Moors, French, Spaniards and Englishmen, Catholics, Protestants, Jews, Mohammedans, intermingled and confounded, form a various and motley population. The town is well supplied, the sea is well stocked with fish, Barbary furnishes cattle and Spain produces game, fruits and vegetables in abundance. The Bay of Gibraltar affords a safe anchorage under the guns of the works, there are no dry docks but every species of repair which can be done out of them may be executed at Gibraltar.

A magnificent bombproof naval storehouse is now erecting, the expense of which is estimated at £180,000. The Public Library at Gibraltar is a most excellent institution, the books were originally collected by subscription and some difficulty occurring about a house in which to place them the British public erected this building for that purpose. Had it been placed a little more square to the front it would have had a better appearance from without; within it is extremely well fitted up, the books are generally English though there is a selection of the best Spanish works, a few French authors – I was surprised not to find a larger proportion of military works, but I think the subjects are mostly miscellaneous.

I spent two days in viewing the works. Previous to the siege of 1781 the fortifications towards the land consisted of the works which cover the town, of the Devil's Tongue – a name which the Spaniards have given to a mole which, running out into the sea, gives an enfilading fire on the right of the approaches – of the upper and lower lines, of Willis's battery and the rock mortar. The upper and lower lines are each divided into two, the former into hammer and pincers and the latter into Kings and Queens. The communications between them are kept up by galleries in the rock which are consequently secure. Willis's Battery is higher up the rock so, though probably 1,200 feet above the level of the neutral ground, it was three times silenced during the siege by the famous 68-gun battery, which the Spaniards erected in one night and which was finally destroyed in the sortie.

But the most wonderful works are those which have been erected since the siege. The upper and lower union galleries, Willis's galleries, St George's and Cornwallis's paths are not merely galleries of communication but actual batteries excavated in the living rock; they have been sufficiently proofed to ascertain that neither the smoke nor sound will occasion material inconvenience to the artillerymen in working them. Till the guns here were fixed the Spaniards would not believe that guns could be placed in such a situation and conceived them erected only for show or to give an ideal appearance of strength.

I am not aware that an attack against Gibraltar can be made in other than three ways, all of which have been tried and all in vain – namely, on the land side; two, by storming from boats; three, by landing a party on the back of the rock by surprise.

The first two plans were fully tried in the siege of 1781–3 and the latter was attempted in the beginning of the last century by 500 Spaniards who bound themselves by a sacramental oath to obtain possession of the place or perish. They succeeded in landing and gaining St Michael's Cave undiscovered but they were here betrayed by an hermit who was in their secret and put to the sword by the garrison.

One great part of the Rock on the land side is not only inaccessible but incapable of being rendered otherwise by a besieger. It is against the north-east point only that an attack may be directed. Besides the works, when cavaliers are piled on cavaliers this part of the fortification is covered by an inundation which, though only four feet deep, is rendered impassable by its muddy bottom and by a ditch which crosses it in the middle. The attackers, therefore, would be necessarily reduced to Bay side barrier or [?] Forbes Barrier, two gates or rather sallyports placed upon slender necks of land, the one running between the bay and inundation, the other between the inundation and the foot of the Rock. On these points are directed the fire of about 400 pieces of ordnance, including fifteen 68-pounders, cannonades, each capable of discharging some 900ozs or musket balls. To this tremendous fire the attacking columns would not only be exposed while forcing the barriers and escalading the works but even previous to their arrival at the inundation, for from the circumstance of the north-west part of the Rock and farther into the neutral ground to the north-east, many of the guns obtain a reverse fire upon the inundation and render it impracticable to form covered approaches up to its brink. They also prevent the erection of breaching batteries there which would considerably increase the difficulty of an escalade. There is, besides, the enfilading fire from the Devil's Tongue, a fire not easily silenced, for the mole is too narrow to be hit without difficulty and, being in the water, is not subject to ricochets.

Two. The security of the sea side may be fairly deduced from the actual failures of the attack to 1782, for although the intended plan was not on that occasion perfectly carried into execution, yet it probably was as nearly so as any complicated plan of that nature ever will or ever can be, and certainly a more formidable plan of attack can scarcely be imagined, add to this the fortifications on that side have been considerably increased since that era.

Gibraltar may be considered as a fortress which an happy combination of nature and art has rendered sufficiently impregnable to answer every useful end. It is true that in contemplating this magnificent piece of military architecture one is tempted to regret that the town is situated where it is. Could the flat ground on the north-east side been escarped and thrown into the sea, the place would have been rendered more perfect than it, at present, is. This is, however, the regret of a visionary engineer, for it is sufficiently strong as it is as to answer every purpose and defy every enemy except famine or one of those wonderful accidents which occasionally occur in the history of military transactions.

After viewing the works everyone who visits Gibraltar should extend his walk by Middle Hill and the Signal House to St Michael's Cave, and from thence by St Misery to St George's Tower, or O'Hara's Folly. General O'Hara wished to erect this tower with sufficient height to look into Cadiz bay but finding that impracticable, he converted it into a second signal house. It has, however, since been destroyed by lightning; the point where it is situated is 1,472 feet above the level of the sea and the highest in the garrison.

From hence he should go up the hill and down Mediterranean Steps to Mediterranean Battery, hence by Levant Cave Magazine to Windmill Hill, through the hole in the wall to Europa, advance by Europa and back by Buena Vista and Rossia. Near St Michael's Cave is a mortar excavated in the Rock, for the purpose of throwing stones on a particular point in the Bay. From Mediterranean Steps you see a St Michael's Cross, made by General O'Hara and Captain Douglas, formerly Town Major. They had descended the Rock to this point when the tremendous precipices around them affected their nerves and, though both men of known courage, they waited in the same spot in fearful but motionless anxiety till they were discovered and drawn up by ropes.

There is a fine example of the effects of contrast in ascending Mediterranean Steps. You proceed almost in one instance through a low, excavated passage when the propect is confined to a few feet from the ground. On emerging you see at once the overhanging rock on which St George's Tower is situated 900 or 1,000 feet above the spot where you are. You are so close that the eye is unable to take in the immense angle under which the rock is [?] and is almost tempted to give up the attempt of seeking the summit. I did not see this in cloudy weather but probably the effect is increased.

The following is the artillery at present actually mounted in Gibraltar:

Iron Ordnance:		Brass Ordnance:	
42-pounders	27	26-pounders	2
32-pounders	88	18-pounders	2
26-pounders	8	12-pounders	23
24-pounders	230	6-pounders	14
18-pounders	52	3-pounders	2
12-pounders	50	10-pounder Irish howitzers	17
6-pounders	10	8-pounders	21
4-pounders	4	$6\frac{1}{2}$-pounder howitzers	4
68-pounders of cannonades	15	10-pounder Irish Mortars	1
24-pounders of cannonades	21	$5\frac{1}{2}$-pounder Mortars	1
13-pounder Irish Mortars	26	$1\frac{2}{5}$ Mortars	1
10-pounders	6		
8-pounders	1		

Total number of pieces of ordnance: 626

All the Spanish lines and posts in the neighbourhood of Gibraltar have been dismantled. In the beginning of the present contest the Spaniards were continually requesting supplies of guns, etc from the garrison for their armies in Valencia and other parts of Spain. The Governor, I believe Sir Huw Dalrymple, represented that it would be much fairer to furnish them from the Spanish works than the English ones and, after a little hesitation, the Spaniards acquiesced and the whole of the guns have been brought into the fortress, where those which have not already been sent off by sea still remain.

Appendix B

Cocks's library is known to have included the following:

de Saxe: *Reveries*
Essai Generale de Fortification
Jomini: *Traite de la Grand Tactique*
Memoirs of Prince Eugene
Lloyd: *History of the Seven Years War*
Tempelhoff: *translation of above*
Memoir sur la guerre de Pyrenée par M.B*** (sic)
Treatise de la Guerre de la Vendée par M. Bouchon
Histoire de Cartes dernier compagnie de M. de Turenne Publie 1782 par le complie de Brimbard sous le nom de Beaurzan
Hassell's *Statistique Europienne*
Stuart: *Elements of Philosophy of the Human Mind*
St Pierre: *Theory of the Tides*
Blair's *Sermons* and his *Lectures*
Buonaparte: *The Secret Cabinet*
Rousseau: *Nouvelle Eloise*
Ferguson: *Lectures*
Adye: *Bombadier*
Caesar's Commentaries
Walton: *History of English Poetry*
Percy: *Ancient Ballards*
Milford: *Grecian History*
Dulles: *Mathematics*
Spenser: *Faerie Queen*
Milton: *Paradise Lost*
Campbell, Thomas: *Gertrude of Wyoming*
Defoe: *Robinson Crusoe*
Hammond: *Love Elegies*
Scott: *The Lady of the Lake* and *Sir Roderick's Vision*
Allison: *On Taste*
Rational Recreations, including Experiments in Pneumatics, Hydrology & Pyrotechnics
St Evremond
Tacitus
Vergil
Shakespeare
Pope

Appendix C

Observations on Piquets
Of attacking small parties of the enemy

TAKE THE WORLD and all the different tribes and nations into which it is divided and you will find more cowards than brave men. More fights are determined by the ill conduct of the beaten than the valour of the conquerors. Few men in modern armies are much interested in the success of the master which they serve, or feel sufficient principle to fight from a sense of duty, at any rate if they begin in this way they get tired of doing so every day. Other motives of action are required, variety, expectation of plunder, the fear of contempt from their comrades, the fear of punishment and the hope of reward from their officers, or if these won't do, brandy.

It is evident that a soldier who requires these stimuli is not always ready for action; oppose men prepared to fight to such men attacked unexpectedly and you have them already half beaten, and more especially if you meet them without an officer. A serjeant may be able to command as well as an officer but soldiers will not fight so well under him because they know his report will not afterwards affect their character so much.

I have said take the world in general, but British soldiers are different from others in their vices and their virtues, their excellencies and their defects. I do not think I am over-partial to my countrymen who have but too many military faults, but I will give them the credit of valour. With a Briton self is everything. He is more afraid of disgracing himself in his own eyes than in those of the world. Everyone else, what ever his merits, is usually an object of contempt, hence he has what few others have, a motive of intrepidity constantly operating. An acute moralist observes that the great end and object of our existence is sensation. A Briton is very subject to ennui and the spur given to his system by a feeling of danger is, to him, an actual pleasure. If there is a man in the world who likes fighting for fighting's sake, it is a British soldier.

With such men opposed to men of the common run, you may attempt things which, at first sight, seem almost desperate in the way of small skirmishes, going out with the design of attacking should an opportunity occur, you risk nothing against a patrol or foraging party of the enemy which has probably come out with very pacific intentions. They will always be well satisfied if they defend themselves, all you must make sure of is that you really attack them unexpectedly, and you are sure of success. Our men will do their duty and *they* will probably not do theirs, with cavalry especially because they can gain nothing, for even if they repulse us our horses will carry us out of their way.

With cavalry against cavalry the affair is generally very simple. Keep two-fifths in reserve to cover your retreat in case of disaster, to secure prisoners and help wounded or dismounted men, and attack sabre in hand with the remainder the instant they see you. Regularity of attack is of little consequence. I have no faith in the shock of cavalry. If you can bring the bulk of your people on a flank or a small party of the enemy, so as to be pretty sure of cutting down two or three men and getting two or three backs turned directly, it will be a good thing.

Men act on these occasions a great deal by instinct and example and when one man turns his back, others do it without knowing why and sometimes without being frightened. On these occasions your dragoons should hussa and flourish their sabres. I know very well that the point gives worse wounds than the edge and perhaps exposes the men less, but I repeat that in cavalry combats more is done by frightening your adversary than hurting him. Prime in imnibus praeliis [?] oculi vincutur, Tacitus Germanicus. The action of cutting gives a man a tremendous air and countenance, he is worth two or three sneaking rascals pinking with the point of their sword.

When your enemy has fairly turned his back that is the moment to bring the point into play. I need not tell a dragoon in pursuit always to ride up on his adversary's near side, but even then you can only cut at his head or his back, the one is probably defended by a skull cap the other by a strong pouch belt, and in French soldiers by a rolled cloak. Neither of these are easy to cut through. On the other hand the whole of the left side is exposed to the point. You will very likely give him here a mortal wound but even if you do not, he will probably shrink when he feels your sabre and lose his balance on the off-side of his horse, and in this case you have him prisoner. These rules accord with the principles of the sword exercises as taught in our service.

In attacking small parties of infantry not sufficient to form a square it is still more requisite to be quick in your attack; you must, however, be very careful that there is no ditch or wall behind which they can shelter themselves before you reach them and where you cannot get at them. If there is nothing of this sort and no house into which they can throw themselves, charge in line and your files open. This order, which is sometimes called the charge au forager, increases your apparent numbers and renders it more difficult to hit your man. At the same time advance your reserve towards their flank as if to cut them off.

Infantry who do their duty are really a formidable arm to cavalry but the latter have appearance on their side, and there are few infantry who will stand cavalry when taken unprepared in an open place. A serjeant of the 16th Dragoons of the name of Baxter, patrolling with five dragoons, fell in with an officer and 42 infantry cooking. He rode at them hoping to surprise them but they got to their arms, began firing and killed one of the men. Being an intrepid fellow he persevered, dashed in among them, sabred one or two and so frightened the rest that they threw down their arms. Some Portuguese peasants helped to secure them and he brought forty prisoners to the regiment.†

If the infantry consists of 200 or 300 men and is strong enough to form a square, it is best to let them alone if there is no particular object to be gained by their defeat. If any military object beyond the destruction of the square renders it

---

†16 November 1810.

necessary to attack them, it must be done in the principles described in the other section. Your success, even if you do succeed, will cost so much that the destruction of the square will not counterbalance the loss of men and horses and therefore should not be attempted except with a further military object in view.

Of Piquets

The object of piquets is to enable the troops in the rear to relax in security. The instant therefore an alarm becomes sufficient to oblige them to turn out and load their baggage the piquets are no longer useful and, if there be any risk in their retreat, should fall back on the main body. They naturally form the skirmishers and support and the advanced and rear guard. Piquets of Observation merely look out.

Piquets of Support are expected to stand their ground at certain times in order to give the troops in the rear more leisure.

Piquets of this description should always have piquets of observation in their front. The stronger the piquet the more difficult it is to keep it in constant alertness.

When the country is plain and open, piquets of observation, with a grand guard at some distance in the rear covering the encampment, are alone wanted. The piquets of observation should not be too strong, three reliefs of the vedettes are only required, when there are too many, officers sometimes think themselves bound in honour to skirmish, perhaps get a man or horse wounded and in bringing them off get into a scrape.

It is necessary that an officer should ascertain that the enemy is coming on seriously before he thinks of leaving his post. I need not impress this on young men of spirit but when once this is certain, with a piquet of observation he should always retreat in time. The grand guard should fall back at the same time, only observing to support any piquet that is accidentally pressed.

When the country is cramped and enclosed so that the piquets have a bad look out, piquets of support may be necessary; for these I would always employ infantry. A few infantry skirmishers will prevent the enemy's cavalry from galloping into your encampment and as they are only required in an enclosed country, their retreat is secure.

The most disagreeable country for outposts is an open country affording no shelter for infantry, but when the unfavourable nature of the ground deprives you of a good look out, there you must have a strong piquet or two of support, formed of cavalry. These piquets are again supported by the grand guard. If the enemy comes on with infantry you must, for the most part, retire skirmishing. He will seldom give you an opportunity of doing anything good, but then again infantry cannot come on very fast. If he advances with cavalry you must endeavour to charge the head of his column and oblige him to deploy a few squadrons. This gives time. If you are hard-pressed you can always retreat à la debordage and rally behind the first defile or broken ground.

By night infantry should always furnish the piquets if there is any shelter for them. They are more formidable to the enemy and a sentry is not so easily seized or killed on his post as a vedette. Besides, night work takes less out of the effective strength of infantry than cavalry, the cavalry should be employed in patrolling. If, however, the country is quite open I do not wish to see infantry. In case of attack the cavalry cannot direct them and are embarrassed how to help them.

If the country is just so far enclosed to allow of infantry by night, but to make it too dangerous to risk them by day, they should be ordered off before daybreak and the cavalry piquets should then mount and patrol to the front. By night the vedettes or sentries should be posted with a view to the security of the piquet only. The security of the post should be maintained by patrols. Fewer vedettes are required by night than by day. By day the whole country must be watched, by night only the accessible ground.

Piquets should change their ground at night but I do not like their falling back without object. If possible, they should be moved at night by a defile; by day, they should be in a hollow or among trees. Piquets must always recollect when attacked to make a great firing whether they stand their ground or not, in order to give the alarm. The officers of piquets should make their men acquainted during the day with the ground they will have to patrol at night. Three patrols of communication are usually sufficient.

Note The NCO of the piquet is responsible that the reliefs take place properly and that the vedettes have their proper orders. When the dragoons are tolerably intelligent it is not necessary that he should go round every relief, he may content himself with posting the relief till every man has been once on vedette, and afterwards only parading them.

It is an invariable rule for the piquet to be constantly accoutred; all the horses must remain saddled and half those of vedettes must be constantly bridled. The best time for foraging is usually in the afternoon but you must rather go without forage than let your people go out of sight of the vedettes if you forage to the front. When part of the piquet is foraging the remainder should usually be bridled. If you can forage to the rear this is not necessary as you can send one or two at a time. Half an hour before dawn of day the whole piquet must be mounted and patrols are then usually sent a little way to the front.

Fires should not be allowed in an advanced piquet but it is a good deception to make a few near the day post and there establish your night post, two or three hundred yards off. If the enemy thinks of surprising you he makes right for the fire and, not finding you, is at a loss and stops, when the glare discovers him to you. These fires may be kept up by the patrols. If the weather is so cold as to absolutely require a fire it should be concealed behind a house so as to mask it as much as you can and make several of those false fires besides.

When very near the enemy the piquet may be mounted and moved to a fresh spot once or twice in the night, to keep them alert. It is not an easy matter to keep people awake all night, they generally droop towards morning. To prevent this set them singing, smoking or drinking coffee, the last plan especially is capital. If a fellow is inveterably drowsy, make him mount his horse, go the vedettes and count the enemy's fires. A good piquet officer is very invaluable, an officer who allows himself to be surprised on piquet is disgraced for ever. Young men should bear this in mind.

On Chains of Posts

Chains of posts or outposts may be classed under three heads:

> Those covering an army in position.
> Those covering an army extended in cantonments.
> Those which cover a line or frontier.

An army assembles in position when so near the enemy that it may, in a few hours, be brought into action.

If so close that the whole army is obliged to be under arms, the outposts in front are composed by day of small cavalry piquets in the open ground and small infantry piquets in enclosed ground, both forming a chain of vedettes and sentries in front. The cavalry piquet should be supported as much as possible by light infantry, which may keep the enemy's tirailleurs in respect and prevent them picking off the vedettes. By night, infantry piquets are substituted for the cavalry and the latter are placed in reserve forming a second line of piquets furnishing patrols along the line of sentries. Frequent patrols of cavalry must in such cases be in motion on our flanks, which must endeavour to get on, and even round, the flanks of the enemy and discern any movements he may make in the night preparatory to an attack the following day. The rattling noise which accompanies the movement of artillery, the kindling and extinguishing of fires, everything must be observed and immediately reported to the officer on duty for the night who, in armies of any size, will generally be a general officer. Should anything important be observed a second report must also be made to Headquarters. Parties of observation should likewise be detached to the rear of the enemy if practicable where, by gaining high and commanding ground, they may observe what is going on in his lines of operation to the rear.

When an army is separated in cantonments but at no great distance from the enemy, a detached corps of light infantry or cavalry is usually formed in front to take the outposts of the army. If there are several grand routes by which the enemy may advance, considerably separated from each other, an advanced corps is sometimes attached to each, communicating by patrols and exchanging reports of what each may learn. These corps furnish the chains of cavalry posts in front, which again give the piquets of each post a certain portion of country to watch.

These posts may be supported by infantry as mustered in tents, but the great body of the infantry should be encamped or cantoned near some position where they could make a stand against any reconnaissance force of the enemy, or even keep his army partially in check till the troops in the rear can assemble. These positions should be strengthened by field works.

When the country is so open and the enemy so near that he could reach the position in less than a night's march, the whole of the troops forming the outposts should be turned out at least half an hour before dawn of day and formed in the alarm posts. The baggage should likewise be packed and sent off an hour before dawn three miles to the rear, or still further if there be any defile which it may clog up or impede the movement of troops.

A chain of posts is formed to cover a line or frontier when the two armies have taken up stationary cantonments at some distance from each other. From half a regiment to a brigade are then generally stationed on the great routes communicating between the enemy and ourselves. These posts should be one or two days' march in front of the infantry cantonments. If the enemy is two days' march or upwards from these posts, they may content themselves with pushing forward on the different routes in front, subaltern officers' parties about a day's march each. These parties should be relieved every three days, they should send forward daily patrols to the front, about half a march. The officers should endeavour to learn the cantonments of the enemy in their front and get daily reports through the peasants that no change has taken place at any of them. They must inform the officers who relieve them of all they have heard.

Note When the two armies are assembled en masse and an engagement is expected, but still they are some hours' march from each other, a large body of cavalry, principally light, is pushed forward as near the enemy as possible to observe his movements. The general officer commanding this body should endeavour to extend his chain of piquets and parties so as to outflank the enemy, and thus he must try to bring forward his own flank parties so as to get them on the flank of the enemy. He must observe which heights command the greatest extent of country and must keep possession of them as long as possible, and even should he be obliged to abandon them, if an opportunity occurs of re-obtaining a momentary possession it is right to take advantage of it. He must observe on which side the enemy appears most jealous of our observations and must diligently push them on that direction. It is not always the highest hills from whence you observe the best. If the enemy is as strong in cavalry he will endeavour to prevent their reconnaissances; this will give rise to a variety of skirmishes. In these affairs you must not allow yourself to be bullied because the result of a petty action of this kind previous to a battle has sometimes a great effect on the spiritual and moral force of both armies. At the same time you should usually avoid a general affair, first because it will distract your attention too much from the observation of the enemy and, secondly, because it will weaken the cavalry which will perhaps be wanted to strike a blow in the ensuing engagement. Infantry officers and aides de camp are always crying out for a grand cavalry affair for they desire no better diversion than to get up on a hill and see the mêlée, which is certainly a very entertaining spectacle, but in my opinion on the eve of an engagement which may decide the fate of a campaign an officer ought to prefer his duty to his vanity.

If the ground is very woody and enclosed, infantry may be necessary to support the detached cavalry, but it is better if possible to do without them. They must on no account ever be separated from the army by a plain. The old Austrian armies were enabled to carry on their duties to greater perfection than we can because they always had a multitude of light troops which never entered into the body of the battle and which, in consequence, they had no wish to spare previously. Our army, which is differently organised, has no light troops which cannot act in line when necessary. Cavalry cannot be expected to do these duties well unless thoroughly rationed, at least with corn; it requires great exertions of man and horse, the officers must show all their zeal, activity and intelligence.

At night the detached cavalry must still remain near the enemy but they should cover themselves if possible by a ravine or a redoubt. If this is not the case, after feeding they must bridle up for the night; at all events, they must be mounted and ready before daybreak and remain so until their patrols have made a report of what the enemy is about.

The only case where the officer commanding can indulge in any general action of cavalry is when our army is much superior to the enemy and consequently he can less afford to lose men and horses than ourselves.

Hints for a Patrol

I make three classes of patrols.

(1) Patrols of reconnaissance or discovery.
(2) Patrols of security.
(3) Patrols of communication.

Patrols of reconnaissance are sent out from the troops doing the outpost duty or sometimes from the army by order from headquarters. They are under charge of an officer, vary from 6 to 8, to 50 or 60 dragoons, and make a separate turn of duty. Their strength must depend upon the openness of the country and the distance they have to go from their own posts. Every patrol requires separate rides but I will suppose two cases which will give a general idea of the conduct to be pursued by all.

Let the country be unenclosed but broken by valleys, streams and woods and let us suppose the patrol has orders to proceed the distance of 10 or 12 miles from the outpost on a given road unless it should previously meet the enemy.

A patrol of this sort would find some riflemen very useful to leave in a wood or in some enclosed ground on the road to cover its retreat. It must be careful, however, that the infantry in its retreat will not have above a mile and a half, or two miles, of open country to cross lest, if pressed, its ammunition should be expended too soon. If there is no infantry the patrol must take the same precautions from the moment that it leaves the outposts as it otherwise would do from the time it left the infantry.

It should consist of a captain, subaltern and 25 or 30 dragoons. The patrol will march with an advanced guard of an NC officer and 6 dragoons; it will keep about 500 yards in front. When it happens to get out of sight of the patrol by hopping a hill or turning a corner it will leave a dragoon who will keep the patrol in sight; the advanced guard must not go out of sight of this dragoon. Three dragoons from the advanced guard will be 400 yards in front and one of them another 100 yards further still. This advance must not lose sight of the non-commissioned officer and the motions of all must be regulated by those of the patrol.

The distances I have mentioned are not to be scrupulously observed but varied according to the facility or difficulty of keeping up the visual communication between the different links of the chain. If any commanding heights be near the road the non-commissioned officer of the advanced guard should ride up them or send a trustworthy dragoon to their top.

Note A In so doing this he must creep quietly up the height, leaning on his horse's neck so that if he discovers the enemy from the top he may come back and only show the appearance of a horse grazing without a rider. If the guide of the advanced guard is to be trusted he should first ascend and look round if the height be immediately on the road; if the heights be out of the road it would lose time to send him there.

The non-commissioned officer of the advance must report everything he sees or hears to his officer – dust, horses or mules grazing, smoke, troops of peasants, shots fired, drums beating. If he observes anything suspicious he must halt the advance, concealing it as much as possible, and wait till the officer has reconnoitred. The non-commissioned officer and dragoons of the advance guard, especially those most in front, must accurately observe the tracks on the road they are passing and likewise on the different crossroads in order to ascertain if they are used by the enemy. They must likewise stop and examine all peasants or others whom they meet.

Besides the advance guard, the officer must send out one or two intelligent dragoons to each flank in order to ascend the heights, observe the crossroads and meet peasants. These men should be occasionally relieved. The officer should have made all the previous enquiry possible as to the nature of the country and arranged in his own mind how he would retire to either flank in case he was cut off.

At setting off, he should provide two guides, one to go with the advanced dragoon, the other to remain with himself and explain the names of the different villages he may see, where respective roads lead to and other questions relative to the country. The instant the advanced guard or the flankers make any signal he must halt the whole patrol and ride to the man who makes the signal. He should leave on the commanding heights, at a distance of every two or three miles, a file of dragoons; this chain must look out that the enemy does not cut the patrol off or form any ambuscade in the rear to attack them on their return. If the dragoons thus left observe a party of the enemy equal to, or stronger than, the patrol coming in its rear, one dragoon should immediately ride off to apprise the patrol if he is able to avoid observation. The other should conceal himself and watch the motions of the enemy. Should the enemy discover him, he must make off in a contrary direction to that in which the patrol has marched, in order to mislead the enemy. If it is impossible to report to the patrol without being discovered, both dragoons must remain concealed in observation till the enemy ferrets them out, or till it is evident that the enemy's party has got scent of the patrol, either by information or by observing their traces. In this case, it is indispensable to warn the patrol as soon as possible. One dragoon should do this while the other keeps as near the enemy as he can, firing occasionally to give the patrol notice where the enemy is.

Note B If a party of the enemy appears to the rear decidedly inferior to the patrol, the dragoons must watch them narrowly and if they dismount, or go carelessly to forage in a village or farmhouse, the patrol, on its return, may make some of them prisoners. Dragoons left on a chain of this sort must have orders to remain till dark and if the patrol has not then returned, to return themselves.

The officer commanding the patrol should be provided with a tracing of the country and a glass. He must question all peasants and even send to houses and villages near the road. In this sort of enquiry he must, of course, be guided by the time he has to spare. He must make his men march quietly and encourage them to look out individually and point out anything they observe. He may judge of their capacity by the remarks they make. His worst horses he should leave in the chain behind.

Note He should constantly point out the direction in which their own outposts are and make them observe it by some hill, steeple, or other remarkable object; then, in case they are separated from the patrol, they will not be at a loss.

These little rules and precautions may appear oftentimes unnecessary but if an officer accustoms himself to do them habitually, they will become as natural and as much part of the patrol as taking open order is part of the foot parade.

If the officer has a river to pass on the patrol which is not generally fordable, he must enquire very particularly as to the bridges and points that may be crossed and he must leave two or three dragoons within sight of it with the same orders as the chain I have before mentioned. They must fire a particular number of shots, nine for instance with two intervals at the end of each three, in case the enemy occupied the bridge. If the patrol comes to a large wood it must halt at the distance of half a mile; if there are any heights which look down into the wood it must be well reconnoitred from them. The advance guard must then send a patrol of two dragoons forward while two other patrols of three dragoons each turn to the right and left, skirting the edge of the wood.

The first cross tracks these flank patrols on entering the wood come to, one must halt at the entrance while the others proceed, 7 or 800 yards into the wood. On their return they may halt at the entrance and the third man may proceed further up the outside edge of the wood. If all these patrols return without meeting anything suspicious the advanced guard may proceed through the wood and to the first height beyond it while, if the wood is not very large, a dragoon goes round it, right and left, and meets the advanced guard on the other side. After these precautions the patrol may advance.

Note If the enemy is discovered to occupy the wood with infantry the patrol must not pass it but, having made what observations it can as to their force and whether encamped in the wood or on the march, it must return.

If cavalry is in the wood the patrol must be guided by their numbers as to advancing or returning.

If the patrol approaches a large village or town it should halt at the distance of a mile, or a mile and a half, and in such a situation as that by hiding a flank behind a wood or hill it may appear stronger at a distance than it is. The officer should then move with the advanced guard towards the village, making for some height from where he can look down into it. If he finds one, he must reconnoitre it carefully from thence for 10 minutes or a quarter of an hour. If there be none such, he must spread his party at the distance of 200 or 300 yards from each other, forming an arc, rather convex, towards the enemy, and in this manner proceed to within 350 or 400 yards of the village. The dragoons must all keep their eye on the officer. When he arrives at the above-mentioned distance he will halt about 10 minutes, diligently observing the town; in the meantime the dragoons on the flanks must move gradually forward till they form the arc of a circle concave towards the town, no dragoon approaching nearer than 350 yards.

If any peasants come out in this interval they must be examined. If they say the town is not occupied by the enemy they must be kept in hostage till their information is proved, and threatened with death if it turns out false. If any peasants are seen in the neighbourhood, or coming towards the town, they must be detained. One must be sent in while his companion or his horse is kept as a pledge of his fidelity.

If no peasants are seen, as sometimes happens where a town has been nearly deserted in consequence of the war, the two flank dragoons must ride round the town on each side, gradually approaching it; at the same time the guide may be sent in. If nothing of the enemy is observed, a single dragoon may ride through the town and meet those who ride round it.

Note If the enemy is discovered to occupy the town the officer should endeavour to make out whether he is cantoned there or only there by chance on a foraging party, or on the march. He will probably be able to make this out by the way in which his vedettes or sentries are posted. He must endeavour to form a judgement of the numbers in the town by the fires, by those he may see, or by the baggage animals grazing near it. If the enemy does not disturb him he need not fall back far but remain at the distance of a third or half a mile, watching the town for half an hour or an hour. If a party of cavalry comes out after him he must retreat at a round pace to the point where he has left the patrol; this must make the most of itself and will probably cause the pursuing enemy to check.

Altogether, if he has observed the precautions laid down and has not the ill fortune to be embarrassed in his rear by any chance party of the enemy, he is pretty sure of half a mile start, which is quite enough. He should not draw sword except in extremity.

If a piquet of cavalry turns out in front of the town and is so situated as to prevent you getting any sight of it, and if it is not stronger than your advance and you can get near it without being observed, it may sometimes be right to charge it and drive it from its post, which will only occur when your orders are positive to reconnoitre the town. You must make your observations as quick as possible and then retreat at a trot.

If the distance to which the patrol is sent be so great that it cannot leave a chain behind for security, it should endeavour to return by a different route, with the same precautions as it advanced. If the patrol is out above four-and-twenty hours it should guide itself by the same rules as a party of observation, which in fact it then wholly becomes. If a patrol finds itself wholly cut off it must conceal itself for the day and retreat in the night, and if necessary divide or even disperse. On the whole a patrol should keep its horses as fresh as possible for fear of accidents. It should avoid engaging till it has fulfilled its object but if, on its return, an opportunity occurs of making prisoner it should not let it slip.

Let us now suppose that a patrol of eight men under a subaltern is sent off in a country enclosed by walls or hedges so that troops can only move by the roads. No slow or weak horses should be allowed on such a duty. The principles of this patrol are the same as those of the former. If any great road cross that on which the patrol is moving a single dragoon should be left within sight. This man should not ride after the patrol in case the enemy come in the rear but fire a shot or two and retreat, when necessary, towards his own outposts. A particular spot should be fixed on where the patrol may look for him on their return, that if they miss him from thence they may suspect something is going wrong. If this dragoon sees the patrol coming back pursued he must post himself on a height like a vedette and fire a shot as if to alarm troops in his rear. The patrol must conduct itself when approaching woods and villages by the same rules as the former. It is not a bad plan to time a patrol of this strength so it may arrive at the point where it expects to meet the enemy just before sunset, in case its retreat will be secure if it knows the country.

If a patrol does not understand the language of the country sufficiently to comprehend what the peasants say it should endeavour to get their reports in writing.

Patrols of reconnaissance are sometimes sent out at night, especially after a day's skirmishing when it is not known what points the enemy continues to occupy and what he has abandoned. Two or three dragoons are sufficient for this duty, they must proceed in the direction ordered till challenged by the enemy or till they reach the point ordered them. They must diligently observe all fires and listen for all noises. One man should occasionally dismount and examine tracks of the road or go to a little distance where his hearing is not disturbed by the breathing and stamping of the horses and listen with his ear to the ground. One dragoon should be thirty or forty yards advanced and all with their carbines sprung. If it is a moonshiny night the dragoons should have their cloaks on so as to conceal their white belts.

The French generally make their sort of patrols much stronger than we do with 12 or 20 men. But with good horses like ours such numbers are unnecessary and therefore wrong. The French infantry always beat the Reveille one hour before daybreak, which is therefore a very good time to have this sort of patrol out.

Patrols of Security are sent out from the advanced piquets, their object is to examine occasionally those points in front of the line of vedettes where information may be gained but which it would be imprudent to occupy constantly.

Daybreak and before sunset are the common times for these patrols but these periods should not be always the same. In most countries it is scarce possible to place vedettes so but what the enemy can get near them by some route or other unobserved, these deficiencies are made up for by patrols of security. They should consist of two, three or four dragoons and should explore all ravines, woods, villages, where it is probable the enemy might conceal himself if he meditated any attempt on the piquets.

In doing this one dragoon should always remain behind to warn the piquet if the rest of the patrol is carried off. These patrols should find out by the traces if the enemy is in the habit of patrolling near the vedettes.

Patrols of Communication are sent from piquet to piquet to ascertain that all is well. They are principally required in the night when it is impossible to post the vedettes so thick as to form a complete chain.

When infantry find the night piquet, cavalry should be attached to give the patrols of communication. Two dragoons are sufficient who should ride ten or twelve yards one behind the other. If they fall in with the enemy they must fire. if the country is very enclosed the infantry sometimes furnish patrols of communication.

The patrols of communication by night should occasionally stop and listen as before mentioned, there is usually a general communication all around the posts at daybreak before the relief takes place and the reports go off.

Appendix D

Cocks's list of the guns at the 1812 siege of Badajoz – March 24

Our batteries are as follows, reckoning from the left:

No 1: Three 18-pounders.
Three 5½-inch howitzers.
This battery furnishes a direct fire against Picurina. It is a good deal exposed to Pardeleiros but the Engineers have covered it very well by a high epaulement on the left and traverses between each gun.

No 2: Four 24-pounders, likewise Picurina.

No 3: Four 18-pounders. Furnishes a direct fire against the right face of the redoubt of San Roch.

No 4: Six 24-pounders.
One 5½-inch howitzer.
Furnishes a direct fire against the right face of La Trinidad bastion, an enfilading fire against the left face, a direct fire against the curtain between La Trinidad and San Pedro and a direct fire against the right flank of Santa Maria. It was ordered to fire only on La Trinidad.

No 5: Four 18-pounders. Furnishes a direct fire against the salient angle of the redoubt of San Roch and the left face of La Trinidad.

No 6: Three 5½-inch howitzers. Against the right flank of San Pedro. This battery is a good deal exposed to San Cristobel.

The enemy, as near as I can observe, has opened the following embrasures but I cannot see whether or not they all have guns in them:

Castle: One
Demi bastion of San Antonio: Face 6; Flank 2
Prolongation of ditto with the curtain: 2
Bastion of San Pedro: Left face 4; Flank 4
Redoubt of San Roch: Left face 4
Curtain between San Pedro and Trinidad: 2
Bastion of La Trinidad: Right face 4; Flanked angle 1; Left face 4;
Left flank 4
Curtain between Trinidad and Sta Maria: 2
Bastion of Sta Maria: Right face 5; left ditto

More batteries were subsequently added. He gave the French list on 1 April, as follows:

	guns
From the Castle against Nos 4 & 5:	1
Flank of San Antonio on Nos 7, 8 & 9:	2
Prolongation of ditto on Nos 7, 8 & 9:	2
Battery in front of the Castle on Nos 7, 8 & 9:	6
Flank of San Pedro on Nos 7, 8 & 9:	4
Curtain of San Pedro on No 5:	1
Trinidad, howitzers, on Nos 7, 8 & 9:	2
Curtain of Trinidad and Santa Maria on Nos 7, 8 & 9:	1
Bastion of San Roque Flank on Nos 7, 8 & 9:	4
Face of bastion of San Roque on Nos 7, 8 & 9:	3
Pardeleiros on Nos 7, 8 & 9:	1

Making a total of 27 guns

There were also 2 or 3 mortars. There were three embrasures in the flank of San Antonio but only two had guns.

Appendix E

The Siege of Badajoz, April 1812

17 March The front to be attacked is that between the bastions of Santa Maria and La Trinidad but it will be first necessary to take the detached redoubt of Picurina. The front which we attacked last year has been severed by an inundation formed by damming up the little river which ran under the castle . . . The hill in front of Fuerte Santa Cristobel has been occupied by an advanced redoubt, the three ravelins between Pardeleiros and the river have been repaired and the salient angles of the covert way on that side countermined. The enemy has done nothing to the point we mean to attack, probably thinking that the counter guard, which covers La Trinidad with the stream which runs at the foot of the glacis, placed it on a par with the rest. Ground to be broke this night . . .

18 March Last night the approach to the first parallel was commenced on the capital of the bastion of La Trinidad; it consisted of four zigzags and followed the crest of the hill as much as possible to avoid the wet, making 1,400 yards of work, commencing 850 from Picurina.

Note A The second branch of the zigzag had a direction given it nearly parallel to the place, with a view to support the trenches in front in case of a sortie.

The first parallel, 250 yards from Picurina, which is 400 from the body of the place, was commenced. We had 200 extra men on the working party, probably they were not employed in the trenches. The night was rainy and windy which prevented the enemy from discovering us.

In working, it is usual to allow at night one man to each four feet and to calculate that in twelve hours they will have got themselves under cover, that in twenty-four hours there will be cover for infantry and in forty-eight the trenches will be completed to the breadth of nine feet and depth of three. Parallels require another day as they must be twelve or fourteen feet wide, provided with a better parapet and should have two banquettes. Batteries may be finished in forty-eight hours ready for the guns and the guns may be got in in a night. Our zigzags are to be ten feet by three and our parallels twelve by three. There is a road leading to the town crossing our zigzags, this has been left open to facilitate the passage of our guns.

19 March Completed the zigzags and continued the parallel; it ought to have been completed but the rainy weather and the soil prevented the men from getting on so fast as they otherwise would have done. The right of the parallel not affording cover by morning, the men were obliged to withdraw. To the right it will be only three to four hundred yards to the place. The soil is a mixture of chalk, sand and clay and the rains appear in the course of time to have washed the clay from the tops of the hills into the valleys.

A battery for four embrasures was commenced opposite Picurina.

At 1am this morning the enemy made a sortie with 1,500 infantry. The principal column debouched from the gate near the detached ravelin of St Roch† and advanced by the Merida road to the unfinished part of the parallel forming that part which was occupied. Our covering party gave way and ran; however, they rallied and drove back the enemy who did little other mischief besides carrying off 150–200 entrenching tools. The principal object of this sortie was to cover a reconnaissance made by forty hussars who advanced at full speed from St Roch and got as far as the Engineer encampment. No one saw them until almost among the artificers and they nearly took General Picton. They took some officers but could not get them off; I do not think they learnt much. Our guns were parked in a hollow and I do not believe they saw them . . .

Headquarters encamped today and I remained with them. The enemy throws few shells and his fire is altogether slack. It is said he has 100,000 shot but only 8,000 shells and is short of powder. He is otherwise well provided.

20 March The besieging army can scarce find its allowance of men for duty, 200 were deficient tonight on the working party. The parallel was sufficiently completed to afford cover along its whole extension. A second approach to the right is wanted, it would facilitate the relief but we have not men to do it without losing time, the first of objects.

Note The further you proceed in a siege the more you want two approaches. If therefore you are in a hurry to get your first parallel established, you may very well neglect the second approach till you are constructing your batteries, when you will probably have men to spare. The four-gun battery was nearly completed and the platforms laid. Another six-gun battery was commenced to the left and others to the right. No battery will open till twenty-four guns or howitzers are ready . . .

21 March Completed the four-gun battery and continued the parallel and the other batteries. The weather still continues rainy and the troops are rather short of tents. Much greater use has been made of musketry this siege than any other and the good effects are very apparent. Picurina has scarcely dared to fire a gun and the ravelin of St Roch has been kept in very good order. The enemy brought down two field guns this morning from Cristobel on the other side of the Guadiana, they enfiladed part of the parallels but did no great mischief, our tirailleurs kept them in order. The enemy appears particularly jealous of our right, a very large proportion of his fire was in that direction . . .

22 March Completed the parallel and continued the construction of the battery, the enemy again brought two field guns to enfilade our parallel, covering their left with a epaulement of sandbags against our riflemen. They occasioned a few casualties but their practice was bad . . . We are constructing five batteries, two to the left of six and four embrasures against Picurina, one direct against the face of San Roch and two enfilading ones against the left face of La Trinidad and the left face of San Pedro . . . The pontoon bridge was swamped this morning in consequence of the sudden rise of the river.

---

†This is St Roque on the maps. Cocks spells it correctly later.

23 March The batteries Nos 1 and 2 being completed; the guns were got in last night ... The enemy again brought down his two field pieces. His fire was altogether slack; as yet in the whole siege he has not fired above 7 or 800 shells. He is working in the ditch in front of the curtain between San Pedro and the Castle. His first design appears to have been that of establishing a redan there, but I think he has now given up the idea and is working at a sort of trench to cover musketry from bastion to bastion... A Spaniard has brought a letter to Lord Wellington he was entrusted to carry from Phillipon† to Soult. He says that: 'Within these few days the English works have assumed a formidable appearance; that he will do his best to prevent being taken by a coup vivre but if not relieved must alternatively surrender.' Lord W gave the Spaniard what he said he was to have had from the French, being 512$.

24 March Owing to the dreadful shower yesterday afternoon the batteries were not completed and no more guns taken in last night. This was of little importance as owing to the failure of the pontoon bridge we should not have had sufficient shot over to open tomorrow.

Our working parties were employed on completing the batteries, draining the trenches and carrying shot to the batteries. Not above twenty men per embrasure can work at once in a battery. A 100 shot per piece is the complement. Our powder is placed in a depot near the last of the trench from whence the battery magazines are fed, but enough is never brought into any battery magazine to occasion serious damage. This is a much better plan than the French who bring their powder into the battery magazines by which serious casualities sometimes occur; an accident of this sort silenced their fire for two days at Ciudad Rodrigo.

The enemy withdrew their field pieces early this morning in consequence of the approach of the 5th Division. By 3 pm the investment was completed. All the enemy's cattle was withdrawn within the wall, they have upwards of 300 oxen and a good many sheep. At 3 pm fifteen or sixteen French hussars came out from behind Pardeleiros and galloped towards our piquets; their object appeared to get into the prolongation of our parallel and see if our guns were in the batteries. I do not think they would see this. The enemy has constructed a small place d'armes behind Picurina, in the covert way, from whence he has placed a small mortar which threw a few shells, very weak [?], at battery No 1. In general the enemy's fire today has been slacker than ever, he is probably reserving his shells till our fire begins to silence his guns but why he does not fire more round shot I cannot imagine, unless he is short of powder; to the right our parallel is ever within range of grape ...

Cocks then listed all the batteries and these can be found in Appendix D.

25 March Our working party last night did not exceed 600 men, they were employed in clearing and draining the trenches and carrying shot and ammunition. The remainder of our guns were brought in by the Merida road and though the night was fair and light they were not discovered and were all mounted without loss soon after midnight. The weather seems set in to be fine. The enemy

---

†The governor of Badajoz.

has opened four new embrasures in the curtain between San Pedro and La Trinidad.

Nos 1 and 2 batteries opened their fire about 10 am against Picurina. They did not produce all the effect that was expected, the ditch of Picurina is very deep and the scarp mostly cut out of solid rock; it is likewise so well covered by its glacis that it cannot be seen. The parapet is of earth, well rammed of a stiff, adhesive nature and left at the natural slope. The only injury the fort suffered was in the embrasures and a few palisades near the salient angle.

By twelve, the other batteries had opened against the respective defences and guns. They soon had manifest superiority over the fire of the place and the defences of the left face of the ravelin of San Roch were nearly destroyed as low as the corden; some spherical case were thrown against such parts of the works as were not opposed directly or by enfilade. They appeared to me to produce good effect in quietening the enemy's fire.

Note Spherical case would be found more useful to fire from a besieged town on the trenches than on any other occasion. I think the balls should be larger; at present, a man, if struck at all is struck by a great number but in the long run one large ball will give a worse wound than a number of small ones. Upwards of 2,500 rounds were fired. We had a howitzer and 2 guns disabled and another dismounted. Although Picurina was so little damaged the Earl determined to escalade when it was dark. The execution of his arrangements was left to Maj-Gen Kemp.

It was determined to attack in three columns altogether, making from 4 to 500 men. The right column was composed of detachments of the 88th and 45th; it was directed to sortie from No 2 battery and force its way into the communication between Picurina and the body of the place. It was then to divide, one half to make front towards the town and charge whatever attempted to come out to the assistance of the troops in the fort, the other half was to cut away the palisading which closed the rear of the fort and force their way in.

The centre column, composed of detachments of the 74th, 83rd and a few Light Division, debouched from No 1 battery and was ordered to escalade by the angle of the shoulder of the right.

The left column, formed of detachments from the 74th and 77th, was to proceed by the inundation and attack the left flank of the work. The first half was then ordered to clear away everything by their fire while the other half pushed into the place under their protection.

The attack commenced about nine. The right and centre columns succeeded in making their way in; the left column, having foolishly thrown away their ladders hoping to get in without them and having likewise missed their hatchet men, failed, and unfortunately continued their fire upon the fort after our men were in, by which a good many were knocked down.

The enemy had 250 within. It is closed to the rear, the scarp is 18 or 20 feet high, the covert way and gorge well palisaded; these however, are as usual close to the glacis and therefore easily got over. I know not to account for the practice of placing them here, unless it is to prevent the attacker from using them as cover for his musketry. The enemy did not defend himself well, the instant our people got on the crest of the parapet they mostly threw down their arms or ran into the guard room.

Note This, however, brought our people to a stand, confusion natural to an attack by detachments instead of corps took place and at this instant the enemy made a feeble attempt to sortie in relief of the place. He was instantly driven back by part of the right column but a panic spread among our troops and they began to evacuate the fort. The enemy perceiving this, sallied from the blockhouse to complete our rout. Nothing however could be more [?]. Our men were rallied by General Kemp and closed with the enemy before he could get back to the blockhouse. Resistance ceased. A few endeavoured to escape by swimming the inundation but they were drowned. Half the enemy were bayonetted and the rest taken . . .

26 March 450 men composed the working party last night. The right of the first parallel with batteries 3 and 4, 5 and 6, being at second parallel distance, about 300 yards, it was unnecessary to advance them, the left only was to be altered, which had hitherto been kept at a distance by the Picurina. The new trench commenced between No 3 battery and the Merida road, from thence it extended to Picurina and from Picurina to the inundation. Although this makes a distance of near 700 yards yet the party worked with such speed as to have completed cover by daybreak. I think this inundation is as much in our favour as against us for it covers our left flank completely.

Note And renders a sortie very perilous to the enemy as his retreat is confined to a single point. It is kept up by closing the arch near the ravelin of San Roch by which the water formerly ran off. This arch may be seen from many points and I should conceive might be opened by our shot.

The firing was slack today on both sides, the enemy appeared completely cowed and his defences being a good deal ruined scarce dared to show his face. Our people were sparing of their fire, there being a lack of shot till about 1 pm.

The defences by the left face of San Roch were today almost wholly destroyed. The bastion of La Trinidad was completely kept in order by No 4 battery, the parallel of its right face was beat down by a direct fire and the left face enfiladed. No 3 did considerable damage to the curtain between Trinidad and San Pedro. No 1 was ready to silence the right flank of San Roch bastion in case it endeavoured to annoy us, but it was silent so it was not thought necessary to waste ammunition on it. Our guns, firing on ricochet had 2° elevation with a charge of 2 lbs.

27 March We had last night 1,200 men at work and the enemy's fire was so slack as to enable us to work by open approach all night. A battery to hold eight 18-pounders was traced out and commenced in the communication of Picurina; it communicated with the 2nd parallel by a zigzag of two branches, which broke off to the right of Picurina. This zigzag was continued to the rear so as to form a communication with No 1 battery. Another battery was commenced in rear of the 2nd parallel and to the left of Picurina to hold twelve 24-pounders, and a third was traced to the left of the eight-gun one to hold two 24-pounders and four 18-pounders. The men were well under cover by morning along the whole of these works. These batteries will be called Nos 7, 8, and 9 if numbering from the left.

The second parallel was completed. As we work nearer the place we get men covered from the enemy's fire but it is astonishing he makes so little use of Trinidad and Pardeleiros; the defences of San Roch are nearly destroyed ...

28 March ... We are in want of good sappers and of gabions. The sapper volanti consists of a number of men running forward, each carrying a gabion and setting them down close together in the direction of the proposed trench. The men lie down, each behind his gabion, till all are arranged, when they all begin to fill together.

Lord Wellington's principle in besieging is to open one or more breaches, according to the strength of the garrison, as soon as possible. They should be sufficiently near to enable the attacking columns, in case of success, to communicate shortly after entering, and yet should be so far that the troops defending one breach cannot see what passes at the other. To enable his troops to advance the assault he directs all the fire he has over and above the breaching batteries or those defences which flank the points to be breached, disregrading that part of the enemy's fire which only bears on the trenches or the batteries.

In the present siege the points to be breached are the faces of La Trinidad and the flanks of the adjoining bastions; the fire of batteries Nos 3, 4, 5 and 6 is ordered to be directed on these works and on the ravelin of St Roch.

By this system, although the enemy's fire may be superior on the whole, yet ours is superior in the most critical points. It perhaps occasions a few more daily casualties and the artillery are usually averse to it for men naturally wish to fire at whatever annoys them but it saves means and it saves time and, in the end, to save time is to save men ...

At a siege the killed and wounded should never be brought back to their encampment, the former should be buried as quickly as possible, the latter conveyed direct to a hospital; an exception may sometimes be made in favour of wounded officers ...

29 March The same number of men were at work. Batteries Nos 7 and 9 were continued and platforms of the latter were laid. The approach was continued by sap towards the salient angle of the ravelin of St Roch. A sap was carried near the river towards the left face of St Roch; some trenches of communication were dug. A battery for four $5\frac{1}{2}$-inch howitzers was commenced in front of No 4 battery and another for two to the right of Picurina.

The enemy opened rather a heavy fire at daybreak from Pardelieros, Santa Maria and the curtain between Trinidad and San Pedro and the Castle. It produced no effect, our batteries fired but little. No 6 has been broken up. Our musketry kept the enemy in very good order but could not prevent his firing some shots from St Roch and occasionally throwing a shell from a small mortar he had there.

30 March The working party consisted of 800 men. No 9 battery and the 4 howitzers opened at daybreak.

Note A The former endeavoured to breach the right flank of Santa Maria, the latter enfiladed the right face of La Trinidad and the counterguard in front with the ditch and covered way. The enemy answered them by a heavy cross fire from the Castle, the right flank of Santa Maria and Pardeleiros. Batteries Nos 7 and 8 were continued and the platforms laid.

Note B No 7 battery is considerably exposed to Pardeleiros and, in consequence, requires to be well traversed and covered by a high epaulement to its left flank. Old No 4 battery was broken up. The sap continued towards the ravelin of San Roque and a battery traced for six or ten 18-pounders to breach the left flank of San Pedro. An approach was begun from the first parallel to communicate with the 3rd and [?] battery.

The enemy has formed a battery for 5 guns in the prolongation of the flank of San Antonio. He has taken away the 2 field guns he had in front. In the course of tomorrow and the next day a fire of fourteen 24-pounders, nineteen 18-pounders and six $5\frac{1}{2}$-inch howitzers will be opened on the place at the distance of 3–400 hundred yards. A few days will probably effect a breach. If there is no obstacle in the ditch to prevent our throwing ourselves in and arriving at once at the foot of the breach, there will be no difficulty in marching to the counter scarp by the further side of the inundation, but if the counter scarp is revetted and so deep as to prevent this, or if there is any considerable depth of water in the ditch, it will be necessary to sap up to the crest of the covert way in order to blow away the counter scarp in the one case, or make a passage over the ditch in the other. This sap must communicate and be supported by the approaches. It will therefore be necessary either to destroy the dyke or to make a bridge across the inundation, thus connecting the sap with our present approaches or to begin new ones on the other side the river. The success of the first measure is very doubtful.

Note If judged necessary, I would prefer to take possession of the ravelin of St Roch, after which I think we could ascertain the nature of the dyke.

The second will be difficult and dangerous but practicable.

The third will be most secure and most expeditious if we have sufficient men, but it will double the number of our covering party in order to protect the new approaches from sorties out of Pardeleiros.

The enemy continues a galling fire of musketry from St Roch with a small mortar, he has also a gun in the flanked angle of La Trinidad. One of our magazines exploded this morning at half past 8 am; it was situated in the ditch of Picurina, resting against the scarp, a live shell fell into the ditch, rebounded from the counter scarp on the magazine and instantly exploded. 10 or 12 men were hurt including 4 English gunners killed and about 2,000 lbs of powder lost.

31 March 700 men composed the working party last night, 500 this morning. Batteries Nos 7 and 8 opened their fire at 10 am. The fire of both was directed against the left face of La Trinidad. For the first three hours they each fired by salvoes, concentrating against two points near each extremity of the face and endeavouring to penetrate through the revetment. Their practice was good and they had considerable effect. The enemy brought a heavy fire upon them from the Castle from 4 guns in the left flank of San Pedro, from the 2 field guns in La Trinidad, from a gun in the right flank and another in the face of Santa Maria, from a gun in the flank of St Roch and another in Pardeleiros. The batteries however were low and well covered and the casualties few. After 1 pm they left off firing salvoes and the practice was not so good.

The best way to make a breach is to mark a square by two vertical and two transverse lines and then knock at the area which may be supposed loosened but we are too far off for such delicate practice. No 9 continued its fire against the right flank of Santa Maria. The defences suffered considerably and the angle of the epaule appeared much injured.

The battery against the left flank of San Pedro and its communication to the rear was continued but not completed. It is scarce possible to work at this parallel by day on account of the musketry fire from the covert way of St Roch. Batteries Nos 3, 4 and 5 fired very little.

It is believed that there is but little water in the ditch of the front attack, perhaps there may be a lunette. I should conceive a resolute fellow might look in during the night.

Note At night three batteries were ordered to fire two shot or shell every five minutes, making six in five minutes . . .

1 April 800 men at work besides a working party of artillery bringing in ammunition. The battery against the flank of San Pedro is contained; it will be No 11 if ever it is completed, but it lies so low and is so much exposed to the enemy's fire that I do not think it will be practicable to live in till the fire be further reduced.

Note A A battery on the crest of the glacis would be much less exposed because, being closer, less fire could be brought to bear on it. Its communication (No 11's) was completed and the sap carried on farther to the right. The other batteries were repaired and the embrasures put in order. The batteries Nos 7, 8 and 9 continued their fire with great effect and good practice.

Note B The enemy has been working at the breach in the night with 200 men, and a deserter says he lost 40 killed and wounded. The enemy kept up a heavy fire but it was not so warm as yesterday, probably his artillerymen are fatigued, his practice was not good and he sometimes fired in salvoes, which I cannot account for. I believe he complains of his powder which is Spanish but in general Spanish powder is considered better than French which has not sufficient saltpetre.

Our batteries are so well constructed that the enemy's fire does not slacken ours. The flank of San Pedro was kept quieter than yesterday by an enfilading fire in ricochet from No 5. In general, enfilading fire will not produce effect against a flank, here it evidently is. The enemy was very jealous of it and made it hot. A shell burst while the Earl was there in the very battery, this is the third or fourth time he has been in the trenches.

In fact this fire need not be regarded would we march straight to the breach, but the more we see of the nature of the inundation the more reason is there to believe there is water in the ditch. There is certainly water in front of the right face of Trinidad and the ditches appear on a level before both faces. I believe the Earl considers this point as ascertained. His project in consequence is this, to take the ravelin of San Roque and thus get at the head of the inundation and let it off, perhaps this will likewise let off the water in the ditches but should they be separately dammed up it will at least enable us to sap to the crest of the glacis and make a bridge over the ditch if necessary. But before we can keep possession of San Roque it will be necessary to quiet the flank fire. Measures will be taken tomorrow.

It will be necessary to silence the battery in front of the castle before we assault otherwise our men will be too much exposed after carrying the place. The Earl thinks that the gorge of the ravelin is closed by a wall and endeavoured to open it today by throwing shot from the howitzers in No 4 into the terreplein, expecting they would ricochet against the inside of the wall. These howitzers have 6°, 6½°, 7° elevation, they produce no effect, the practice of their natures being incorrect. Finding that the howitzers would not do, a 24-pounder was turned on it from the left of No 7.

A deserter came in this evening and he says there is no water in the ditch and no [?] in the town.

2 April 800 men at work. The sap was continued beyond the ravelin to within 50 yards of the inundation. Battery No 11 was completed; it is all placed, being oblique both to the curtain and the flank of San Pedro ... The enemy's fire was much slacker than the two preceding days, the breaches improve. Ever since the siege, the enemy has kept out three cavalry vedettes in front of Pardeleiros, one of them sees our breaching batteries in reserve, our riflemen drove them in today closer to the fort.

3 April The cavalry vedettes have disappeared this morning, a little circumstance of this sort has a great effect on the morale of troops. An attempt was made last night to blow up the dam which retained the inundation, it was not very well managed and failed. It will be renewed tonight and perhaps San Roque taken possession of. Part of the breaching guns are endeavouring to open its gorge.

Anson's Brigade, being ordered to relieve Le Marchant's at the outposts, I thought it no longer right to remain absent though my notification has arrived as major in the 79th Regiment. I am attached to the 16th Dragoons. I join that regiment this evening at Almendralejo. Before I left the trenches the breach of La Trinidad appeared nearly practicable. Almendralejo is 7 leagues from Badajoz.

7 April ...This afternoon we got intelligence of the glorious storm of Badajoz, which took place last night. General Picton with the 3rd Division were to escalade the Castle, the 4th Division to storm the breaches and the face of La Trinidad and the adjoining flank and curtain, the Light Division to storm the breach in the bastion Santa Maria, part of the 5th Division to escalade the bastion of San Vicente next the river, a brigade of Portuguese to make a false attack on Pardeleiros.

The attack commenced at 10 pm. The Engineer Officer conducting the Light Division being killed, they got compounded with the 4th. They found the ditch full of water but not so deep as to prevent their wading. The defence of the breach by Philippon was excellent in arrangement and resolution.

Appendix F

Cocks's Military Thoughts Section in the Journal, begun August 1811

Loiza
Military Ideas. Section 1:

(1) Operations are military movements, tactical or strategical.
(2) The base of operations is that line behind which a general may reasonably hope for temporary security and where he forms his magazines and depots.
(3) The object of operations is that point which the intermediate efforts of the offensive army are directed.
(4) The lines of operations are the routes by which communications are carried on between the base and the object. They should be considered relatively to the advance and retreat of armies and the facility of moving convoys, stores, sick, etc.
(5) The lines of manoeuvre are transverse to the lines of operation and are the routes by which an army is able to change them. These lines are of accidental operation.
(6) The territorial lines of action are those districts or country by which you can get at your enemy and he at you. These lines are sometimes confounded with the lines of operations, but in fact one of the former includes all the latter that an army can possess at the same moment.
(7) The usual bounds of territorial lines are tracts of mountainous country, the sea or navigable rivers without bridges. Of these, the first circumscribes military operations more than any other feature of nature and the sea is likewise a complete boundary, unless there is a fleet at the disposal of the army. In most states one finds certain points of political consequence but not military strength, such as capitals, great mercantile establishments, which contribute the faible of states. However, when so near the line of action as to enter military combination they embarrass you as they must be covered, but they do not embarrass your adversary as he has nothing to fear from them.
(8) The importance of faibles depends on the nature of the government and is usually more ideal than real. When the Athenians embarked by the persuasion of Themistocles they got the better of prejudice, by giving up their faible all the inconvenience resulting from it vanished. Frederick had no faible, Berlin was twice occupied in the Seven Years War. On the other hand, the Austrians scarcely ever dared to uncover Vienna, every demonstration in that direction paralysed them. Buonaparte had no faible in his Italian campaign. Defeat would have finished his fortunes but then he cared not what became of France. He procured the same advantage in the German campaigns by removing the line of action far from his own faible to that of his adversary.
(9) The line of defence or cantonment is that extended line an army occupies when not in immediate danger of attack. The object of extending is to facilitate

subsistence and the degree of extent is limited by the time in which the enemy can attack.

(10) The line of battle or position is the constructed line occupied by an army when collected previous to fighting.

(11) The theory of war is like the theory of Natural Philosophy, taken alone its results cannot be trusted but it enables you to arrange your ideas and draw conclusions from what you see and what you read.

(12) Grand effects arise from a just conception and skilful use of the three following combinations:

Firstly, the choice of the individual lines of action.

Secondly, strategy, which is the science of bringing into the field of action larger masses than your adversary in proportion to your total force.

Thirdly, tactics, or the science of bringing to the point of contest in action a larger proportion of the force present than your adversary.

Section Two: Of territorial lines of action, bases and lines of operation, etc:

(1) The choice of lines of action depends on these considerations:

Nature, when most adapted to your troops and least to those of your adversary and where most favourable to subsidence.

The strength of the respective armies, that is the number and quality of the troops, the state of their equipment and the talents of their chiefs.

The local distribution of the forces, the situation of your own and your adversary's faible, political considerations.

(2) It is advantageous to act on the offensive because the offensive army acts on ascertained data, the defensive one on supposed data.

(3) An army can act offensively when it can fight its adversary.

(4) The army acting offensively chooses the line of action but when both can act offensively the army which can make the initiative movement chooses it.

(5) An inferior army may sometimes enable itself to act on the offensive by making the initiative movement and thus choosing a line of action favourable to the quality of its troops. These considerations prove the advantage of making the initiative movement.

(6) An army should not advance when it can no longer act on the offensive, if it cannot fight it is only going forward to retrace its steps with certain loss when its adversary advances. If circumstances render a long retreat necessary, it is often more advisable to make a movement on the line of manoeuvre and seek a new base and new lines of operation than to try to regain your old ones by a movement directly retrograde. Your enemy will be less prepared to follow you up.

There is no number 7.

(8)–(9) When you are much nearer your enemy's faible than he to yours you may uncover and neglect your own, providing you threaten his. In such cases, if the country produces supplies sufficient for your army while following up the *victory*, it is right to fight and fight with all your heart and soul and strength, seeking all to gain all. For first, as you are manoeuvring freely against an adversary embarrassed to cover his faible the chances of a battle are in your favour, and secondly, a victory is conquest because it leads to your adversary's faible, a defeat is only retreat because your own is out of danger.

(10) It is probable that in order to threaten your adversary's faible you may be obliged to give up your line of operations, but I do not fear this, for a moving army, even in disaster, is not easily surrounded.

(11) It is nevertheless necessary that in such a case battle should not be delayed because your enemy, close to his base, is accumulating, while you, at a distance, or perhaps wholly separated from yours, are diminishing.

(12) Short campaigns, concluded by decisive battles, occasion less human destruction and draw less deeply on resources of nations than long, fatiguing campaigns, even without a battle. Besides, indecisive campaigns are disastrous to both parties, decisive ones only to one.

(13) Since an army advancing in the daring way described in numbers (8)–(9) sets its hopes of success on a victory and its fears of disaster on the insecurity of its retreat, it obviously becomes the policy of the opposing army in the first place, to choose, if possible, a position covering its faible, where it cannot be attacked without manifest disadvantage, and secondly, to increase the difficulties of the advancing army in keeping up communications to the rear.

(14) If the position just chosen is inattackable, and not to be turned, the advancing army has got into a scrape, which it must be got out of as it can. But this can seldom be the case, the lines of Villafranca are almost unique and if there is a chance of success still it should attack. Though the chiefs of the defensive army fight with their backs to the wall, their soldiers do not, on the contrary, the soldiers who attack *do*. Victory will be conquest and perhaps the more complete the more unexpected; defeat will be only retreat which you must submit to if you do not fight, and though experience teaches that a well-managed retreat is not so disastrous an operation as it is sometimes thought, yet it always occasions a degree of loss in sick, wounded, stragglers and stores, and above all strikes a blow in the spirit and moral force of the army. Fight, therefore, if it be possible and if you retreat afterwards you will only have lost a few thousand men more.

(15) Altogether then, the nature of the territorial line is combined with the strength and disposition of the armies and should enable you to act offensively at any point of the line. Secondly, they should be chosen in a country furnishing supplies independent of the magazines, sufficient to gain and follow up a victory.

Note When an army is so near its adversary as to remain necessarily in position, foraging parties cannot go out, but such a state of things cannot last long and an army may always carry 8 or 10 days' biscuit along with it.

Lastly, they should always lead to your adversary's faible and be at a distance from your own.

(16) Wars are glorious and results splendid when such territorial lines present themselves and chiefs know how to profit by them. But they sometimes are not to be found and then war must be carried on by principle, more regular and more cautious.

(17) This system which may be the [?] of [?] invasion has never been comprehended by Austrian generals. Controlled by court orders and responsible to the Aulic Council, they always appear to have been instructed to leave no part of the

Austrian territories exposed to the incursions of the enemy. Every part has consequently become a faible and they have, of course, manoeuvred to disadvantage. It was the Ancients who understood this system. Alexander owed all his conquest to it. When Hannibal was at the gates of Rome, the Senate sent an army to Africa. Charles XII had some idea of it but he was a mad man and his means were insufficient, moreover, fortune was against him.

Had Frederick II been opposed to Austria alone I think he would have adopted it, but it is Buonaparte of the Moderns who has taught most in this branch of war. Lord Wellington would, perhaps, follow his example but Lisbon, our point of departure, has hitherto been a most embarrassing faible. The French Generals in Spain have no faible, what is Madrid or Seville more than any other town?

(18) When your own faible is as much threatened as that of your adversary's you cannot uncover it. If the forces are nearly equal you can only manoeuvre till an opportunity offers of striking a blow.

(19) When the supplies of the country cannot be depended on, either from their actual insufficiency or their being placed beyond your reach, you must form a new base as you leave your old one, and always preserve your lines of operation secure.

(20) An army which has only a single line of operation proceeding from a single point as the base, possesses no territory except that on which it stands, for there is no other point to which a detachment of the enemy cannot advance in safety.

(21) Its lines of operation are consequently insecure and ineffective. Frederick was obliged to raise the siege of Olmutz in 1758 because he had only a single line and advantage was taken of this to carry off his convoy.

(22) An army possessing two lines of operation forming a very acute angle is nearly in the situation of an army with only a single line if the enemy is able to manoeuvre against both. In 1758 Frederick, when at Koenigsberg had only two lines of operation, by N [?] and Trattenau, forming an acute angle. Dorn took a position which deprived him of the latter and Laudohn, with a detachment, manoeuvred against the former. Laudohn was not strong enough to maintain his ground because Frederick was retreating with his whole army and, of course, dislodged him. But had Frederick's army been occupied, Laudohn would have cut off his convoys.

(23) But when the extreme lines of operation projected from the base form a right or obtuse angle, the army advances on correct principles because no detachments can venture into the triangle, all transport on the intermediate routes is therefore secure.

(24) In this case the army is likewise master of the resources of the included country.

(25) When one of the flanks of your lines of operation is covered by inaccessible country, less development is required.

(26) Routes will sometimes serve as line of operation for supplies which are impracticable to heavy artillery, or the stores necessary for a siege. This is especially the case in Portugal and Spain where supplies are usually conveyed on mules. A river or a lake may serve as an excellent route for supplies but be no line of retreat.

(27) When your own base outflanks that of your adversary you may commonly turn and separate him from all his magazines without losing your communication with more than a part of your own.

Section Three: Of Strategy

(1) Strategy is the science of bringing a proportionally larger force than your enemy to the point required for the line of action.
(2) The effect of an army on a given point is compounded of its disposable force and the rapidity with which that force can move.
(3) An army can move with greater rapidity in corps than in mass because, in a cultivated country, corps can usually supply themselves without convoy and because small columns move faster than large ones.
(4) Moreover, the development along the line of action which is given to an army by division renders it less easy to judge its real intentions.
(5) But an army must not risk division within reach of the enemy.
(6) An army in march, dividing in order to facilitate subsistence, gains nothing by separating its column above a day's march, for columns cannot forage above half a march to the right and left.
(7) But when a quarter development is proposed in order to mislead the enemy, you risk nothing provided you have so combined your movements that you can always concentrate before he can.
(8) To ensure this your lines of operation must be interim to those of your *enemy*.
    This principle is [?] in the invasion of Bohemia in 1756 and the campaign of 1760.
(9) An army, therefore, advancing on the line of action may advance with advantage to itself by different corps, but these corps must have a direction concentric to the point where they meet the enemy and when the decisive effort is to be made. However, the lines of operation of these corps should be interim to those of the enemy, but if this is not practicable the corps must always be nearer to each other than the enemy is to any one of them.
(10) When you have established interior lines of operation you may bring the mass of your force to bear, first on one, and then on the other and taking advantage of natural obstacles and keeping the enemy in check with a small force on one line, you may overwhelm him on the other and thus successively.
(11) If you are inferior to your enemy, your lines of operation, even though interior, should not be too far asunder, otherwise the enemy may gain access to the part of the line you have weakened.
(12) But if you are superior, it will sometimes answer to isolate the enemy to a considerable distance, for very large masses are cumbrous and cannot be all brought into action. Two armies of 50,000 each have a better chance of beating two armies of 36,000 than one army of 100,000 has of beating one of 60,000.
(13) The same principles taken conversely apply to retreats, for here, working only to get clear of your enemy and while certain he cannot bring you to action, eccentric retreats are to be preferred, but the columns must afterwards pursue a concentric direction to the point where you mean to stand.

(14) Lines of cantonment or defence are regulated by the same system. The position is then the point of union and if the enemy is free to advance without interruption to this point, every cantonment, at least of infantry, should be two days' march nearer it than he is. If then there are partial positions and the enemy may be kept in check, the distance of the cantonments may be regulated by the time the troops attached to these positions can maintain themselves in them.

Thus in the cantonments of Cartaxo, the Light Division was, in fact, farther from the lines and their own position than the enemy on the side of Rio Maior, but there was a position of Alcoentre when the 3rd Division on that side could have maintained themselves till the retreat of the Light Division was secured. Altogether, however, it should be recollected that greater caution is necessary in the disposition of lines of cantonment than in the combinations of advancing corps because, in the one case, the enemy has the initiative movement, in the other you have.

(15) An army advancing must direct its efforts against the centre, or one of the flanks of the enemy, or else must wholly avoid him and go beyond one extremity of his line.

(16) The last of these cases belongs to the war of invasion.

(17) The attack on the centre of the line of defence is only advisable where, from your superiority, or from your having the initiative movement, you are certain of penetrating the enemy's line of defence. The consequences will then be very decided but this is not often practicable because if he can keep you at all in check the army is more quickly assembled in mass on the centre than any other point.

(18) In general it is most advisable to concentrate on one flank of your enemy's line of defence and endeavour to fall on his extreme corps and roll up the others successively. Such combinations give you every chance of bringing the greater part of your army in mass against isolated division; enable you, if successful, to manoeuvre at once towards your enemy's faible and do not risk your own retreat in case of failure.

(19) It is more difficult to lay down principles of defensive rather than of offensive warfare because, after all, defensive operations must spring from the offensive ones to which they are opposed. All that can be done is consider in principle what your enemy ought to do and this you must endeavour to prevent his being able to effect.

(20) If your lines of operation are not inferior to those of your enemy it is contrary to all principle to extend in order to make him extend. You thus give him an opportunity of bringing into action against corps [?], both Dumouriez and C [?] committed this fault in 1792. Why was not General Valency at the Battle of Genappes?

(21) In countries which allow of manoeuvre an inferior army can draw advantage from its very inferiority, for it can manoeuvre with greater facility . . . [?], even equal armies should not wait an attack, much less should inferior armies. I do not like these unexpurgable positions like Busaco, they are certainly necessary to armies that cannot manoeuvre, such as ours in 1810, but what is the use of gaining a victory if you cannot follow it up?

(22) An army covering a siege should never wait to be attacked by a relieving

army, many a town has been taken in a field of battle half a dozen leagues off. A covering army can never prevent a town being relieved except by a battle. Beresford's decision in fighting at Albuera, if it was his own, almost makes amends for his other blunders.

(23) Altogether then, strategy teaches to disperse when you do not mean to fight and when your enemy cannot make you fight, for dispersion facilitates subsistence, gives rapidity to movement and deceives the enemy. But when there is a chance of fighting, concentrate in mass and always bear in mind that victories are the means not the ends of war, the commencement not the conclusion of exertion; they are, too, even easier to gain than to turn to account . . .

It is interesting to recall that Cocks was a contemporary of Clausewitz, 1780–1831, and the latter must have been pondering the beliefs which ultimately formed his book, *Vom Kriege*, at the same time as Charles was also wresting with military science.

Sources

Unpublished Material

Eastnor Archives
 Letters and diaries of Major The Hon. Edward Charles Cocks
 Letters of John Sommers Cocks, 2nd Baron Somers, later 1st Earl Somers
 Letters of Margaret, wife of above
 Letters of Captain The Hon. John Somers Cocks, later 2nd Earl Somers
 Letters of The Hon. James Somers Cocks
 Letters of The Hon. Margaret Maria Cocks
 Letters of Elizabeth Cocks, great-aunt of Edward Charles
 Diary and letters of The Rev Treadway Russell Nash, DD
 Miscellaneous letters from other relations and friends of the family

Thomas Somers Cocks archives, in the possession of J. V. Somers Cocks, Esq.
 Letters from Major The Hon. E. C. Cocks to Thomas Somers Cocks, Esq.
 Jacquier's Hotel document, February 1808 with reference to ECC and TSC
 Testimonial for John Day, Cocks's servant, 19 June 1809
 Letter from R. T. Cocks to his brother, Charles, 20 July 1855
 Portrait of Thomas Somers Cocks

Surrey County Record Office
 Somers Cocks Papers

Barclays Bank Ltd, Cocks, Biddulph Branch, Whitehall, London
 Banking documents of the Cocks family in the eighteenth century

The Viscount Combermere
 The Stanhope papers re Sir Stapleton Cotton

Public Record Office
 Regimental Returns. WO17 16th Light Dragoons and 79th Foot
 Wills and probate, E. C. Cocks and T. R. Nash
 Documents relating to the RMC Marlow

Chester County Record Office
 Tomkinson Papers and Owen MSs, on loan

British Newspaper Library
 Berrow's Worcester Journal, 1785-1812
 The Courier, 1785-1812
 The Morning Post, 1785-1812

National Army Museum
  Journal of the Regimental Officer during the recent campaign in Portugal and Spain under Lord Wellington: Lt Col P. Hawker
  Wyld's Atlas

British Library
  Hardwicke Papers. Add MSs 35646 f39
  Joseph Sydney Yorke. Add MSs 35395
  Yorke Papers. Add MSs 35395 f45
  Lord Hill's Correspondence, 35,059ff

Gloucester County Record Office
  Baptismal records: Redmarley d'Abitot, 1791
  Lady Guise's Daybook, 1801-6. Info on Highnam Court

Hereford and Worcester County Record Office
  The Palfrey Papers
  Justices Commission, 26/7/1807. Ref: Q/JC/5. ECC becomes a JP

Victoria Library, Westminster
  Rate Books for Westminster, 1785-1806
  Baptismal record, St James's, Piccadilly, 1786

St George's, Hanover Square
  Baptismal records, 1790, by courtesy of the incumbent

West Sussex County Record Office
  Lovell Badcock Papers Add MSs 1367

Medical Diagnosis
  The Royal College of Surgeons of England
  R.C.F. Catterall, Esq, FRCS, who diagnosed Cocks's clubfeet from evidence in the letters exchanged between the parents

Published Sources

Berridge, E: *The Barratts at Hope End*
Brett-James: *Wellington at War*
Burke's Peerage 1889
Clausewitz: *On War*
Combermere & Knollys: *Memoirs and Correspondence of Field Marshal Viscount Combermere*. Ed. by Lady Combermere and W. Knollys 1866
Commons Journals 1807-9
Cobbett, W: Parliamentary Debates 1807-9
Dictionary of National Biography
Fitzclarence: *A Manual of Outpost Duties*
Fortescue, Sir John: *History of the British Army 1808-12*
Guedalla, P: *The Duke*
Hooper, W: *Reigate: its story through the ages*

Hibbert, C: *Corunna*
Jones, Lt Col Sir John T: *Journal of the Sieges carried on by the Army under the Duke of Wellington in Spain.* Vol 1, 3rd edition 1846
Jameson, Captain: *Historical Record of the 79th*
Longford, E: *Wellington, The Years of the Sword.* (Panther edition 1972)
Ludlow Beamish, N: *History of the King's German Legion.* (London 1832)
MacLeod, C: *Robert Emmet. Noted Irish Lives.* (London 1935)
Napier, W. F. P: *History of the War in the Peninsula. 1807-10; 1810-12.* 2 volumes
Oman, C: *The Peninsular War*
Pelet, J. J: Ed. D. D. Horward. *The French Campaign in Portugal 1810-11*
Schaumann, A. L. F: Ed and translated by A. M. Ludovici. *On the road with Wellington*
Somers & Hervey-Bathurst: *Eastnor Castle,* Ledbury, Herefordshire
Somers Cocks, J. V: *The History of the Cocks Family.* 1966
Tomkinson, W: Edited by James Tomkinson. *The Diary of a Cavalry Officer in the Peninsular War and Waterloo campaign, 1808-15*
Weller, J: *Wellington in the Peninsula 1808-14*
Whittingham: *A Memoir of the Services of Lt-Gen Sir Samuel Ford Whittingham, KCB, KCH, GCF,* Ed. Major General Ferdinand Whittingham, CB. (London 1868)
Wellington, *The Despatches of Field Marshal Arthur, Duke of Wellington during his various campaigns,* Compiled by Lt-Col Gurwood 1834-8

Selected Bibliography

Brett-James, A: *Life in Wellington's Army*
Bryant, Sir A: *The Years of Endurance*
Bryant, Sir A: *The Years of Victory, 1802-12*
Barnett, C: *Britain and her army*
Chandler, D. G: *The Battle of Salamanca*
Colby, R: *Mayfair; A Town within a Town*
Glover, R: *Peninsular Preparation*
Glover, M: *Wellington as a Military Commander*
Glover, M: *Britannia Sickens*
Gray, D: *Spencer Perceval*
Kincaid, J: *Adventures in the Rifle Brigade*
Namier & Brooke: *History of Parliament. The Commons 1754-1790*
O'Connor, Sir James: *History of Ireland 1766-1924.* Vol 1
Parkinson, R: *The Peninsular War*
Postgate, R. W: *Robert Emmet*
Rudorff, R: *War to the Death. Sieges of Saragossa. 1808-9*
Robinson, C. W: *Strategy in the Peninsular War 1808-14*
Schere, M: *Recollections of the Peninsula*
Stepney-Cowall: *Leaves from the Diary of an Officer of the Guards*
Stanhope, Earl: *Conversations with the Duke of Wellington*

Thoumine, V. R. H: *Scientific Soldier. A life of General Le Marchant*
Thomas, P. D. G: *The House of Commons in the Eighteenth Century*
Ward, S. G. P: *Wellington's Headquarters*
Wheeler, Private: Ed. Liddell Hart. *Letters of Private Wheeler*

References

In this section I have used the following abbreviations:
ECC   – Edward Charles Cocks
JSC   – his father John Sommers Cocks, later 2nd Lord Somers and eventually 1st Earl Somers
MC   – Margaret Cocks, wife of above, mother of ECC
MMC – Margaret Maria Cocks, sister of ECC
TSC   – Thomas Somers Cocks, cousin to ECC
W.D. – Wellington's Despatches
Captain The Hon. JSC – John Somers Cocks, younger brother of ECC

Introduction
1. Tomkinson, p217
2. Tomkinson, p218
3. Tomkinson, p218
4. *Saturday Review*. 14 April 1894. Palfrey Collection, Worcs CRO
5. Nash Diary. Eastnor Archives, 29 July 1786
6. Parish Record, St James's. Victoria Library, Westminster
7. Somers Cocks, p37f
8. Somers Cocks, p87f
9. Eastnor Archives. 1st Earl's box. Letters between JSC & MC, 1786–9 and R. C. F. Catterall, Esq, FRCS
10. Elizabeth Cocks to JSC, 2 Sept 1789
11. ECC to MC, 6 Feb 1804
12. Somers Cocks, facing p117
13. St George's, Hanover Square, Registers, 1790
14. Burke's Peerage, 1889
15. Tomkinson, p210–11
16. ECC to The Rev Philip Yorke, 12 Jan 1812
17. ECC to MC, 10 Oct 1799
18. Eastnor Archives. ECC box. Paper written by MC
19. ECC to JSC, 11 June 1803
20. ECC to JSC, 13 June 1803
21. ECC to JSC, 7 Aug 1803
22. ECC to JSC, 16 July 1804
23. PRO WO17 1076 Regimental Return 16th Light Dragoons, Sept 1805
24. ECC to MC, 6 Feb 1804
25. History of Parliament Trust and Commons Journals, Vol LXIII

26. Commons Journal, Vol.LXIII
27. Eastnor Archives. ECC Box. Paper written by MC
28. Complete Peerage. House of Lords Record Office
29. Surrey CRO Somers Cocks Papers 371/1/37
30. Tomkinson, p212
31. Tomkinson p129
32. Hibbert, p62-3
33. ECC to MC, 2 March 1809
34. ECC to Captain The Hon. JSC, 29 April 1809

Chapter three: Talavera
1. ECC, 9 Aug 1809
2. ECC to JSC, 4 March 1810
3. Weller p104

Chapter four: Andalusia
1. ECC, 7 Dec 1809
2. ECC, 11 Jan 1810

Chapter six: Between the Coa and the Agueda
1. ECC, 27 May 1810
2. ECC to The Rev Philip Yorke, 10 July 1810
3. ECC, 16 May 1810
4. ECC, 30 June 1810
5. ECC, 30 June 1810

Chapter seven: Wellington's Eyes and Ears
1. W.D. Vol 6, 26 July 1810, Alverca to Brig-Gen R. Craufurd
2. Tomkinson p37
3. Tomkinson p35
4. W.D. Vol 6, to Lt-Gen Sir S. Cotton Bt, 3 Aug 1810
5. W.D. Vol 6, to Lt-Gen Sir S. Cotton Bt, 16 Aug 1810, half past 6am
6. W.D. Vol 6, to Lt-Gen Sir S. Cotton Bt, 31 Aug 1810
7. Tomkinson p38
8. W.D. Vol 6, to Lt-Gen Sir S. Cotton Bt, 3 Sept 1810
9. W.D. Vol 6, to Lt-Gen Sir S. Cotton Bt, 6 Sept 1810
10. Lovell Badcock Papers Add MSs 1367
11. W.D. Vol 6, to Lt-Gen Sir S. Cotton Bt, Gouvia 2pm 10 Sept 1810
12. Pelet p156
13. W.D. Vol 6, to Lt-Gen Sir S. Cotton Bt, 15 Sept 1810
14. W.D. Vol 6, to Marshal Beresford, Gouvia, 15 Sept 1810
15. W.D. Vol 6, to Lt-Gen Sir S. Cotton Bt, Corticao, 20 Sept 1810
16. W.D. Vol 6, to Lt-Gen Sir S. Cotton Bt and to the Earl of Liverpool, 20 Sept 1810

Chapter eight: The Fighting Squadron
1. ECC, 27 Sept 1810

Chapter ten: No Man's Land
1. W.D. Vol 7, to C. Stuart, Esq, 3 March 1811
2. W.D. Vol 7, to ECC Cartaxo, 26 Feb 1811

Chapter fourteen: More Reflections
1. ECC, 4 July 1811
2. ECC, 8 July 1811
3. ECC to his mother, 19 Aug 1811
4. ECC, 20 July 1811

Chapter sixteen: Heartache
1. ECC to his sister, 11 Sept 1811
2. ECC, 1 Dec 1811
3. See Schaumann, pp281 and 318 for his descriptions of this tale
4. ECC to TSC, 10 Sept 1811
5. ECC, 14 Sept 1811
6. See Schaumann, pp281 and 318
7. ECC, 14 Sept 1811
8. See Schaumann, pp281 and 318
9. ECC to TSC, 2 Oct 1811

Chapter seventeen: Autumn Activities
1. In the possession of J. V. Somers Cocks, Esq.

Chapter eighteen: Ciudad Rodrigo
1. In the possession of J. V. Somers Cocks, Esq.

Chapter nineteen: Winter Letters
1. ECC, 1 Feb 1812
2. Tomkinson p126/7
3. Tomkinson p129

Chapter twenty: All Points of the Compass
1. ECC, 3 May 1812

Chapter twenty-one: Salamanca
1. ECC to TSC, post-script written on 23 July to a letter of 19 July 1812

Chapter twenty-two: Sweet Success
1. Tomkinson p214

Chapter twenty-three: Siege of Burgos
1. ECC, 18 Sept 1812

Chapter twenty-four: 8th October 1812 and its Aftermath
1. Tomkinson p209
2. Tomkinson p217
3. Longford p363, Panther edition of *The Years of the Sword*
4. Tomkinson p209
5. Tomkinson p210

6. Brett-James, Wellington to Beresford, Oct 1812
7. Tomkinson to Captain The Hon. JSC, 9 Oct 1812, Eastnor Archives
8. Wellington to Lord Somers, 11 Oct 1812, Eastnor Archives
9. Miss H. P. Carew to MMC, September 1815
10. Tomkinson p217

Index

Agar, George C. 159.
Albuquerque, Duc d', 45, 50, 53, 55.
Alexander the Great, 238.
Alexander I, Czar, 148.
Alexander, Lt W. J. 60.
Alorna, Marquis d', 78.
Anson, Maj-Gen George, 159, 167, 204.
Archer, Lt-Col Clement, 149, 179n.
Areizaga, General Don Carlos de, 45, 46.
ARMY, PENINSULAR
  DIVISIONS
  First, 102, 105, 131, 144, 161, 162, 182–185, 188, 192, 197–199, 200.
  Third, 120, 144, 161–163, 165, 183, 188, 234, 240.
  Fourth, 132, 144, 161, 162, 183, 234.
  Fifth, 144, 165, 183, 228, 234.
  Sixth, 142–144, 183, 184, 197, 198, 200.
  Seventh, 103–105, 108, 120, 131, 144, 183–5.
  Light, 59, 68, 103, 105, 144, 149, 161–163, 165, 170, 183, 229, 234, 240.
  Erskine's Division, 102.
  BRIGADES
  Guards, 28–30.
  Heavy, 19, 76, 122.
  Highland, 193.
  Portuguese, 197.
  Alten's, 144.
  Anson's, 36, 84, 102–103, 108, 125, 234.
  Bock's, 184.
  Bradford's, 183.
  Le Marchant's, 150, 234.
  Slade's, 85, 102–103, 120, 149.
  Stuart's, 55.
  REGIMENTS
  Cavalry Regiments
  1st (Royal) Dragoon Guards, 67, 68, 70–74, 85, 108–109.
  2nd Dragoon Guards, 101.
  3rd Dragoon Guards, 82, 150.
  4th Dragoon Guards, 150, 168.
  5th Dragoon Guards, 150, 170.
  Heavy Dragoons, 114.

11th Light Dragoons, 120–121, 125, 134, 142, 144, 150.
13th Light Dragoons, 120.
14th Light Dragoons, 18–20, 25, 28–30, 64, 72, 76, 108–109, 145.
16th Light Dragoons, 16–18, 25, 27, 29, 30, 33, 34, 39, 60, 64, 72, 79, 85, 87, 90, 97, 98, 108, 125, 128, 141, 149, 158, 161, 188, 204, 213, 234.
20th Light Dragoons, 29.
23rd Light Dragoons, 37.
1st Hussars, KGL, 60, 62–64, 72, 79, 84–85, 87, 97, 98, 103, 108, 125, 128, 131, 144, 150, 183.
2nd Hussars, KGL, 120, 121, 125, 142.
Chasseurs Britanniques, 104, 108.
General Madden's cavalry, 120.
INFANTRY REGIMENTS
The Guards, 105.
3rd, 28.
5th, 144, 163.
7th, (Royal Fusiliers), 68.
24th, 201–202.
40th, 23, 162.
42nd, 162, 193.
43rd, 165.
45th, 163, 165, 229.
48th, 17.
52nd, 82, 165.
60th, 29.
71st, 102, 107.
74th, 163, 229.
77th, 229.
79th, 55, 56, 102, 104, 107, 171, 179, 182, 192, 195, 196, 204, 234.
83rd, 229.
87th, 144, 183–185.
88th, 163, 165, 229.
95th, 82, 165.
Brunswickers, 109.
Caçadores, Portuguese, 62, 71, 103, 106, 148, 165, 197.
Artillery, 144.

250

Capt Ross's troop, 62.
Capt Bull's guns, 85, 103.
Ashworth, Capt R. 64.
Atty, Capt, 91.
Aulic Council, 237.

Badcock, Lt Lovell, 76-78.
Bailey, Mr, 23.
Barrier, Gov. Ciudad Rodrigo, 161, 170, 174.
Baxter, Sgt, 213.
Beauchamp, Lord, 185, 201.
Belli, Capt John Henry, 34, 64, 103, 108, 110.
Beresford, General William Carr, Marshal of the Portuguese army, 25, 27, 28, 30, 59, 78, 99n, 111, 114, 204, 241.
Bergmann, 108, 143.
Berkeley, Admiral Lord, 173.
Bessières, Marshal, 107, 109, 132, 144.
Bevere, 15-16.
Bicknell, 168.
Blake, Lt J. 103, 108.
Blake, General J. 120, 123, 159.
Blunt, General, 93, 97.
Bock, Maj-Gen Baron von, 184.
Bodleian Library, 159.
Bogie, Bugler Charles, 195.
Boughton Monchelsea, 149n.
Boverick, F. 41, 56, 87, 91, 127, 151n, 195.
Bowes, General, 184.
Brennier, General, 102, 106, 107.
Bromesberrow Place, 16.
Browning, Elizabeth Barratt, 206.
Brotherton, Maj, 145.
Bruton, General, 195.
Bull, John, 125, 186, 192.
Buonaparte, Joseph, 36, 46, 185, 187, 188, 196, 201.
Buonaparte, Napoleon, 17-21, 41, 60, 73, 102, 107, 134, 148, 185n, 190, 191, 235, 238.
Butler, Samuel, 167n.

Caffarelli, General, 187
Cameron, General, 29, 147.
Campbell, 54, 55.
Campbell, Maj-Gen Alexander, 142-143.
Capons, Brig-Gen, 46.
Carew, Harriet, 151.
Casamajor, 168.
Castanos, General, 53, 84.
Castleditch, 15, 56n, 87, 143n, 151, 177, 192, 205.
Castlereagh, Lord, 28n, 31.
Cathcart, Lord, 15.
Cavendish Square, 95, 143.
Cervantes, 45.

Chambers, 168.
Charles XII, 238.
Childe Harold, 199.
Churchill, Mrs, 182.
Clausel, Marshal, 192, 193, 195, 201.
Clive, H. G. 159.
Cobbett, William, 39.
Cochrane, Colonel, 142-143.
Cocks, Biddulph Bank, 15, 20n.
COCKS, MAJOR THE HONOURABLE EDWARD CHARLES
  Birth and Childhood, 12, 13f. Cornetcy, 16. Lieutenancy, 17. MP, 17. Captaincy, 17. Sails for Lisbon, 21. Andalusia 1809, 23f. Oporto campaign, 27f. Begins journal, 33. Talavera campaign, 34f. Succumbs to fever, 37. Kindness of Wellington, 34. Examines Elvas, 34. Accompanies Cotton to Cadiz, 43. Gibraltar, 207f. Andalusia 1810, Intelligence operations in the Sierra Morena, 45f. Writes to Wellington, 48f, 50f, 77. Retreat to Cadiz, 53. Siege of Cadiz, 54f. Spanish/Portuguese frontier outpost operations, 1810. 60f. First intelligence operation for Wellington, 67f. Busaco and the retreat to the Lines, 82f. Mentioned in despatches, 79, 92, 128. Operations against foragers, 92f, 97f. Visits England briefly, 100. Returns and battle of Fuentes d'Onoro, 101f. 2nd siege of Badajoz, 111f. Negotiations for a majority, 122, 128, 159, 169f. Brevet majority, 115, 128. Second intelligence operation for Wellington, 127f. Falls in love, 139f. Depression, 147-148. Holiday in Oporto, 147f. Winter amusements, 149, 151, 167. Siege of Ciudad Rodrigo, 161f. Regimental promotion, 171, 175, 186. 3rd siege of Badajoz, 226f. Entertains brother James, 177f. Holiday in Lisbon, 179. Salamanca campaign, 182f. Capture of Madrid, 191. Advance to Burgos, 192. St Michael Hornwork operation, 193. Brevet Lieut Colonelcy, 195. Arranges purchase regimental lieut colonelcy, 195-196, 200f. Death, 204.
  Quotes Wellington: 104, 115, 148-149, 165, 170, 195. Approval of Wellington, 24, 25, 36, 88-89, 94, 96, 107, 120, 122-123, 126, 166, 170, 183, 188.
  Criticises: Attitude of British officers, 40, 41, 142. Spanish military practices, 54-55. Craufurd's operations, 10/11 July 1810, 64-65. 11th Light Dragoon operations, 121, 142.
  Discusses: Political decisions, 19-20. Religion, 136. Oporto strategy, 29-30.

251

Talavera campaign, 34f. Novels, 91, 125.
Retreats, 130. Turning an army, 130.
Generals, 130, 136. Orders of battle, 131.
Columns of march, 131. Lines of operation,
132, 235f. Battles, 135. An officer's attitude
to his men, 148. Billeting troops, 150.
Faibles, 235f. Education suitable for an
officer, 153f. Military strategy, 184, 235f.
Enemy strategy, 84-85, 94-95, 134f, 137,
144f, 187, 188. Allied strategy, 87-89, 94-
95, 96, 144f, 170f, 193. Patrol duties, 218.
Outpost duties, 216f. Piqueting, 120-121,
214f. Fighting, 212f.

Comments on: Spanish attitudes, 23, 135.
Spanish people, 125, 135. Spanish generals,
45, 46. Spanish guerillas, 125, 134-135.
Portuguese people, 71, 80, 99, 135, 170.
Portuguese troops, 122, 129. Enemy tactics,
87. Army reform, 126. Courage, 129.
Honour, 132, 156. General R. Craufurd,
166. Spanish women, 40.

Maxims: 80, 105, 130f. 150.

Cocks, Charles Lygon, Lt-Col, Coldstream
Guards, (1821-1885), 12, 206.

Cocks, Charles, 1st Baron Somers, MP, (1725-
1806), 17.

Cocks, Jane, 151.

Cocks, Ensign James, Grenadier Guards,
(1738-1758), 101.

Cocks, the Hon James Soṁers, (1790-1856), 15,
16, 34, 141, 167, 173, 174-177, 179, 182, 182f.
186-188, 190-192, 205, 206. Letters to from
ECC, 39, 40, 90, 98, 125, 128, 168.

Cocks, Capt the Hon John Soṁers, (1788-
1852), 15-17, 101, 115, 112f, 115, 128, 134,
143f, 149, 150-151, 159, 168, 169, 176n, 204-
206. Letters to from ECC, 24, 84.

Cocks, John Sommers, 1st Earl Soṁers and 2nd
Baron Soṁers, (1760-1841), 13, 15, 16-17,
34, 100, 143n, 205, 206. Letters to from ECC,
25, 34, 36, 37, 72, 92, 134, 141, 159, 169.

Cocks, Margaret, née Nash, 2nd Lady Soṁers,
(1760-1831), 13, 15, 173, 183, 186 188, 192,
206. Letters to from ECC, 19, 21, 23, 93, 115,
134, 149, 193. From James, 173, 176, 183,
186, 187, 188, 192.

Cocks, the Hon Margaret Maria, (1791-1853),
15, 16, 206. Letters to from ECC, 43, 91, 98,
109, 124, 133, 151, 182, 187, 191, 198.

Cocks, Lt-Col the Hon Philip James, (1774-
1857), 182.

Cocks, Richard, (Baptised 1564. Died 1623), 15.

Cocks, Thomas Somers, Banker, (1781-1859),
15, 45, 101, 128, 172n, 199, 206. Letters to
from ECC, 19, 20, 21, 23, 30, 38, 63, 73, 93,

95, 107, 112, 122, 127, 133, 141, 143, 151, 158,
170, 171, 175, 177, 179, 180, 183, 186, 187,
191, 192, 195, 200. From John Somers, 150.

Colborne, Colonel, 162.

Cole, Maj-Gen Sir Galbraith Lowry, 68, 71, 76.

Collyer, 175, 179.

Colville, Charles, Maj-Gen, 162.

Combermere, see Cotton.

Cooke, General, 201.

Cordemann, 79.

Cotton, Lt-Gen Sir Stapleton, later Field
Marshal Viscount Combermere, 12, 13, 16-
18, 20, 23-25, 27, 34, 40, 43, 59-64, 71, 73, 77,
78, 79, 90, 101, 111, 112n, 115, 118, 128, 134,
150, 167, 204.

Cox, Governor, Almeida, 71, 73.

Cradock, General Sir John, 18, 23, 24.

Craufurd, John, 159.

Craufurd, Maj-Gen Robert, 59, 60, 63, 64, 65,
67, 68, 71, 82, 162, 165, 166.

Creevey, Thomas, 143.

Cuesta, General Don Gregorio de la, 18, 20, 21,
23, 24, 33, 34, 37, 38, 50.

Cunningham, 95.

Dalrymple, General Sir Huw, 210.
Day, John, 151n.
Dubreton, General, 195.
Dekin, Lt, 97, 128, 143.
Dereham, Colonel, 39.
D'Erlon, see Drouet.
Dickson, Maj, 103, 112, 115, 162.
Don Quixote, 44, 45.
Dorn, 238.
Douglas, Capt, 209.
Down House, 16.
Drawbridge, Sgt, 169.
Drouet, General, Comte d'Erlon, 94, 174, 180,
201.
Dublin, 16, 17.
D'Urban, Lt-Gen Sir Benjamin, 9, 206.
Dyter, John, Trumpet Major and Sergeant, 171,
187.

Eastnor, 15, 16, 206.
Eastnor Castle, 177, 205.
Eastnor Church, 192.
Egerton, 95-96.
Elder, Colonel, 62.
Eliot, 171.
Emmet's Rebellion, 16.
Emmet, Robert 158.
Erskine, Maj-Gen Sir William, 128.
Escurial, 110, 192, 193.

Fenwick, Maj, 92, 96.
Ferguson, 159.
Fletcher, Colonel, 114, 162.
Foster, Lt, 116.
Framingham, Colonel, 112.
Frazer, Lt, 202.
Frederick the Great, 59, 131-132, 151, 154, 167, 235, 238.
Freire, General Manoel, 123.
Frere, John Hookham, 51, 55.
Fulton, Lt-Col, 195-200, 201.

Gabriel, Capt Robert, 150, 206.
Gardener, Mrs, 56, 87.
George 111, 114n.
Gibbs, Maj, 162.
Gibraltar, 43, 53, 55. Appendix A.
Gilbert, 95.
Gloucester, 16.
Gordon, Colonel, 37, 39.
Gordon, Capt Alexander, ADC to Wellington, 145.
Gordon, Mr, 43.
Gorse, Trumpeter, 172.
Gort, 17.
Graham, Lt-Gen Sir Thomas, 162, 180, 182, 183.
Grant, Major Colquhoun, 143, 148.
Grant, Lt Hugh, 193.
Great George Street, 143.
Grueben, Capt, 65.
Gurwood, Lt John, 165.

Hamilton, General, 120.
Hannibal, 238.
Hardwicke, 3rd Earl of, 17, 39, 206.
Hargood, Admiral, 123n.
Hargood, Maria, 123.
Hawker, Lt, 115.
Hawker, Lt-Col Peter, 39.
Hawkes, 95.
Hay, Maj-Gen Andrew, 103.
Hay, Lt William, 127, 141, 145, 171.
Hereford, 206.
Hervey, Major Felton, 28, 30, 129, 158, 161.
Heyderwick, Capt, 202.
Highnam Court, 16.
Hill, General Sir Rowland, 27-28, 59, 68, 71, 72, 80, 82, 94, 118, 120, 139, 179, 180, 190, 193, 201.
Holmes, Lt, 202.
Houston, Maj-Gen William, 105, 111.
Hudibras, 167.
Hunt, 118.

Innes, Capt, 56.

Jacquier's Hotel, 159.
Johnson, Samuel, 167.
Jomini, Baron Antoine, 96n, 143.
Julian, Don, 67, 70-73, 76, 102-104, 106, 139-141, 148, 183.
Junot, General, 88.
Junta, Supreme, 18, 33, 40, 46, 51.

Kellermann, General, 38.
Kemp, Maj-Gen, 229, 230.
Knipe, Capt, 104, 109.
Krauchenberg, Capt, 79, 103, 108, 129, 143.
Krokenburgh, Capt, 62, 64, 84, 143.

La Foix, 180, 188.
La Motte, Captain, (The Royals), 68.
La Motte, Colonel, (French), 104.
Landemann, Capt, 56.
Langwerth, Maj-Gen, 39.
Laudohn, 238.
Lawrie & Co, 196, 201.
Lawrie, Maj, 179, 184, 195, 197.
Ledbury, 15.
Le Marchant, Maj-Gen, 150.
Lewis, 143.
Lindsay, Capt, 53.
Linsingen, Capt, 85, 92, 143.
Liverpool, Earl of, 79, 100.
Loison, General, 28.
Long, Maj-Gen, 120-121.
Loy, General, 120.
Lutchens, Capt, 121.

Macdonald, Lt, 62.
Mackenzie, Sgt Donald, 195.
Mackenzie, Sgt John, 195.
Mackenzie, Maj-Gen, 25, 35, 36, 37.
Maitland, General, 190.
Manners, Lord Charles, 149.
Marlow, Royal Military Academy, 153.
Marmont, Marshal, 109, 120, 127, 132, 134, 139, 143-146, 149, 159, 161, 174, 175, 177, 183, 185, 187, 188, 195, 201.
Massena, Marshal, 60, 67, 78, 81, 82, 85, 88, 90, 92-96, 100, 101-104, 106-107, 109, 120, 144, 170.
Mayne, 162.
McGreachy, Maj, 118.
McKinnon, Maj-Gen, 163, 165.
Meyer, Maj, 103, 108.
Miguelets, 135.
Montbrun, General, 146.
Montijo, Conde de, 51.

253

Moore, General Sir John, 18, 19, 20, 183.
Mortier, Marshal, 38.
Murray, Capt, 85, 141.
Murray, Colonel George, 30, 137.
Murray, General J. 28.
Myrtle, 56, 57.

Nairac, Capt Robert, 9.
Napier, Maj William, 12, 13, 165.
Napoleon, see Buonaparte.
Nash, Margaret, see Cocks.
Nash, DD, Rev Treadway, 15, 16, 100, 167, 175.
Ney, Marshal, 38, 71, 76, 88, 131.
Nickolls, Thomas, 19, 151.

Obelisk, 206
O'Farrell, 53, 54.
O'Hara, General, 209.
O'Fin, Colonel, 145.
O'Loughlin, 55.
Orange, Prince of, 205.
Ordenanza, Portuguese, 109.
Owen, Lt Hugh, 12, 13, 18, 59n, 206.

Pack, Maj-Gen, 165, 183, 204.
Paget, General Sir Edward, 28, 30.
Palafox, 51.
Parque del, Duke, 45, 51.
Peacock, Maj-Gen, 173.
Pelly, Maj R. 141, 179n.
Perémond, 175.
Philippon, General, 174, 228, 234.
Picton, Maj-Gen Sir Thomas, 82, 105, 111, 112, 162, 183, 227, 234.
Pilgash, 49.
Piquets, Observations on, 212 and Appendix C.
Pole-Carew, Agneta, 100, 158, 199, 206.
Ponsonby, Maj Frederick, 17, 167, 176, 191, 204.
Poten, Ernst, 143.
Price, 122, 175, 177, 195, 196, 201.
Prosser, 95.

Redmarley d'Abitot, 16.
Reigate, 15, 17, 141, 176.
Reigate Priory, 17, 143n, 177.
Renant, see Reynaud.
Rennie, Sir John, 12, 206.
Reynaud, 106, 148, 149, 165.
Reynier, General, 60, 67, 68, 71, 72, 74, 78, 82, 88.
Ridge, Maj, 163.
Roche, Colonel, 46, 48, 50.
Romana, Marquis de La, 51, 91.

Ross, of the Guards, 38.
Rousseau, 159.
Ross, of the Engineers, 162.

Saavedra, 51.
Sanchez, Don Julian, see Don Julian.
Saunders, of the Horse Artillery, 123.
Saxe de, Maurice, 17.
Schaumann, Augustus, 139n, 140–141.
Schultz, 168.
Sea Flower, 100.
Sebastiani, General, 34, 38, 55, 123.
Serain, General, 48, 49.
Sherbrooke, General Sir John, 44.
Siego, Camillo, 139–140.
Siego, Josepha, 139, 140–141, 143, 147.
Simon, General, 82.
Skerrett, Colonel, 201.
Slade, General, 67, 68, 185.
Smirke, Robert, 177.
Somers, John, Lord Chancellor, 15, 143.
Somers, Mary, 15.
Soult, Marshal, 18, 24, 25, 27, 28, 33, 37, 38, 110n, 118, 120, 123, 126–127, 134, 137, 175, 176, 190, 193, 196, 201, 228.
Soult, nephew of the Marshal, 79, 174, 175.
Stanhope, Maj the Hon Lincoln, 122, 128, 141, 151, 171, 186.
Stewart, General the Hon Charles, 28, 30, 31n, 133.
Stewart, Lt, 100.
Stockdale, 39.
Strenuwitz, 70.
Stuart, Charles, 74, 99, 169, 173.
Stuart, General, 108.
Sturgeon, Maj Henry, 158, 185, 186.
Suchet, Marshal, 144, 159, 196, 201.
Swetenham, Capt, 57.

Talbot, Lt-Col, 64.
Tempelhoff, 143, 153.
The Times, 39.
Thompson, 71.
Thong, 196.
Tomkinson, Lt William, 12, 13, 15, 18, 27, 59, 70, 71, 74, 76, 82n, 98, 99n, 151, 158, 167, 179, 204–205.
Trant, Colonel Nicholas, 24, 109, 148.

Urbino, 23.

Valency, General, 240.
Vandaleur, Maj-Gen, 165.
Vestot, 167.
Victor, Marshal, 24, 25, 27, 33, 34, 37, 38, 46.

Vigodet, Brig-Gen, 45.

Wales, Prince of, 191.
Walton, Capt, 168, 169.
Weller, Jac, 116, 144.
Wellesley, Marquis, 100.
Wellington, Arthur Wellesley, 1st Duke of, 12, 13, 18, 24, 25, 27, 28, 29, 30, 33, 34, 36, 37, 38, 39, 46, 47, 48f, 59, 60, 64, 65, 67, 68, 71, 73, 74, 76, 77, 79, 81, 82, 84, 88, 89, 92, 94, 96, 97, 99, 100, 101, 103, 104, 105, 106, 107, 109, 110, 111, 114, 115, 118, 120, 122, 123, 124, 126, 127, 128, 133, 137, 139, 140, 142, 143, 144, 145, 148, 149, 150, 158, 159, 162, 163, 165, 166, 169, 170, 171, 174, 175, 176, 177, 179, 180, 182, 183, 185, 186, 187, 188, 191, 192, 193, 195, 196, 197, 200, 201, 204, 205, 206, 233, 238.
 1st Peninsular operations, 18. Returns to Portugal, 24–25. Oporto campaign, 27–30. Talavera campaign, 33–39.
 Proposed defence of Portugal 1810, 59. Rejects relief of Ciudad Rodrigo, 60. Defends honour of 16th LD, 64n. Orders Cocks on first intelligence mission, 65. Writes Craufurd re Reynier's advance 26 July 1810, 68. Requests Cotton to reinforce Cocks, 71. Writes Cotton re Cock's destruction of Castel Mendo mills, 73. Writes Brit. Ambass. re Guarda, 74. Writes Cotton re further reinforcement of Cocks and the mvt of French cannon, 76. Receives letter from Cocks, 77. Mentions Cocks in despatches, 79. Massena's outflanking mvt at Busaco, 82. Mentions Cocks in despatches again, 92. Sends Cocks out against foragers, 97. Writes Charles Stuart re fever in As Caldas, 99n. Writes to Cocks, 100. Recommends Cocks for brevet majority, 101. Fuentes d'Onoro, 102f. Remark at dinner table re battle, 104. Sends Cocks out on patrol, 105. Loss of Almeida, 106. Leaves for Alemtejo, 110. 2nd siege, Badajoz, 111f, 228f. Comment to Maj Dickson, 115. Aborts siege, 118. Takes up new line, 120. Encourages Cocks in promotion plans, 122. Deceived by Engineers at Badajoz, 123. Sends Cocks on another intelligence mission, 127. Cocks dines with, 128. Having quarters whitewashed, 133. Reconnaissances, 137. Determined to prevent re-victualling of Rodrigo, 139. Siego affair, 140. Aftermath of Almeida affair, 142. El Boden 143–145. Discusses El Boden with Cocks, 148–149. Recommends Cocks for purchase of regimental majority, 159. Siege of Ciudad Rodrigo, Comments on tactics, 162–163. Remark to Gurwood, 165. Rebuke to Barrier, 170. Anxious to assist Cocks in promotion, 175. Approves his plan for, 177. Prophesies battle, 182. Nettled by Marmont, 185. Salamanca, 186–188. Enters Madrid, 191. Advances north, 192. Forms light companies with Cocks commanding, 193. Awards Cocks brevet lt colonelcy, 195. Siege of Burgos, 200–201. Grief at Cocks's death, 204. Writes to Lord Somers, 205. Remark at graveside, 206.
Westminster School, 16.
Weyland, Lt R. 103, 108.
Wheatley, Maj-Gen, 182.
Whippy, 95.
Whittingham, Colonel, 56, 190.
Wilson, Sir Robert, 25.
Wisch, Cornet, 65, 67, 68, 70.
Wood, Lt, 142.
Woodbridge, 17, 19.
Worcester, 16, 206.
Worcestershire Provisional Cavalry, 16.

York, 176.
York, Duke of, Commander-in-Chief, 122, 159.
Yorke, Rev Philip, Letters to, 24, 135, 153.
Yorke, Philip James, 153, 156n.